# Think Before You Like

## ALSO BY GUY P. HARRISON

*Think: Why You Should Question Everything*

*Good Thinking: What You Need to Know to Be Smarter, Safer, Wealthier, and Wiser*

*50 Popular Beliefs That People Think Are True*

*50 Simple Questions for Every Christian*

*50 Reasons People Give for Believing in a God*

*Race and Reality*

# Think Before You Like

### Social Media's Effect on the Brain and the Tools You Need to Navigate Your Newsfeed

## GUY P. HARRISON

 Prometheus Books

59 John Glenn Drive
Amherst, New York 14228

Published 2017 by Prometheus Books

Cover images © Gonzalo Aragon / Shutterstock; WonderfulPixel / Shutterstock
Cover design by Liz Mills and Nicole Sommer-Lecht
Cover design © Prometheus Books

Inquiries should be addressed to
Prometheus Books
59 John Glenn Drive
Amherst, New York 14228
VOICE: 716–691–0133 • FAX: 716–691–0137
WWW.PROMETHEUSBOOKS.COM

21 20 19 18 17    5 4 3 2 1

Library of Congress Cataloging-in-Publication Data Pending

Printed in the United States of America

*For Marissa*

# CONTENTS

# ACKNOWLEDGMENTS

Every book is a team effort and I am deeply grateful to the following people for their critical contributions to this one: Jade Zora Scibilia, Timothy Redmond, Steven L. Mitchell, Hanna Etu, Jose van Dijck, Jacob Silverman, Benjamin Radford, Sean Prophet, Catherine Roberts-Abel, Bruce Carle, Mark Hall, Jill Maxick, Cheryl Quimba, Nicole Lecht, Liz Mills, Garth Humphreys, Carrie James, Daniel K. Minto, Joshua Compton, Dean Burnett, Elke Feuer, Gerald Kane, Miki Hardisty, John Michael Strubhart, Ian Liberman, Miriam Metzger, Bo Bennett, Jake Farr-Wharton, William Poundstone, John Higginson, Kelly Frede, Leticia Bode, Leo Igwe, Maya Indira Ganesh, Kevin Hand, Frances Booth, Jeremy Kocal, Bong Manding, Brendan Nyhan, Tim Raynor, Peter Boghossian, Robert DeAngelo, Susanna Cline, Adam Alter, Angela Russell, Nathan Lee, Cameron M. Smith, and Joy Holloway-D'Avilar.

# INTRODUCTION

Something big is happening. Much of human culture is changing in a way that may come to redefine what it means to be a "normal" member of society, to be human. Evolution—change, transition, upheaval—is nothing new, of course. This moment, however, has a heavy feel to it, as if something profound is gaining momentum. This is so big that it may join the short list of all-time game changers: bipedalism, brain expansion, tool making, control of fire, language, music, sea travel, agriculture, pastoralism, civilization, mathematics, philosophy, industrialization, aviation, spaceflight, and social media. Wait, social media? You cannot be serious. *Social media?*

How can anyone think of Facebook, Snapchat, Instagram, Twitter, and so on as catalysts for some looming deep and revolutionary shift for all of humankind? Aren't these nothing more than glorified time-sucks that enable us to share inane videos, brag about the minor triumphs of our common lives, call strangers mean names, and gobble up fake news? Aren't these social media platforms just a way for companies to track us, spy on us, and sell off the crumb trails of our private lives to the highest bidder? How can social media possibly matter?

Look a little deeper and it becomes clear that the explosive popularity of social media is an important global phenomenon, a force that may be restructuring humanity. For all the banality and ethical concerns, Facebook and other platforms seem to be fulfilling the great promise of the Internet: to connect and tie our species together like never before. Soon there will be many tens of billions of devices connected to the Internet. We are in the process of wiring the world and ourselves rapidly and completely. *Think Before You Like* addresses some of the challenges and dangers that come with online connection, networking, and interaction. Some concerns are external, such as the way social media companies collect and profit off users' "private" data. They also manipulate people's minds, hook them in ways not so different from how casinos manage to keep gambling addicts planted in front of slot machines for hours. Other concerns are internal. Most social media users are not aware of the natural and standard human cognitive biases, mental shortcuts, perception problems, and emotional weak spots that can and do trip them up online. This book can help with that.

Acknowledging serious problems does not mean we must fear, hate, or reject social media. A bit of awareness and personal dedication to good thinking can be enough to significantly elevate and make safer the social media experience. It should not surprise us that billions have been drawn to one form of social media or another. We are primates, social creatures who find it not only enjoyable but also necessary to form social bonds and maintain near-constant communication with others. The worst fate for a prisoner, for example, is not the threat of violence, regret, boredom, bad food, or even torture. It's isolation. Prison administrators use solitary confinement as the ultimate punishment for prisoners who refuse to follow rules. Separate a human from humanity, and you move to kill something important within him or her. People need people; and social media feeds the hunger, to some degree. These various platforms help us do what we must: communicate, share feelings, gossip, teach, learn, brag, envy, hate, and love.

If the trends hold, its seems that everyone eventually will be connected within multiple, overlapping digital networks. Facebook, still so young, now has more than two billion users.[1] WhatsApp and YouTube claim a billion each.[2] QQ and WeChat are both moving toward a billion users.[3] Do you know about Baidu Tieba? If not, you might one day soon because more than 600 million of your fellow humans are already on it.[4] Even with user overlap, we can see that social media is big and getting bigger. But let's not get carried away.

Social media sites are great for keeping in touch with old friends and finding new ones. Everybody loves it when Facebook helps people raise funds for a beloved teacher's cancer treatment. But, as with any other far-reaching human endeavor, this one comes with a few negatives. Terrorists love social media, too, and some use it to their advantage, as do criminals, bullies, and imbeciles who spread nonsense. Social media platforms are tools that can be used to build or to destroy.

This book is neither an endorsement nor a condemnation of social media. I have no idea if the good will outweigh the bad in the long term. And, when realistic virtual reality and augmented reality arrive in force, social media is sure to morph and evolve rapidly. All that can be said with certainty today is that there is an urgent need for all users to arm themselves with knowledge about how social media companies operate, how our brains function online, and what steps we can take to protect ourselves.

This is not a book aimed at dumb or gullible people. This book is for smart, reasonable people, just like you. The social media arena is a place where millions of human minds are manipulated and steered for someone else's gain. High intelligence or traditional educational accomplishments won't be enough to protect you. There is no place for arrogance here. Those who believe they could never fall for a silly belief already have. Those who think they are above being exploited online and made vulnerable make the easiest marks. Awareness about the realities of various social media ecosystems can be off-putting. But don't be afraid. Be prepared. Don't turn off social media, necessarily; but use it wisely.

Guy P. Harrison
California, 2017

# Chapter One

# WILD AND WIRED:
# NAVIGATING THE NEW CULTURES OF CONNECTIVITY

**We're going to connect everybody.**
—Mark Zuckerberg, cofounder of Facebook[1]

**You're an interesting species. An interesting mix. You're capable of such beautiful dreams, and such horrible nightmares. You feel so lost, so cut off, so alone; only, you're not. See, in all our searching, the only thing we've found that makes the emptiness bearable is each other.**
—*Contact* (1997 film)[2]

**We are at a moment of temptation, ready to turn to machines for companionship even as we seem pained or inconvenienced to engage with each other in settings as simple as a grocery store. We want technology to step up as we ask people to step back.**
—Sherry Turkle, professor of the social studies of science and technology, MIT[3]

**Social media is bullshit.**
—B. J. Mendelson, writer[4]

I s Earth a social planet? It certainly seems so, given the preva-lence of social media. It's everywhere; nearly everyone is online and connected. And it's not just people. If anything, we humans were late to the party. Our Internet may seem ultra-cool and revo-lutionary to us, but the general concept is neither new nor unique. Many of the life-forms we share this planet with have used and relied on their own complex, extended social networks for many millions of years. Bacteria, for example, generally regarded as one of the simplest forms of life, are not so simple that they don't use "quorum sensing." This is a kind of social media action-network that enables them to keep track of how many of their "friends" are nearby. These tiniest of creatures send signals to one another in the form of molecules called autoinducers.[5]

Not only do some bacteria communicate with one another and maintain social ties, they also "resolve conflicts" within their networks and even send "friend requests" to bacterium who are outside their social circle. "Our study shows that bacteria living in biofilm communities do something similar to sending electronic messages to friends," said Jacqueline Humphries, a UC San Diego researcher.[6] "We found that bacteria from one species can send long-range electrical signals that will lead to the recruitment of new members from another species."

Plants do it, too. Look around your backyard, a city park, or a forest and you see grass, bushes, and trees. What you don't see is nature's Internet; but it's there. Most plant life on Earth is wired together into vast underground social networks provided to them by fungi. This organic and natural information superhighway serves an estimated 90 percent of all land plants.[7] Their Internet has been around for millions of years. It is made up of long, thin fibers called mycelium, and through it plants share information and nutrients, including carbon.

Much like our Internet, bad things can happen on the "wood wide web," too. Some plants use their connectivity to steal nutrients from other plants. Some send toxins via mycelium to harm rivals. Plants even have privacy issues like us. The dodder vine, for example, is a parasitic plant that attaches to other plants to suck water and nutrients from them. The dodder also does something that is similar to what social media companies are up to with their users' information. The dodder takes in data, in the form of RNA molecules from the host plant, and uses it for its own good. If the host is about to flower, for example, the dodder will flower too. This is because sometimes plants die after flowering and the dodder doesn't want to be stuck with a dead host without completing its flowering cycle.[8] Given the ubiquitous and complex connectivity we find in nature, it feels a bit like we are behind. But we're catching up fast.

## THE GLOBAL LURE OF SOCIAL MEDIA

| Percentage of Internet Users on Social Media:[9] | |
| --- | --- |
| Middle East | 86% |
| Latin America | 82% |
| Africa | 76% |
| United States | 71% |
| Six European Nations (France, the United Kingdom, Germany, Italy, Poland, and Spain) | 65% |

## WHAT HAVE WE BECOME?

I was sitting in the corner sweet spot of a local coffee shop, lost in writing and minding my own business, when two women marched in side by side. It was probably the clicking of their heels on the tile floor that drew my mind away from my search for the next sentence. They bought drinks and sat down at a table near mine.

Before my brain could reboot and slide back into work mode, I noticed something that would have been viewed as bizarre, mysterious, and even otherworldly only a couple of decades ago. The two women, who were obvious friends, as indicated by their earlier behavior at the counter, were not talking. They did not so much as glance at one another. Over the next ten minutes or so, they never spoke. Instead they stared down at their phones and busied themselves poking and swiping on miniscule touch screens in total silence.

**ONLINE COMMUNITIES**

| Estimated Number of Users | |
|---|---|
| 1. Facebook | More than 2 billion[10] |
| 2. WhatsApp | 1.3 billion[11] |
| 3. YouTube | 1.3 billion[12] |
| 4. Facebook Messenger | 1.2 billion[13] |
| 5. WeChat | 938 million[14] |
| 6. QQ | 869 million[15] |
| 7. Instagram | 700 million[16] |
| 8. QZone | 638 million[17] |
| 9. Tumblr | 550 million[18] |
| 10. Twitter | 328 million[19] |
| 11. Sina Weibo | 313 million[20] |
| 12. Baidu Tieba | 300 million[21] |
| 13. Skype | 300 million[22] |
| 14. Snapchat | 300 million[23] |
| 15. Viber | 250 million[24] |
| 16. Line | 220 million[25] |

None of the coffee shop behavior I observed was unusual for America or most other societies today, of course. Smartphones and social media sites and apps are saturating the planet. More than three-quarters of the US population, 77 percent, owns a smartphone now; and 92 percent of America's eighteen- to twenty-nine-year-olds own one.[26] Smartphones are most common in South Korea, where nearly 90 percent of the entire population owns one, and 100 percent of eighteen- to thirty-four-year-olds do.[27] Seventy-seven percent of Australians, 74 percent of Israelis, and 71 percent of Spaniards have a smartphone.[28] It is remarkable how these handheld devices have become so important so fast. Americans check their phones, on average, nearly fifty times per day.[29] Those in the eighteen- to twenty-four-year-old bracket do it *eighty-two times per day*, on average. Within five minutes of waking up, more than 40 percent of people have already looked at their phones for the first time of the day. More than 30 percent of smartphone owners check them five minutes before going to sleep. And around half of all smartphone owners take a peek at some point in the middle of the night. Collectively, American eyes are engaging with those tiny screens about eight billion times per day.[30]

---

Every sixty seconds, Facebook users upload an average of **136,000 photos** and update their status **293,000 times**.[31]

---

Soaring smartphone ownership is helping to drive the explosive growth of social media. Nearly seven of every ten Americans, 69 percent, now use social media. This is up from just 5 percent in 2005. Among US Internet users, 71 percent are on at least one social media platform. Eighty percent of Americans in the eighteen-to-twenty-nine-year-old range are social media participants.[32] A Pew survey of forty countries found that a median of 76 percent of Internet users use social media networks. These high rates are present in many countries. In Jordan, for example, 90 percent of internet users are on social media sites, Indonesia 89 percent, the Philippines 88 percent, Venezuela 88 percent, and Turkey 87 percent.[33] It seems clear that a significant factor in social media's current appeal is that a person is able to carry around a vast network of friends and contacts in one hand. Mobility has arrived, and people like it.

---

### SOCIALIZATION RUNS DEEP

Researchers in San Diego have grown "mini-brains" from stem cells.[34] The tiny clusters of networked neurons resemble an embryonic human brain, and striking differences have emerged between them based on the source of the stem cells. Cells taken from people with Williams syndrome, a condition that makes one prone to hyper-socialization, grew neurons with an unusually high number of connections. Mini-brains grown from cells taken from donors with autism, a condition marked by low socialization, had fewer connections.

Tech writer Alexis C. Madrigal described the most successful of all smartphones, the iPhone, in the *Atlantic*:

> The iPhone is the single-most successful product of all time. One billion iPhones have been sold. They underpin the most valuable company in history, and have catalyzed a whole new technology industry that's an order of magnitude larger than the one built around PCs. . . . The iPhone is the ur object of our time. A version of it is attached to the vast majority of adults. We sleep with them. We spend more time with them than [with] our children. The success of other technology companies, media empires, romantic relationships, and political campaigns depends on reaching people through them. . . . In short: the iPhone is the Pocket Crystal, and we are all enchanted.[35]

That's not hyperbole. It's difficult to overstate the role smartphones now play in modern culture. More and more, they contain our lives, or at least enough of our lives to cause extreme stress, if not panic, when one goes missing for a minute. It's the new human appendage. The smartphone also has become the pseudo-cocktail of our time. Held in one's hand, or at least in-pocket ready for quick draw, it makes us feel that we are okay, connected and engaged with something important, somewhere else. And it never fails us when an awkward moment threatens. The smartphone helps us feel normal and unflappable in social settings. You may be the wallflower at the party, but no one has to know when you have a smartphone. You are not alone in a crowd because you are unattractive or lack charisma. No, the only reason you are not the center of attention is because you are too busy for the boring flesh-and-blood people close by. You have legions of more important digital folks to tend to. There is much liking, swiping, scrolling, sharing, and posting to be done. Who has time for here, for now?

No one need ever again suffer boredom either. Why expend mental energy contemplating life, fantasizing, or conjuring up an original thought? Dispatch all daydreams and whip out your smartphone to check those urgent and spectacular social media updates that might be coming waiting for you. Retweet a retweet and keep those Snapchat streaks alive by any means necessary. Thanks to smartphones and the constant tug of social media chores, we can now fit in by not fitting in. Facebook and all of the rest are never more than inches and seconds away now. The phone is no longer a phone—a device for talking to other humans—but a portal into many worlds and many lives. It is our personal wormhole, a mobile and magical time-suck that enables to do both good and evil to ourselves and others. "Those little devices in our pockets are so psychologically powerful," said MIT professor Sherry Turkle in a memorable TED Talk, "that they don't only change what we do; they change who we are."[36] In her book *Alone Together*, she wrote: "We love our objects. But enchantment comes with a price."[37]

---

### TELL US WHAT YOU REALLY THINK

Anti–social media critic Janelle Randazza sounds off in her book, *Go Tweet Yourself*:

> No one cares if you're going for a walk, eating lunch, playing the banjo, or taking a nap. And we care even less if you tell us in a mere 140 characters. . . . The more we talk, the less we listen and the more Facebook friends, Twitter followers, and LinkedIn connections we acquire the greater the chance that any sliver of meaningful contact we could forge will get lost in the din of nudges, pokes, prods, and virtual two-steps. . . . Social networking is akin to a zombie invasion that is eating our brains, leaving us vapid nodes who somehow believe there is importance in telling the world we're buying a carton of milk.[38]

---

My observations in the coffee shop struck me as profoundly odd that day only because I had social media on my mind. I imagined one woman calling—more likely, texting or messaging—the other woman the night before or that morning to suggest that they meet for coffee to chat. Apart from the brief moments they spent walking into and then out of the shop, however, they never spoke or even looked at one another. Not a single word. A question came to mind: Contrary to the claimed benefit, could social media be making us less social?

I stepped back in time mentally and considered how strange this behavior would appear to someone from the past. A fourth-century nomad, medieval lord, or even a twentieth-century sociologist might find it unimaginable, even inhuman, perhaps. But today this is common and normal. Hundreds of millions of friends, family members, and acquaintances routinely share time and physical space—all while ignoring one another. At any given moment, a considerable portion of humanity is lost in one cyber-subculture or another. Somehow these digital dimensions are able to compete for and win our attention. They steal it away from real human beings who are an arm's length from us.

I then stepped back in a different way. I observed the women from outside my species. In my mind, I became an alien anthropologist, just in from another world, on expedition to study twenty-first-century *Homo sapiens*. I wondered, are these life-forms fully dependent on the ubiquitous tiny handheld devices, or do they simply enjoy having them close? Is this a symbiotic relationship? Does the device gain something from the relationship? If so, what does the device take from them? And who benefits more, human host or device? I speculated that perhaps it is someone or something on the other side of the tiny screens they find so compelling. If something is there, this remote entity should be the focus of further study. Given the well-documented pervasiveness of supernatural beliefs on this planet, it occurred to me that this could be yet another manifestation of humankind's deep hunger and habit for religious ritual. Are they praying to new gods through their devices? That might explain the devout silence and entranced stares so common here. By gently cradling and continually massaging the devices with their fingers, do they work to satisfy some digital divinity, or are they searching for something yet unfound?

Hopelessly derailed from my writing for the moment, I walked outside and found more of the same. Everywhere I looked, people stared down at smartphones in their hands. Some were alone, but there were also multiple clumps of people. Like the two women inside, they were together and yet not. *How bizarre*, I thought. Has humanity been seduced by some weird smartphone fetish? Are a handful of Silicon Valley hypnotists on their way to entrancing all of humankind? Are billions of people on a social media sleepwalk to nowhere? In that moment, I turned judgmental. It all seemed so pathetic. *What is wrong with these people? Don't they have lives, real lives?* Then I raised my phone to check my Facebook feed. Had to see how many likes had accumulated under my cute and clever comment about . . . something. I can't remember what.

## WHAT IS SOCIAL MEDIA?

For millions of years, our ancestors formed important social links and shared information through them. Therefore, at the most basic level, social media today is not changing humankind so much as tapping into what we have always been. Online social networks are a new way to do an old thing. This is who we are; this is what we do. A million years ago in Africa, any typical individual *Homo erectus* relied on connectivity to survive. She may not have been wired in to LinkedIn or Snapchat, but we can be sure that she was connected. She had a social network and it was vital to her. She made daily use of it to stay informed, to enhance her safety, and to be human. Closer to our time, networks of fast-striding distance runners kept the vast Inca Empire connected. In different places in different times, horses, ships, trains, and planes delivered the information to maintain and build connectivity. Then came the telegram, radio, telephone, and telecommunication satellites to quicken the pace and extend the tentacles further and deeper. We always have been linked to others. What is different about the present moment is that we now possess the ability to connect to vastly more people over greater distances than ever before, and do so instantaneously. Whether this will enhance or debase our humanity in the long run remains an open question.

### A DEFINITION

"Social media" is an evolving and slippery concept because of fast-changing computer technology and the diverse nature of the Internet itself. The Internet is social; it's all about making connections, so why would we define only a portion of it as "social media"? Much like defining *religion* presents the challenge of being precise without excluding, pinning down *social media* can be difficult because being accurate, fair, and comprehensive means drawing very wide boundaries. Therefore, the most useful way to think of social media may be as *the total of websites, networks, and apps that allow people to connect, create content, and share information*. This definition is vague and simple but useful. The key is the relative ease of two-way communication that makes social media so different from the old, traditional one-way process of information sharing that governments, corporations, news publishers, and PR agencies once relied on and dominated.

Another reason we must loosely define social media is because it won't be tomorrow what it is today. Given the pace of technological change, it's not difficult, for example, to imagine some direct mind-to-mind interface showing up in the near future (more on that in chapter 6). Furthermore, VR (virtual reality) and AR (augmented reality) seem close to landing with force and shaking up the world. Social media might turn out to be the biggest game changer in all of history. That sounds like crazy hyperbole—until you consider what is coming soon.

Facebook sure seems to think something big can be achieved with virtual reality. In 2014, the company bought Oculus, a VR startup, for $2 billion.[39] The general vision for this exciting technology is grand, extending far beyond gaming applications. It's likely that VR will become so good, so capable of fooling our brains into believing that we are actually having a real physical experience, that we may quickly come to want or rely on it for several hours per day, for both for work and play. A key challenge in the coming decades may be in figuring how to get ourselves off the couch to do things in the real world. It will be tough when a pair of VR goggles can deliver convincing social encounters, realistic fantasy adventures, romance, sex, travel, and a whole lot more, straight into our brains. We already have some people spending several hours per day on Facebook and Twitter; so what will people with such inclinations do when VR enables them to hold hands with a Facebook friend on a beach in Hawaii while the sun sets, or punch some Twitter troll's avatar senseless in a virtual back alley?

Will this turn out to be great, horrible, or a murky mix of both? Jeremy Bailenson, founding director of Stanford University's Virtual Reality Interaction Lab, anticipates significant benefits coming from fast-improving VR technology but is also concerned about possible negative consequences: "I worry what happens when a violent video game feels like murder. And when pornography feels like sex. How does that change the way humans interact, function as a society?"[40] The future of social media is unknown. We can be sure, however, that things are going to get very interesting very soon. Hang on.

Gerald Kane, an information systems expert and McKiernan Distinguished Fellow at Boston College's Carroll School of Management, has studied social media for more than a decade and concludes that there is no such thing as social media. He maintains that it is misleading to think of these sites and apps as entities that are somehow fundamentally unique on the Internet. "Social media is just the Internet," he declared in a popular TED Talk back in 2014.[41] "Social media is exactly what the Internet was always supposed to be, and it has just evolved over time." Kane cites a quote by no less than World Wide Web founder Tim Berners-Lee to back him up: "I designed it for a social effect—to help people work together—and not as a technical toy." Kane dismisses the notion that social media might be a fad. "We haven't seen anything yet," he told me.[42] "Social media will completely change how organizations run. Of course, I also see social media increasingly augmented with other digital technologies such as analytics, AI, and AR/VR [augmented reality/virtual reality], so the distinction between 'social media' and other digital tools will be less clear." Kane predicts that the online landscape of the future will look more like the world of a 150 years ago than the one fifteen years ago. He compares an increasingly connected online world to that of a small town where everyone knows everyone.

"Social media is simply a tool," he continued,

> It can make things better and worse. It can enable us to keep up with friends and family across the globe, and it means that teenagers can't ever escape the bully tormenting them. It means we can get information instantaneously, and it means that people can try to manipulate that information for their own ends. How we use it is far more important than simply *that* we use it. Yet, the "right" way to use it continually changes as the platforms and their capabilities change. The "right" way to do things in 2007 may not be the right way in [the future].

Kane is not alone in taking the long view. For instance, in his book *Writing on the Wall: Social Media—The First 2,000 Years*, digital technology expert Tom Standage makes the point that social media have been around for centuries. Today's blogs, he writes, are the new pamphlets; social media platforms are the new coffeehouses; and media-sharing sites, the new books. He feels that the rebirth of social media today is indeed a profound shift, but it is also a return to the way things used to be.[43] Media expert June Cohen adds that "old media"—newspapers, radio, and television—aren't really all that old. "Books and newspapers became common only in the last two hundred years, radio and film in the last hundred, TV in the last fifty. If all of human history were compressed into a single twenty-four-hour day, media as we know them emerged in the last two minutes before midnight. Before that, for the vast majority of human history, all media were social media. Media were what happened between people. . . . Media were participatory. Media were social."[44]

Cohen believes that what we are seeing today with the rise of social media is "neither the unprecedented flowering of human potential nor the death of intelligent discourse but, rather, the correction of a historical anomaly. There was a brief period of time in the twentieth century when 'media' were understood as things professionals created for others to passively consume. Collectively, we have rejected this idea."[45] Cohen is correct. While social media is widely thought of as something new, it's more precisely the newest form of our oldest obsession. Social media did not begin with Facebook's launch in 2004. It began when our most distant ancestors collaborated with others, shared something in some way. Social media began for "us" in the proverbial primordial pool.

## HOW MANY FRIENDS DOES IT TAKE TO FILL A BRAIN?

> **Human nature is deeper and broader than the artificial contrivance of any existing culture.**
> —Edward O. Wilson,
> *The Creation: An Appeal to Save Life on Earth*[46]

The more you think about the social media phenomenon, the more mysterious it all seems. Is all of this posting, liking, sharing, snapchatting, tweeting, trolling, emoji plastering, and so on making us more human or less human? Anyone with a smartphone in her or his pocket and access to the Internet carries the potential to connect with billions of people. Think about that: a gargantuan chunk of humanity only a few finger-taps away. I'm not sure what that means, but it certainly seems significant. Our world has become smaller; or maybe humankind has become larger? Just how valuable and useful

| Communication and Connectivity Milestones | |
|---|---|
| Oral Language | more than 100,000 years ago |
| Art | 40,000 years ago or more |
| Written Language | more than 5,000 years ago |
| Electric Telegraph | more than 200 years ago |
| Telephone | more than 160 years ago |
| Radio | more than 120 years ago |
| Electric/Digital Computer | more than 80 years ago |
| ARPANET | 1969 |
| Internet | more than 50 years ago |
| E-mail | 1972 |
| World Wide Web | 1989 |
| Blogs | 1994 |
| Six Degrees | 1997 |
| Friendster | 2002 |
| Baidu Tieba | 2003 |
| LinkedIn | 2003 |
| MySpace | 2003 |
| Skype | 2003 |
| Flickr | 2004 |
| Facebook (college only) | 2004 |
| YouTube | 2005 |
| QZone | 2005 |
| Facebook (everyone) | 2006 |
| Twitter | 2006 |
| QQ | 2006 |
| Tumblr | 2007 |
| Spotify | 2008 |
| Sina Weibo | 2009 |
| WhatsApp | 2009 |
| Pinterest | 2010 |
| Viber | 2010 |
| Instagram | 2010 |
| Facebook Messenger | 2011 |
| WeChat | 2011 |
| Snapchat | 2011 |
| Line | 2011 |

are large and extensive online networks of people, anyway? Oxford University anthropologist Robin Dunbar studies social networks and concludes that our brains evolved an upper limit of about 150 for an individual person's number of friends and alliances that can be made use of. Beyond that, we are just fooling ourselves, because it takes time, work, and cerebral real estate to build and maintain meaningful relationships. "With social media, we can easily keep up with the lives and interests of far more than a hundred and fifty people," Dunbar told the *New Yorker*. "But without investing the face-to-face time, we lack deeper connections to them, and the time we invest in superficial relationships comes at the expense of more profound ones. We may widen our network to two, three, or four hundred people that we see as friends, not just acquaintances, but keeping up an actual friendship requires resources."[47]

I have thousands of Facebook friends, but how many of them will loan me twenty bucks if I hit hard times? Can you list more than 150 friend names that you currently interact with in some way, first and last name, right now off the top of your head? How many people are you comfortable sharing your most important dreams, hopes, fears, and secrets with? Our online networks may be vast, but how intimate are they? Some social media users seem to be engaged in a strange game of collecting digital people as if they were points in a basketball game. Why? For what ultimate purpose?

What does it mean to have thousands of social media friends and followers? I have written six books prior to this one and primarily through them I have connected with many interesting people around the world. I interact with some of them in meaningful and rewarding ways. They have proven to be pleasant, positive additions to my life. They certainly feel like actual friends. I have encountered some of these social media friends off-line, in person, and was relieved to find out that they were neither serial killers nor dangerous sexual deviants. (Or, they were polite enough to hide it from me if they were.) Some of my social media friends, however, seem mysterious to me, perhaps even a bit of a concern. It's nothing they have said, no image they posted that makes me wonder, only that I'm not sure what it is exactly that we do for each other. We just seem to kind of be there, floating in cyberspace, tethered to one another for some unknown purpose.

Given the emphasis on numerical feedback that is common to

social media sites and apps, it may be easy for some to become pre-occupied with the number of friends or followers they have. After all, a widely accepted measure of modern fame is how many Twitter followers a celebrity has. One of the first things that catch the eye when visiting a Facebook or Twitter page is the displayed number of notifications or interactions. But placing too much value on quantity of friends or volume of friendly encounters may be a mistake. According to Dunbar, a small core of around five close relationships is far more important to our well-being than a vast collection of hundreds or even thousands of casual online acquaintances.[48]

## CONVERSATIONS IN THE DARK

Social media, for the most part today, doesn't do nuance well. It can be difficult to "read" people, no matter how plain and straightforward their typed words may be. That's why sarcasm is a risky proposition online and probably not worth the effort in most cases. That little, telling inflection of voice or partial grin that gives away true intent face-to-face is missing in a tweet or a Facebook comment. I've made this mistake in the past by posting a comment in which I wrote something so absurd that "everyone would know I was joking." But, of course, not everyone did and some people took my words to be literal. It's important to know that nonverbal information—facial expressions and body language, for example—make up the *majority* of information transferred between two people talking while sharing the same physical space. All or most of that is lost in most online exchanges. Even audio and video conversations on Skype are truncated versions of the evolved and traditional form of human face-to-face communication, which is detailed and complicated, with most of it occurring at the subterranean, subconscious level of our minds. Much of what we say is supported, embellished, or contradicted by miniscule cues of voice tones and cadence, eye movements, hand gestures, and stance. The subconscious sees much that the conscious mind misses.

For better or worse, online communication is stripped down, bare-bones communication. This is good when it leads us to focus on the message rather than the possibly unrelated traits of the messenger such as gender, age, religion, skin color, and so on. I like the idea of this but sometimes worry about the downside that accompanies it. For example, I often respond to comments or questions about some idea in one of my books or articles through social media. Usually it consists of a straightforward answer to a simple question or a brief exchange of ideas, and everyone goes away happy. Occasionally, however, I connect with someone who just doesn't quite understand my point or my position on something, and I find it difficult to figure out exactly what they are trying to communicate to me. I wonder, in these cases, whether the person behind the stream of words is sincere or is trying to troll me for sport. I almost always proceed as if the person is sincere. Better to err on the side of respect and kindness, I figure. But I sometimes suspect that a person is just having his version of fun and wasting my time by pretending to be incredibly stupid or stubborn. Face-to-face, I would almost certainly be able to pick up something in the person's facial expressions or body language to identify what's really going on. But online, I'm handicapped, in the dark and disadvantaged. I'm less human because I can't take advantage of my primate senses that have been honed over a vast stretch of time to read the silent messages of friends, kin, and enemies during face-to-face interactions.

It can be easy to strike up a new friendship online but so too is it easier to be mean. Are most Twitter trolls polite and compassionate people off-line? Are they consistent jerks during their waking hours, or does something about social media, the relative anonymity or distance maybe, change and empower them to be cruel? What about romance and sex online, not in the pornography industry but between civilians? There is a lot of love and lust to be found in cyberspace. I receive about two or three Facebook friend requests every week from extremely attractive women. Most are wearing sexy bikinis and strike lustful poses that catch my attention. But before I welcome these lonely beauties into my personal online space, something called critical thinking taps me on the shoulder and reminds me that skepticism is demanded when something seems too good to be true. So I consider a more likely scenario, for instance, maybe there is a large, excessively hairy, basement-dwelling male lurking behind those provocative photos.

In a later chapter about addiction we will explore the strange relationship between deep brain processes and social media engineering, but it's never too soon to think about your own motivations to keep coming back to one or more of these sites. What is the hook that is working on you? Is it the people, the friends and family who are there, and nothing else? Or could it have something to do with the way these platforms are set up and how they operate that reels you back in again and again? I feel good when a silly string of words I put together gets a couple of hundred "likes." But why? Who cares? Is such a fleeting trickle of dopamine in my brain really worth investing an hour of time reading Facebook instead of Shakespeare? Has the tiny digital thumbs-up on Facebook or the Twitter heart become the applause our time, the coveted stamps of approval for a new age? If so, I suspect we may have lost something. If social media have become a major part of modern society—and they have—then we must be curious about what their impact is. The questions are obvious. How are all of these online social networks changing human culture? How might they be changing us as individuals? What is going on in our subconscious minds while we are online? Are these sites turning people into cyber-addicts? For all the talk about it, how important can privacy really be when hundreds of millions give theirs away so casually to social media sites? What does it mean for society and democracy when millions of people experience intellectual isolation inside of the electronic echo chambers that have come to be known as filter bubbles? Why does fake news fool so many people? What is the future of social media? It would be irresponsible not to consider such questions.

This book is a call for everyone to *pay attention*. Give some thought to the role of social media in society and in your personal life. "There's something happening here that's really unprecedented," declares Robert Epstein, a psychologist at the American Institute for Behavioral Research and Technology, "Technologies are rapidly evolving that can impact people's behaviors, opinions, attitudes, beliefs on a massive scale—without their awareness."[49] *Pay attention.*

## ARE WE BECOMING "EFFICIENT SHADOWS OF OURSELVES"?

How many of us look around, take in the surrounding physical environment, and strike up conversations with strangers anymore? Could we be losing the will, the ability even, to accept where we are during a given moment and to reflect on what is occurring around us? Often these days the odd one out, the deviant, is the person who is *not* hunched over and staring at a tiny screen with lifeless eyes. I spent time in Switzerland and Sweden while writing this book, and, just as it is in the United States, I observed most people in most public spaces deeply absorbed in their smartphones.

Go to a playground or park in many societies today, and you are likely to find dedicated parents who cared enough to take their children outside to play under the Sun. But are they *there*? Are they with their child? Do they enjoy seeing their daughter or son play and laugh? Are they sufficiently present to cheer on the child's successful crossing of the monkey bars? Or is the glare of that little screen too bright for them to see anything beyond it? How many children and teenagers have lost some of the love and wisdom offered to them because Instagram and Snapchat felt more interesting and important than a parent, older sibling, or teacher?

Have some of us made a fool's bargain? Have we traded some of life's deepest rewards for fleeting and soon-forgotten micro-doses of dopamine? Politics and culture commentator Andrew Sullivan has struggled to balance his online and off-line lives. He is concerned with where social media is taking us. "We have gone from looking up and around to constantly looking down. . . . Has our enslavement to dopamine—to the instant hits of validation that come with a well-crafted tweet or Snapchat streak—made us happier? I suspect it has simply made us less unhappy, or rather less aware of our unhappiness, and that our phones are merely new and powerful antidepressants of a non-pharmaceutical variety."[50]

Sullivan worries that investing so much into virtual networks compromises our flesh-and-blood networks and diminishes our daily experiences. He continues:

> By rapidly substituting virtual reality for reality, we are diminishing the scope of this interaction even as we multiply the number of people with whom we interact. We remove or drastically filter all the information we might get by being *with* another person. We reduce them to some outlines—a Facebook "friend," an Instagram photo, a text message—in a controlled and sequestered world that exists largely free of the sudden eruptions or encumbrances of actual human interaction. We become each other's "contacts," efficient shadows of ourselves.

Jaron Lanier, a technology expert and virtual reality pioneer, is one of social media's toughest critics. He believes our "digital hive is growing at the expense of individuality,"[51] that so much social media activity may be lessening the perceived value of a human being. He also advises social media users to stop calling themselves "users" because they are being "used."[52]

"Anonymous blog comments, vapid video pranks, and lightweight mashup's may seem trivial and harmless," Lanier writes in his notable book, *You Are Not a Gadget*, "but as a whole, this widespread practice of fragmentary, impersonal communication has demeaned interpersonal interaction. Communication is now often experienced as a superhuman phenomenon that towers above individuals. A new generation has come of age with a reduced expectation of what a person can be, and of who each person might become."[53] He continues, "The time is come to ask, 'are we building the digital utopia for people or machines?' If it's for people, we have a problem."[54]

Alexis C. Madrigal, author of *Powering the Dream: The History and Promise of Green Technology*, wrote in the *Atlantic* about what he sees as Facebook's lack of accountability for how it is impacting human interactions:

> Facebook must accept the reality that it has changed how people talk to each other. When we have conversations at home, at work, in cafés, and in classrooms, there is not an elaborate scoring methodology that determines whose voice will be the loudest. Russian trolls aren't interjecting disinformation. My visibility to my family is not dependent on the quantifiable engagement that my statements generate. Every word that I utter or picture that I like is not being used to target advertisements at me. The platform's own dynamics *are* a huge part of what gets posted to the platform. They are less a mirror of social dynamics than an engine driving them to greater intensity, with unpredictable consequences.[55]

## THE NEXT BIG BRAIN

Any productive conversation about the prominence and future of social media must include the rise of automation and artificial intelligence (AI). We are now witnessing the arrival of smart machines into our lives at unprecedented levels and, among other things, this will have a major impact on our Internet and social media experiences. It is important that we be aware of how fast this is happening. For example, Watson, the IBM supercomputer, may be known to most people for its 2011 victory over human champions on the game show *Jeopardy*, but it has been up to much more important work since then, like reading through millions of medical journal articles and assisting doctors with finding the most effective treatments for cancer patients. AI will do many wonderful things for us. Lives will be enhanced, made more efficient, and even saved, thanks to supercomputers. When a machine can absorb an amount of information equivalent to reading a million books per second—without ever forgetting a single word—amazing things can happen. But all may not go smoothly. Theoretical physicist Stephen Hawking told the BBC in 2014 that artificial intelligence could bring about the end of the human race. "Once humans develop artificial intelligence," Hawking warns, "it will take off on its own and redesign itself at an ever-increasing rate. Humans, who are limited by slow biological evolution, couldn't compete and would be superseded."[56] Other notable figures who fear that AI might harm humanity in the future include Bill Gates, Steve Wozniak, and Elon Musk.[57]

Musk, speaking at the National Governors Association summer meeting in 2017, seemed frustrated that people were not more concerned about the possibility of super-intelligent machines sweeping humanity aside. "I have exposure to the very cutting-edge AI, and I think people should be really concerned about it," he said.[58] "I keep sounding the alarm bell, but until people see robots going down the street killing people, they don't know how to react, because it seems so ethereal." Musk believes government regulation is needed but the laws must come before rather than after a major AI disaster. "AI is a rare case where we need to be proactive about regulation instead of reactive. Because I think by the time we are reactive in AI regulation, it's too late. AI is a fundamental risk to the existence of civilization."

A possible digital apocalypse is not the only concern. One 2017 study predicted that 38 percent of US jobs will be lost to automation by 2030; Germany may lose 35 percent; and the United Kingdom, 30 percent. Remember, change is not only coming; it is happening now. AlphaGo, a Google supercomputer, defeated Ke Jie, the world's best Go player, in 2017. Go is an ancient game of pure strategy, more demanding than chess. "AlphaGo is improving too fast," said Jie after the loss.[59]

| Potential Jobs at High Risk of Loss to Automation by Early 2030[60] | |
|---|---|
| United States | 38 percent |
| Germany | 35 percent |
| United Kingdom | 30 percent |
| Japan | 21 percent |

It feels inevitable, doesn't it? Ever-smarter machines are likely to be almost everywhere soon, doing many of the things we do now, only better. But for all the warnings and concerns, how can we resist the progress AI may bring? So many conveniences and so many potential solutions to our greatest problems may be waiting just around the corner, thanks to the coming wave of superintelligence. Cosmologist Martin Rees, former president of the United Kingdom's Royal Society, says experts may disagree about the rate of change but not the direction. In the long run, Rees believes, humankind's tenure as the great influential force on Earth will probably shrink to near insignificance: "[In] a long-term evolutionary perspective, humans and all they've thought will be just a transient and primitive precursor of the deeper cognitions of a machine-dominated culture extending into the far future and spreading far beyond our Earth."[61]

I recently walked into a Panera Bread restaurant in Southern California and was taken back by the absence of human employees. No one was behind the counter, and no employees were in sight in the dining area. I wondered if the place might have been closed and someone forgot to lock the door. I figured it out once I spotted the computerized sentries waiting to take my order. Soon after paying a machine with a credit card, my take-out order appeared on the appropriate counter several feet away. I assume the food was prepared and placed there by human hands, but can't be sure. I left without any interaction with another human taking place. It was a fast and smooth experience, just as I would have preferred. Driving home, however, I wondered if I had just glimpsed our future: Very efficient, but a little lonely, too.

## "WE'RE NEVER GOING BACK"

Sean Prophet, a Los Angeles television editor, is a big believer in social media as a positive force with staying power. Don't fight it, he says, get onboard. "This is a permanent change to human interaction," he said.[62]

> We can debate all day long whether that is a good or bad thing. But so long as computers and networks exist, it will be a reality. Social media is an integral part of the lead-up to the technological singularity,[63] which will represent an always-on connection from every human brain potentially to every other human brain. We ain't seen nothin' yet. The naysayers are suffering from a tremendous lack of vision. Whatever changes are happening now will become permanent. We're never going back.

Randall, aged thirty-two, is a heavy social media user and father of a baby girl. He wonders what the future holds for her in an increasingly wired world. "I am concerned for my daughter, who I know will soon enough discover how to use computers and smartphones. Considering how rapidly technology has advanced in my lifetime thus far, I can't imagine just how much more it will grow by the time she begins developing an online relationship between herself and her friends, and what kind of problems she will encounter."[64]

Kelly, a California college student, inhabits the Facebook, Instagram, and Snapchat worlds. She loves them for the assist they provide to her love life. The challenges of a long-distance relationship with her boyfriend are made easier with social media. "Talking on the phone or [through] e-mails can only go so far," she said, "but being able to send a funny Snapchat photo or post a short video of my day is a valuable way to feel connected despite distance."[65] Social media also helps her to stay close to her family in the same ways. She credits Facebook as a significant aid to her studies as well. "I'm in a master's program, and a lot of the schoolwork is very independent and isolated at times. By joining a group for our class on Facebook, it's extremely easy to check in with classmates and make sure I am doing the work correctly or have the accurate dates for quizzes, tests, etc."

Kelly is aware of the irony lurking behind the social media in our lives. What is billed as social often seems antisocial. She says these sites and services "often serve as a blockade to connection. People can become mindless about checking their phones for social media updates and miss out on their current reality," she said. "When two people meet face-to-face, social media often sneaks into the time they are sharing. Simply checking one's phone during a conversation disrupts the connection between people and can become a barrier to real-life experiences."

Bong Manding is a registered nurse who spends about five to six hours per day on social media. He says it can lead people into shallow and superficial behavior, but it's definitely not all bad. "We yearn for more likes and more comments to stroke our ego," he said.[66] "On the other hand, if we use social media the right way, it's got a lot of tremendous benefits. Helping other people through posting to GoFundMe—awesome. Sharing feel-good videos—awesome. It lifts our morale and much more. The best of all is that we learn a lot just by being on social media. We get to talk to people from the other side of the world. The Internet makes this world smaller and people closer. You foster sense of community, cultivate friendships, argue intellectually, inspire and get inspired. Social media is awesome."

Author Elke Feuer of Florida points out the often-conflicting nature of social media that push us together while simultaneously pulling us apart. "In some ways, social media has connected us more, making us more human from the connections we make," Feuer said.[67] "However, where it falls short, is when it's not supplemented with in-person connections, which are equally important to sustain real relationships. While social media [and the]Internet have benefits, I'm concerned about the disconnection they're creating and the misconceptions people have about hurting others online and how easily they can do it without consequences. I'm also concerned about how easily people share private elements of their lives on the Internet without realizing the damage they're doing—because what goes out in the cyber world can't be undone."

Feuer makes an important point. There was a time when slipping on a banana peel—literal or figurative—might be fodder for humiliation, but it had a short shelf life. In most cases, there was a good chance it would fade soon and normal life could resume. If the mistake or crime rose to the level of media coverage, one could take some comfort in the knowledge that by the end of the week most of the newspapers containing the damaging article or photograph would be wrapping fish or lining birdcages. Now, however, the damning information, and continued torment, is only a quick Internet search away, possibly for the rest of one's life.

---

### WANT MORE TWITTER FOLLOWERS?

A study conducted by Georgia Tech researchers[68] concluded that the best way for non-celebrities to increase the number of their Twitter followers is to focus on sharing more content that is useful or interesting to others and less personal information. News and other informational content attracts followers at a rate thirty times higher than tweets about one's lunch, current mood, or other highly personal topics. Twitter is based on weaker social ties than platforms such as Facebook; therefore, the researchers recommend very few, if any, tweets about negative personal topics such as a death in the family, unemployment, and poor health. Overuse of hashtags also seems to repel potential followers.

---

It's a big question but one worth tackling: Will the Internet, and today's most popular social media platforms in particular, turn out to be mostly good or bad for us? "It's too diverse a medium to narrow down specifically," answers Dr. Dean Burnett, a psychiatry instructor at Cardiff University in Wales. "Books can be incredibly enlightening or utterly stupid, but nobody attributes one outcome to the entire medium. That would be like seeing gambling addicts in casinos and saying buildings are bad for us."[69] He's right. Social media is what we make of it. And therein lie both problems and opportunities, potentials that run in many directions. I remind readers that throughout this book we will explore some of the worst aspects of social media but none of this erases all of the good that comes from it today, nor does it negate social media's potential to do remarkable, positive things for humankind in the future. It is too easy to blame social media for things individual people do with it. Yes, there are serious problems that demand our attention and correction, but don't become lost in the technology. Do not make the mistake of believing that these problems are not tied to who we are and how we conduct ourselves. From casual users to billionaire owners, *people* create the social media universe. AI hasn't taken over the world yet. We still run things and deserve any blame for outcomes we don't like. The good news here, of course, is that human-created problems can usually be fixed or alleviated by humans.

Leticia Bode, an assistant professor at Georgetown University, researches the intersection of communication, culture, and technology. She has an interesting perspective on privacy issues and other challenges related to the rise of these platforms. "I think social media is a symptom more than a cause," she said.[70] "In general, societies are becoming more open, and that openness will likely lead to both greater use of social media and greater empowerment of women. Social media platforms mostly replicate what exists in the off-line world. That means they reveal people and politics at their best *and* at their worst. The Internet doesn't make us more or less human, but sometimes it makes our humanness more visible and more observable."

## TRUSTING TOOLS

Evolutionary biologist Richard Dawkins calls the Internet "a work of genius, one of the highest achievements of the human species."[71] And social media platforms may well turn out to be the most powerful, impactful expressions of the Internet. Welcome to the revolution, comrade. All of your clicking, poking, snapping, swiping, and tweeting is changing . . . something . . . somehow. We are remaking the world, our cultures, maybe humankind itself. Let's hope it's for the better, right?

Thomas Rid, a political scientist and expert on information technology, writes in his book *Rise of the Machines*: "Machines are about control. Machines give more control to humans: control over their environment, control over their own lives, control over others. But gaining control through machines means also delegating it *to* machines. Using the tool means trusting the tool. And computers, ever more powerful, ever smaller, and ever more networked, have given ever more autonomy to our instruments. We rely on the device . . . trusting it with our security and with our privacy. The reward: an apparatus will serve as an extension of our muscles, our eyes, our ears, our voices, and our brains."[72] No one is suggesting that Snapchat is about to become

Skynet[73]; however, it could be argued fairly that most people who commit considerable portions of their life to the Internet and social media sites have given little, if any, thought to the potential risks. And, make no mistake, there are significant risks that accompany our ever-increasing connection to and dependence on the Internet and its darling, social media platforms and apps. For example, the Internet has no backup. What if it breaks? Some might say that's a silly question, but there is no easy answer to it.

Our thinking can become derailed when we see technology as something separate from the life-forms that make and use it, namely, people. The near-global digital network that connects billions of computers and smartphones may feel at times like something left to us by an advanced alien species. But it wasn't. Remember that human technologies reflect not only the brilliance and the positive, the best hopes of their creators, but also their limitations, their flaws, and sometimes their worst temptations, too. "Technologies can never be relied on to solve problems in the absence of social action; one of the dangers of fetishizing technology as an actor in its own right is that it obscures this point," explains UK science writer Oliver Morton.[74] "Good solutions will rarely, if ever, be implemented through technology alone. And technology will never be the last word on anything; there will always be something new to try, some other galling thing to seek to set right. The centuries of ceaseless technological change are not going to come to an end; they may only just be getting going. A clear understanding that technology does not have its own agenda but serves the agenda of others, and that it necessarily creates new needs almost as effectively as it meets old ones, will make this change easier to navigate responsibly. But it will never bring changes to a halt."

When it comes to the future of the Internet and social media, much may be confusing and unknown now, but we can be sure that we are neck-deep in an online, data-driven upheaval. Regardless of our level of participation, we all are both beneficiary and victim. A wired world inhabited by a deeply tangled and intertwined humanity is a good thing. Except when it's a bad thing, of course. Like most human inventions and milestones, this one is messy and promises to get messier. History shows that this is our way. My guess is that after news arrived about the invention of airplanes, it didn't take more than five minutes before someone said, "Hey, I bet we can use this to kill people."

## DIGITAL GROOMING FOR THE MASSES

Kelly Frede, a University of Southern California graduate student with a degree in biological anthropology, says that all of this online social networking fits well with our primate profile:

> Socializing is one of the most rewarding activities humans can perform, so it's no surprise we use the highest technology to socialize. Humans and other primates are innately rewarded when they socialize; their brains are flooded with serotonin, dopamine, and oxytocin when they spend time with others. We also have mirror neurons that allow us to feel connected or related to others. When one chimpanzee watches another chimp "fish" for termites, mirror neurons light up their brain, allowing for one chimpanzee to learn the behavior of the other. For humans, we can extrapolate this form of learning to the Internet. Watching a video of a friend can excite mirror neurons and make you feel more connected. Our brains interpret social media as reality, so we get that "happy" cascade of neurotransmitter release when we use social media.[75]

Frede likens tweeting back and forth, posting pics of food on Instagram, and validating a Facebook friend's status update to primate grooming:

> Social media is a social reward in human society, just like grooming is a social reward to baboons. Social media also provides an outlet to manipulate our social circles online. Instead of having to groom a fellow chimpanzee, we can "like" our co-worker's post to become closer and move up the social hierarchy. We may think of social media as an inferior form of technology because it "just" lets us connect to others, but socialization is what has allowed our species to survive for hundreds of thousands of years and continues to do so through new forms of technology.

Frede's comments ring true. I often spend time observing the bonobo chimps at the San Diego Zoo, and I'm always struck by how social they are. Writing this book made me even more aware of it. When one bonobo wanders off to be alone

> at the edge of the habitat, for example, he or she will soon
> rejoin the others, or another bonobo will come over and make
> physical contact, as if to check and make sure that everything
> is okay. Absolute and lasting isolation seems foreign, if not
> dreadful, to them—as it is with us. Socializing and communi-
> cating ideas and feelings to others is so important to humanity
> that I wonder how far we will go in pursuit of it. Will we one
> day connect and share ourselves through electronic means to
> such a degree that billions of us become a single entity? Would
> that bring us the peace and contentment we seek?

Social media, for all the tech, gadgetry, and dehumanizing aspects, really is quite human. It allows us to be more of ourselves in some ways. We can follow our hearts to tweet out calls to feed the hungry, or we can torment a teen and drive her to suicidal thoughts. One way to get a feel for what people really think about social media is to read the graffiti on the wall. "When you quit social media, you find out who your real friends are, which is hardly any of them," says "Marcus" in a comment posted on YouTube.[76] "You are not friends [with] most of the people on these social networks. You are just another number and another way to relieve boredom." Someone who goes by the screenname "Captain Crunch" adds: "Facebook and any social network of that magnitude is the biggest tool fabricated by the control system. Not only is it unnatural and misinforming but it's destroying social interaction and self-preservation. How many hrs a day do ppl dedicate to pointless popularity contests when they could be applying themselves to so many different things??" Finally, "The Robot That Stole Your JAWB!" says, "Social media is garbage, it's the perfect medium for narcisistic [sic] idiots that feels like erybody [sic] wants to know how much their shit weighted [sic] today, nobody truly 'shares' things, they only 'show' stuff, when is the last time you had a deep or half meaningful conversation with somebody on Facebook? Fuck social media, the land of superficiality and empty narcisism [sic]."

Social media may have spread faster and farther than the Black Death managed to in the Middle Ages, but that doesn't mean every platform is the perfect fit for everyone. For example, citing too much hate coming at him, former basketball star and current TV sports commentator Charles Barkley says he made the decision to "elim-inate social media from my world. I think social media is just for losers to feel like they're important. They get to voice their opinion on every single thing in the world."[77] I have long believed that one of the most appealing traits of social media is that it gives us the ability to talk and be together without having to talk and be together. I lean toward introversion, so I am perhaps more tuned into this than many others are. It is significantly easier and more comfortable to interact with people when the Internet serves as a buffer. This is not about being antisocial or disliking people. It's a comfort thing and a consideration of personal energy reserves. This appeal may not be exclusive to introverts. "Technology is seductive when what it offers meets with our human vulnerabilities," writes Sherry Turkle, professor of the social studies of science and technology at MIT.[78] "And as it turns out, we are very vulnerable indeed. We are lonely but fearful of intimacy. Digital connections and the sociable robot may offer the illusion of companionship without the demands of friendship. Our networked life allows us to hide from each other, even as we are tethered to each other. We'd rather text than talk."

Facebook and other social media platforms offer users a fast and easy way to make new friendships and maintain old ones. This has obvious appeal in a time when so many people live highly mobile and urban lives. We often find ourselves alone in crowds of strangers and even physically close, real-world friendships are much different now than they were for most of human history and prehistory. During our hunter-gatherer days, intense friendships and close alliances were necessary for day-to-day survival. This is no longer the case for many in the modern world, however, and our relationships may feel less satisfying as a result.[79] Social media engagement may be irresistible in part because it promises at least a tiny taste of something we hunger for: membership in a band, clan, or tribe and the feeling of close interdependence with others that comes with it. Even if these online connections may be imperfect or shallow, it should not surprise us that people have flocked to social media in such high numbers. After all, real-world loneliness is awkward and uncomfortable. For some it may be closer to agony. It certainly isn't healthy. Loneliness, according to recent research, can be more destructive to our health than obesity, drug use, or smoking cigarettes. A 2017 *New Scientist* editorial declared loneliness an "epidemic" and "public health disaster," one that is "dreadfully damaging" to the mental and physical well-being of millions.[80]

Loneliness, scientists have only recently discovered, can increase inflammation in the body.[81] Excess inflammation is a significant problem that has been associated with depression, Alzheimer's disease, and obesity. And loneliness is far more common than you might expect. Researchers say that feelings of loneliness strike anyone at any point in life. One doesn't even have to actually be alone to feel lonely and suffer its consequences. It's likely to occur when a person's social expectations don't match the reality of his or her life.[82] It can happen to anyone.

Social media may one day be a source of relief for the serious problem of loneliness. But that day is not here yet. In fact, some believe that social media *causes* loneliness, depression, and other negative states.

## DOES FACEBOOK MAKE YOU SAD?

There have been many studies published over the last several years that suggest high-volume use of social media platforms, Facebook in particular, may cause depression, anxiety, and other mental health problems. Young people could be more vulnerable to these problems. For example, Canadian researchers who looked at more than seven hundred students in grades seven through twelve, reported a link between more frequent use of social media and mental health problems.[83]

Researchers at the University of Pittsburgh School of Medicine found a similar connection with young Americans, aged nineteen to thirty-two. Those who reported most frequently checking their social media accounts were 2.7 times more likely to suffer depression.[84] The researchers controlled for other factors that might cause or contribute to depression. However, lead researcher Lui yi Lin warned about the challenge of untangling cause and effect with these kinds of studies. "It may be," she said, "that people who already are depressed are turning to social media to fill a void."[85] Lin offered some additional important points to consider:

- "Exposure to social media also may cause depression, which could then in turn fuel more use of social media."
- "Exposure to highly idealized representations of peers on

social media elicits feelings of envy and the distorted belief that others lead happier, more successful lives."
- "Engaging in activities of little meaning on social media may give a feeling of 'time wasted' that negatively influences mood."
- "Social media use could be fueling 'Internet addiction,' a proposed psychiatric condition closely associated with depression."
- "Spending more time on social media may increase the risk of exposure to cyberbullying or other similar negative interactions, which can cause feelings of depression."

As you review the relevant research, there does *seem* to be many scary, negative consequences swirling around heavy social media use. On the other hand, millions of people go online daily, use social media frequently, and seem to escape unscathed. A 2015 Pew Research Center study reported that "the frequency of Internet and social media use has no direct relationship to stress in men."[86] That same report also found that the use of social media is linked to *lower* stress levels in women. Perhaps all we can be sure of at this time is that "too much" time on social media is unhealthy. "Too much," however, must be defined by each individual.

There is the possibility that social media may prove to be more helpful than burdensome to mental health problems. For example, algorithms might soon be sifting through mountains of social media data to screen people for mental health issues. Hopefully this would be done to help them get treatment rather than to discriminate against them, of course.

Two researchers, Harvard's Andrew Reece and Christopher Danforth of the University of Vermont, showed in 2017 that an AI program could identify people who had been diagnosed with depression, with a 70 percent accuracy rate, based on nothing more than photos users posted on Instagram.[87] Subtle differences such as variations in the use of color filters and brightness levels applied to photos were enough for the program to pick up on and identify people with depression. Human analysts could not match the computer program's success rate. Reece and Danforth wrote: "These findings support the notion that major changes in individual psychology are transmitted in social media use, and can be identified

via computational methods."[88] Privacy and abuse concerns notwith-
standing, there is fascinating potential for good here. In the future,
millions of people may routinely submit their social media accounts
for algorithmic analysis in order to reveal mental health problems
that might otherwise go undiagnosed and untreated.

A pertinent question is what so much screen time now might
mean for children and teens later in life. Jean M. Twenge, professor
of psychology at San Diego State University, studies the effects of
digital technologies on people and describes a looming disaster for
the current generation of young people—she calls them "iGen"—who
spend hours per day on their smartphones. "Rates of teen depression and suicide have skyrocketed since 2011."[89] Twenge warns: "It's
not an exaggeration to describe iGen as being on the brink of the
worst mental-health crisis in decades. Much of the deterioration
can be traced to their phones. . . . There is compelling evidence that
the devices we've placed in young people's hands are having profound effects on their lives—and making them seriously unhappy."

## WILL WE MISS PRIVACY?

> The gradual erosion of privacy is not just the unim-
> portant imaginings of fastidious liberals. Rather, the
> loss of privacy is a key symptom of one of the funda-
> mental social problems of our age: the growing power
> of large public and private institutions in relation to the
> individual citizen.
> —David Burnham, *The Rise of the Computer State*[90]

Chapter 5 addresses the general issue of privacy online. It will
shed light on the tireless and near-omnipresent algorithms that are
always out there, working and learning everything possible about
you wherever you go online. George Orwell may have grossly under-
estimated just how bad things could become. The constant surveillance, collection, and analysis of your data matters to you. Out-of-
sight must not mean out-of-mind when it comes to your personal
information and online habits. These hidden data-gathering processes impact your off-line life in many ways. Based on your digital
profile alone, there are companies that probably know you better

than your friends and family know you, and, in some ways, better than you know yourself.[91]

While working on this book, I interviewed or surveyed a wide cross section of social media users, more than one hundred, and was surprised to discover how few of them, especially among those under the age of twenty-five, are concerned about this constant monitoring, collecting, saving, and trading in the details of their lives that many companies and governments are engaged in. Most don't know much about it; and, among those who do, few seem worried. We are now years into the post–Edward Snowden[92] era. One might reasonably have thought that the widespread loss of privacy for hundreds of millions of people would be common knowledge and at least a bit distressing for most people of any age. Jacob Silverman is the author of *Terms of Service*, a hard-hitting book about social media. He stressed to me that there is indeed a big problem here worth everyone's attention: "I think many people simply don't realize that everything they do online is being surveilled by massive corporations and that data about their activities is freely traded among companies and governments."[93]

Silverman added that the constant customization of personal online experiences is another huge problem being overlooked: "[Many people] don't understand how their own behaviors and data production are used to filter information, social media timelines, and search results—producing what's commonly called a 'filter bubble,' in which people only see content designed to flatter their tastes or beliefs."

Don't ignore the dark side of social media. Don't pretend it's not there. Ignorance can only make it worse. "It's a digital data vacuum cleaner on steroids, that's what the online ad industry has created," explains Jeff Chester, executive director of the Center for Digital Democracy.[94] "They're tracking where your mouse is on the page, what you put in your shopping cart, what you don't buy [as well as what you do buy]. A very sophisticated commercial surveillance system has been put in place."

Lori Andrews, a law professor and activist for Internet privacy rights, explains that we are all shadowed by a digital double now. These doppelgangers have been pieced together from our searches, purchases, shopping trends, and social media activities. Your second "you" may even have more of an impact on your opportunities online than your off-line, real world characteristics do. For example, while online you might be shown ads for merchandise, tickets, or services with price points based not on your credit history or income but on your age, neighborhood, gender, skin color, and websites visited in the past—all based on data mined from your online activities.[95] "As behavioral advertisers increasingly dictate a person's online and off-line experiences, stereotyped characterizations may become self-fulfilling," Andrews warns. She continues:

> Rather than reflecting reality, behavioral analysis may inevitably define it. When young people from "poor" zip codes are bombarded with advertisements for trade schools, they may be more likely than their peers to forgo college. And when women are routinely shown articles about cooking and celebrities, rather than stock market trends, they will likely disclaim any financial savvy in the future. Behavioral advertisers are drawing new redlines, refusing to grant people the tools necessary to escape the roles that society expects they play. Our digital doppelgangers are directing our futures and the future of society.[96]

You are not the sum of your Google searches, Amazon purchases, and Facebook likes. Your online activities should not define you as a person. But, increasingly, they do. Part of the problem is that many people have been swayed by the sweet talk of a wonderful wired-world in which online social networks serve, fix, entertain, heal, and satisfy all wants and needs. For years now, young billionaires have been declaring lofty and gallant goals for the platforms that enrich them. For example, Mark Zuckerberg declares that his company, Facebook, will be key to ushering in the "global community," a true planetary culture that connects everyone, prevents harm, and enables faster progress.[97] Many have lined up behind such promises for the glorious march to cyber-utopia. But no one seems exactly sure of the details—how to get there and what it will look like once we arrive—only that we must move toward it. It's the mission itself that seems to matter most right now, and that mission is to connect everyone and share everything toward transcending borders, improving education, ending war and racism, sparking democratic revolutions, and generally saving us from ourselves. All of this can be accomplished thanks to "free" social media sites and apps. And to join in this noble adventure, all we need do is let them know everything about our private lives.[98]

I'm firmly opposed to encouraging irrational fears about anything, so I'm reluctant to paint too harsh an image here. But the "free" gift of participation on these social media platforms can be imagined as little Trojan horses that we happily welcome and wheel into the center of our lives. Millions of people enjoy, trust, and rely on social media activity; some give social media engagement something near to religious devotion. While our minds sleep in the glow of digital screens, however, little hoplites in the form of algorithmic digital spies and saboteurs spill out from the belly of the beast to conduct their endless espionage missions. Ignorance and indifference won't help us. As we will see, this challenge can be controlled to some degree and defended against in meaningful ways.

Silverman points out a couple of pertinent facts relevant to the cyber-utopian promise. First, that these exact same promises related to new communication technologies were made by others in the past. He quotes radio pioneer Guglielmo Marconi: "The coming of the wireless era will make war impossible, because it will make war ridiculous."[99] And, second, Silverman reminds us that the future is already here. The Internet, digital communication, and all of those "revolutionary" Apple products are everywhere—yet utopia eludes us. "Instantaneous global communication has failed to stop war, genocide, or famine; women remain second-class citizens in large parts of the world; authoritarian propaganda travels as easily online as human rights reports and in some countries, more easily; smartphones have become the preeminent surveillance tool for corporations and governments alike." He continues:

> While many once foresaw digital capitalism as the harbinger of an era of widespread prosperity, legacy industries such as newspapers have crumbled, and income inequality is now higher than ever—particularly in San Francisco, home to many technology industry employees who are shuttled daily on private buses to and from massive suburban campuses, where they're showered with amenities and services and never have to interact with residents in surrounding communities.[100]

For me, the most fascinating—and troubling—aspect of social media today is the uncertainty of it all. We just can't be sure where it's going in the near or long-term future. Sure, Facebook may bring us all together and help create one big happy human tribe. Or, it may divide and sort us into several million psychologically distinct digital silos, stirring conflict and dumbing down humanity to horrific levels.

William Poundstone, a thoughtful critic of human cognition and culture, is the author of several books, including *Head in the Cloud: Why Knowing Things Still Matters When Facts Are So Easy to Look Up*. He believes that social media has made and will continue to make a significant impact. "To be human is to change, and connectivity is part of that," he told me. "You see people crossing the street, or eating in restaurants, and they're all glued to their phones. You almost want to tell yourself it's a fad and it will pass. But think how much more immersive—and addictive—our devices will be in ten years. I don't pretend to know where we're going, but it's a big and fundamental change."[101]

At this point, no one knows enough to either cheer on or condemn social media without reservation. The landscape is changing under us every moment as countless invisible bridges connect a scattered humanity. The Internet and social media have made a significant and lasting impact on us in a brief time. And more is coming. We have added a new layer to our existence and cannot afford to ignore what appears to be a total and permanent rewiring of humanity, if that is indeed what this is. We cannot be passive about this or fail to give due attention. Yes, this means we must devote something more than a 140-character tweet, two-line Facebook post, or Instagram pic to the matter. We need to invest in some deep thinking about what it means to have more Facebook friends than flesh friends. Are we okay with so many people devoting considerable time and mental energy to sharing and retweeting other people's humor and wisdom instead of making an effort to create some of their own? Isn't it worthy of a parent's concern when a young daughter feels compelled to devote hours of daily effort to maintain an online persona? Shouldn't someone, maybe all of us, be concerned when a teenager becomes a full-time publicist charged with upping the Q-Rating of a client which is herself? "There was a time when," writes Randi Zuckerberg in her book *Dot Complicated*, "if you wore the wrong kind of clothes to middle school, at worst the only people who would notice would be the clique of mean girls at the cool-kids table. Now, the cool-kids table is everywhere."[102]

Online social networks can change the ways we view our relationships with others and how we fit into the world. These platforms reveal and display our connections to people in a new way. We now can look at a compilation of names and think to ourselves: *I know these people; I'm tied to all of them in some way, big or small*. Doing

this can give life to our networks, make them seem more important. Like everyone, I had friends in high school and college, and I
have made connections along the way in professional life. Prior to
engaging with social media sites, however, I never owned a list of
my friends or mapped out my social network. It existed only as a
vague cluster of faces who came and went somewhere in my mind.
Today, thanks to social media, I am able to scroll through a digital
list of thousands of names and headshots representing people I have
crossed paths with at some point and share a social connection with
to some degree. Ironically, seeing all of these people compiled in
one place for easy viewing on a computer screen makes them seem
more real than they would be if they had existed only as memories
or occasional contacts. "What makes social network sites unique is
not that they allow individuals to meet strangers," danah m. boyd
and Nicole B. Ellison write in the *Journal of Computer-Mediated
Communication*, "but rather that they enable users to articulate
and make visible their social networks."[103]

Social media sites are sometimes criticized for cheapening or
making a farce of friendships; but in this way, at least, they allow
us to better visualize, understand, and possibly develop a greater
appreciation for our existence as social creatures.

## WHAT DOES "FREE" COST?

A key reason social media platforms have become so popular is that
they are billed as free to users. What's odd about this is that they
are not free to their users. There is a price—and it's a considerable one. Users pay for access to the popular social media sites not
with cash but by pouring out much of their lives, knowingly and
otherwise. Your life is the currency by which you gain admission.
Your age, education, location, profession, and personal preferences
become ammunition to be used for or against you by marketers,
governments, employers, landlords, political operatives, and more.
Baby photos, tearful comments about breakups, political rants, and
photos of drunken adventures are all fair game. Social media companies aggregate, identify, and quantify users' online movements
and behaviors. "One mistake is to think social media are 'free,'"
Poundstone explains, "You're paying for them, just in ways you can't

see. Another is to think you're not affected by online advertising. Everybody thinks it's those 'other,' gullible people who fall for sales pitches. But we can't all be right. Online ads are a quarter-trillion-dollar industry."[104]

### YOUR FIFTEEN MINUTES OF FAME
### NEVER HAS TO END IN CYBERSPACE

**We've all been raised on television to believe that one day we'd all be millionaires, and movie gods, and rock stars. But we won't. And we're slowly learning that fact. And we're very, very pissed off.**
**—Chuck Palahniuk, *Fight Club*[105]**

What drives so many to devote time and energy to posting, commenting, and interacting on social media? Maybe this feels like the best or only way to be heard in an increasingly crowded and noisy world. I remember in the first weeks and months of my career as a journalist, I would get a rush of positive feelings when I saw my name in print. No matter that it might have been attached to a meaningless, mediocre article about nothing that was buried deep in the newspaper or magazine. If it had my name on it, it was a big deal. It's embarrassing to admit this publicly, but it felt like fame. And I liked it. Having my name seen by the public meant on some level that my existence was confirmed. I was real. I mattered. *I am published; therefore, I am*. Those moments of exhilaration faded over time, however. Today, even when I see my books on shelves in bookstores, I don't feel anything close to that first high of a simple newspaper byline. But I do remember. Maybe this is what many people who publish so much of their lives on social media sites are chasing. We all want to exist out in the light. We all want to be famous or popular, or at least matter to some degree. What is American pop culture today but a vast greenroom filled with delusional hopefuls anxiously awaiting the call to center stage? I imagine that anonymity might feel like death to some these days. And here comes social media to the rescue, offering everyone, regardless of status or ability, a readily available micro-dose of fame.

There must be something to that. Facebook earned $27 billion in advertising in 2016, and Google made $90 billion that year.[106] It's difficult to imagine this much money flying into the coffers of these social media companies on a yearly basis if they weren't selling something that businesses find value in. Clearly the playbook of surveilling users and exploiting their data for targeted advertising is a winner. At least for now. There is always the possibility of a public backlash at any time. If enough people were to become aware and get upset about how much of their lives is being harvested and sold, they might demand change or simply leave these platforms for others that offer more privacy.

It is important that every social media user, from mere dabblers to full-blown cyber-addicts, pause and let this soak in. Every click, share, like, search, tweet, photo, video, and comment is captured, saved, and tossed into various vats of data that define you. This is the digital brew that becomes your online identity. Algorithms determine who you are in digital form, and all of this happens beyond your vision and reach. You have no right to review it to see how much they know or check it for accuracy. For better or worse, you are what you do online, as transcribed by unknown numbers of algorithms.

I sometimes wonder what my digital profile looks like—not the profile I construct but the profile that is created by my data behind the scenes. I'd like to think that my profile shines as a charming fitness enthusiast, avid book reader, nature lover, and advocate for science and reason, but I doubt it's that simple or flattering. For instance, as a writer forever researching something new, I've read several issues of al Qaeda's disturbingly slick, well-designed online do-it-yourself-terrorism magazine. I've chatted at length with someone behind a white supremacy site—she was far more friendly and articulate than one might expect. For research pur-poses, I have attended two KKK rallies and one Neo-Nazi picnic. I probably e-mailed some friend or family member about one or more of those outings—*Hey, sorry, can't make lunch this Saturday. Gotta go to a Nazi potluck*—which means there is a digital record somewhere indicating that Guy P. Harrison goes to organized hate rallies. How might a soulless algorithm, one that perhaps lacks the flexible and insightful judgment of a human being, make use of that information? I also have an odd mix of Facebook friends, fans, and followers. Some are tofu-saturated, magic-crystal-believing liberals and others are fire-breathing, bombs-away right-wingers. For a science fiction short story, I once conducted an extensive series of Google searches while trying to come up with a fact-based estimate of how many millions of people a lethal lab-produced airborne virus might kill if it had an incubation period of two to three weeks in the host, during which time victims showed no symptoms so they could remain mobile and spread the virus farther. Come to think of it, it's worrisome that no one from the US government has ever knocked on my door to ask me a few questions. I also have a teenage son living in my house. I don't want to even begin to imagine what he may have been Googling over the years—on an Internet account with my name attached to it.

Do I have anything to worry about? Do you? Are there misinformation and misinterpretations out there that could be bad for us? We can't know, because the companies that barter in the shadows with our private thoughts and activities don't have to tell us what they know—or, what they think they know—about us. This should worry everyone because, unlike inaccurate credit reports, we don't have the legal right to check them. We can't petition to have harmful errors and misjudgments corrected when we don't even know that they exist.

Personally, this gives me pause; but maybe this is not a big deal. Maybe it's a good thing. "I don't believe there is any information worth protecting that is available via my social media accounts," said Natasha, a Florida attorney active on five social media platforms.[107] "I personally like advertisements being targeted toward consumers' desires and needs." I too like the way Amazon recommends book titles to me based on previous purchases and page visits. I've been introduced to many great books over the years in this way. But here's the colossal problem: Most people know relatively little about any of this. Too many people seem to know nothing at all about what is going on behind the scenes. If a person understands that virtually every move made on a social media site is logged, stored, saved, and sold—and he or she is okay with that— then fine, no problem, take the risk. While researching this book, however, I was shocked again and again by encounters with bright, well-informed social media users who knew almost nothing about the collection of "private" data that these companies are engaged in. People must become aware of this reality. As we will see later in this book, people can suffer when unseen algorithms nibble away at their souls one click at a time. I assume the main reason so many people aren't aware of what is going on is because social media companies don't make it clear to their users that they are trading in the data of their lives. Why would they tell? They can't be proud of what they are doing; because even if it's not illegal or unethical (users agree to allow it in most cases), it looms as a potential PR disaster for them nonetheless.

---

### A CONNECTED SPECIES

- Globally 3.2 billion people are using the Internet, of which 2 billion are from developing countries.
- Between 2000 and 2015, global Internet penetration grew seven-fold from 6.5 percent to 43 percent.
- For every Internet user in the developed world, there are two in the developing world.
- Four billion people from developing countries remain offline, together representing two-thirds of the population residing in developing countries.
- Of the 940 million people living in the least developed countries (LDCs), only 89 million use the Internet, which corresponds to a 9.5 percent penetration rate.
- The proportion of households with Internet access increased from 18 percent in 2005 to 46 percent in 2015.
- Mobile broadband penetration reached 47 percent in 2015, twelve times greater than in 2007.
- The proportion of the population covered by a 2G mobile-cellular network grew from 58 percent in 2001 to 95 percent in 2015.

Source: International Telecommunications Union[108]

## WHAT A CONNECTED WORLD IS DOING TO US

Less than 1 percent of the world's population was using the Internet back in the early days of the 1990s. Today, however, about half the world's population is online. This equates to more than 3.5 billion people.[109] This fast spread has meant tumultuous times for traditional news media companies. The way we interact with information has changed in profound ways. Thanks to the Internet in general and social media in particular, the way millions of people get and process news is significantly different from what it was only a couple of decades ago. Where gatekeepers once determined what information we would read, hear, and view, we now have . . . ourselves? Yes, you are now your own news editor and publisher. There is still plenty of accurate news out there, but you have to think before consuming more than ever because of the sheer volume and accessibility to lies and nonsense. Social media serves as fertile ground for lies, error, fake news, and an endless tsunami of stupidity. Good luck if you aren't adept at critical thinking.

Social media has empowered and energized bad ideas and beliefs like nothing we have seen before. A ridiculous claim can now move around nations and even the entire world at lightning speeds to bore straight into the minds of millions of people. Just ask Mario Gazin, the owner of a Brazilian mattress factory. His company's sales began to decline rapidly, and then he lost an order for one million units. Why? Because of a claim spread on WhatsApp. Someone recorded a message claiming that Gazin had made a literal deal with Satan to sell more mattresses. The story spread like wildfire, particularly among Brazil's large evangelical population.[110] People just didn't want to do business with someone who was doing business with the devil. Of course, the person who made the post presented no evidence nor logical support of the claim. He or she just threw it up on the wall of cyberspace and people believed it.

The greater personal independence and choice that come with mass online connectivity are good things because our news and information should not have to be spoon-fed to us by paternalistic governments and corporations. Part of being an adult is taking responsibility for your decisions and actions. However, there is the problem of how well this diverse and abundant flow of information can work when so many people seem determined to operate with a childlike willingness to believe just about anything they encounter on social media, no matter how unlikely or absurd it may be. "Some people observing the media landscape today have wondered whether truth even matters anymore," write media experts Bill Kovach and Tom Rosenstiel in their book, *Blur*, "Perhaps," they speculate, "in the new information age reality is simply a matter of belief, not anything objective or verified . . . . Rather than trying to find out what is going on, they have already decided. Perhaps, in a sense, we have already moved from the age of information to the age of affirmation."[111]

Sadly, that seems like a fair description of much of the current culture. Kovach and Rosenstiel point out that this is not the entire story of what has happened, though:

> Old journalism's problems have much more to do with loss of revenue due to technology than a loss of audience. . . . The most fundamental change is that more of the responsibility for knowing what is true and what is not now rests with each of us as individuals. The notion that a network of social gatekeepers will tell us that things have been established or proven is breaking down. Citizens have more voice, but those who would manipulate the public for political gain or profit—be it corporations or the government—have more direct access to the public as well.[112]

## THE CONNECTED BRAIN

Some people are sure that social media is just another fad, one destined to vanish as fast as it arrived. It is difficult to imagine its extinction any time soon, however, because its key features soothe, if not accommodate, some of our deepest needs and desires. And the numbers don't lie. *Billions* are doing it. These online social network activities are behavioral expressions of who we are as a species. Humans have always been social creatures, and there are no signs of this changing. Social media is a new way of doing an old thing. Therefore, so long as the Internet survives, it is probable that online social media will remain popular and relevant in some form as well. With hindsight, it is easy to see why millions would have flocked to social media.

## FACEBOOK

### Headquarters

1 Hacker Way, Menlo Park, California 94025

### Employees

20,658 employees

### Statistics

- More than 2 billion monthly active users
- 1.32 billion daily active users on average
- 1.15 billion mobile daily active users on average
- Approximately 85.2 percent of daily active users are outside the United States and Canada

Source: Facebook[113]

## FACEBOOK DOMINATES THE SOCIAL MEDIA ECOSYSTEM

| Percentage of US Adults Using | | | | |
|------|------|------|------|------|
|      | Facebook | Pinterest | Instagram | LinkedIn | Twitter |
| 2016 | 68% | 26% | 28% | 25% | 21% |
| 2014 | 58% | 22% | 21% | 23% | 19% |
| 2012 | 54% | 10% | 9% | 16% | 13% |

Source: Pew Research Center[114]

| | | Facebook | Instagram | Pinterest | LinkedIn | Twitter |
|---|---|---|---|---|---|---|
| | **WHO IS ON SOCIAL MEDIA?** | | | | | |
| | Total | 68% | 28% | 26% | 25% | 21% |
| **Sex** | Men | 67% | 23% | 15% | 28% | 21% |
| | Women | 69% | 32% | 38% | 23% | 21% |
| **Age** | 18–29 | 88% | 59% | 36% | 34% | 36% |
| | 30–49 | 79% | 31% | 32% | 31% | 22% |
| | 50–64 | 61% | 13% | 24% | 21% | 18% |
| | 65+ | 36% | 5% | 9% | 11% | 6% |
| **Education** | High School or less | 56% | 19% | 18% | 9% | 14% |
| | Some college | 77% | 35% | 31% | 25% | 24% |
| | College graduate | 77% | 32% | 33% | 49% | 28% |
| | Less than $30,000 | 65% | 29% | 23% | 16% | 18% |
| | $30,000–$49,999 | 68% | 27% | 27% | 11% | 16% |
| | $50,000–$74,999 | 70% | 30% | 29% | 30% | 26% |
| | $75,000+ | 76% | 30% | 34% | 45% | 30% |
| **Location** | Urban | 70% | 34% | 26% | 29% | 22% |
| | Suburban | 68% | 24% | 29% | 26% | 21% |
| | Rural | 65% | 25% | 20% | 15% | 19% |

Source: Pew Research Center[115]

We are an obsessively social life-form in servitude to an insatiable hunger for peer interaction and networking.[116] We can't help ourselves when it comes to connecting, watching, showing, sharing, envying, bragging, and so on. Communities are the foundation of not only our species but also our genus. Socializing helped make us what we are today. Introverts are common, making up about a third to half of the population,[117] but true hermits are exceedingly rare.

Lifetimes are spent gathering evidence of our significance, no matter how flimsy or fleeting, in the form of social recognition and acceptance from other people. Admiring people, wanting to be like them, gossiping about them, asserting dominance, being submissive, showing off, comparing and judging, these are all human activities that predate, well, humans. Perhaps Facebook, Instagram, Snapchat, Twitter, and the rest were made inevitable or at least predicted by the rise of *Australopithecus afarensis* and *Homo erectus* in prehistoric Africa so long ago. They used the power of small social networks to help them survive and find some comfort in difficult environments. We might imagine the earliest grunts and calls, coupled with their crucial alliances, as the dawn of social media.

## IS SOCIAL MEDIA THE NEW SOCIAL CAPITAL?

It may be tempting to explain the explosive success of social media as one more case of herd mentality, just another fad with people copying people. That may explain it in part, but there is more to it. This cultural phenomenon is not only remarkable because many hundreds of millions of people have signed up for Facebook, Instagram, Snapchat, and so on, and use them; what makes social media so interesting and important is that vast numbers of people are spending significant amounts of time on these platforms and doing many different things with them. Clearly this young and growing digital ecosystem means something to many people of all ages and diverse backgrounds. But why? Why does a significant portion of humanity want or need to have an online network of friends, followers, and acquaintances?

Some people may charge that puttering around in a digital fantasyland with a few friends on Facebook or Snapchat is a lame and trivial diversion, the contemporary equivalent of watching mindless sitcoms back in the 1980s. But there is something going on here that may have far more significance than is readily apparent. "Social capital," a sociology term meant to attribute value to real-world or off-line social networks, is relevant to social media. Our social connections, the bonds with other people with whom we share our lives in intimate or tangential ways, have a profound impact on our lives. Both the quality and quantity of these connections impact much of what matters to us, from our careers to our love lives.

Perhaps the staggering popularity of social media platforms, achieved in such short time, is associated with—though not causal to—a decades-long trend of slipping and fading connections. Americans, for example, have become much less tied to one another and to their traditional social institutions. The typical American is no longer strongly connected to extended family, neighbors, colleagues, and clubs as was once the case. Involvement in such clubs, civic groups, religious gatherings, and other forms of active "belonging" have all plummeted over the last fifty years.[118]

This is not a uniquely American phenomenon. Many societies around the world have been experiencing the same trend. And I've witnessed this firsthand. I lived in the Cayman Islands for some twenty years, and it is common there to hear older people complain about what they see as the erosion and loss of a once-close-knit community in which "everyone knew everyone." Social involvement, awareness, and commitment to traditional institutions were at high levels there thirty years or more ago. People felt that they could rely on one another. All of that has faded significantly, they say, to the detriment of the Cayman Islands. Many older Jamaicans have expressed the same sentiments to me about their homeland.

**US SOCIAL TRENDS AT THE CLOSE OF THE LAST CENTURY[119]**

| Attending Club Meetings | Down 58% |
|---|---|
| Family Dinners | Down 43% |
| Having Friends Over | Down 35% |

One of the more interesting and provocative books about the weakening of traditional (off-line) social networks in the United States is

Robert Putnam's *Bowling Alone*. Although it was published back in 2000, before the creation of Facebook and other broadly successful platforms, I believe his work can help us understand some of social media's attraction and the hold it has on so many people today. Putnam, a professor of public policy at Harvard, points to social capital as a critical measure of a society's strength and overall vitality. For readers who are not familiar with the concept of social capital, it may be helpful to think of it as the flesh-and-bones or *living human* version of money, property, infrastructure, land, and resources. In Putnam's words:

> Whereas physical capital refers to physical objects and human capital refers to the properties of individuals, social capital refers to connections among individuals—social networks and the norms of reciprocity and trustworthiness that arise from them. In that sense social capital is closely related to what some have called "civic virtue." The difference is that "social capital" calls attention to the fact that civic virtue is most powerful when embedded in a dense network of reciprocal social relations. A society of many virtuous but isolated individuals is not necessarily rich in social capital.[120]

Putnam found that social capital plunged over the last few decades of the last century. Americans now vote less, attend fewer club and civic meetings, go to fewer religious services, entertain friends and extended family at home less often, and so on. "For the first two-thirds of the twentieth century a powerful tide bore Americans into ever deeper engagement in the life of their communities," writes Putnam, "but a few decades ago—silently, without warning—that tide reversed and we were overtaken by a treacherous rip current. Without at first noticing, we have been pulled apart from one another and from our communities over the last third of the [twentieth] century."[121]

Why has social capital declined in the United States and in other societies? Putnam, again, writing before the age of Facebook and Twitter, lists multiple factors that have contributed to this unraveling of old, off-line social networks: (1) *television*, which may account for as much as 40 percent of the decline; (2) *suburban sprawl*, because when people are spread out over larger geographical areas, social involvement becomes more difficult and time-consuming; and (3) *living alone*, which makes it more difficult to connect and build social ties with others and with traditional social institutions.

Before attempting to connect the decline of social capital to the rise of social media, it is important to make clear its value. Consider the following benefits of social capital, according to Putnam:[122]

- Social capital enables people to **solve problems**, especially bigger, collective problems.
- Social capital **"greases the wheels"** of a community with trust and cooperation helping to make business and social contacts efficient and productive.
- Social capital makes it easier for one to recognize how his or her success or failure may be linked to the success or failure of others. It stimulates and nurtures a sense that **we're in this together**, which can make working to achieve collective goals more desirous.
- Civic connections may be as potent as **marriage and wealth** when it comes to predicting life happiness.
- **Children benefit** from high levels of social capital. The quality of their development is strongly tied to the levels of trust and reciprocity in society.
- Having solid social networks make communities **safer and more functional** because people work together and watch out for one another. Where social capital is low they do not. (As such, Putnam concludes that poverty has less to do with the cleanliness and crime of an area than social capital.)
- Communities with high social capital **do better economically** and can better withstand social and economic challenges.
- Joining and participating in one social group cuts in half your **odds of dying** in the next year.
- Social capital allows for the **flow of helpful information** that is useful or necessary to achieving community goals.

The decline of social capital is a compound problem because social capital is composed of two types: "bonding capital" and "bridging capital."[123] Bonding capital is the sum of connections between people who are *alike or have similar interests*. Bridging capital is the sum of connections between people who are *not alike or do not share similar interests*. Putnam describes bonding capital as a kind of "sociological glue," a human adhesive, and bridging capital as a "sociological WD-40," a human lubricant.[124] Bridging capital is of great importance to societies with highly diverse populations, such as the United States. Bonding capital, for all its virtues, can also be destructive; this would be the case when one group is tightly bonded together but devoid of external bonds. Neo-Nazi groups, al Qaeda, and ISIS, for example, have high *bonding* social capital but little *bridging* capital, which helps fuel their destructive ideologies. If bridging capital sets the stage for greater cooperation and overall harmony, then maybe social media really can save the world because it seems capable of inspiring and nourishing this, even as the problem of filter bubbles (see chapter 2) encourages the division.

## HAVE ONLINE CONNECTIONS REPLACED OFF-LINE CONNECTIONS?

The reason I suspect that the explosive rise of online social networks is a direct reaction to the decline of social capital is because it was the perfect fit with perfect timing. This *proves* nothing, of course. Coincidences happen every day, and maybe this is one of them. But I find it hard to believe that more than a billion people would be devoting so many hours per day cultivating Facebook profiles if they were going to club meetings and religious services, keeping up with union activities, focused on various civic duties, and holding a regular Thursday-evening card game with the neighbors. With all of that going on, who would have time for social media?

Facebook, Instagram, Twitter, and so on all sprouted up within a social ecosystem in decline. When Americans, and others around the world who were experiencing the same trends, found themselves alone and isolated at home, night after night, with their televisions and little else to occupy them, a hunger grew. They were in violation of the primate directive to make and maintain social networks. This set the stage perfectly for the new online ecosystem that offered them at least a form of human connection and involvement, however imperfect and ultimately unsatisfying for some. And they could engage in it without having to leave home or even get up off the couch—perfect. Social media provided people with a new outlet to express one of our oldest and deepest universal urges. Of course it proved irresistible to millions. We can't, however, conclude that social media or even the Internet at large is behind the loss of social capital, which Putnam points out:

The timing of the Internet explosion means that it cannot possibly be causally linked to the crumbling of social connectedness. . . . Voting, giving, trusting, meeting, visiting, and so on had all begun to decline while Bill Gates was still in grade school. By the time that the Internet reached ten percent of American adults in 1996, the nationwide decline in social connectedness and civic engagement had been underway for at least a quarter of a century. Whatever the future implications of the Internet, social intercourse over the last several decades of the twentieth century was not simply displaced from physical space to cyberspace. The Internet may be part of the solution to our civic problem, or it may exacerbate it, but the cyberrevolution was not the cause.[125]

---

### HOW MANY FACEBOOK FRIENDS DO YOU HAVE?

- 39% of adult users have between 1 and 100 Facebook friends
- 23% have 101–250 friends
- 20% have 251–500 friends
- 15% have more than 500 friends

The average (mean) number of Facebook friends is 338. The median (midpoint) number of friends is 200, meaning half of all Facebook users have more than 200 friends and half have fewer than 200. Younger users have larger friend networks than older users. Twenty-seven percent of those in the eighteen-to-twenty-nine-year-old range have more than 500 friends in their network. Seventy-two percent of users age 65 and over have 100 friends or fewer.[126]

---

## THE IMPACT OF SOCIAL MEDIA

A 2016 Pew study on the US presidential campaign of that year found that social media equaled local TV news as the "most helpful" source of political news for Americans.[127] Only cable TV news was more popular. Social media ranked ahead of news websites, news apps, radio news, network nightly news, and newspapers. Most interesting, however, is what seems to be in store for the future. Young people aged eighteen to twenty-nine named social media as their preferred source for news about the presidential campaign. Thirty-five percent said that they rely on social media first; this is concerning due to the tailored experience social media users face each time they open up their social media apps, as we'll explore in a moment. Among this age group, news websites and news apps came in second with 18 percent; and cable news, third with 12 percent. As evidenced by these findings, it is clear that American society, and the rest of the world, are changing fast. No one may accuse social media of being trivial or irrelevant. These sites and apps have become a key information source for millions of people.

An issue in need of immediate attention is one almost no one recognizes: Many of the same features and benefits that make social media attractive and popular also enable and magnify cognitive biases, prejudices, and high levels of irrational belief—perhaps more than any form of media ever has before. One could hardly dream up a better environment to nurture confirmation bias, subconscious fears, and general cognitive laziness. Chapter 4 addresses these problems in depth. Critical thinking, skepticism, and awareness of standard mental processes are essential to the individual on social media. Out in popular culture today, Facebook friends and Twitter followers are fast replacing professional editors and producers of national newspapers and TV network news as the selectors and arbiters of information. One of the best things about social media is that it eliminates traditional gatekeepers. One of the worst things about social media is that it eliminates traditional gatekeepers.

## THE RENAISSANCE OF NONSENSE WILL BE DIGITIZED

We are a silly species; there's no denying that. You only have to look at the constant avalanche of ridiculous and unlikely things we humans believe to be true. From astrology to auroras, from ghosts to the gazer who heals,[128] many people line up, ready to believe with cash in hand. Yes, we have the most powerful and capable brains on Earth and, yes, we have achieved many wonderful and impressive things in a relatively short time. But Mozart's music and smartphones can't redeem or hide our lust for the ludicrous. Suckers for empty promises, false hopes, and pseudoscientific babble, we are our own worst enemies. Few people take the time to learn how brains process sensory input in misleading ways and how subconscious biases influence conscious thinking. The result is a global population teeming with easy targets for nonsense and deception.

To get a sense of just how bad things are here in the early days of the twenty-first century, consider these statistics: Three out of four American adults hold one or more paranormal/supernatural beliefs such as spirit channeling or magic crystals.[129] Haunted houses are real, according to 40 percent of adults in Great Britain.[130] Nearly a quarter of all Canadian adults think that some people carry on two-way conversations with dead people.[131] As a by-product of their religious beliefs, more than 40 percent of adult Americans think that Earth is less than 10,000 years old.[132] This is about as wrong as one can be, and on a basic fact that is easy to check. Based on a convergence of verifiable evidence from multiple scientific disciplines, it is clear that Earth is much older than 10,000 years. Our planet has an origin date of approximately 4.56 billion years ago. Saying that Earth is only a few thousand years old is as far off the mark as claiming that the Moon is only a third of a mile away or that New York City is about twenty feet from Los Angeles. But, as disturbing as these kinds of belief statistics can be to those who place a high value on reason and reality, it may get much worse in the near future due in large part to the power of social media.

Today, social media serves as a vast playground, a virtual paradise in which irrational beliefs run free. "We have passed through the looking glass and down the rabbit hole. America has mutated into Fantasyland," laments Kurt Andersen, novelist and host of the award-winning radio show/podcast *Studio 360* in his book, *Fantasyland: How America Went Haywire*.[133] "The old fringes have been folded over into the new center. The irrational has become respectable and often unstoppable."[134] The positive features of Facebook, Twitter, YouTube, and other platforms become powerful negatives when used by con artists, crackpots, and the sincerely deluded. This mostly borderless environment with few rational, competent, and ethical gatekeepers allows just about anyone to promote fraudulent or unjustified claims to audiences of potential millions. The freedoms, convenience, and long reach available to a social media user should not be bad things—but they are when they are used in ways that spread bogus conspiracy theories, medical quackery, and other lies that can and do have real-world, sometimes life-and-death, consequences.

The good news, though, is that social media has the potential to be the solution to its own problems. Skeptics, scientists, experts, and all reason-loving people can use its powers too. They can spread evidence-based ideas, rational perspectives, and accurate information. The hang-up, however, is always how receptive people can and will be to evidence-based claims and skeptical analysis of their irrational beliefs. Most people probably want to be on the right side of truth and reality, but how many know how to get there? It's not as easy as you might think; sometimes, trying to convince someone to question critically a closely held irrational belief can prove tricky.

Social media presents a constant danger to those who have not activated their personal force field of skepticism. The point of this book is that everyone using social media needs to be careful. Being human makes you vulnerable to being led astray in a variety of ways. It's not difficult to adopt safe strategies and make them habits; but it won't happen naturally. Unfortunately, we tend to overestimate our ability to spot lies and absurdities. Most people have no problem recognizing how bad others are at thinking logically; but that sharp perceptive ability often fails us when we look in the mirror.[135] False confidence is a key problem, because it fools people into thinking they can't be fooled. But, of course, all we have to do is point at the shocking sample of belief statistics listed previously. Almost anyone can believe almost anything. No one can deny that irrational belief and runaway cognitive biases are more than a fringe nuisance. This is a global human problem that, to some degree, burdens everyone in every society. Problems are inevitable when the natural state of a social media user is to be susceptible to the power of story over statistics, to be a willing prisoner of both unfounded fears and hopes, and to surrender reason to nonsense because it feels polite, fashionable, or expedient to do so. The good news is that with a specific awareness and certain key skills, anyone can plunge into social media and come out with both their dignity and their connection to reality undamaged.


## WHY TERRORISTS LOVE SOCIAL MEDIA

Some people believe social media will do nothing less than save the world by ushering in a new age of connectivity, mass education, and positive interaction between distant and diverse peoples.

Maybe. Facebook, or some successor to it, may well end up being the critical component to humankind finally achieving a sustainable and peaceful global civilization. Others, however, warn that social media might help to finally drown us all in a sad cesspool of fear, hate, and stupidity. After all, some of the world's most violent and destructive groups currently use social media to organize and grow their ranks in pursuit of dark goals. The FBI stated that it is "highly confident" that Omar Mateen, the man who killed forty-nine people and wounded fifty-three others at an Orlando nightclub in 2016, was "radicalized at least in part through the Internet."[136]

Emerson T. Brooking and P. W. Singer, two experts on the relationship between social media and conflict, charge social media with "expanding the causes and possibly the incidence of war, and extending its reach."[137] Writing in the *Atlantic* they cite the troublesome "us versus them" narrative that social media often supports. These platforms also "expose vulnerable people to virulent ideologies, and inflame even long-dormant hatreds." Brooking and Singer conclude: "Social media has already revolutionized everything from dating to business to politics. Now it is reshaping war itself."[138]

United States Senator Robert Portman said during a Senate subcommittee hearing on terrorism and social media that ISIS, the terrorist group committed to establishing an Islamic caliphate by violent means, has "pioneered a distinctive strategy of targeted online recruitment" through the posting of "sleek viral videos and messages" via social media:

> ISIS, of course, specializes in savagery—violence inspired by delusions of sectarian conquest from another age. Yet it has effectively deployed modern technology of the information age to spread its propaganda and recruit killers to its cause. ISIS has developed a sophisticated information warfare capability. . . . As [former FBI] Director James Comey has noted, even if we were able to keep foreign terrorists physically out of the United States, online communication and social media allow ISIS to, as he said, "enter as a photon and radicalize somebody in Wichita, Kansas." ISIS has weaponized online propaganda in a new and very lethal way. The damage wrought by that weapon is considerable: Orlando, 49 dead; San Bernardino, 14 [dead]; Fort Hood, 13 dead; the Boston Marathon, 3 dead and hundreds wounded. Each of these killers was reportedly radicalized to some degree by online jihadist content. And so many other attacks

inspired by means of social media have, thank God, been thwarted. Indeed, experts tell us that throughout last year, social media played some part in the radicalization of all of the 60 people arrested in the United States for criminal acts in support of ISIS. . . . Online propaganda, amplified by social media and Peer-2-Peer (P2P) communication, is now a key weapon in ISIS's arsenal.[139]

It's not only execution videos and promises of divine approval via violence that show up on these networking sites. ISIS has used social media to present a utopian vision of the caliphate, the fundamentalist Islamic world empire, it seeks to create. One such video showed ice cream being served to the smiling and cheerful residents of an ISIS-occupied city.[140]

Senator Portman stated that while not all terrorism recruitment occurs online, the greatest threat to the United States is that of the lone-wolf terrorist—a person who is radicalized in physical isolation from recruiters, "often in front of his computer screen with access to online jihadist content and videos that create a sort of virtual training camp."[141] Facebook and Twitter have taken steps to reduce the use of their platforms by terrorists. Twitter has shut down more than 100,000 ISIS-linked or ISIS-friendly accounts.[142] Facebook has removed many offending users as well. The senator said these moves have been helpful but the online presence of ISIS "remains strong." In the wake of recent terror attacks, Facebook has been sharply criticized and accused by some of not doing enough to purge and block terrorists from its platform. Facebook has responded by committing to use a combination of AI and human expertise to identify and eliminate accounts used by people aligned with ISIS or other terror groups.[143] How effective this will be remains to be seen.

Never forget that social connections, whether in the physical or digital world, have no inherent moral purity or goodness about them. They can be used to enlighten or to dim minds; to entertain and enrich existence or waste time; to improve lives or end lives. Social media has been a key tool for many terrorist organizations in the twenty-first century, especially jihadists. ISIS, for example, made effective use of it to organize, recruit, and plan operations. These particularly violent apocalyptic religious fighters amplified their successes and drew more fighters to their ranks by the thousands via Twitter and other social media platforms. ISIS fighters did this by posting images and videos that could be viewed and shared by people far away. "The rise of social media as well as the use of the Internet more broadly to disseminate propaganda and connect people to extremist groups . . . has reshaped the jihadist scene," says a New America report on terrorism.[144] "Many extremists today either maintain public social media profiles displaying jihadist rhetoric or imagery or have communicated online using encrypted messaging apps."

*Wired* magazine declared in 2016 that ISIS was "as much a media conglomerate as a fighting force."[145] In the same article, *Wired* cited experts who say that digital propaganda has motived "more than 30,000 people to turn their backs on everything they've ever known and journey thousands of miles into dangerous lands, where they've been told a paradise awaits."

Few people may realize just how good ISIS and others have gotten at using social media for their cause. They don't tweet "*Allāhu akbar*" and leave it at that. The increasing quality of the material promoted on social media activity is alarming. The video of caged Jordanian pilot Muath al-Kasasbeh being burned alive by ISIS, for example, was a sophisticated production far beyond the simple and bland al Qaeda videos of the early 2000s. I watched the entire twenty-two-minute-long video of the pilot's execution. (I do not recommend that anyone do so.) Beyond the abject horror of seeing a trapped man killed in such a way, I was also struck by the terrorists' effective use of music, sharp editing, and diagrams of al-Kasabeh's F16 jet and weaponry. Most potent was the theme, the message behind the grisly killing of a man. Video clips of numerous bombings of ISIS targets by Jordan and Western nations were included. Destroyed buildings and injured or dead civilians were shown, all in an attempt to place a moral context of judgment against the pilot. One especially unpleasant scene showed a dead child, presumably killed by a Western-made bomb. In the film production, all of this ultimately led up to pilot al-Kasabeh's forced walk among the rubble of a neighborhood left in ruins, presumably by enemy bombs. Muscular masked men wearing Special Forces–style uniforms and gear stood guard as al-Kasasbeh walked toward his execution. This was followed by the horrific and barbaric act of burning alive a man trapped in a cage. The video spread to unknown numbers people through social media. Most Western news media, however, chose not to show or even mention the central theme of the video in their reporting, instead covering only the execution itself; as such, many in the West are unaware of the ultimate purpose of ISIS's video, and, therefore, of the effects it could have on those who are susceptible to recruitment efforts.

The power of social media to help terrorists is evidenced by the destructive legacy of jihadist recruiter Anwar al-Awlaki. Hellfire missiles fired from two US drones killed him in Yemen in 2011, but is he really gone? Even in death al-Awlaki continues to recruit, thanks to social media. His videos live on, drawing in new people to fight and die for the al Qaeda/ISIS version of Islam. Because of social media's continuing growth, al-Awlaki may be more successful and influential now than when he was alive.[146]

It is difficult to imagine ISIS or any other currently active terror organization taking down civilization. But what if another group were to come along in the near future, perhaps one with a more rational foundation and less insane sales pitch? What if the next hurricane of human hate utilizes social media to even greater effect, recruiting not tens of thousands but tens of millions? Maybe some future generation will look back on our problems with ISIS in the early twenty-first century as mere foreshadowing for the greater catastrophe that followed. Then, of course, there is the optimistic scenario in which a fully networked population prospers under a bright cloud of Big Data put to good use for the benefit of all. Perhaps this would fall short of the singularity—the moment when AI soars out of sight—but there would be plenty to appreciate and celebrate.

Using the past and the present as a guide, it is easiest to imagine a complex and messy future ahead. The safe bet is that social media will continue to be a source or conduit of both good and bad outcomes. Big picture aside, however, the priority for the individual user is to stay sharp and think clearly amidst all of the noise and turbulence. Intellectual self-preservation is the priority online. This is not as selfish or shortsighted as it may seem, for the individual who values truth and lives a life grounded in reason is best able to nudge others toward a safer and more rational world. Remember, just as propaganda, fraud, and delusions travel with force throughout social media, so too can truth and reality—if enough of us want them to.

*Chapter Two*

# WELCOME TO YOUR VERY OWN CUSTOMIZED, BIASED BUBBLE OF PSYCHOLOGICAL REINFORCEMENT, MANIPULATION, AND LIES

**Facebook has a fundamental characteristic that has proven key to its appeal in country after country—you only see friends there.**
—David Kirkpatrick, author of *The Facebook Effect*[1]

**We are still coming to grips with the role that Facebook plays in American democracy.**
—Brendan Nyhan, professor of political science, Dartmouth College[2]

**We used to say that seeing is believing; now Googling is believing.**
—Michael P. Lynch, philosopher[3]

**The algorithms that orchestrate our ads are starting to orchestrate our lives.**
—Eli Pariser, author of *The Filter Bubble*[4]

I was trapped inside and didn't even know it. For a period of probably five or six years, I was partially blind and deluded, drifting about in a filter bubble of my own creation. It didn't cause me any major problems, but, looking back, it likely did have a slight negative impact on both my personal and professional lives. I had set up a system on my computer and smartphone that would spoon-fed me science news throughout the day, every day. If somebody discovered a new bat species in a rainforest somewhere, I was going to know about it. How can this not be a good thing? What could possibly go wrong? Over time, however, my catered diet of science news led me to develop what I now look back on and see as a distorted, unrealistic view of the society around me. I came to assume that everyone was keeping up with science news and was aware of all of the latest discoveries and advancements. After years of one awkward encounter after another with people who hadn't heard anything about the new exoplanet just found or the latest hominin fossil pulled from the Earth in Africa, it slowly dawned on me that I was projecting my personal information intake onto others. I was living inside a *science news* filter bubble and thought everyone was in there with me, when, of course, they weren't.

## WHAT IS A "FILTER BUBBLE"?

Filter bubbles are personal online zones of customized news, entertainment, and social media posts; tailored search results; targeted ads; and so on that can be so specific and consistent to an individual that the flow of this information places the recipient at a risk of developing a distorted worldview on one or many issues. Opposing viewpoints, contrary arguments, as well as random and novel ideas can become rare or nonexistent inside a filter bubble. Algorithms serve up whatever information is deemed most likely to make you happy and content—reality and your personal growth be damned. Remember, social media platforms are hell-bent on keeping you engaged often and for as long as possible. There just isn't a lot of priority given to helping you become well-rounded and worldly. Filter bubbles help keep users feeling good, self-assured, and stuck to these sites and apps. Political activist Eli Pariser, author of *The Filter Bubble*, is credited with coming up with the name that is now in wide use.[5] Some refer to this problem as being in an echo chamber or silo. Whatever you call it, don't allow yourself to become lost in them unaware.

Thanks to my daily diet of science news, my subconscious mind had drifted to the assumption that everyone was diligent about staying on top of science news, just like me. But, of course, relatively few people do. I can remember many times feeling confused as to why the smart, educated person I was having a conversation with wasn't aware of some fascinating science news that I brought up. As far as my work, I am sure that I wrote some news articles and commentary pieces that were not as good as they could have been if I had not been operating under the assumption that *everyone* knew at least something about some science idea, fact, or discovery. The solution to my problem was not to stop paying attention to science news, of course, but to adjust my awareness and keep in mind that most people were not inside this particular filter bubble with me. Since then, I try to avoid launching into conversations with people under the blind assumption that they are avid science fans, too. I haven't stopped bringing up science news with just about anyone, anytime, and anywhere; I just try to be more sensible about it.

That simple lesson of my own filter bubble experience stuck with me. As political filter bubbles floated across the American landscape like hot-air balloons during the wild and raucous 2016 US presidential election season, I felt frustrated and sad for the minds entombed within them. People couldn't understand how the other side could be so wrong about so much when the news and facts were so plain and obvious. I knew that millions of people had no idea that their online activities had left them intellectually compromised, far more biased and myopic, than they otherwise would have been. Daniel J. Boorstin, the late historian and Librarian of the United States Congress, saw the potential problem of blind bias and irrational beliefs running amok long before the Internet and digital filter bubbles. He wrote this in 1961: "We risk being the first people in history to have been able to make their illusions so vivid, so persuasive, so 'realistic' that they can live in them."[6]

Filter bubbles are a significant problem now and could become much worse in the near future as algorithms become more sophisticated and ubiquitous. It is important for social media users to be aware of this challenge and take practical steps to counter it as best they can in their lives. To be clear, I am not anti-filter-bubble in a total sense. Filters can be good; and I will argue later in this chapter that certain kinds of filters are necessary for a life well lived. Furthermore, some bubbles can be useful, too, to a degree. The key is to consciously choose the right filters, inhabit the right bubbles (as best we can), and be aware that online information comes to us under the influence of someone else's bias or agenda. We also must accept the hard truth that it is virtually impossible to escape all filter bubbles all of the time. There simply is too much going on beyond our view to completely control the flow of information. The issues addressed in this chapter, filter bubbles and fake news, are serious challenges and raise an important question: Is social media a threat to social unity and democracy? You could make a strong case, for example, that Facebook is ripping the world apart, flinging us into ever-deeper echo chambers by playing to our subconscious desires and weaknesses. What a terrible irony it will be if one morning we all wake up to discover that we have connected online only to end up disconnected.

---

### RISE OF THE ALGORITHMS

An algorithm is a collection of steps or procedures used to solve a mathematical or computer problem. Think of them as flowcharts put into high-tech action. Named after Muhammad ibn Musa al-Khwarizmi, a Persian mathematician who lived in the ninth century, today algorithms determine our customized search engine results and sort out all of the data harvested from us as we move around from website to website. They also help to create social media filter bubbles, working in conjunction with our own human biases that drive us to seek out the kinds of ideas, news, and people who confirm our beliefs and feed our hopes. Be aware of them because algorithms often determine our Internet and social media experiences.

Historian Yuval Noah Harari writes in his book, *Homo Deus: A Brief History of Tomorrow*, that all organisms are algorithms, humans included. We are, he explains,

> an assemblage of organic algorithms shaped by natural selection over millions of years of evolution. Algorithmic calculations are not affected by the materials from which the calculator is built. Whether an abacus is made of wood, iron or plastic, two beads plus two beads equals four beads. Hence there is no reason to think that organic algorithms can do things that non-organic algorithms will never be able to replicate or surpass. As long as the calculations remain valid, what does it matter whether the algorithms are manifested in carbon or silicone?[7]

## Hacking Humanity

Harari suggests that twenty-first-century technology may "enable external algorithms to 'hack humanity' and know me far better than I know myself." This, he writes, could lead to the end of belief in individualism and the total ascendance of algorithms:

> People will no longer see themselves as autonomous beings running their lives according to their wishes, but instead will become accustomed to seeing themselves as a collection of bio-chemical mechanisms that is constantly monitored and guided by a network of electronic algorithms. For this to happen, there's no need for an external algorithm that knows me *perfectly* and never makes any mistake; it is enough that the algorithm will know me *better* than I know myself, and will make *fewer* mistakes than I do. It will then make sense to trust this algorithm with more and more of my decisions in life choices.[8]

The trend is clear, the momentum undeniable. We are running, full-speed, into an algorithmic future. More and more human activity will be aided, influenced, or *determined* by whatever an algorithm decides. The role of algorithms in human culture will be widespread, deep, and profound. Harari goes so far as to speculate that ultra-complex and ultra-capable algorithm networks could supplant traditional human belief systems.

"The new religions are unlikely to emerge from the caves of Afghanistan or from the madrasas of the Middle East," he writes.

> Rather they will emerge from research laboratories. Despite all the talk of radical Islam and Christian fundamentalism, the most interesting place in the world from a religious perspective is not the Islamic State or the Bible Belt, but Silicon Valley. That's where high-tech gurus are brewing for us brave new religions that have little to do with God, and everything to do with Technology. They promise all of the old prizes—happiness, peace, prosperity, and eternal life—but here on Earth with the help of technology, rather than after death with the help of celestial beings.[9]

**There is a large proportion of the population living in what we would regard as an alternative reality.**
—Stephan Lewandowsky, cognitive scientist, University of Bristol[10]

There are two major problems with filter bubbles. The first is that the individual Internet user is under continual refinement and categorization. It never stops. And it's only going to get worse in the immediate future. As algorithms improve and multiply, they are going to place us in ever-tightening, more confining bubbles. Sometimes their work is appreciated, of course. For example, I like it when Amazon recommends a great book, one that an algorithm decided I might like, based on my past purchases. But I don't necessarily want an algorithm to create distance between me and a few of my friends on social media simply because we have different tastes in books or music or movies. And by no means do I want an algorithm to shield me from reality or filter out facts because the goal of the coders who wrote it is to keep me happily surfing the Web, liking friends' posts, watching videos, purchasing things, and shedding personal data at every stop.

Another significant problem with filter bubbles is that the creation and maintenance of them is a mystery to us. We, the typical people who use the Internet and social media, don't know and can't know for sure what is going on behind the scenes. All we know is that our online experiences are automatically sorted, categorized, and customized to "serve us." Yes, conveniences and comfort may come with this kind of tailored online isolation, but consider the costs.

"In the filter bubble, there's less room for the chance encounters that bring insight and learning," writes Pariser in *Filter Bubble*. "Creativity is often sparked by the collision of ideas from different disciplines and cultures. . . . By definition, a world constructed from the familiar is a world in which there's nothing to learn. . . . Personalization can lead you down a road to a kind of informational determinism in which what you've clicked on in the past determines what you see next—a Web history you're doomed to repeat. You can get stuck in a static, ever-narrowing version of yourself—and endless you-loop."[11]

To be fair, social media has no monopoly on bias and filtered presentations of knowledge and news. Just take one glance at cable news in the United States today. Those who rely heavily on CNN, Fox News, and MSNBC for their news might easily develop the belief that there is no world beyond America's borders. Or, if there is, nothing much happens there worth knowing about. Cable news presents a massively misleading view of the world. It is detrimental because the absence of information is a huge obstacle to sensible and productive decision making. While critics fixate on internal American political biases, left vs. right, of these media companies, no one seems to notice that they all share a common and more severe bias against basic reality.

Natasha, a Florida litigation attorney, sees a significant problem in filter bubbles, even as she is an enthusiastic user of Instagram, Snapchat, Facebook, LinkedIn, and Twitter. She says that social media is her primary means of communication and an "integral part of life."[12] She loves having the ability to connect with people and keep track of friends and family members but dislikes how social media can sometimes "create a false sense of connection" with people. When it comes to the filter bubble problem, however, her frustration level soars:

> This is a huge problem, because now, more than ever, someone can find extensive support—often completely baseless and unsupported—for whatever position they may choose to take. There is literally a community for every position. [But] I kind of like it because it allows me to research different positions, and that can be mind-blowing. For example, this guy I sat next to on a flight went into a long rant about the earth being flat, people not being 'free,' the earth being less than a thousand years old, etc., etc. I was blown away, and within minutes I found page after page [online] of people supporting these exact claims. Some people will hear something, look online, see social media posts or websites saying the same thing, do zero *real* research, and just run with it.

Some Facebook users understand how easy it is to end up in a filter bubble, through no fault of their own. "I think it's safe to say that the majority of people who use social media tend to follow or have followers who are similar in beliefs and viewpoints," said Camille, a forty-year-old user of Facebook and Instagram.[13] "So most people are in their own little vacuum online or the star of their personal reality show. What is really worrisome is how social networks like Facebook edit your timeline based off of past likes you may have made, thereby resulting in a watered-down timeline which then turns in to a very concentrated feed. So even if you're not trying to be in a bubble, the algorithms can give you a polarized view if you're not careful."

John Michael Strubhart is a retired teacher living in Texas who spends two to three hours per day on social media, three-fourths of that on Facebook. "The filter bubble is definitely a thing," he said.[14] He continues,

> I do have a filter bubble, but I know where its boundary is; and beyond that boundary, I do explore. For example, I actively oppose actions taken by the Trump administration, but I do look for reasoned arguments in support of some of the positions that the administration takes. I also look for what motivates Trump supporters. That information has to be sought outside my filter bubble. The trick at that point is to find reliable information and staying objective in assessment of that information. I haven't found anything that makes me change my objections, but I do gain insight into the reasons or motivations behind the stance of the Trump administration and its supporters. I'm not averse to calling bullshit on claims made within my circles, though. . . . My social media circle consists of people who have the same general values as I do, but I have plenty of friends and family members [within it] who don't share all of those values.

Angela Russell, aged thirty-three, is concerned about the filter bubble problem. "My husband and I talk about this all the time," she said.[15] "Both of us consider ourselves to be somewhere between liberal and conservative. But both of our Facebook feeds seem to be increasingly far left. I don't watch much live news. I have 4.5- and 6-year-old daughters, and it's hard to find the time. I worry that relying on Facebook to keep me posted on what is going on in the world is not the most effective strategy to keep my worldview well-rounded. With that being said, the news media has become so polarized and biased itself [that] sometimes that I wonder if there's any true way to be honestly informed."

## CONFIRMATION BIAS VS. THE QUEST FOR TRUTH

**Once you start looking for confirmation bias you see it everywhere.**
—Dean Eckles, social scientist and statistician[16]

There is a deeper reason why life inside a social media filter bubble feels cozy even though it can be problematic and deprive us of fuller, richer lives. *Confirmation bias* is a natural and standard process of the human subconscious mind. It's always on, working to keep us feeling smart and rational, even as it builds unrealistic, sometimes bizarre fantasy worlds inside our heads. We all have this bias, but few of us realize just how relentless and influential it can be in its mission to support or confirm our observations, conclusions, and beliefs. It is the reason we so often see someone blatantly ignore or sidestep powerful evidence and logic when these things conflict with the person's previously held belief. Many committed creationists who believe the Earth is less than ten thousand years old demonstrate this every time they overlook, ignore, or reject the immense accumulated scientific evidence that reveals an Earth that is billions of years old. This is a cognitive process that people—you and me included—don't naturally recognize when it's happening. We believe ourselves to be consistently fair and honest when it comes to assessing the world around us. But we fail at it every day of our lives, in large part due to confirmation bias.

The tailor-made mini-worlds that confirmation bias helps to create can boost our self-esteem and make us feel profoundly confident about our beliefs, which is precisely the point. *Cognitive dissonance*, the mental conflict that happens when one belief collides with an opposing or contrary belief inside a human mind, doesn't feel good. It may bring on anxiety, confusion, perhaps even desperation. Confirmation bias works to prevent or put out those fires by pointing to the agreeable stuff while blinding us to challenging or contradictory information.

---

### IGNORANCE *ISN'T* BLISS

Are you floating around inside a political filter bubble—one where your views and opinions are backed up by almost everything you see, read, and hear? If so, you need some help. Fortunately, there's an app for that. Launched in February 2017, Read Across the Aisle keeps track of the political news its users read throughout the day. If a user's news exposure for the day is heavy on one side, a meter will show this and the app will suggest that he or she explore some news over on the other side of the spectrum. The goal is to get more people exposed to opposing views and news coverage. As the app's founder, Nick Lum, said, "We can't just hunker down in our filter bubbles and hope that things get better. We have to take a step to get outside of our bubbles."[17]

---

"Confirmation bias is the mother lode of cognitive biases," declares Bo Bennet, author, teacher, and host of *The Dr. Bo Show*.[18] In discussing this particular bias with me, he explains,

> This is the tendency to search for, interpret, focus on, and remember information in a way that confirms one's preconceptions. In this context, this affects what sources we go to for information. We like when reality agrees with us, not when it disagrees with us, so if we have a strong belief that lizard people are ruling the planet in secret, we might choose to get our news from such sources that promote this idea—and, yes, there are several. The confirmation bias also helps us to conveniently "forget" those facts that contradict our views, and at the same time, helps us to remember all the information that supports our views. Be committed to the truth, no matter what that truth may be. This will help mitigate this bias.[19]

A helpful way to come to terms with your confirmation bias is to see it for what it is: cheating. Plain and simple, this is cheating. You do it, I do it, everyone's subconscious mind is constantly prepared to behave dishonestly when it comes to observing, learning, and thinking. The human brain has no shame. It will, without hesitation, notice, fixate on, and remember every available scrap of information that confirms whatever assortment of good, bad, or wacky ideas it currently harbors. At the same time, the brain is no less diligent at ignoring, denying, and forgetting information that contradicts or challenges beliefs currently residing within the skull fortress. This is how horoscopes, for example, can impress so many people and solidify their belief in astrology. A typical fan of this popular pseudoscience is likely to forget the majority of horoscopes that fail to accurately predict the future and offer nothing specific and relevant to his or her life. Due to confirmation bias, however, the one or two horoscope that do happen to hit the mark to some degree will be valued and remembered.

Michael Shermer is the founding publisher of *Skeptic* magazine and a longtime researcher of irrational beliefs and cognitive biases. Our hunger to verify what we believe, he concludes, is the beast within that we cannot afford to ignore: "The study of cognitive biases has revealed that humans are anything but the Enlightenment ideal of rational calculators carefully weighing the evidence for and against beliefs. And these biases are far reaching in their effects. A judge or jury assessing evidence against a defendant, a CEO evaluating information about a company, or a scientist weighing data in favor of a theory will undergo the same cognitive temptations to confirm what is already believed."[20]

Confirmation bias is a clear and present danger to your ability to reason, make sound decisions, and maintain a sensible worldview while on social media. Know it. Respect its power to lead you astray. This is a problem that is thriving now in our digital, connected culture; but it's not new. Confirmation bias has been challenging us for a long time. English philosopher Francis Bacon wrote of it back in the sixteenth century:

> The human understanding when it has once adopted an opinion . . . draws all things else to support and agree with it. And though there be a greater number and weight of instances to be found on the other side, yet these it either neglects and despises, or else by some distinction sets aside and rejects; in order that by this great and pernicious predetermination the authority of its former conclusions may remain inviolate. . . . And such is the way of all superstitions, whether in astrology, dreams, omens, divine judgments, or the like; wherein men, having a delight in such vanities, mark the events where they

are fulfilled, but where they fail, although this happened much oftener, neglect and pass them by.[21]

It alarms me that so many people are willing to believe first and ask questions later. I have discussed this at length with many people who carry around an extensive collection of extraordinary beliefs in their heads (astrology, psychics, bigfoot, Loch Ness monster, ghosts, ESP, alien abductions, and so on). They seem primed to believe at a glance, almost as if by thoughtless reflex. But most tell me that they only believe these things because it makes logical sense to, because there is ample evidence for them, and, in some cases, because personal experiences confirmed them. They present their state of belief as the sensible end result of their patient and careful consideration of good evidence, as if it would be irrational not to believe. I believe that they sincerely feel this way because that is exactly what confirmation bias leads to. It makes the unbelievable feel undeniable.

People who do not understand confirmation bias often end up in bad places where the most ludicrous beliefs seem sensible, proven, perhaps even inevitable and indisputable within their heads. It is crucial that you are aware of the cherry-picking tactics of a human mind and understand the lengths it will go to protect a belief. This is why it is so important that you do not go around casually accepting claims and believing claims simply because they feel good or seem to make sense at a glance. Once inside the mind, an idea can lay down roots and forever seem to the host to be correct and sensible, no matter how inaccurate or nonsensical it actually is. Respect this bias. It's powerful. It shapes your life. Once the subconscious mind begins its silent and endless process of editing your life experiences to protect and nurture it, a lie or a misperception may infect you for the rest of your days.

I anticipate that right about now some readers are thinking to themselves that they don't really need to worry much about confirmation bias, because they are too smart to allow themselves to be negatively impacted by it. Pardon me while I giggle at that misguided notion. One thing about confirmation bias that cannot be stressed enough is that *everyone* has it and *everyone* uses it. Counterintuitively, being highly intelligent and having an impressive education often makes you *more* vulnerable to the problem of confirmation bias rather than less vulnerable.

## THE FILTER YOU WANT, THE BUBBLE YOU NEED

To live in a world like ours, filled to the brim with delusion and dishonesty, a filter is necessary. All who would make an effort to lean toward reality and appreciate truth must adopt and use the filter of good thinking. By applying skepticism, critical thinking skills, and the scientific method with force and consistency in daily life, we can filter out much of, if not most of, the nonsense and fraud that rain down on us every time we turn on a computer or look at our smartphone or walk out the front door. This is the filter of science and reason, an invaluable though not 100 percent reliable way of sidestepping cognitive blunders. Use it.

There is also one specific bubble I recommend inhabiting. Everyone should move into this one, immediately. Let's call it the *Reality Bubble*. This is a big one, spacious enough to contain everything that is real and true. This is where you want to be. Living in it doesn't mean you can't bring in fantasy, fiction, and wild dreams with you, only that those things are not to be passively mistaken for reality. And this filter bubble is a bit different than most because its walls are permeable. It allows in different opinions, weird claims, and evidence that doesn't match known reality—but only long enough to give them a fair hearing. If they can't hold up to a little scrutiny and skepticism, they are ejected or wither and die in the bright light of the Reality Bubble.

Social media enthusiast Sean Prophet of Los Angeles believes that critical thinking can pop any filter bubble that is sustained by ignorance and misinformation. He sounds to me like a proud resident of the Reality Bubble: "I don't care at all personally about filter bubbles," he said.[22] "I care about how people know what's true. I want to stay firmly locked in a fact bubble for as long as I live. I think filter bubbles are only a problem for people who don't know how to determine what's true. As such they are a threat to our democracy. They help keep ignorant people ignorant. But they do almost nothing to keep smart people from becoming smarter."

Imagine someone with a fast and brilliant mind, an intellect well above average. She is very observant, notices detail better than most, and has a great memory to boot. Confirmation bias can flourish in such a mind. This is because she will notice, observe, and retain evidence at a higher rate than lesser minds. And—with confirmation bias unchecked—she will do all of this in a manner that supports her previously held beliefs and conclusions. I have observed, studied, met, and interviewed many conspiracy theory enthusiasts over the years, and a trait common to most of them is an active, hardworking mind. Unlike the typical casual believer in demons or jinn/genies, these people are much less passive and tend to invest significant effort into researching and confirming their pet conspiracy theories. Of course, what is unfortunate for them is that they do it with the confirmation bias in full effect.

## HOW TO BEAT THE BIAS

**The eye sees only what the mind is prepared to comprehend.**
—Robertson Davies, *Temptest-Tost*[23]

Now that we know the human cognition machine includes this stealthy bias dedicated to making us feel good and confident about our ideas and beliefs, what can we do about it? We can't responsibly ignore it and go about our lives, because this bias goes too far and our already tenuous relationship with reality suffers for it. Know going in that confirmation bias is difficult to combat and impossible to defeat. It operates in the dark, beneath our consciousness, so we are never fully aware of it. Only the fool believes confirmation bias cannot trick him or her into not only holding onto but also spreading and vigorously defending silly or dangerous beliefs. No one escapes this problem, so everyone should rise to the challenge and attempt to tame and counteract it as much as possible. Don't be a passive, self-made fool. Fight.

We can reduce confirmation bias by consciously steering our minds in new and different directions. Deny the instinct to duck and run from ideas and evidence that contradict your beliefs and cause you discomfort. Run toward them. Take them on. The goal is not to be loyal to a belief at all costs. The target is truth. Expose yourself to the other side of the tracks. Remember, your confirmation bias has been cheating every day, rain or shine. It never calls in sick. For years it has been working on your behalf, building a worldview for you that feels so right, so sensible, so unnecessary of challenge that you just might be sleepwalking when it comes to judging and assessing the accuracy of ideas and evidence that don't align well with what you believe. If you want to always at least dwell in the vicinity of truth, then you must be honest enough to be humble. Admit that you are not perfect. If you can do this, then it becomes less difficult to see that some of your beliefs, views, attitudes, and ideas may be wrong. From there, it's an easy step to giving thought and consideration to the answers you "know" to be wrong. *Listen* to your intellectual enemies. Separate claims, ideas, and evidence from the person delivering them to you. Maybe you have good reason to see that person as bad, repulsive, or untrustworthy, but so what? Their words may still contain some truth that will benefit you. Don't waste too much time, of course, but always consider the seemingly absurd. Give it a fair, if brief, hearing, because maybe the idea only seems farcical to you because of the big, bad confirmation bias in your mind.

Seek out, hear, and know the opposing viewpoint of as many issues as possible. I have done this for years out of respect for the power of confirmation bias, and it has become habit for me. For example, nearly every day I expose myself to some heavily biased news that feels in my gut like dishonest, vile propaganda that is opposed to almost everything I know to be true and feel to be good. I have social media connections with many people who, it seems, disagree with me about everything. So long as they don't send me death threats, I'm happy to have them in my life because their presence is reassurance that I'm working to keep my mind open. Not only do such people keep me on my toes, but they add to the richness of my existence as well. I seek out contact with those on the other side because I don't want to live in a comfortable but dull rut of constant reinforcement. I get enough cheerleading and backslapping for my views, so I seek out diversity, surprises, and intellectual challenges, too. It's not always easy to do, but I consistently make an effort to listen intently and with an open mind when a true believer tries to sell me on some claim that I already know a lot about and have judged previously to be spurious. I sometimes experience a minor psychological reward, a tingle of positive feelings, when doing this because I recognize that I'm trying. I'm making a real effort to be intellectually honest and fair, and that makes me feel good about where my mind is pointing. I want my own ideas, beliefs, and conclusions to be tested, because I know that some of them are almost certainly wrong. Should these supplements of awkward conversations and the consumption of overtly biased news help expose some bogus idea squatting inside my mind, then I become wiser and closer to reality. Assess your life, online and offline. Do you have a network of friends who pretty much all think the same way about the same things? If so, not only is your life is not only duller than necessary, but also you are living in a confirmation bias paradise. Change your world. Dip your mind's toes into foreign waters, not occasionally but daily. If you are a conservative, fundamentalist Christian and all of your Facebook friends are as well, then you have built for yourself a make-believe world within which your confirmation bias is smothering some of your brain's potential for honest analysis and deep thinking. Virtually all of the comments and news articles you see on your newsfeed will reinforce what you already believe rather than challenge you to think in new ways. It is exposure to different ideas that inspires deep, reflective thinking. Without them, it is difficult to grow and improve as a human. If you are a liberal atheist and your social media networks are dominated by nonbelievers with views and motivations similar to yours, then you are not conducting your life as a worldly person, at least not online. You are no better than the stereotypical hick who refuses to leave his porch and explore what's out there. Why not just save the electricity? Turn off your computer and shout at the wall instead so that you can enjoy the pleasing sound of your echo?

Everyone on social media can benefit from networking with people who are not necessarily aligned with them on the usual laundry list of issues. A wimpy, vegan pacifist can be Facebook friends with a red-meat-eating, macho gun enthusiast. It's possible. Assuming both are reasonably civilized and respectful, two people with contradictory views on one or several issues have the potential to interact online with positive and beneficial results for both. Sure, they may never see eye-to-eye on diet or open-carry gun laws; but that's okay, at least by connecting and interacting they may expose themselves to new knowledge and possibly better ideas. They are pushing back against the steady pressure of confirmation bias.

## WHEN CONFIRMATION BIAS JUST ISN'T ENOUGH

As if subconsciously engaging in a pattern of selective observation and remembering didn't cause enough problems, we also have *motivated reasoning* to contend with. Motivated reasoning is the *conscious* act of collecting information with a bias. This is where things can really go off the rails. Imagine injecting the effective yet stealthy confirmation bias with a cocktail of steroids and HGH, followed up with an extra-large espresso. Motivated reasoning is how we level up our selective thinking. It is as if we are not content to let our subconscious mind create these lopsided, often bogus cases in our heads, so we consciously work to help things along as well. It's like noticing that your house is flooding and deciding that turning on all of the faucets might help.

Motivated reasoning is how we end up with smart people arguing to no end that the Holocaust never happened[24] and NASA faked the six Apollo Moon landings.[25] The more popular and durable conspiracy theories show motivated reasoning in full bloom. With bias as its guide, a committed human mind can build up a remarkably dense and complex defense of just about any crackpot claim. Think of someone who spends a year in a library researching euthanasia. However, this person reads and cites exclusively from books and journal articles in favor of this controversial issue while never opening any works opposed to it. By the end of the year, this researcher will be able to present a thorough and perhaps impressive argument on the merits of euthanasia. But can we respect this presentation? Can we trust it? Can the researcher trust himself or herself? Of course not, and this is why confirmation bias coupled with motivated reasoning is a nightmare scenario of delusion and denial about which we need to be fully aware. We easily recognize the problem with someone else doing one-sided research that fails to incorporate or even acknowledge the big picture. Yet this is precisely what many people do on social media every day. They spend months and years of their lives "researching" one side of a very long list of topics and issues. Most who do pay attention to competing ideas usually do so only to attempt to destroy them. The ultimate payoff for those with the courage to listen to opposing views and consider contrary evidence is a richer life, one that is closer to reality and less vulnerable to mistakes and manipulation.

## TWIRLING THE COGNITIVE KALEIDOSCOPE

Drew Weston, a professor in the Departments of Psychology and Psychiatry at Emory University, used an fMRI (functional magnetic resonance imaging) to learn more about motivated reasoning. He and his colleagues scanned the brains of people who were strongly Republican or strongly Democrat while the participants assessed comments by a Republican and a Democratic politician. Both politicians contradicted themselves, but the test subjects excused the candidate of their party and condemned their rival party's candidate. No surprise there. What was amazing, however, was that their brains did not show the kind of activity during this process that one might have predicted. The part of the brain where most reasoning occurs was inactive. The parts that lit up were those associated with emotion, conflict resolution, and reward. Don't miss that last one. Yes, you read that correctly: reward. In other words, we get to enjoy a nice little chemical treat in our brains when we manage to push aside or explain away troublesome input that threatens a belief or idea we have already latched onto. "We did not see any increased activation of the parts of the brain normally engaged during reasoning," Weston said.[26] "What we saw instead was a network of emotion circuits lighting up, including circuits hypothesized to be involved in resolving conflicts. Essentially, it appears as if partisans twirl the cognitive kaleidoscope until they get the conclusions they want, and then they get massively reinforced for it, with the elimination of negative emotional states and activation of positive ones."

After learning about how confirmation bias and motivated reasoning affect each and every one of us, you may feel a bit down about social media and your engagement with it. But do not despair; it may help you to know that many people from all walks of life apply good thinking online every day, too. It's not foolproof, but it does help. This is the crowd you want to emulate. They understand that there are challenges, not only out there on the Internet, but also inside their own minds. Being aware of your confirmation bias and other subconscious challenges is step one. Step two is doing something about it, deciding not to be an easy target for external or internal threats to reason. *Think* your way around the Web. *Think* your way through social media. It's not so difficult, and it doesn't necessarily diminish the experience in any way. Apply critical thinking over enough time, and it becomes effortless, almost automatic. Ian Liberman, a sixty-five-year-old author, teacher, and game maker, says he spends about four hours per day on Facebook and Google Plus. He believes that social media is neither good nor bad but neutral. "You can be frivolous in what you do or you can contact individuals that are highly intellectual," he said.[27] "[It all] depends on the makeup of the user. For me it [social media] brings the world closer with meeting individuals, and researching themes and news. That is a positive thing. I use critical thinking to choose where I go to fulfill those objectives."

## REALITY WARPED: THE FIGHT AGAINST FAKE NEWS

> **In the case of news, we should always wait for the sacrament of confirmation.**
> —Voltaire, letter, August 28, 1760[28]

Social media came under heavy fire after the 2016 US presidential election. Many fake news articles went viral during the campaign and penetrated millions of minds, possibly affecting, maybe determining, the election result. It is unknown whether or not or to what degree fake news had an impact, because measuring its influence on voters is difficult, if not impossible. What we do know is that lies dressed up as respectable news have found social media to be a fertile environment in which to thrive.

How concerned should we be about fake news? Is it a crisis or a joke? If it is a real problem, what can be done? Numerous experts, from political scientists to philosophers, from leading journalists to business leaders, agree that fake news is a serious problem in need of immediate attention. Apple CEO Tim Cook, for example, believes fake news is "killing people's minds" and says that governments and corporations need to do more to fight it.[29] "It has to be ingrained in the schools, it has to be ingrained in the public," Cook told the *Telegraph*. "There has to be a massive campaign. We have to think through every demographic. We are going through this period of time right here where unfortunately some of the people that are winning are the people that spend their time trying to get the most clicks, not tell the most truth."

## THE GREAT PROPAGANDA PANDEMIC OF 2016

It is important to avoid exaggerating the significance of fake news and the 2016 election. It seems clear that this is a problem worthy of concern, but it's not as new a challenge as some seem to think. Disinformation—aka lying and spinning—has always been a part of politics, of course. Does anyone doubt that history's first politician told a few lies to the first voter? During the US presidential election of 1800, the *Connecticut Courant* warned its readers what a Thomas Jefferson victory would mean for America: "Murder, robbery, rape, adultery, and incest would be openly taught and practiced, the air will be rent with the cries of the distressed [and] the soil soaked with blood."[30] Not so different from the fake news of our time. But, still, we must recognize that the Great Propaganda Pandemic of 2016 was a significant moment in the history of outrageous lies dressed up as legitimate news. It is not difficult to see how the stage was set for it. Trust in traditional news media had plummeted; half of all Americans relied on Facebook to serve up their news; both Donald Trump and Hillary Clinton were deeply disliked by huge portions of the population;[31] and overlapping social media networks made it easy for a provocative lie to reach millions of screens in a single afternoon. Moreover, research has shown that social media users tend to trust a news story based on their relationship with the person who shared it rather than the original source or author of the story.[32] This means that when people see a *New York Times* or *Wall Street Journal* article, for example, that has been shared by someone less trusted, they are less inclined to believe it than articles produced by dubious or unknown sources. Worst of all, most people don't seem to even notice or remember the source of a news story they read. They tend to recall the social media platform they found it on but not the actual source that produced the story.[33] This a significant problem because identifying sources and assessing their trustworthiness is a key factor in spotting fake news. In addition to all of that, most people, then as now, are vulnerable to being fooled by fake news because they have poor critical thinking skills.

But wait, there's more. The 2016 fake news crisis or amusing sideshow—depending on how you view it—was set up by three trends that had been in motion long before. For decades now, newsrooms have been cutting staffs. Many good newspapers have either gone away or are now mere shadows of their former selves. Then there was the rise of hyper-partisan news sources like AM radio talk shows and cable news shows that prioritized political bias over facts and accuracy. Finally, the Internet has for years now been providing people the opportunity to inhabit their own little filter bubbles where they can consume steady diets of one-sided, politically slanted news as well as flat-out lies and propaganda. In retrospect, the stage was set for millions of people to be manipulated by ridiculous and dishonest articles pretending to be news. In 2016, social media hosted the perfect online storm of political fraud and human credulity.

After the smoke cleared somewhat, it was clear that Donald Trump's campaign had made brilliant use of social media data far beyond any benefit they may have gained from fake news. They drilled down and connected data points, got to the personal preferences, concerns, and psychological profiles of millions of people so that they could precisely target them with the most effective ads. Micro-targeting in political campaigns is not new, of course, but this was something at a level never seen before, according to expert observers.[34]

The Trump campaigners won largely because of their "expert manipulation of social media," writes Sue Halpern in the *New York Review of Books*. She continues:

> Donald Trump is our first Facebook president. His team figured out how to use all the marketing tools of Facebook, as well as Google, the two biggest advertising platforms in the world, to successfully sell a candidate that the majority of Americans did not want. They understood that some numbers matter more than others—in this case the number of angry, largely rural, disenfranchised potential Trump voters—and that Facebook, especially, offered effective methods for pursuing and capturing them. . . . What our Facebook president has discovered is that it actually pays only to please some of the people some of the time. The rest simply don't count.[35]

---

## BIGGER THAN POLITICS

It is important that no one mistake references to President Trump and his 2016 campaign by me in this book as a politically based attack against him, his supporters, the Republican Party, or conservatives in general. The crisis of poor critical thinking is not exclusive to one group or one ideology; it rises far above mere politics of the moment. This is about humankind and our collective future—whether we will move toward becoming a more rational species or stumble into some sad abyss, a self-inflicted dystopia of delusion and deceit. Tribal loyalties be damned, we are in this together. David Helfand, a professor of astronomy at Columbia University and advocate for science and reason, dubs this the "Misinformation Age."[36] He believes that it is not only more difficult today for individuals to make decisions, given all of the lies and bogus beliefs flying about social media, but also a "disaster for the formation of rational public policy." Helfand continues: "A counterinsurgency is definitely called for. But our actions will be ineffective if they are politicized and unpersuasive unless we scrupulously abide by the principles of a scientific mind."

Again, this is bigger than politics.

---

## DECLINING TRUST IN NEWS, RISING BELIEF IN LIES?

Trust in traditional news sources has been declining in America for years, and this trend, combined with the popularity and utility of social media platforms, helps to explain how fake news was able to penetrate so far and wide in recent years. Gallup has looked at American trust in news media since 1972; and it found that 2016 saw the lowest ever recorded levels of trust.[37] Less than a third of American adults, 32 percent, in that year, said that they had "a great deal" or "fair amount" of trust in the media. The high point of these Gallup surveys came in 1976, when 72 percent of Americans trusted the news. For a decade now, a minority of Americans say that they trust news media a great or fair amount.

## AMERICANS' VANISHING TRUST IN NEWS MEDIA

|  | A Great Deal of Trust | A Fair Amount of Trust | Not Very Much Trust | No Trust at All |
|---|---|---|---|---|
| **2016** | 8% | 24% | 41% | 27% |
| **1997** | 10% | 43% | 31% | 15% |
| **1972** | 18% | 50% | 24% | 6% |

Source: Gallup News Services[38]

Gallup suggests that the bizarre and contentious 2016 presidential campaign explains the all-time low of 32 percent. Republicans plunged to an astounding low of 14 percent having great or fair trust in the news media. "With many Republican leaders and conservative pundits saying Hillary Clinton has received overly positive media attention, while Donald Trump has been receiving unfair or negative attention," Gallup stated, "this may be the prime reason their relatively low trust in the media has evaporated even more. It is also possible that Republicans think less of the media as a result of Trump's sharp criticisms of the press."[39] It is important to point out that this vanishing trust in news media is not what it seems to be on the surface. People are *not* trusting the media less than before. If they were, then they would be more skeptical and analytical about what they read and hear. What has been happening is that specific trust in *older, traditional news sources* has been slipping, not for news in general. If people were becoming less trusting of *all* news, then they wouldn't be such easy targets for fake news.

## TODAY THE BUCK STOPS WITH YOU

**We've reached the summit of bullshit mountain . . . and you have to wonder if we'll find our way down again.**
—David Remnick, editor of the *New Yorker*[40]

The most important thing to keep in mind as we explore fake news in this chapter is that we are all on our own now. In the past, the public could rely, at least somewhat, on traditional gatekeepers such as newspaper, television, and radio editors and reporters to seek out information, analyze facts and events, judge relevance, and then accurately relay the facts to us. It doesn't matter that they fell well short of doing this perfectly every time. Even with all of their biases and failures, the gatekeepers of the latter half of the twentieth century did a much better job than millions of people currently are doing for themselves.

Lies, hoaxes, and propaganda flourish in the hyper-fast, connected ecosystem of social media. The winds have shifted, and most people are failing to adjust their sails accordingly. Like it or not, we all are publishers and editors now. It falls on every social media user to be his or her own fact-checker, and there should be some responsibility for what we "publish" in the form of a tweet, comment, or share. Shirk this responsibility and you condemn yourself to a state of high vulnerability before the countless liars and opportunists who are working hard to exploit, manipulate, or make a fool out of you. That's in addition to the multitudes of sloppy thinkers who unwittingly spread nonsense and propaganda throughout social media.

The flow of information is no longer limited to a few sources. News today comes at us from a thousand directions, often from new or unknown sources. The once dominant television news broadcasts and newspapers were imperfect, but at least they were known by all and could be counted on to be accurate and truthful most of the time. Today's social media is a dark jungle by comparison. "The major new challenge in reporting news is the new shape of truth," said Kevin Kelly, a technology expert and co-founder of *Wired* magazine.[41] "Truth is no longer dictated by authorities, but is networked by peers. For every fact there is a counterfact. All of those counterfacts and facts look identical online, which is confusing to most people." I perhaps find it easier to appreciate the need to be skeptical and thoughtful of news more than most, thanks to my time spent working as a print and television journalist. Because of those experiences, I have long recognized that skepticism and fact-checking are essential to daily news consumption. I have seen firsthand how the sausage gets made, and how images and stories are cherry-picked for impact. For most of my life I have had the benefit of an internal firewall to protect me from fake news, because I understood that all news is potentially fake news. Before the Internet and social media existed I recognized that there are fallible and biased humans behind every news article, every TV and radio report. Fortunately, we all can come out of the current fake news era better off than ever. To achieve this, however, we first must admit our innate vulnerabilities and commit to applying critical thinking to *every* piece of news that comes our way, from any source.

## WAIT, WHAT IS FAKE NEWS?

The considerable confusion, sincere and otherwise, surrounding what constitutes "fake" has made addressing this form of news more challenging. Merely inaccurate or disagreeable information does not necessarily qualify as fake news, as some politicians have claimed in an apparent attempt to muddy the waters and deflect criticism. Trump did this repeatedly in 2017.[42] For example, he actually tweeted: "Any negative polls are fake news."[43] Syrian president Bashar al-Assad tried this tactic as well. When a reporter for Yahoo! News asked him about human-rights violations, including an Amnesty International report claiming that thirteen thousand prisoners were killed at the Saydnaya Prison between 2011 and the end of 2015,[44] President Assad shrugged it off as fake news: "You can forge anything these days," he said. "We are living in a fake news era."[45] No, a news story or presentation of credible information is not fake news merely because it upsets someone. That can't work, because everything upsets somebody.

So what is fake news, then? Fake news is deceitful news. It includes lies, propaganda, hoaxes, and fraudulent clickbait created for the purpose of making money for somebody somewhere. This form of journalistic treachery is not new, but it has been taken to unprecedented heights thanks to the speed, reach, and convenience of social media networks. In the old fake news model, one person saw a tabloid headline at the grocery store checkout line—"President Kennedy and Batboy Found Alive in Secret Planned Parenthood Facility!"—and, if gullible enough to believe it, might share the lie later at home with a few friends or family members. It would then promptly die a natural death within hours or days. Today, however, one person looks at her phone while standing in line at the grocery store, sees a fake news story on her Facebook News Feed—"Hillary Clinton Confesses to Carrying Donald Trump's Love Child"—and, if gullible enough to believe it, shares the lie with potentially *millions of people*. An individual today can possess a staggering potential to spread good or bad information due to the overlap of so many social networks. A shared bit of information can easily jump from network to network so that a person with fewer than two hundred Facebook friends, for example, might be able to help push a story on to thousands, if not millions, beyond his or her immediate network.

---

### SIGN OF THE TIMES

Oxford Dictionaries chose "post-truth" as its 2016 International Word of the Year. Oxford Dictionaries editors reported a 2,000 percent increase in the use of this word from 2015. "Fueled by the rise of social media as a news source and a growing distrust of facts offered up by the establishment, *post-truth* as a concept has been finding its linguistic footing for some time," said Casper Grathwohl, president of Oxford Dictionaries.[46] "I wouldn't be surprised if *post-truth* becomes one of the defining words of our time."

---

I suggest the following as a concise and useful definition of fake news: *Fake news is dishonest news that has been crafted and published for the specific purpose of misleading readers, listeners, or viewers with knowingly false information*. This is about intent. A poorly researched and poorly written news article with errors that was produced by an incompetent or slack journalist not in the service of a nefarious hidden agenda does not qualify as fake news. That is journalism's version of negligent manslaughter. The charge of journalistic premeditated murder, fake news, is appropriate only when someone *intentionally* lies with a specific goal in mind. That goal can include anything from garnering clicks for profit to making political gains.

The reason we can't apply the "fake news" label based on errors alone is because no reporting is error-free. If mistakes were the deciding factor, then all news sources would be purveyors of fake news—because none of them are perfect. Political bias also has been cited by some as an identifying trait of fake news. This is wrong as well. Bias in reporting may be bad journalism but, in many cases, it's still journalism. For example, Fox News and MSNBC have clear right and left political leanings, respectively. However, on any given day both can and do produce news packages that can't fairly be condemned as politically biased. Although these straightforward reports may indeed serve a larger theme that is overtly biased, they are not propaganda or fake news in isolation.

## PEELING THE *ONION*

The Onion, Inc., is a media company that specializes in news satire. It began in print back in 1988 and launched a website in 1996. Its writers are brilliant at imitating real news delivery in the presentation of absurd, funny stories, commentaries, and videos. All of those who are capable of laughter will find much to enjoy in the Onion's efforts. Though most of its material includes kernels of truth within, and sometimes boulders, the punchlines are clear punchlines, at least to most people. But like intentionally deceptive fake news, *Onion* stories often fool people. Its articles have been taken as true by many people and organizations, including a US congressman,[47] a FIFA vice president,[48] Fox News,[49] and the *Beijing Evening News*.[50] One of my personal favorites from the *Onion*—"Conspiracy Theorist Convinces Neil Armstrong Moon Landing Was Faked"—was good enough to end up reported on as true in not one but two Bangladeshi newspapers.[51] Despite all of this, however, the *Onion*'s work as well as that of others in the same vein do not deserve the "fake news" label. They should not be filtered away, banned, or attacked for what they do. Humor need not be a casualty in anyone's war against fake news. A joke is not a lie. Satire is not fake news. The burden falls on news consumers to think critically so that they may separate one from the other.

## JOURNALISM 101: SPECIAL EDITION FOR THE MASSES

A significant yet often overlooked problem that helps fuel the spread of fake news is general ignorance about news. It's shocking how little many people understand about journalism, and this lack of knowledge makes them more vulnerable to fake news. In the flurry of media coverage about fake news after the 2016 US presidential election, almost no attention was devoted to this root problem. To be clear, I'm referring not to awareness about current events or being able to name current world leaders but rather to a common ignorance or misunderstanding of how news itself is crafted, categorized, and presented. This may seem unbelievable to some, but it's true that many people, possibly most, cannot consistently recognize and understand the differences between and the intended purposes of news reports, editorials, op-ed pieces, feature stories, letters to the editor, and even reader comments posted at the end of an online article.

As a journalist and editor with experience in almost every aspect of the business, I have published countless newspaper, magazine, and web news articles. I know firsthand that even the most basic, straightforward, short, and innocuous news article or photograph has the potential to confuse people. More than once, for example, I have had to spend significant amounts of time explaining to someone why I had the audacity to express my opinion in a clearly identified *opinion column*. I also have had to explain that quoting someone in my news article does not mean that I necessarily endorse what the person said. This points to a significant failure by news media companies. They assume that the public understands how journalism works. But most people don't, and this leaves them vulnerable to fake news. News providers should concern themselves more with the media literacy of their readers, listeners, and viewers. Elevating media literacy throughout society needs to be a priority. All schools and every parent should attempt to educate young children about news. These concerns I have about the public's understanding of basic journalism are based on more than personal anecdotes.

In November 2016, the Stanford History Education Group published *Evaluating Information: The Cornerstone of Civic Online Reasoning*, which examined the findings of its eighteen-month study on how well middle school, high school, and college students can assess the credibility of news and social media information they commonly encounter online.[52] The researchers analyzed thousands of responses to fifty-six tasks from students across twelve states. The students were diverse. For example, some attended "under-resourced, inner-city schools" in Los Angeles, and others "well-resourced schools" in suburbs outside of Minneapolis. The college students were from six different universities, including Stanford, an elite school with a 94 percent applicant rejection rate, and large state universities that admit the majority of students who apply.

The testing was intended to identify basic competence from incompetence. The researchers say they did not attempt to catch students with tricky questions or nitpick minor distinctions. They showed students screenshots of news webpages, Facebook posts, and tweets. Students were asked to evaluate the material to see if they could discern news articles from ads, judge the reliability of photos and websites, and so on. The goal was to discover whether "digital natives," young people who have always known the Internet and are online as much as or more than anyone these days, were savvy thinkers in cyberspace. Spoiler alert: What the study found is disturbing and suggests that the next wave of American adults may be no better than the current generation when it comes to intelligently assessing news. "Easily duped" is how the researchers described America's online youth.[53] They asserted, "Many assume that because young people are fluent in social media they are equally savvy about what they find there. Our work shows the opposite."[54] The Stanford History Education Group investigators write:

> In every case and at every level, we were taken aback by students' lack of preparation. For every challenge facing this nation, there are scores of websites pretending to be something they are not. Ordinary people once relied on publishers, editors, and subject matter experts to vet the information they consumed. But on the unregulated Internet, all bets are off. . . . Never have we had so much information at our finger-tips. Whether this bounty will make us smarter and better informed or more ignorant and narrow-minded will depend on our awareness of this problem and our educational response to it. At present, we worry that democracy is threatened by the ease at which disinformation about civic issues is allowed to spread and flourish.[55]

To better understand how severe the challenges are, consider these brief highlights from the Stanford History Education Group study:

- More than 75 percent of middle school students correctly identified news stories and traditional advertisements.[56]
- Middle school students struggle with native advertising, the increasingly common practice of presenting ads in ways that make them look like real news. A native advertisement fooled more than 80 percent of the students—even though it was clearly identified by the phrase "sponsored content." Some students even saw this and noted it but still believed that it was an authentic news article. "This suggests that many students have no idea what 'sponsored content' means and that this is something that must be explicitly taught as early as elementary school."[57]
- The researchers showed high school students a photo of flowers from an image-sharing website. The photo was accompanied with the claim that the flowers have "nuclear birth defects" as a result of Japan's 2011 Fukushima Daiichi nuclear disaster. Fewer than 20 percent of students challenged the source of the photo or the claim. Nearly 40 percent of students argued that it was strong evidence of nuclear contamination because the photo showed conditions near the power plant.[58]
- A majority of university students failed when tasked to evaluate a tweet. Only a few of the students recognized that the tweet relied on data from a professional polling firm, which would make the information more credible. Less than a third of the students noted that the political agenda of the organization that authored the tweet might have influenced the content.[59]
- More than half of the university students failed to even click on the link provided within the tweet they assessed. "These results suggest that students need further instruction in how best to navigate social media content, particularly when that content comes from a source with a clear political agenda."[60]

## NOT ROCKET SCIENCE

Sam Wineburg, and Sarah McGrew, authors of the Stanford study discussed above, observed professional fact-checkers conduct online searches to learn how they sort out real news from fake news in contrast to typical college, high school, and middle school students. Three things stood out among the professional fact-checkers when compared to the students:

1. Professional fact-checkers read "laterally." They "jump off the original page, opening up a new tab, Googling the name of the organization or its president. Dropped in the middle of a forest, hikers know they can't divine their way out by looking at the ground. They use a compass. Similarly, fact-checkers use the vast resources of the Internet to determine where information is coming from before they read it."[61]
2. Professional fact-checkers don't trust the "About" page on a site. "They don't evaluate a site based solely on the description it provides about itself. If a site can masquerade as a nonpartisan think tank when funded by corporate interests and created by a Washington public relations firm, it can surely pull the wool over our eyes with a concocted 'About' page."
3. Professional fact-checkers don't trust Google. Instead of relying on Google's presentation of pages as a reflection of reliability (which would be a misunderstanding of how the search engine's algorithms work), "the fact-checkers regularly scrolled down to the bottom of the search results page in their quest to make an informed decision about where to click first."[62]

"None of this [fact-checking] is rocket science," write Wineburg and McGrew in an article published by *PBS NewsHour*. "But it's often not taught in school. In fact, some schools have special filters that direct students to already vetted sites, effectively creating a generation of bubble children who never develop the immunities needed to ward off the toxins that float across their Facebook feeds, where students most often get their news. This approach protects young people from the real world rather than preparing them to deal with it."[63]

If you are a parent, please make it a point to explain to your children or teenagers that an Internet search does not call up websites that have been expertly and thoroughly vetted for truth or ranked by a measure of accuracy, as many assume. Make sure that they understand that Google and other search engines merely present links to sites based on what algorithms determine is relevant to the search, and sometimes ads are placed at the top of the search results which can mislead some people. Search algorithms involve factors such as inbound links and usage of keywords. So, while it's not exactly a popularity contest, it may help to think of search results that way. If you search for "psychic," for example, most of the top results likely will be links that endorse and encourage belief in supernatural mind reading. You must go deep to find links that lead to skeptical perspectives and alternate explanations for how psychics do what they do. Google is not the ace librarian at your local library. To its credit, however, Google did promise in 2017 to work at tweaking its system so that at least some generic searches will be less prone to presenting webpages of outright lies or nonsense.[64] This is a complicated issue, however, because we shouldn't want one company—or government, for that matter—deciding for us what is true or not. Ideally, we all should be able to think for ourselves. Given the current state of critical thinking, however, it's probably best if Google does pull some weeds to reduce their infestation of so many human minds. But don't wait on the engineers to come up with the magic algorithm that will keep you safe. Think for yourself today. Assume a skeptical stance now.

Brendan Nyhan, a professor of political science at Dartmouth College, researches misinformation in politics. He points out that technology and social media are allowing people to consume and spread news faster than ever before. We may be "supercharging" the process of spreading false information among like-minded people, he said.[65] Nyhan studied the effect of fact-checking during the 2016 US presidential campaign and found reason for hope. "The findings were encouraging," he told me, "because we found some evidence of responsiveness to fact-checks even among the respondents we expected to be most resistant to them." He continued,

My coauthors and I conducted an experiment in which we corrected misleading rhetoric from Trump's convention speech suggesting that crime in the US had increased dramatically. It is actually way down from historical highs over the medium to long term. There was a very slight uptick in 2015, but relative to twenty years ago, it has declined dramatically. We provided corrective information to people saying that official statistics show that the crime rate is down substantially. That intervention was effective at reducing misperceptions about crime increasing, even among Trump supporters, whom you might expect to be most resistant. We thought that result was encouraging. Some of the findings in this field, including my own, can be pretty depressing. I take that study to mean all hope is not lost, and there's still a lot of room to learn what's most effective in responding to misinformation.

## VISIBLE LISTENING

Carrie James is a principal investigator for Project Zero,[66] a research organization within the Harvard Graduate School of Education. She has done extensive research on the activities of young people online, including their challenges when it comes to discerning credible news from fake news. "While concerns around fake news are at a peak now, good tips for scrutinizing online sources with a critical eye have been around for some time," she told me.[67] "I like the advice[68] of Common Sense Media from their recent news literacy effort focused on parents and kids. ['Filtered experiences' feels like a bigger challenge. Recent political events—including the fact that Trump's election blindsided many in the US and beyond—reveal the degree to which many of us operate in echo chambers and filter bubbles. . . . We all need to be proactive in seeking alternative sources of news [and] information and truly diverse perspectives on the critical issues of our time. So all of us need to be examining our online friending and following habits, looking for opportunities to broaden the array of perspectives to which we are exposed. And once we've diversified our networks, we have to be willing to listen attentively to what others have to say, with an intent to understand and learn."

Related to this, James says that a key theme in her recent work has been strategies for "visible listening" in online conversations. Visible listening refers to a form of deep learning whereby one more thoughtfully probes and reacts to information. With so much attention placed on speed and quantity—the number of followers, likes, retweets, and so on—James hopes for a rise in the *quality* of social media interactions. "I co-direct an online global learning community[69] for which we've designed a dialogue tool kit,[70] a set of lean structures intended to support visible listening and mindful commenting. Our end goal is to help youth, our primary audience, develop the skills and dispositions to slow down, listen attentively to others, and engage meaningfully with individuals from diverse backgrounds, especially in online contexts."

## THE BOUNDLESS NATURE OF BELIEF

After having researched and written about irrational beliefs and the weird inner workings of the human mind for many years, I have been rendered virtually incapable of being surprised by what some people are willing to believe. To be human, I have learned, is to be capable of embracing any absurdity. I've had conversations with intelligent, highly educated people who think the Earth is hollow and contains huge secret subterranean cities. Otherwise sensible people have tried to convince me that a preacher can heal AIDS and cancer by extending his hand toward the sick and calling down the Holy Spirit. I've seen genuine fear in the eyes of people who "knew" the world would end soon by supernatural means. I once dated a woman who was haunted by a nagging concern that ghosts and demons might cause her harm. I know from experience, therefore, that even the most ludicrous and unreasonable fake news story can and will be accepted by some people as true. Wherever good thinking is scarce or absent, *anything* can be packed and sold as fact.

Consider the strange case of Edgar M. Welch. The twenty-eight-year-old father of two and North Carolina resident drove 350 miles to Washington, DC, then walked into the Comet Ping Pong, a kid-themed pizza restaurant, and opened fire with a military-style rifle. (Fortunately, nobody was injured in the attack.) Why did Welch do this? Because he was determined to break up an alleged international, satanic child sex-slave operation that Hillary Clinton and other top Democrats were running out of the restaurant. Why did he believe that such terrible crimes were being committed there? He read it on social media, of course.[71] "I just wanted to do some good and went about it the wrong way," Welch later told a *New York Times* reporter.[72]

He added that he dislikes the term "fake news" and suggested that use of the label is a way of degrading news articles that don't come from established media sources. Welch wasn't the only person taken in by this particular false claim, as tens of thousands shared it.[73] Comet Ping Pong received hundreds of death threats.[74] No less than former National Security Adviser Michael T. Flynn, who was at the time an influential member of President Trump's cabinet, used social media to promote the false Clinton child-sex-slave claim and other fake news stories.[75] His son and aid, Michael G. Flynn, did as well. The son even tweeted the following message *after* Welch had been arrested for the shooting incident: "Until #Pizzagate proven to be false, it'll remain a story. The left seems to forget #Podesta Emails and the many 'coincidences' tied to it."[76] Harvard's Howard Gardner, a leading developmental psychologist who has dedicated much of his life trying to understand how people think and learn, asks one of the key questions for the times we live in: "Do people really want to know the truth in the digital era?"[77] Not at all, it seems; even the most minimal effort to separate fact from fiction takes the wind from the sails of most fake news stories, and yet here we are, with people in positions of authority promoting fake news. Gardner wrote a particularly moving essay published on his website in reaction to the explosion of online fake news. You can feel sadness and frustration in his words:

> As if to finish the final funeral of truth, we have an electorate, many of whom do not seem to care about rampant lying; and the creation of a new category—fake or false news: news which is simply made up for propaganda purposes and is then circulated as if it had been carefully researched and validated. . . . Until 2016, I had assumed that truth was a widely accepted goal—we might even say a widely accepted good—even though, of course, it is not always achieved. . . . But I have had to come face-to-face with an uncomfortable, if not untenable situation: if we don't agree about what is true, and if we don't even *care* about what is true, then how can we even turn our attention to what is good, let alone care about what is good, and what is not?[78]

It is long been common to hear concerns about voters being educated and informed on important issues. But the fake news/social media phenomenon of 2016 highlights a new aspect of this problem. Twenty or thirty years ago, the agreed-upon solution to the problem of misinformed voters was getting more people to consume more news. That goal no longer makes sense, however, because "the news" has become so fractured, so much of it partisan, unreliable, inconsistent, dishonest, or self-serving. More news alone is not the answer. At this moment in history an unprecedented number

## WHEN REAL JOURNALISTS SPREAD FAKE NEWS

Anthony C. Adornato has done some important research on the problem of fake news. The former television news reporter and anchor is now an assistant professor of journalism at the Roy H. Park School of Communications at Ithaca College. Adornato conducted a nationwide survey of news directors at network affiliate television stations, and what he found is disturbing: There has been, for some years now, a strong trend toward traditional and established news media outlets covering social media posts as news. This has led to a rise in these newsrooms spreading false information. A third of those surveyed by Adornato said they had reported information from social media that was later found to be false or inaccurate. Most disturbing, says Adornato, is that of those stations that have a social media policy, "nearly 40 percent said the policy does not include procedures for verifying social media content before it is included in a newscast."[79]

of human beings are under constant mental assault by countless streams of nonsense and lies. It is possible today, thanks in large part to social media, for a typical person to be a dedicated and constant consumer of news and yet simultaneously be profoundly ignorant of world events and even of basic realty. News has never been perfect, of course. It has always included plenty of bias, incompetence, and lies; but at one time there was at least the common practice and understanding that the news was meant to inform the public about facts and actual events, to steer people in the general direction of truth, at least most of the time. That's gone now.

At the dawn of the Internet age, optimism and utopianism were common. One could scarcely go five minutes in the early 1990s without hearing someone go on about the glorious new age of free and accessible knowledge, and all that the Internet was going to deliver. A borderless world was at hand. The Internet was to be the great equalizer. A new age of enlightenment was upon us. And yet here we are today, awash in a digital disaster of misinformation and fake news. What happened?

The challenge of an ignorant and misinformed public is no longer as simple as getting more people to pay attention to the news, because news is such a significant part of the problem. But this must be addressed and remedied somehow because bad information combined with bad thinking raises the likelihood of people making disastrous decisions in the voting booth and in their lives, generally. "If we cannot ensure that we are receiving credible news and information," warns Rory O'Connor, an author and documentary filmmaker who has written about social media, "the implications for our democracy, which depends on an active, informed citizenry, are enormous."[80] President Barack Obama believes that fake news on social media and the confusion it sows pose a threat to nothing less than freedom and prosperity: "We won't know what to fight for," he said.[81] "And we can lose so much of what we've gained in terms of the kind of democratic freedoms and market-based economies and prosperity that we've come to take for granted."

Miriam Metzger, associate professor at UC Santa Barbara, is an expert on the social uses and effects of communication technology. She also studies issues related to the credibility of digital information. "I see two findings in the research, and in some ways they are at odds," she told me.[82]

> One is that most people prefer news that they think is objective and presents all important perspectives. The other is that people prefer and gravitate toward information that they believe is congenial to their political perspective. More interestingly, the research seems to indicate that people have a hard time identifying bias in news that they feel is attitude-consistent. A hypothetical example might be a Republican feeling that Fox News is more "fair and unbiased" than a nonpartisan news source. Yet people often feel that "objective" news is biased. This is known as the "Hostile Media Effect."[83]

While Metzger says the research hasn't caught up sufficiently at this point to say anything definitive about how vulnerable social media leaves a typical user to believing fake news, she does suspect that the breadth of information transfer through social media may be a significant factor. "Social media are another channel through which people are exposed to news—real or fake—and so from a simple distribution perspective, social media help to transmit news to people who might not otherwise seek it out or see it at all. There has always been fake news—think tabloids—but one possible effect of digital media generally is that it is harder to know which sources are legitimate purveyors of news and which are not." She continued, "For example, in the print era we all knew that the *National Enquirer* was a purveyor of fake news, so it wasn't taken as serious news. Today, the plethora of sources of information available and accessible online make knowing each one impossible, and so too discerning which are credible and which are not. Always be skeptical," she added. "Don't accept anything at face value. Think. Read widely."

## CONTRADICTORY "FOUNTAINS OF FACTS"

"Knowledge is power; capture it and you capture power in a democracy," states Michael Lynch, a professor of philosophy at the University of Connecticut who studies the impact of technology on human society. He is concerned about today's unprecedented ease of access to "alternative facts."[84] "There is nothing to fear from information when counterinformation is just as plentiful," he says.[85] When so many contradictory "fountains of facts" are just a click away from anyone with a computer or smartphone, the notion of building or maintaining an informed electorate becomes a far more complex challenge. For Lynch, the bigger worry now is not about who controls the content, but rather who controls the *flow* of that content. "It is no coincidence," he writes, "that we are now seeing Big Data companies like Facebook sponsor presidential debates."

It is important to recognize that the mere presence of real news amid fake news is not a solution. Even reducing the amount of fake news doesn't necessarily mean that everyone will turn to real news. As Lynch points out, people must know and understand real information, too. "There are reasons to think we are no closer to an informed citizenry . . . than we ever have been. Indeed, we might be further away." He continues:

> Searching the Internet can get you to information that would back up almost any claim of fact, no matter how unfounded. It is both the world's best fact-checker and the world's best bias confirmer—often at the same time. . . . The very availability of information can make us think that the ideal of the informed citizen is more realized than

it is—and that, in turn, can actually undermine the ideal, making us less informed, simply because we think we know all we need to know already. . . . We no longer disagree just over values. Nor do we disagree just over the facts. We disagree over whose source—whose fountain of facts—is the right one. And once disagreement reaches that far down, the daylight of reason seems very far away indeed.[86]

"Facts are the closest thing we have to a national religion," writes Matt Taibbi in *Rolling Stone* magazine, lamenting this new era of alternative facts.[87] "In America, where sex-tapers become royalty and monster trucks massively outdraw Shakespeare, even advertisers aren't supposed to just lie. The truth is the last thing here that isn't openly for sale."

## WHO BELIEVES THIS STUFF?

How did the United States, one of the wealthiest and most educated societies ever, end up here? Why are so many Americans willing to believe almost anything? How can someone in a high government position utter the phrase "alternative facts" and receive nodding agreement from millions of Americans? Kurt Andersen, author of *Fantasyland: How America Went Haywire*, thinks that, for many, extreme credulity has become one of the components of being a proud American. Accepting crazy claims and stupid ideas is now seen as an aspect of freedom—the freedom to be fooled, if you will. Andersen writes: "Being American means we can believe any damn thing we want; that our beliefs are equal or superior to anyone else's, experts be damned. Once people commit to that approach, the world turns inside out, and no cause-and-effect connection is fixed. The credible becomes incredible and the incredible credible."[88] Andersen maintains that the United States has become unique among developed nations: "Treating real life as fantasy and vice versa, and taking preposterous ideas seriously is not unique to Americans. But we are the global crucible and epicenter. We invented the fantasy-industrial complex; almost nowhere outside poor or otherwise miserable countries are flamboyant supernatural beliefs so central to the identities of so many people. This is American exceptionalism in the 21st century."[89]

BuzzFeed, a news site that focuses on digital media, studied the fake news problem by analyzing more than a thousand posts on six "hyperpartisan" Facebook pages. Three of the pages were right-wing and three were left-wing. BuzzFeed determined that the right-wing pages had the higher rate of fake news. Thirty-eight percent of right-wing posts examined were false or mostly false, compared with 19 percent of false or mostly false left-wing posts.[90] Regardless of whether anti–Hillary Clinton fake news articles drew more media attention and outnumbered anti-Trump fake news, it would be a mistake to view this as a conservative or right-wing problem. Fake news is a *human* problem.

"I certainly don't blame people who are being misled," said Nyhan, the Dartmouth political science professor who studies misinformation in politics. "I feel that we too often blame the public for being human beings rather than the politicians and media sources that deceive them. People reading their social media feeds and being deceived are the victims, not the perpetrators. But it is important to be careful about what we share. We have to be responsible and avoid spreading misinformation, and retract and correct when we do."[91]

### FACEBOOK AND FAKE NEWS

| Fake News from Unreliable Sites | vs. | Accurate News from Reliable Sites |
|---|---|---|
| 8,711,000 shares, reactions, and comments on Facebook | | 7,367,000 shares, reactions, and comments on Facebook |

Source: BuzzFeed study of Facebook and fake news during the last three months of the 2016 US presidential election.[92]

BuzzFeed analyzed Facebook posts and found that some fake election news articles outperformed real election news from nineteen major news outlets combined. In total engagement on Facebook (liking, reacting, commenting, and sharing), fake news beat real news—and by a significant amount.[93] Over the last three months of the campaign, made-up stories from dubious sources were more popular than accurate articles from more established sources such as the *New York Times*, the *Washington Post*, the *Huffington Post*, and NBC News. In the closing weeks of the campaign, the twenty top-performing fake stories from hoax and hyperpartisan sites generated 8,711,000 shares, reactions, and comments on Facebook. The twenty best-performing election stories from nineteen major news sites generated 7,367,000 shares, reactions, and comments (see the table provided above).

## TRUMP'S TRIUMPH PUTS FAKE NEWS IN THE SPOTLIGHT

Of the top twenty fake news articles, seventeen were clearly anti–Hillary Clinton or pro–Donald Trump. The two most successful false stories, according to the BuzzFeed study, were the pope endorsing Trump, and Clinton selling weapons to ISIS.[94] There may be a psychological reason for this imbalance, as evidenced by a recent study by UCLA.

A 2017 University of California–Los Angeles study found that the degree to which one is liberal or conservative can predict how likely he or she is to believe news or information about a danger. Conservatives tend to be more concerned about risk and danger than liberals are. This makes them more vulnerable to falling for false dangers. This does not mean conservatives are generally more gullible. The study addressed the specific topic of danger. If another study focused on fake news that centered on a benefit in change or progress, I suspect liberals would probably believe it at a higher rate than conservatives would. "Social conservatives see safety in the status quo, while liberals see opportunity in change," said anthropologist Daniel Fessler, the study's lead researcher.[95] Because the world is filled with both dangers and opportunities, we cannot say that one way is right and the other wrong, Fessler explained. If a danger is real, liberals may suffer by ignoring it. If a perceived danger is false or insignificant, conservatives may suffer due to unnecessary actions or by missing out on opportunities because of unwarranted caution.

There is, of course, no limit to this kind of thing. A few creative con artists and an infinitely gullible public form a near-perfect symbiotic system. And don't assume that the fakers care about politics.

In 2016, for example, some enterprising teenagers in a small town in Macedonia profited off the US presidential election by pumping out wild but untrue pro-Trump fake news stories.[96] These particular news reports traced back to some 140 websites with American-sounding names such as "USConservativeToday.com."[97] When an irresistible story goes viral, those views and shares turn into money via pay-per-click ads on the webpages. The perpetrators of the fraud cared nothing about Trump winning. They were in it for the money.[98]

The most disturbing revelation from the 2016 election cyber-subterfuge was the creative and concerted effort by the Russian government to influence it in Trump's favor. This included the use of not only hacked and leaked Democratic Party e-mails but also fake news delivered through social media. The Central Intelligence Agency, the National Security Agency, the FBI, and the Office of the Director of National Intelligence all concluded that this really did happen.[99] Former CIA and NSA director Michael Hayden described Russia's interference in the 2016 presidential election the "most successful covert influence operation in history."[100] Even if Russian-sourced fake news stories had no significant impact on how people voted in that election, we can view the event as a warning. In the coming years, it now seems likely, if not inevitable, that many powerful entities with considerable resources are likely to weaponize social media as a component of their propaganda wars.

The most successful fake news stories tend to have a too-good-to-be-true feel. This should always ring alarm bells for savvy news consumers and good critical thinkers. All social media users are targets for this kind of thing, because the ever-present goal is to grab attention and get clicks—whatever it takes. One successful fake news story claimed that Academy Award–winning actor Denzel Washington had declared his support for Trump's campaign. It was the perfect snare for any Trump supporters who were hungry for ammunition to counter accusations of racism against their candidate. The article was shared hundreds of thousands of times before election day, even though it was untrue.[101] The piece originated from a website named "American News." Even the fastest glance at this site, however, should make it obvious to anyone that it is not in the business of producing accurate and honest news. But those who are not in the habit of pausing to think before believing fell for it. Those who did not check the source or look for corroborating reports were sitting ducks. Desire defeats reason all of the time. One of the core principles of good thinking is to be mature enough to seek out and accept what is real, rather than blindly pretending that comforting hopes and beliefs are real. People want to believe something, so they naturally suppress or ignore the impulse to doubt and verify. When something feels too good to be true, be more vigilant, not less so.

Another bogus article that went viral claimed that Hillary Clinton bought $137 million worth of illegal arms.[102] It came from a clearly suspicious website named "What Does It Mean." There are countless sham websites that are nothing more than clickbait factories producing extreme and absurd articles designed to catch the eye of gullible people—which, to some degree, means all of us.

Although Hillary Clinton got it the worst during the campaign, Trump took some hits, too. One particularly embarrassing Trump quote moved through social media circles. It helped portray him as exploitive and cynical, a must-share for Trump haters. According to this post, Trump told *People* magazine back in 1998 that Republicans were dumb and believe anything they hear on Fox News. But he never said it. It was a made-up quote designed to damage his campaign.[103]

---

**TOP FIVE FAKE NEWS STORIES PRIOR TO THE 2016 US PRESIDENTIAL ELECTION, AS RANKED BY SHARES, REACTIONS, AND COMMENTS ON FACEBOOK[104]**

1. "Pope Francis Shocks World, Endorses Donald Trump for President, Releases Statement" (Source: *Ending the Fed*)
2. "WikiLeaks CONFIRMS Hilary Sold Weapons to ISIS . . . Then Drops Another BOMBSHELL! Breaking News" (Source: *Political Insider*)
3. "IT'S OVER: Hillary's ISIS Email Leaked and It's Worse Than Anyone Could Have Imagined" (Source: *Ending the Fed*)
4. "Just Read the Law: Hillary Is Disqualified from Holding Any Federal Office" (Source: *Ending the Fed*)
5. "FBI Agent Suspected in Hillary Email Leaks Found Dead in Apparent Murder-Suicide" (Source: *Denver Guardian*)

Source: BuzzFeed study[105]

Did the fake news that spread like a pandemic via social media play a meaningful role in the 2016 presidential election? Maybe, but who can be sure? Most people vote the way they do for more than one reason. The bigger question is, what can be done about this serious problem that did not go away after the election? Google, Twitter, and Facebook responded to the charge of being massive conduits for hoaxes, lies, and propaganda by promising to get tougher on fake news. Less than one week after the election, Google announced that it would stop making its AdSense advertising network available for use by fake news websites, and Facebook changed its policies to include a ban on ads that promote fake news.[106]

Political misinformation researcher Nyhan says that fake news made up a small portion of the total information people consumed during 2016 US election. "I would hardly define it as the reason Trump won, as some people have suggested," he said.[107] "I don't think there's any evidence to support that claim. But those stories were shared millions of times on Facebook, and we do need to take seriously the way the purveyors of fake news have found large audiences. It has become financially attractive to mislead Americans with bogus news stories. . . . A perverse financial incentive was created. Facebook and Google are starting to take steps to counter that threat. I'm concerned about partisan misinformation more broadly. I think that's a very serious concern. We depend on some kind of a shared basis in factual reality to have a public debate about what our government is doing and should be doing."

Facebook's founder and CEO, Mark Zuckerberg, denied in a post that his company had influenced the election either way: "After the election, many people are asking whether fake news contributed to the result, and what our responsibility is to prevent fake news from spreading. These are very important questions and I care deeply about getting them right. . . . Of all of the content on Facebook, more than 99 percent of what people see is authentic. Only a very small amount is fake news and hoaxes. The hoaxes that do exist are not limited to one partisan view, or even to politics. Overall, this makes it extremely unlikely hoaxes changed the outcome of this election in one direction or the other."[108]

Zeynep Tufekci, an associate professor at the University of North Carolina School of Information and Library Science, was not impressed with Zuckerberg's response: "In holding fast to the claim that his company has little effect on how people make up their minds,

Mr. Zuckerberg is doing real damage to American democracy—and to the world."[109] Internet media expert Jose van Dijck, of the Netherlands, told me that she believes there is clear need for more responsibility from social media companies. "Platforms like Facebook should realize they cannot hide behind the excuse of being a 'mere' technical facilitator or 'mediator' between content and users. Now that the US population receives 50 percent of their news through [Facebook's] News Feed, Facebook should behave like a responsible news organization and take care of the content it distributes—whether it is racial slurs, copyrighted material, or fake news."[110]

---

### FINANCIAL FAKE NEWS

It's not just the "Hillary Clinton Shoots Bigfoot" type of articles that fool gullible people. Fake news can strike anywhere and potentially snare anyone. In 2017, hundreds of articles were published on top financial news sites that were found to be misleading and biased fake news. They were written by people who had been paid to promote certain biotech stocks. This was according to enforcement actions by the US Securities and Exchange Commission. The payments received by the writers were not disclosed to readers. According to the SEC charge, twenty-seven individuals and entities "posted bullish articles about [publicly traded] companies on the Internet under the guise of impartiality when in reality they were nothing more than paid advertisements."[111]

---

Based on discussions I had and surveys I conducted with more than one hundred experts and laypersons after the election, there seems to be a popular belief that banning, censoring, and/or labeling fake news will fix this. But these steps alone are unlikely to succeed. It reminds me of America's "War on Drugs." Fighting only the supply side of the equation while ignoring the demand is probably not a winning strategy. The reality is that people, not just the bogus news articles, are a key part of the problem, too. It's time for social media users to take responsibility for the beliefs they allow to enter their minds. Convincing people to embrace good thinking on social media would rob the purveyors of fake news the target-rich environments they have enjoyed. Therefore, the priority target in this fight should not be the bogus articles themselves or even the sources that spawn them. Those things still matter, of course, and should be given due attention, but the decisive battles will take place within human minds. The fundamental challenge here is that some people can't or won't apply critical thinking skills while consuming news and information online. The idea of banning or blocking fake news strikes me as accepting or, worse, encouraging and enabling a culture of passive stupidity. We are not rocks. We are human beings capable of reason and analysis. We all have remarkably powerful brains. The potential for good thinking is always present, in everyone. Properly and consistently applied, critical thinking skills can defeat fake news almost every time.

Perhaps stung by global criticism for their role in enabling a culturally corrosive free-for-all of lies and idiocy, Google and Facebook promised to make significant changes in 2017 toward improving the situation. In addition to their previously mentioned promise to reduce the financial incentive by restricting ad sales to fake news producers, Google now allows people—actual human beings—to flag hoaxes, overt propaganda, and the worst of the conspiracy theories. Google also said that it has tweaked its algorithms to push "low-quality content" further down in search results.[112] In April 2017, Facebook announced that it would continue working to make it easier for users to be aware of related articles and third-party fact-checkers before reading an article.[113] It will take time to see if it's effective, but this is a sensible approach because once a lie or a bad idea gets into a human mind, it can be difficult to extinguish it. Better that more credible information is available earlier rather than later. This is similar to how preventive vaccines are always preferable to after-the-fact cures.

## HOW TO KEEP FAKE NEWS OUT OF YOUR HEAD

- **Be skeptical of everything.** Online or off-line, never accept any claim, story, or news article as 100 percent true. Always leave a door slightly ajar for escape. Take the stance that all knowledge is *provisional*. Hold on to some humility and uncertainty so that you don't tie yourself too tightly to a mistake or lie. Doubt is a good thing. Skepticism is not cynicism. Thinking critically does not mean you are closed-minded or negative. Doing so is safe and wise. We should approach *all* news we encounter in this way, regardless of the source. The BBC and the *New York Times* make mistakes every day. No journalist is perfect every time—and sometimes one of them just plain lies.[114] You don't have to rise to a state of paranoia, but you should maintain a high level of awareness and concern about what you are taking in. Dishonest people are out there, every day, hoping that you will be lazy in a key moment they can exploit.

---

### WINDOW INTO THE MADNESS

People have always been sloppy thinkers, and the act of one person transmitting crazy ideas to other people predates civilization. What is new today is that this phenomenon of spreading lies and false beliefs has been energized and ampli-fied by the Internet and social media. For most of human exis-tence, most crackpot notions were localized, their growth constrained by communication limitations. Now even the most absurd and unlikely claims can thrive, reaching millions.

Before the Internet, Alex Jones, the man behind InfoWars, a prolific conspiracy-theory-factory of a website, would have struggled. He might have barely managed to entertain five or six gullible people at his local Starbucks with talk of a NASA child slave colony on Mars[115] or the Sandy Hook Elementary School massacre having been a government false-flag opera-tion.[116] Today, however, Jones has the ear of millions of fans, including, it seems, a US president. In December 2015, then can-didate Trump appeared on Jones's show and declared to the host: "Your reputation is amazing. I will not let you down."[117]

Today anyone can observe the reach and popularity of someone like Alex Jones. Millions of clicks, shares, likes, com-ments, and retweets give evidence to a significant problem. The Internet has empowered those who would spread misin-formation and encourage the most ludicrous beliefs. But at the same time, it also gives the rest of us a window into the madness. Thanks to the Internet and social media, we can observe irrational beliefs in real time as they surge through society. The key question is, having seen the problem, are we smart enough and responsible enough to formulate and implement necessary solutions?

- **Consider the source.** While we cannot trust any source completely and without reservation, the reputation of a source is a key step in assessing a news article. One of the first things I do when I encounter a news article, post, or anything online is to look at the source. I rarely, if ever, read the entire text of a news story without first noting the source. When many people land on a webpage, however, they begin reading the content. Even if they are thoughtful enough to be concerned with errors, bias, and dishonesty, they make the key mistake of assuming that any problems present will become apparent while reading. This is not necessarily so. Before I waste my time and risk letting lies or nonsense creep into my mind, I ask myself the following questions: Who is behind this website? Who wrote the material? Who took this photo and wrote the caption under it? Who is paying the bills here? If I don't know the answers to at least some of these questions, or if there is a clear agenda at work that compromises truth and reality, I'm out. I may still read the article, but my capacity to absorb it as fact shrinks to almost nothing. Before believing, I will need to see more of the same information from better sources.

  Specifically related to this, I have watched people conduct Internet searches when trying to find an answer or research a topic, and it is shocking how few people check the source before plunging into the information. This is a critical error that leads millions of people off course in their thinking and worldview. There are many times when an article should be dismissed before reading, simply due to its source. I know this may seem harsh, maybe even closed-minded, but it's not. It's good thinking. There is just too much bad information on the Web. For example, if a middle school student is researching basic facts about the Holocaust for a class project, the last thing she needs to do is land on some Neo-Nazi site and waste her time reading an article that claims it never happened.

- **Google is not a god.** I know, I know; Google is great. How did we ever live without it? But it's still *just* a search engine. It feeds you results based on the query and perhaps your online identity as determined by the algorithms working behind your back. Google is not your personal librarian. It's not an arbiter of truth, a champion of science and reason, or anything else like that. It's a search engine. You put words in, it spits out links to relevant websites. This is merely the starting point and not the end of the research road. You have to think and sort out the wheat from the chaff, the real from the fake.

- **Slow down.** When reading news, it's wise to withhold fully accepting a claim or digging in on a position until you know more, preferably from multiple sources. Did you just read that Kanye West kicked a puppy? Wait and gather more intel before deleting all of his songs from your playlist. Never forget that an important component of news is speed, never more so than today. But while speed is a priority for news media companies, it doesn't have to be yours. Let others rush in and make mistakes. In almost every case, you have the luxury of time. Slow down and get it right. I advise thinking of news, all of it, as a *suggestion* of a possible reality. Think of a news article not as an end point but as a signpost along the way on your journey toward the truth.
- **If no one else is reporting this story, ask yourself why.** If you encounter a lone report that describes the opening of a new habitat featuring a live Bigfoot specimen at the San Diego Zoo or the invasion of South Korea by North Korean killer robots, chances are good that it's fake news. The absence of similar reports by multiples news organizations is a gigantic red flag. Cable news networks are hyperfocused on being fast. If they aren't reporting on a big story, it's probably because they figured out that it's unsupported by evidence or credible sources and unlikely to be true.
- **Understand the difference between opinion and news.** Many people don't recognize the fundamental difference between opinion or commentary and news. Straight news is about the hard facts of an event and may include direct quotes from an interview subject related to the topic. Commentary is an open arena where writers or broadcasters can express feelings, hunches, and opinions. Both are important, of course, but confusing one for the other can lead to problems.
- **Check the URL carefully.** Many fake news sites seek to fool people with a Web address that is similar to a legitimate news site. One common trick is the have a URL that is identical

to a major news company except for a couple of extra letters at the end. For example, ".com.co" is not the same as ".com." At a glance, for example, you might assume that ABCNews.com.co and BostonTribune.com are the Web addresses of real and respectable news organizations. But they aren't. Both specialize in publishing fake news articles. The first one has nothing to do with the ABC News most are familiar with, and the other is not the website of a respected Boston newspaper as one might assume.

- **Don't spread garbage.** Another significant problem is the habit many seem to have of sharing news links after doing nothing more than reading the headline. How can anyone intelligently assess an article without reading it first? About six in ten people, 59 percent, are guilty of this, according to a recent study.[118] In 2016, a satirical site published an article with a catchy headline but gibberish for text. Nearly 46,000 people shared it.[119]

  Please don't do this! In many circumstances, sharing a news article implies an endorsement. Understand that headlines are there to catch the eye, provoke, and excite the mind; and they often are written by an editor, someone other than the person who wrote the article itself. As a result, headline and article do not always share a consistent theme and tone. Most troublesome, however, is that some fake news is designed to look credible at first glance. The lies only emerge somewhere down in the text. The headline may be intentionally written to make the bogus text below it seem respectable. Don't be an accomplice. If you can't bother to read the story and assess its accuracy, then don't share the story. Don't add fuel to a fire that already burns up too much invaluable intellectual capital. Spreading fake news drags us all down. The proliferation of propaganda and nonsense pushes us toward a coarser, more inefficient and dangerous world. When engaged on social media, strive to act in ways that uplift us and help make humankind wiser and more sensible.

- **Videos lie, too.** Fools say "seeing is believing." The wise know that sometimes it goes the other way: "believing is seeing." Our beliefs, as well as fears and hopes, color our perceptions. A devout UFO believer, for example, is more likely to watch a video of a light in the sky and "see" an alien spaceship, clear as day, with an alien crew member waving from one of the windows. A good skeptic, however, would likely see nothing more than a distant, blurry, unidentified light in the sky. This is because the skeptic would know to slow down, take it in with sharpened attention, and resist jumping to unjustified conclusions.

The skill and vigilance needed to defend against fake news will become even more urgent in the near future as new technologies allow people to manipulate and create fake audio and video. This can be done now. The software already exists.[120] And soon the public will have access to the necessary tools as well. When that happens, we are sure to be flooded with videos and soundbites of celebrities, politicians, and others doing and saying things they never did or said. Think of the problems this can lead to. Imagine a faked but convincing viral video of you—or of a world leader—making racist statements or calling for the extermination of poor people. If the current poor state of critical thinking doesn't improve, millions would believe it. We may soon find that literally nothing online can be trusted, no matter how real it appears. A time may come when only the reputation of those who produce and publish a video can be a reliable indicator of trustworthiness.

- **Slow the flow.** Part of the reason fake news has exploded on social media is that it is so easy for one to become fatigued or at least distracted and cognitively compromised by the never-ending avalanche of information. We don't have infinite cognitive energies. The best of us can be worn down to a point where we are more likely to believe nonsense and pass it on to others. An interesting study published in *Nature Human Behaviour* in 2017 revealed this effect, concluding that *everyone* is more vulnerable to falling for fake stories when the flow of news becomes too great to pay close-enough attention.[121] In light of this, it may be a good idea to restrict the volume of your news exposure. Try to be selective. More is not better when it comes to making sensible assessments.

- **Diversify your cognitive portfolio.** Don't attempt to live on social media alone. Sure, there is great stuff out there, but much of it is nothing more than empty calories. Enrich your mental diet by broadening your horizons. Read books and magazines off-line, if only to make sure your brain can still do it. Have more conversations with people who are physically present with you. Take breaks from the Internet on a regular basis. A day or even a week away is unlikely to shatter your life. None of this makes you a Luddite. But it just might help make you an intellectually deeper, more well-rounded person—and someone less likely to fall for fake news.

- **Remember who you are.** We are primates, fresh off the African savannah, and as such we don't automatically do well at identifying irrational beliefs and fraudulent claims for what they are. Our brains, for all their glorious powers, are suckers for a good story, an exciting image, convenient lie, or just plain old gossip. We must pause and *think* so that we may give ourselves the best chance to make the right decision about what to believe. We must second-guess our own minds, as Nyhan reinforced: "Social media is tough. It's important for all of us to be aware of our limitations as human beings. We are all vulnerable to misinformation. It's hard to fact-check every single piece of news that comes across your view. So it's important to be cautious."[122]

Awareness and consistent skepticism can keep us from being pulled down the fake news rabbit hole. Remember that any story that feels perfect or that you just *need* to be true because it supports something you believe in has an automatic advantage in your sub-conscious mind and puts your rational mind at a disadvantage. The mere hint of a "perfect story" has nudges you into a state of weak-ness. This is the precise moment when critical thinking skills and a commitment to skepticism can save you from cluttering your head with a lie and hoodwinking you into becoming an accomplice who shares and spreads fraud. Good thinking is all that stands between you and all of those fake news stories out there designed to make fools out of us.

Benjamin Radford, deputy editor of *Skeptical Inquirer*, is one of the world's most prominent skeptics and promoters of critical thinking. He is also the author of *Media Mythmakers: How Jour-nalists, Activists, and Advertisers Mislead Us*; he had a lot to say about fake news in an e-mail exchange with me:

"Fake news" is a broad phrase covering anything from Internet hoaxes to rumors to propaganda. Though these categories vary widely in cause, intent, toxicity, and in other ways, the good news is that all of these varieties of "fake news" have the same antidote: skepticism and critical thinking. all of these variations can be stopped in their tracks by media-savvy citizens. Though the public love to blame the news media for misinformation—and deservedly so—they are less keen to see the culprit in the mirror. Many people, especially on social media, fail to recognize that they have become de facto news outlets through the stories and posts they share on Facebook, Twitter, and elsewhere. Yes, the news media help spread myriad "fake news" stories—but they are gleefully aided by ordinary people like you and me.[123]

Radford says that although we cannot easily influence or control what a news organization, group, or individual publishes online, we can help by not sharing misleading information and posting propaganda. "It can be as simple as not forwarding, liking, or sharing that dubious news story, especially if it seems crafted to encourage social outrage, before checking the facts. It's too easy, especially in the heat of righteous indignation, to share and spread misinformation. If news organizations can't or won't take responsibility, we as netizens can take that power by refusing to be a conduit for these and other varieties of fake news—or, better yet, debunking it."

## FIGHTING BACK

John Pavley, senior vice president at the media conglomerate Viacom, believes Facebook can do a better job when it comes to fake news.[124] For starters, he says human editors should be in the loop. Algorithms don't exist that can consistently and accurately identify harmless satire, real news, and well-designed fake news—not yet. He also would like to see Facebook give users the option to "dislike" news in addition to "liking" it. Best of all, he recommends Facebook give users a mix of news they are likely to both agree with and disagree with. This is how confirmation bias can be held back a bit, if not tamed.

Pavley also points the finger of blame at each of us as well:

If you want to blame some modern phenomenon for the results of the 2016 presidential election, and not the people who didn't vote, or the flawed candidates, or the FBI shenanigans, then blame the trolls. You might think of the typical troll as a pimply-faced kid in his bedroom with the door locked and the window shades taped shut but those guys are angels compared to the real trolls: the general public. You and me.[125]

Pavley is correct, of course. Fake news only becomes a problem when enough people fail to apply a minimal amount of reason before passing it on to others. It seems at times that the unofficial mantra of social media today is, "Don't think, just share."[126] This must change. Take some responsibility, both for yourself and for the state of social media. It's easy for us to kill fake news. All we need to do is think.

It is wise to carefully consider all proposed solutions to fake news. Some cures could be as bad as or worse than the original problem. Katherine Losse, an early Facebook employee who became Mark Zuckerberg's ghost writer, warns us about this potential issue in a blog post: "Technology companies could very well end up banishing 'Fake News' by moving to publish only news they create and approve, which creates a new monopoly on news and story creation. It is for this reason that as we head into a world dominated increasingly by centralized power, maintaining the ability to tell and write our own stories remains critical."[127] Losse hits upon a critical challenge swirling around the issue of fake news. How do we encourage and preserve the ability of people, everyday people, to publish their ideas and share information on social media freely while still working to maintain acceptable levels of social and journalistic sanity? The answer to that, I suppose, is to find a way to convince everyone of the value of critical thinking so that creative lies and nonsense lose their viral potential.

"How can people be so stupid?" This is a sentiment several people expressed to me during discussions and interviews about the fake news phenomenon. I disagree strongly with the implication that a portion of humanity is hopelessly dim, and I worry that my analysis of fake news here may be misinterpreted by some as blanket condemnation of human brainpower. This is not the case. Nothing in this chapter or in the rest of this book is meant to suggest that humankind is stuck in an eternal loop of one mad belief after another. Perhaps we are, but I opt for optimism. The same half-crazed brain that leads us to believe in ghosts can think them away as well. I concede that we may struggle forever with delusions and irrational beliefs because of our brain's evolutionary history and resulting troublesome ways. But given our no-less-real capacity for skepticism and critical thinking, I believe that we can do better. It may not be natural or easy, but we are fully capable of becoming a more sensible species.

---

### TOO BUSY TO RESEARCH IT?
### CHECK IN WITH THE FACT-CHECKERS

Sometimes we are too busy to play Sherlock Holmes and spend hours trying to track down some slippery detail in a news article to find out whether or not it's accurate. Fortunately, there are shortcuts available. Trustworthy fact-checker sites are ready and waiting to help you sort through the confusion. **Snopes.com**, founded by David Mikkelson in 1994, is the oldest and largest of such sites. This is a good place to make a quick visit when you hear or see something that seems questionable.

The **International Fact-Checking Network (IFCN)** is an international fact-checkers site that was launched in 2015 (www.poynter.org/category/fact-checking). Hosted by the Poynter Institute for Media Studies, the various organizations fact-check government leaders, news articles, and statements by major institutions and companies. They also provide training resources for other fact-checkers.

---

The human brain is routinely lauded for its intellectual and creative abilities. But its greatest power of all is that of flexibility, or neuroplasticity. We can learn new things throughout life, change our behaviors, and literally redesign our brains. We don't have to rely on instincts for everything. Humankind may never completely outgrow its silly ways, but we can always improve, learn from mistakes, do better next time, and chase wisdom at every turn. "We shamelessly yield to impulse and invent reasons afterward," write Ellen and Michael Kaplan in their book, *Bozo Sapiens: Why to Err Is Human*.[128] They continue, "We impute motives to distant figures and events of which, despite the global wash of media, we really know almost nothing. . . . We allow others to impose on us with slippery rhetoric and bogus statistics. We cower from difficult truths and cry after comforting illusions. And yet, astonishingly, here we still are—the masters of creation. For idiots, we have been remarkably successful: our grand entrances may start on a banana peel, our sweeping exits lead into a closet, but we are the stars of this show."

*Skeptical Inquirer* deputy editor Radford wants people to understand that some fake news can have deadly serious consequences. He cites a 2014 incident that occurred in Guarujá, a town near Brazil's largest city of Sao Paulo. Fabiane Maria de Jesus, aged thirty-three, was beaten to death by a mob because they thought she was a witch. Why did they think this?

"Maria de Jesus was suspected of being a witch because of a warning shared on social media," Radford explains.[129] He elaborates,

> The Facebook page for a local tabloid-style news outlet spread an alert claiming that a woman had been seen abducting children for use in witchcraft. It's not clear how the news alert obtained information about the alleged witch's motivations, but a sketch of the supposed child abductor was included with the alert. Because Maria de Jesus looked vaguely like the child abductor, the mob suspected it was her. Administrators for the Facebook page later released a statement denying responsibility for the attack and stating that it had merely passed along the unfounded rumors as a public service and never explicitly claimed the child-abduction rumor was true. . . . When wild rumors are given credence through social media and accepted without question or evidence, the results can be tragic. It's something to keep in mind the next time you share, like, or tweet a sensational news item warning of some threat.

## FINAL THOUGHTS ON THE WAR FOR YOUR THOUGHTS

Strive to make skepticism and critical thinking habitual, largely automatic, or subconscious reactions to your online encounters with news and other information. This won't make you invulnerable and incapable of making missteps, of course, but keeping your guard up, is key to living a safer and more efficient life. Do not forget for one second that you are under constant threat of intellectual assault from countless throngs of deluded believers pushing endless streams of baloney and madness. There also are countless profit-motivated, agenda-driven, and just plain dishonest companies and people who show up and work hard every day with the aim of fooling you for their own gain.

Do not allow yourself to be complacent about this challenge. Fake news matters. Even if you have it all figured out and don't think you can fall for the lies and hoaxes, you still live in this world with millions of other people who are eating it up every day. Delusions lead to danger. Idiocy might lead to the realization of *Idiocracy*,[130] or worse. "Believe in truth," urges Timothy Snyder, a professor of history at Yale University.[131] "To abandon facts is to abandon freedom. If nothing is true, then no one can criticize power, because there is no basis upon which to do so. If nothing is true, then all is spectacle. The biggest wallet pays for the most blinding lights."

Wouldn't it be a cruel irony if social media, created mostly by highly educated liberals in democratic society, ends up enabling dictators and anti-intellectual fascists of many flavors to take and hold power in nations around the world? I find some reason for hope and optimism amid the current explosion of fake news, however. There is a chance that people will be forced, after being suckered and exploited one too many times, to recognize and admit the obvious: We all must think before we believe. Maybe out of embarrassment or simple frustration, we will stop trusting every news story that thrills us, feels good, or otherwise feeds some deep desire. We will realize the need to be skeptical and cautious about *all* news. And that will be progress.

*Chapter Three*

## SOCIAL MEDIA ADDICTION: HARM OR HYPE?

**Never before in history have a handful of people at a handful of technology companies shaped how a billion people think and feel every day with the choices they make about these screens.**
—Tristan Harris, former Google employee,
co-founder of Time Well Spent[1]

**Every time you check your phone in company, what you gain is a hit of stimulation, a neurochemical shot, and what you lose is what a friend, teacher, parent, lover, or co-worker just said, meant, felt.**
—Sherry Turkle, Abby Rockefeller Mauzé Professor
of the Social Studies of Science and Technology
and director of the MIT Initiative on Technology and Self[2]

**You're part of a controlled set of experiments that are happening in real time across you and millions of other people. . . . We've figured out, to some extent, how these pieces of the brain that handle addiction are working; people have figured out how to juice them further and how to bake that information into apps.**
—Ramsay Brown, co-founder of Dopamine Labs[3]

**This is your life and it's ending one moment at a time.**
—Chuck Palahniuk, *Fight Club*[4]

Several years ago, I stayed at the Las Vegas Hilton and explored the hotel's casino during one of my amateur anthropologist moments. I wandered among the natives, hoping to learn something about what they gained by losing money. I saw excited eyes follow a little white ball as it orbited the roulette wheel. Trembling hands motioned the dealer for one more card at the blackjack table. That was all interesting enough, but nothing compared to the sight of the slot machines. Row after row of them stood strong, shining under the lights like the altars of some bizarre future religion. Beeping and flashing, each one had before it what looked to me like a semiconscious human being, frozen in reverent devotion. Was this a symbiotic relationship of some sort, a parasite-host scenario? If so, which were the parasites and which were the hosts?

I continued exploring, up and down the aisles, excited by the profound weirdness around me. I could approach and closely observe these techno-gamblers because I did not exist to them, such was the depth of their spellbound state. The glassy-eyed people stared into intoxicating flickering images of what I guessed was for them a mix of hope, excitement, and, perhaps, danger and despair. The glow of the machines illuminated their vacant faces and I studied their blank expressions. No one looked happy, but neither did anyone seem sad. They were just *there*, doing what one does in front of a slot machine. Play, play, and play again. The minds within these people may have been razzled, dazzled, and excited; but from my perspective, looking at them from a few feet away, they seemed barely alive. They were gone, away in some strange zone of disconnect from the outer world. Most of the players had magnetic game cards clipped onto lanyards worn around their necks. With their cards plugged into the machines, the dangling lanyards between human and machine took on the look of a feeding tube or energy hose, the gambler's umbilical cord. The cards' real purpose, of course, was to make the slow and ceaseless draining of money and time feel more comfortable and convenient. Dropping quarters all night might feel too much like work. And carrying the weight of so many coins or tokens might awaken some of the players to how much money they are losing.

Odd as it all was to me, I stopped short of drawing too many conclusions that night. I was an outsider there, a bewildered visitor, and as such I reserved judgment. I didn't know enough to call it bad or wrong. For all I knew, those were the happiest people on Earth. Besides, I'm sure many of those seated zombies were probably on vacation and would return to lives that did not include long stints of drooling before slot machines. Out of curiosity, I did some research on slot machines after that casino fieldwork. It turns out that the science and engineering behind them is nothing short of amazing.

Slot machines are not silly games. It varies by country, but these high-tech, big-money earners commonly bring in from 70 to 80 percent of a casino's revenue.[5] Over a period of eleven years, the Pennsylvania state government took in $3 billion from all casinos' combined table games, such as blackjack, baccarat, and roulette, while earning an astounding *$17 billion* from slot machines alone during that same period. There are nearly one million slot machines in the United States today, which is equal to about double the number of ATMs, and Americans today spend more money playing them than they do on movies, baseball, and theme parks *combined*.[6] These are brilliantly engineered tease-and-reward boxes. They are designed to keep a human brain engaged with them for as long as possible, because more play means more money.

The details behind the remarkable success of the slot machine pile up fast, but the core concept is simple. To keep a player engaged, you *vary input* so that the player is repeatedly placed in suspense, not sure what will happen next. This builds tension. Then you deliver *adequate rewards*, not so little as to frustrate but not so much as to satisfy. This relieves tension without allowing the player to feel a sense of completion. Repeating the process of anticipation/ tension, followed by reward/release, over and over, keeps players stuck in place, until their money runs out, of course.

Natasha Dow Schull, an MIT anthropologist who has studied gambling, says that slot machines are the most potent form of gambling because they are solitary, fast, and continuous. "When gamblers play, they're going into a zone that feels comfortable and safe," Schull told the *New Republic*.[7] "You're not playing to win, you're playing to stay in the zone—a zone where all of your daily worries, your bodily pains, your anxieties about money and time and relationships, fall away."

Casinos encourage or require players to use those magnetic game cards, or "rewards cards" that I saw in Las Vegas, to track and accumulate valuable details about them. The data enable the casinos to learn how long an identified individual plays, how much he or she typically spends before quitting, and what minimal trickles of success work best to keep him or her playing and spending money.[8] Does any of this sound familiar?

Can you think of another multi-billion-dollar industry today that might be tapping into the same anticipation/tension, reward/release cycle to hook people and keep them engaged and staring at screens for as long as possible? Does anyone you know come to mind, someone who spends a lot time in a state of semi-disconnect while swiping and poking, hoping for a reward, maybe one in the form of an interesting photo or comment to pop up?

---

### YOUR SMARTPHONE VS. SEX, CHOCOLATE, AND SHOES. WHO WINS?

The explosion of smartphone ownership is a key factor in the rise of social media use. Together, these mobile devices and online social networks have found a fruitful symbiotic relationship. Therefore, it can help inform us about where the popularity of social media may be heading by looking at the current affinity for and reliance on smartphones. The Pew Research Center reported in 2017 that more than three-quarters of Americans, 77 percent, now have smartphones and 92 percent of US eighteen- to twenty-nine-year-olds own one.[9] That same Pew study reports that "smartphone ownership rates have skyrocketed in many countries since 2013. This includes increases of over 25 percentage points among the total population in large emerging economies such as Turkey (+42 points), Malaysia (+34), Chile (+26) and Brazil (+26)."[10]

Popularity aside, it's also clear that people *want and need* smartphones to a high degree. I will refrain from invoking the word *addiction*, but some of these human-device bonds are *strong*. A United Kingdom survey by the Physiological Society found that the idea of misplacing or having your smartphone stolen is viewed as a major stress event. "Losing your smartphone" ranked just below "terrorist threats."[11] Among eighteen- to twenty-four-year-olds only, losing a smartphone was ranked close behind "serious illness" as a significant stressor.[12]

Another study, conducted by TeleNav, an international wireless and GPS service corporation, revealed just how deep the love of smartphones can run for some people.[13] It is difficult to know whether we should be disturbed or amused by their findings:

- One-third of those surveyed say they would rather give up sex for a week than their smartphone.
- More than half, 54 percent, would prefer to sacrifice exercising for a week than lose their phone.
- Seventy percent would sooner abstain from alcohol for a week than go without their smartphones.
- Sixty-three percent would choose phone over chocolate.
- Fifty-five percent say they would give up caffeine for a week rather than their phone.
- Twenty-one percent say they would surrender their shoes for a week before their phone.

## THE DEFECTOR

**Every time I check my phone, I'm playing the slot machine to see, "What did I get?"**
—Tristan Harris, former Google employee
and founder of Time Well Spent[14]

Tristan Harris had a job most people would likely consider very cool. He was Product Philosopher at Google, responsible for studying how technology impacts people's attention, well-being, and behavior. But he took the task so seriously that he quit over concerns that there is too much industry emphasis on hooking people with apps and devices—by any means necessary—to keep their eyes on screens solely to harvest data and sell ads. This comes, he believes, at the expense of what could be and should be happening: working toward making technology more helpful and better able to improve our lives. He looks around today, sees people everywhere staring down at phones, and worries that society may have taken a wrong turn.

Harris describes what is going on at many tech companies and social media platforms a "race to the bottom of the brain stem, to get people's attention at all costs."[15] He charges Apple, Google, Facebook, Instagram, Snapchat, and the rest with gaming us, erecting a stealth casino around us and selling us pocket-sized gambling machines.

"If you're an app, how do you keep people hooked? Turn yourself into a slot machine," Harris writes on his website.[16] "The average person checks their phone 150 times a day. Why do we do this? Are we making *150 conscious choices*? How often do you check your email per day? One major reason why is the #1 psychological ingredient in slot machines: *intermittent variable rewards*. If you want to maximize addictiveness, all tech designers need to do is link a user's action, like pulling a lever, with a *variable reward*. You pull a lever and immediately receive either an enticing reward—a match, a prize!—or nothing. Addictiveness is maximized when the rate of reward is most variable." Harris continues:

> When we pull our phone out of our pocket, we're playing a slot machine to see what notifications we got. When we pull it out to refresh our email, we're playing a slot machine to see what new email we got. When we swipe down our finger to scroll the Instagram feed, we're playing a slot machine to see what photo comes next. When we swipe faces left/right on dating apps like Tinder, we're playing a slot machine to see if we got a match. When we tap the # of red notifications, we're playing a slot machine to what's underneath. Apps and websites sprinkle intermittent variable rewards all over their products because it's good for business.[17]

Social media companies make their money based on how long users stay on their sites and apps. So how are they doing with that? "Very well" would be an understatement. In 2016, Facebook took in a whopping $27 billion in advertising, while Google earned an astonishing $90 billion.[18] This money comes as a direct result of keeping people interested, entertained, engaged, hooked, addicted—whatever you call it. Nearly three-quarters of Americans, 73 percent, go online daily; 43 percent go online several times per day; and 21 percent are online "almost constantly." Younger people, ages eighteen to twenty-nine, are dedicating even more time to the Internet, including social media sites, of course. According to a Pew study, 36 percent of these young people are online "almost constantly."[19]

According to a 2016 study by dscouts,[20] a Chicago research firm, smartphone users tap, click, and swipe 2,617 times per day on average. The heaviest users doubled that with 5,427 daily touches. This equates to about a million touches a year, two million for the most active users. The average user engaged with his or her phone in seventy-six sessions per day. The top 10 percent of users averaged 132 sessions a day. "Checking your likes is the new smoking," says comedian Bill Maher.[21]

"Notification numbers appear on the app icon to draw you in, then on the top or bottom menu to draw you in further," explains Mike Elgan, a writer for *ComputerWorld*.[22] "They play the same psychological trick on you that clickbait headlines do—they tell you that there's information you really want to know, but they don't tell you enough to satisfy. . . . The biggest tool in the social media addition toolbox is algorithmic filtering. [They] tweak their algorithms, then monitor the response of users to see if those tweaks kept them on the site longer or increased their engagement. We're all lab rats in a giant, global experiment."

With so much time being invested now, it is clear that wise management of it should be a priority for users. Going online is not inherently bad. What matters is what we do online with all of that time and how well we resist against all of these attempts at psychological manipulation coming at us. It is vital for more social media users to learn and accept what these companies are attempting to do. Simply knowing and always remembering that you are a target, that smart people are working hard to hook you with digital bells and whistles, can reduce the power of these apps, games, and sites. With awareness may come the motivation to better monitor and self-regulate time spent online.

"They run thousands of tests with millions of users to learn which tweaks work and which ones don't—which background colors, fonts, and audio tones maximize engagement and minimize frustration," explains Adam Alter in his important book *Irresistible: The Rise of Addictive Technology and the Business of Keeping Us Hooked*.[23] "As an experience evolves, it becomes an irresistible, weaponized version of the experience it once was. In 2004, Facebook was fun; [today], it's addictive." Alter, an associate professor of marketing and psychology at New York University's Stern School of Business, believes that individuals, companies, and all of society can take meaningful steps to reduce the problem of overuse/addiction. Here are some of his suggestions:

- If the numerical feedback mechanisms (number of likes, retweets, shares, etc.) of many social media platforms help to make them so addictive, then these features can be removed so that users may be less fixated on social comparison and chronic goal setting.

## HOW MUCH TIME?

- On average, people now spend approximately 116 minutes, just shy of two hours, on social media every day. This equates to **five years and four months over a lifetime**. This is more than an average person spends eating and drinking, socializing in person, or grooming over a lifetime.[24]
- Teens now spend as much as **nine hours per day** on social media. This is more time than they typically sleep, and more time than they spend with their parents and teachers.[25]
- **"Filling up spare time"** is the main reason users aged sixteen to twenty-four give for being on social media.[26]
- Thirty percent of all time spent online is now devoted to social media interactions.[27]
- Americans in the eighteen-to-twenty-four-year-old bracket check their phones **82 times** per day on average.[28]
- More than 40 percent of Americans check their phones within five minutes of waking up.[29]
- Collectively, Americans check their screens about **eight billion times per day**.[30]
- The number of Americans who spend **more than 20 hours per week** on the Internet almost doubled between 2008 and 2015, to more than 43 million people.[31]
- About 20 percent of Americans say that they are on the Internet **"almost constantly."**[32]
- Thirty-four percent of girls between the ages of eighteen and thirty-four log on to Facebook **before they go to the toilet** when they wake up in the morning. Twenty-one percent wake up in the middle of the night to read their texts, and 39 percent identify themselves as **Facebook addicts**.[33]
- Each second on Twitter, on average, about 6,000 tweets are tweeted. This is approximately 350,000 tweets per minute; 500 million per day; and around 200 *billion* per year.[34]
- **About three-quarters of the US population** now use a smartphone, tablet, or other mobile device at least occasionally. Of these people, 87 percent go online daily.[35]
- The average Internet user now has about **eight social media accounts**, up from just three in 2012.[36]
- The world's YouTube viewers spend approximately **one billion hours** watching videos each day, a tenfold increase from the 2012 daily rate.[37]

- Some 60 percent of parents think their teens are **addicted to smartphones,** and about half of teenagers agree that they are.[38]
- Close to four in ten Americans, 38 percent, say they **never disconnect** from their phones.[39]
- People view **8 billion videos every day** on Facebook. Snapchat users watch **ten billion videos per day.**[40]

- Office e-mail accounts could be disabled between something like 6 p.m. and 5 a.m. so that workers are not encouraged/forced to constantly check for new work e-mails at home.
- Games could be designed to be more like books with chapters. They could have natural stopping points built into them so that players are not encouraged to always keep playing.
- Children can be introduced to electronic devices and social media at a slow pace and with adult supervision rather than all at once.[41]

All of these problems—Internet addiction, wasting too much time online, sacrificing face-to-face interactions—may be alleviated with balance. By finding a reasonable balance between our online and offline lives, we can have it all. We can have the best of the Internet and social media, all of the many wonderful things they offer us, and we can have each other too. Balance is the key. Alter writes:

> Our attitude to addictive experiences is largely cultural, and if our culture makes space for work-free, game-free, screen-free downtime, we and our children will find it easier to resist the lure of behavioral addiction. In its place, we'll communicate with one another directly, rather than through devices, and the glow of these social bonds will leave us richer and happier than the glow of screens ever could.[42]

Harris now devotes much of his energy to Time Well Spent, an advocacy group he co-founded. The goal is to push tech companies toward making devices and social media platforms less addictive and more useful to people. In other words, "Harris is the closest thing Silicon Valley has to a conscience," as Bianca Bosker wrote in the *Atlantic*.[43] The following is a sampling of the kinds of questions Time Well Spent is raising and encouraging people within the industry to address:

- What if we designed social media to **reduce loneliness**—and made it easier to coordinate with others?
- What if we designed devices to **help us disconnect** without missing something important?
- What if we designed devices to help us **fall asleep** on our schedule?
- What if we designed devices for quick in-and-out uses, **not endless interactions**?
- What if we designed home screens to promote **off-screen choices**, not just on-screen choices?
- What if we designed news feeds to reward the most **in-depth reporting**, not most clicks?[44]

## THE CURIOUS CONCEPT OF INTERNET ADDICTION

Are you or anyone you know addicted to the Internet, to social media? Is that even a real thing? Some experts say yes, others no. One argument against the concept of Internet addiction is that the Internet is a means to *do things*, and if one is addicted to anything it would be to *those things*—gambling, sexting, playing Farmville, posting selfies, and so on—rather than to the Internet itself. It's a point worth considering. After all, repeat drunk drivers have issues with combining alcohol and the act of driving. Roads are not really the problem. Maybe those who find themselves in crisis or living a significantly compromised life have problems with depression or some other mental illness, and social media or Internet use is just the visible outer layer of the real problem. Regardless of whether or not cyber-addition is technically an addiction or valid health issue, this much is certain: Thanks to smartphones, billions of people now have easy and instant access to the targets of their potential compulsion all of the time, anywhere. It's not difficult to imagine, therefore, how people might get hooked to some degree and find their lives becoming a bit degraded, if not derailed, as a result. And should Internet addiction or at least excessive, harmful use be on the rise, as some say, we all had better learn something about it so that we may guard against it. Sure, there is hype, exaggeration, and maybe a fair bit of fearmongering attached to this topic, but this does not mean there is nothing to be concerned about.

Our smartphones and online networks may give us the means to connect in positive ways with astonishing numbers of people all around the world, but they also sometimes harm traditional relationships as well as cause real-world problems for some individuals. If we add true addiction into the mix, we have bad recipe to contend with. Some research has found, for example, that the mere presence of smartphones or digital tablets can negatively impact "closeness, connection, and conversation quality" during face-to-face interactions.[45] The psychological gravity of a smartphone in the room "can interfere with human relationships, an effect that is most clear when individuals are discussing personally meaningful topics."

University of Albany psychologist Julia Hormes led a team of researchers that studied the addictive potential of Facebook. According to their data, an estimated 10 percent of users experience what Hormes calls "disordered social networking use."[46] Returning to the slot machine model, she cites the cycle of variability of input and reward as the key. "New notifications or the latest content on your newsfeed acts as a reward," she explained. "Not being able to predict when new content is posted encourages us to check back frequently. This uncertainty about when a new reward is available is known as a 'variable interval schedule of reinforcement' and is highly effective in establishing habitual behaviors that are resistant to extinction."

Lawrie McFarlane, former deputy minister of health in Canada and president/CEO of the Saskatoon Regional Health Board, worries that skyrocketing Internet use and social media engagement deserve more scrutiny for the sake of safety, especially when young people are concerned. He worries about social media having a negative effect on traditional means of socializing. "Facebook, Twitter, Snapchat and so forth revolve around built-in metrics of attention—Likes, Retweets, Followers and so on—so when we use these apps, we are playing a very addictive game of vying for attention points. As our scores get higher, our desire for attention points increases. When we value another person's opinion, or want to express that we care about them, we pay them in attention points. We desire more and more quantities of attention, while investing less time and energy into the quality of our social lives."[47]

Some research suggests that **1 in 8 Americans** now suffer from what we can at least describe as problematic Internet use. In China, Taiwan, and South Korea, **30 percent or more** of the population may be suffering to some degree with compulsive and harmful Internet-use issues.[48]

Even the most committed fans of Facebook and other platforms stand to learn things by listening to criticisms, even when they're difficult to digest. Here's a bit more of the bad, according to McFarlane: "Social media confronts us with a disembodied form of communication that results in social isolation, crude and primitive uses of language, likely alterations in brain chemistry, shorter attention spans, and a scary lack of self-awareness and meaningful knowledge of others. Moreover, we must not forget that the relevant technology is still, more or less, in its infancy. Text messaging is only two decades old. Digital cellular networks emerged in the early 1990s."[49] McFarlane compares the explosion of social media upon the modern landscape to the Industrial Revolution. A century or so passed, he notes, before societies finally began correcting in earnest the abuses and horrors it inflicted on workers, children in particular. He worries that, once again, it may take an unacceptably long period of time before societies react in meaningful ways to the possible harmful effects of the Internet and social media on children today.

## IT'S COMPLICATED

> **Recent research suggests that use of social networking sites can be addictive for some individuals.**
> —*Journal of Behavioral Addictions*[50]

Addiction is complicated. No surprise there, since it happens in the human brain, the most complex thing we have yet encountered in the universe. Addiction can also be an emotionally charged and contentious concept, with some seeing disease and others seeing only willpower issues. It doesn't help that most of us tend to use the term far too loosely, calling ourselves and others "addicted" to everyday things and behaviors when it's really nothing more than a desire, a tendency, or a mild habit. For example, it may be tempting to point to the frequent use of electronic devices by a teen as addiction, but maybe it's not. Maybe she just uses her smartphone and tablet a lot because they help her do what she wants and needs to do with greater ease and efficiency. We must keep in mind when thinking about Internet addiction that true addiction refers to serious problems with thought-out medical criteria. If we or even a relevant medical professional cannot determine whether a child or teen is *addicted* to computer gaming or social media, we still should be aware and concerned about serious problems that don't require addiction to be present. Excessive media use might harm a child's ability to focus and pay attention in class, for example, or damage emotional well-being. No matter if, when, and how the research community comes to a consensus on Internet addiction, it is clear there are some people who are falling into real problems, problems that require our attention now.[51]

UCLA professor of psychiatry and biobehavioral sciences Gary Small, named one of the world's top innovators in science and technology by *Scientific American*, takes Internet addiction seriously and advises everyone who ventures online to at least be aware of it. "When we think of addiction, we usually associate it with alcohol or drug abuse," he writes in his book *iBrain*.[52] However, the same neural pathways in the brain that reinforce dependence on those substances can lead to compulsive technology behaviors that are just as addictive and potentially destructive. . . . Internet addiction afflicts people from all walks of life: homemakers in their thirties and forties, teenagers, businesspeople in their fifties and older, college students, and even kids under ten. Everyone is at risk of getting hooked on Web applications."[53]

Most addictions of any kind begin with occasional, recreational use and progress from there. Once they reach a higher threshold, negative consequences such as damaged relationships, insomnia, and missing work or school impact the addict's life. "That's the natural narrative arc of any addiction, and the same is true with an Internet addiction," says Anna Lembke, a psychiatrist and addiction expert.[54]

## FROM MY COLD, DEAD FINGERS . . .

Are you addicted, hooked, or a mere casual fan of electronic devices and social media sites they connect you to? Whichever it is, you would be wise to give some thought to how they might be effecting the quality of your sleep. Is it possible that a smartphone, tablet, or laptop is stealing an hour or two of sleep from you at night? If so, you might need to put down the magic boxes and step away. Here are a few things to know that may help motivate you.

Sleep is much more than rest time. Critical brain activity and maintenance take place during the night. It's during deep sleep that our brains sort and file new memories and lay down the neural networks needed to retain any new skills acquired during the day. Cell waste left behind in the brain after a long day of thinking, is cleared away during sleep. Not enough sleep can mean a compromised cleanup job. Leftover debris can lead to less than optimal brain performance the next day and may increase one's risk of Alzheimer's disease.[55] Cancer risk goes up as well when sleep quality go down. And it's the same with diabetes, heart disease, strokes, and obesity.[56] Do not overlook the serious problems sleep deprivation can cause. Bad sleep is incompatible with good thinking and good health. If your devices and Internet or social media activities are compromising your sleep, it's time for change.

If you can manage it, turn off all of your devices at sunset. Read a book or listen to music in the final hour or so right before going to sleep. Keep your smartphone and other devices out of the bedroom so that you won't see them and be tempted to "just check Facebook one more time." There is a physical reason why you should do this, beyond just to resist temptation. Shortwave blue light, which is generated by phones, tablets, and laptops, can reduce melatonin levels in the brain by 22 percent before bedtime.[57] Melatonin is a crucial sleep hormone, and when it's reduced, we can take longer to fall asleep and experience less REM or deep sleep later in the night. If you must stare at a screen right before going to sleep, try adjusting the device's settings to remove the blue light. If your device doesn't do that on its own, there are apps available that can. Television is not as harmful to melatonin rates, by the way. Probably because the screen is relatively far away.[58]

Elias Aboujaoude, a psychiatrist and the director of Stanford's Obsessive Compulsive Disorder Clinic, says there's more physiological evidence than ever that indicates that the Internet is addictive: "There are studies that have looked at people's brains while they're online, and their brains start looking like those of someone who has a substance abuse disorder. Similar pathways seem activated."[59]

Problems related to compulsive Internet use are diverse and wide-ranging. The Center for Internet Addiction reports that perhaps one out of eight Americans has some form of significant problem with Internet use.[60] China was one of the first countries to officially recognize Internet addiction and reportedly has more than 20 million people suffering from it today.[61] As much as 30 percent of the populations of China, Taiwan, and South Korea may be dealing with serious Internet use problems to some degree. There are now more than five hundred hospitals in South Korea that treat Internet addiction.[62]

The Center for Internet Addiction, mentioned above, is a treatment facility that bills itself as the first "evidence-based Digital Detox recovery program," and it was founded in 1995 by Kimberly Young, a pioneer in the field. The center defines internet addiction as "any online-related, compulsive behavior which interferes with normal living and causes severe stress on family, friends, loved ones, and one's work environment." Internet addiction has also been called "Internet dependency" and "Internet compulsivity." The key identifying factor, according to the Center for Internet Addiction, is compulsive behavior that "completely dominates the addict's life. Internet addicts make the Internet a priority more important than family, friends, and work. The Internet becomes the organizing principle of addicts' lives."[63]

The concept of Internet addiction is still relatively new and remains controversial among experts. Even naming it, whatever *it* actually may be, has not yet been widely agreed upon. Some prefer to call it simply "Internet overuse." Other names include the aforementioned Internet dependency and Internet compulsivity, as well as the following: Internet addiction disorder (IAD), compulsive Internet use, problematic Internet use, pathological computer use, problematic computer use, and problematic Internet use. Internet addiction, by any name, is not included in the most recent *DSM* manual (*Diagnostic and Statistical Manual of Mental Disorders*, 5th ed.).[64]

According to the Center for Internet Addiction, there is no single behavior or pattern of behaviors that indicate Internet addiction. Time spent online is much less an important factor than the impact that Internet use is having on one's life. The following are warning signs[65] that may indicate a problem:

- Compulsive use of the Internet
- A preoccupation with being online
- Lying or hiding the extent or nature of one's online behavior
- An inability to control or reduce online behavior
- Internet use that repeatedly interferes with one's life, including work/family life, relationships, and school
- Using the Internet as a means to alter one's mood on a regular basis

Common Sense Media, a parent advocacy group that studies social media use among children and teens, as well as other issues, reports that 59 percent of parents think that their teens are addicted to smartphones and other mobile electronic devices. Interestingly, half of the teens surveyed feel that they are addicted.[66]

The problem isn't limited to children, though. "I really think the only way that I could stop using social media would be if it became unavailable to me," admits Susanna Cline, aged fifty-five, of Tennessee.[67] She says that she spends an average of about four hours per day on social media, mostly Facebook. "Yes, I am addicted to social media. If I were not spending so much time on it, I would have a more organized home and I would make more of an effort to be with friends. I would also write and work on my music much more than I do. . . . I am very concerned, but apparently not concerned enough to cut back. . . . I do contemplate it, though, because it often leaves a bad taste in my mouth."

Florida attorney Natasha spends a lot of time on social media every day but says she could stop if she wanted to. "Actually, I said I was going to deactivate my accounts today so I could focus on some new ideas for my social media platforms. . . . Super ironic." This comment by Natasha makes me aware of the fact that while writing this book, I found it necessary to devote significantly less of my time to social media. Social media, it would seem, can be an obstacle to thinking and writing *about* social media.

Alera, a bright twenty-two-year-old San Diego college student with a global outlook, expresses herself on several social media platforms, mostly Snapchat. She admits to worrying that the two or three hours she devotes to social media on average every day might be too much: "I'm spending time using social media when I could be doing more productive things," she said.[68] "I could stop using social media today, but I would feel disconnected. I think I might be slightly addicted to it, because I depend on it a lot. I use it as something to focus on in awkward situations, use it for some of my news, and as a way to stay in touch with people." Alera appreciates the positives of social media but doesn't deny that there some negatives. "Lack of accountability. Echo chambers. The last election showed me how much of an echo chamber I was living in. I naively assumed that most people agreed with the people I interacted with on social media. Regardless of your belief, you can find numerous think pieces to validate your viewpoint."

> Randall, aged thirty-two, lives in California. He uses Twitter and Instagram sparingly but is on Facebook *a lot* and wonders if he may be approaching the social media addiction danger zone. Millennials are commonly stereotyped as being glued to their phones, but I see many adults similarly fixated on their phones. . . . The most troubling thing about all of this is that I get it. I get how addicting it can be. Like a fellow drug user who tries not to fall completely into addiction, it is easy to see why so many have already succumbed, and, simultaneously, it's easy to reassure myself that I'm not *that* bad. At least, not yet. My wife thinks I'm already too addicted. I disagree, but then again there was certainly a time in my life [when] I didn't check my Facebook updates at least once every few hours or have access to games wherever I went. Maybe I'm already just a phone-distracted moment away from being another statistic.[69]

Randall continues,

> As a person born in the eighties, at one point I most certainly enjoyed daily life with friends without using social media; but as of now, I doubt that I could quit of my own volition. I'm not even sure how I'd respond if I were forcibly removed from Internet access. It's easy to say that I'd be just fine, especially if there were other activities to focus on, but it's been so long since I lived without social media access that I honestly don't know if I'd express symptoms of withdrawal. Even considering it gives me an ever-so-slight pang of anxiety. Controllable,

## THE MIRAGE OF MULTITASKING

Multitasking is often admired as a key skill of super-achievers, those who get more done in less time than other mere mortals. But there's a problem with attempting to juggle three or four tasks at once: It's stupid.

Despite the public's (mis)perception about it, multitasking is actually inefficient and counterproductive. Regardless of how busy and productive people may feel while bouncing their brains back-and-forth between Facebook, Instagram, and doing their homework, they are fooling themselves. They are not doing their best work. By far the best way to get things done well is to tackle them *sequentially*, one after the other, rather than all at once. A strong body of research shows that multitasking can reduce productivity by as much as *40 percent*. The choice is clear: look busy by flitting around unfocused, or pick a single target and perform at your best.

Think of the human brain as big, heavy truck. It's slow to get moving, but once rolling it can take you far. Stopping to change direction means dealing with momentum issues and then having to once again build up to optimal speed from a dead start. Better to drive in a straight line to one destination, then on to the next one, and so on.

A 2017 study used functional magnetic resonance imaging (fMRI) of brains in action and revealed how the normal activities of the brain are disrupted by multitasking. Neuroscientist Iiro Jääskeläinen, one of the study's authors, recommends allowing the brain to do what it does best—focus on one task, settle into deep thought, and get it done. "It's easy to fall into the trap of multitasking," he said.[70] "In that case, it seems like there is little real progress and this leads to a feeling of inadequacy. Concentration decreases, which causes stress. Prolonged stress hinders thinking and memory."

Jääskeläinen views social media as problematic because it often encourages multitasking: "Social media is really nothing but multitasking, with several parallel plots and issues. You might end up reading the news or playing a game recommended by a friend. From the brain's perspective, social media only increases the load."[71]

negligible, but still there. . . . My wife says I'm addicted to my phone, as she often catches me using it while out at restaurants or doing activities. At home, although she uses her phone regularly, I spend even more time on my phone as well as on the PC. It's not a serious area of conflict so far, but it's certainly something she finds annoying enough to point out, which is usually my cue to put the phone down and pay attention.

## WHO'S IN CHARGE OF YOUR LIFE?

> **The one thing you can't Google is what you ought to be looking up.**
> —William Poundstone, author of *Head in the Clouds* and *Carl Sagan: A Life in the Cosmos*[72]

Frances Booth, author of *The Distraction Trap: How to Focus in a Digital World*, says it is still possible to live without social media in the modern world if you desire it. It is also possible, she says, to be a sensible user of social media, one who doesn't let it dominate the daily agenda. It is important, she told me, to be aware of how you feel during and after a session on social media. If engagement on Facebook or Twitter consistently leads to bad feelings, then it's time to do some self-analysis and decide whether or not it's worth it. She doesn't recommend dropping social media immediately if you recognize that there are problems but to seek a solution in structure. "Social media can trigger a whole range of emotional responses. Notice exactly how it is making you feel. Do you want to feel like that? Also, notice whether you are always responding to other people's demands. Set your own agenda, and set boundaries."[73]

"Wasting time" is perhaps the most common charge levied against social media use. Remember, as mentioned previously in this chapter, more than two out of every ten Americans say they are online "almost constantly." Booth says it's not that difficult to take control if you simply set limits and keep them. "Do an accurate assessment of exactly how much time you are spending on social media. You might be surprised at how much time it is eating up. Start setting yourself a set amount of time for each session—for example, thirty minutes. When your time is up, step away! Decide what you want to use social media for. For example, keeping in touch with certain people, as a way of getting information, or for marketing. Keep focused on that aim and watch out for getting distracted and going off on a tangent."

It may be helpful when assessing your time investment in social media to keep in mind the basic truth that the priority for the big and successful social media companies is to make money off your engagement with them. We aren't plugging into charities or nonprofit organizations focused on nothing but helping us be happy and productive citizens. No, these companies are dedicated to serving their *paying* clients first, not you or me. This doesn't mean that they are necessarily evil, of course, only that they are focused on something other than your best interests. Nothing personal, it's just business. But you need to be aware of this reality when attempting to assess how much of your time you are comfortable devoting to social media. It's a relevant factor. They use you to make money in the same way that CNN devotes thousands of hours to covering a missing plane or meaningless celebrity scandals that have zero impact on their viewers' lives. CNN does these things not to enlighten society, obviously, but to make money. Clearly, cable news networks have pushed the viewer's desire to be informed about important current events down their lists of priorities. Their number one mission is attracting and keeping advertisers. Cable news viewers, like social media users, don't stand a chance against the power of all of that advertising revenue. The game is luring in eyeballs and keeping them on screen for as long as possible—whatever becomes of the brains attached to all of these eyes is of little or no concern. Facebook, Snapchat, Instagram, Twitter, and so on engage in a game in which you are not even a player. At best you are the ball, something to be kicked around. So long as you stay on the playing field, they're happy. I say all of this not to upset you but make sure that you know your place in their pecking order. You and I are products, not customers. When you run around in these social media ecosystems, you are working to help billionaires get richer. Understanding this doesn't mean you can't still use and enjoy social media, of course. But do be aware of it.

MIT professor and social media expert Turkle is uncomfortable with excessive use or overreliance of that word "addiction," at least when referring to the bulk of people who are not necessarily

## THE INBOX TRAP: STOP WASTING YOUR BRAIN'S TIME

You and your fellow humans send an estimated 247 billion e-mails per day.[74] All of this writing and sending, receiving and reading of electronic messages eats up human time. In his book, *The Organized Mind*, Professor Emeritus of Psychology at McGill University Daniel J. Levitin explains why so many people check their e-mails and social media accounts so frequently: "Each time we dispatch an email in one way or another, we feel a sense of accomplishment, and our brain gets a dollop of reward hormones telling us we accomplished something. Each time we check a Twitter feed or Facebook update, we encounter something novel and feel more connected socially—in a kind of weird, impersonal, cyber way—and get another dollop of reward hormones. But remember, it is the dumb, novelty-seeking portion of the brain driving the limbic system that induces this feeling of pleasure, not the planning, scheduling, higher-level thought centers in the prefrontal cortex. Make no mistake: email-, Facebook- and Twitter-checking constitute a neural addiction."[75]

Levin, like many time-management experts, advises turning off e-mail notifications on your phone or computer and allotting only a few specific time periods to deal with e-mails, maybe once in the morning, again in the afternoon, and then one last time in the evening.[76] Reading and responding to them in specific and designated chunks of time tends to be more efficient and productive than stopping work to do it many times throughout the day. The first step is turning off that bell, to stop behaving like Pavlov's dogs. Once an e-mail alert is heard or vibration felt, the subconscious mind will not rest until you drop whatever work you were attempting to do and look at it. Obviously the same goes for text messages, Facebook Messenger, tweets, and so on.

destroying their lives due to Twitter trolling, World of Warcraft binges, or even a bit of Facebook obsession. She warns that talking about addiction can suggest to people that, as with most addictions, the only solution is to get rid of the addicting substance. But we all know that the Internet, e-mail, and social media are not going anywhere. And again, attacking only the supply side of the problem does not fix the problem itself. "We will not go 'cold turkey' or forbid cell phones to our children. We are not going to stop the music or go back to the television as the family hearth."[77] She is cautiously optimistic, however. "I believe we will find new paths toward each other, but considering ourselves victims of a bad substance is not a good first step. The idea of addiction, with its one solution that we know we won't take, makes us feel hopeless. We have to find a way to live with seductive technology and make it work to our purposes. This is hard and will take work. Simple love of technology is not going to help. Nor is a Luddite impulse." She encourages skepticism about linear progress and emphasizes a need for humility as key. She believes that the Internet and related technologies are still young, young enough for us to tackle the difficult problems and come up with meaningful solutions before they become impossible problems.

## "I THINK I'M OFF FOR GOOD THIS TIME."

Shanika, aged thirty-four, is a thoughtful New York preschool teacher. She took a break from Facebook because she felt that it was stealing away time she needed for other things. "I felt that I was not able to achieve some of my personal goals—practicing my guitar and getting through my reading list. Facebook was taking up all of my alone time. Instead of spending time thinking or reading or playing, I'd spend it reading posts. I decided to return to Facebook [after a break] because I wasn't hearing from anyone. Although I'd left my personal information for friends to contact me, no one did. While I want to get off of Facebook, I'm afraid of losing contact again with so many people."[78]

Shanika estimates she spent about two hours per day on Facebook. She went on it at home, at work, on the ride home, and before going to bed. "There are so many things I know that I want to do when I have time alone that I am just not doing, and it has been hard to focus because of the distraction [of Facebook]. There is something very enticing about it, checking to see how many people 'like' or agree with a post I make, reading other people's posts, being entertained by videos and memes, being educated by videos and posts, reading opinion pieces. All of these things, but ultimately they have distracted me from things that are important to me that I always say I have no time for."

"I do think that I'm addicted to a certain degree," Shanika said. "There is a part of me that can go on without thinking about it, but only after about a week or two of being away. The initial departure is much more difficult. I have found myself typing 'Facebook' in the search engine when that wasn't what my intention was."

"I don't think social media is necessarily anti-intellectual," Shanika continued.

> I think it depends on how and who uses it. I've come across many posts on Facebook that have made me think about myself and the world. It all depends on the type of people you decide to engage with on it. I do, however, think that the fast and flashy nature of social media decreases one's attention span. I find myself struggling to get through books, a pastime I once enjoyed. I used to be able to zip through at least two to three books a month. Now, I can barely get through one book at all. I feel that it is because I am used to reading through so much information at once on the Internet, having more than one tab open at a time, while simultaneously responding to texts or e-mails or commenting on posts. I recently deleted my Facebook account again, and it is taking me time to get back to the habits I consider good: reading, playing my guitar, writing. It was, for me, like an addiction, and I feel like I am now slowly rebuilding myself again. The last time I deleted my account, it also took me a while to readjust. I think I'm off for good this time.

I sometimes see a wisp of fear in people who spend of a lot time reaching for and staring into a smartphone. They seem at times to be in weird state of urgency, presumably worried that an e-mail or post on social media is in their phone screaming at them, in need of urgent attention. Sure, important information does show up in our inboxes and Facebook feeds every now and then. But how often? How much of this kind of fear and concern is justified? Do truly earth-shattering bits of information come to us through social media on daily basis? For most

## COULD YOU BE SUFFERING FROM "SMARTPHONE-INDUCED BRAIN-DRAIN"?

Before doing anything that requires significant brainpower, you may want to put your smartphone somewhere out of sight—as far away as possible. A fascinating—though disturbing—2017 study suggests that a smartphone's mere presence can so distract one's mind that cognitive performance drops, to a significant degree.[79]

Researchers at the McCombs School of Business at the University of Texas at Austin conducted two experiments with more than seven hundred smartphone users. Results indicate that even when people are able to maintain sustained attention, and do not physically check their phones, the phone's presence still manages to degrade their cognitive capacity. Furthermore, those who self-report a higher dependence on their smartphone show more negative cognitive effects if a phone is present during testing than do those who report less dependence.

To be clear, these experiments were not about the problem of being interrupted by a ping or vibration from the phone while thinking. All phones were turned off or set to silent. Interestingly, those who were asked to place their phones in another room before taking a cognitive test outperformed not only those with their phones near them, but also those with phones in their pockets or a bag nearby. The *mere presence* of the phone, even one not visible, degrades mental function, according to the researchers.

"We see a linear trend that suggests that as the smartphone becomes more noticeable, participants' available cognitive capacity decreases," explained Adrian Ward, lead author of the study. "Your conscious mind isn't thinking about your smartphone, but that process—the process of requiring yourself to not think about something—uses up some of your limited cognitive resources. It's a brain drain."[80]

Ward and his coauthors write: "One's smartphone is more than just a phone, a camera, or a collection of apps. It is the one thing that connects everything—the hub of the connected world. The presence of one's smartphone enables on-demand access to information, entertainment, social stimulation, and more. However, our research suggests that these benefits—and the dependence they engender—may come at a cognitive cost."[81]

people, I suspect, there is no sensible justification for checking their phone every five minutes throughout the entire day. Perhaps social media users can enhance their lives a bit by taking the intensity down a notch or two. This is not a trivial concern. A human brain in a constant state of distraction and urgency is stressed and therefore inefficient.

Never forget that your mind is mostly a bustling hive of thinking and decision making that "you"—your conscious mind—are unaware of. A whirlwind of constant cognitive activity is occurring below the surface. If you are checking your phone more than a hundred times per day, just to make sure you don't miss the greatest tweet of all time, then your capacity for higher thinking is constantly compromised. You won't be your best creatively or when it comes to making sound decisions. In this kind of state, no one can be their best, because it means living in a perpetual crisis behind the scenes, with the silent scream of the subconscious always demanding immediate action: "Check the phone now!" Simply being aware of this may help you exercise more rational control over the almighty smartphone and all of those seductive social media sites.

California State University psychologist Larry Rosen researches how technology and social media impact our anxiety levels. He says that heavy smartphone/social media users are relentlessly tormented by internal cortisol shots that nag them to pick up their phones. "What we find is the typical person checks their phone every fifteen minutes or less," he said in a *60 Minutes* interview, "and half of the time they check their phone there is no alert, no notification. It's coming from inside their head telling them, 'Gee, I haven't checked Facebook in a while. I haven't checked on this Twitter feed for a while. I wonder if somebody commented on my Instagram post.' That then generates cortisol, and it starts to make you anxious. And eventually your goal is to get rid of that anxiety, so you check in."[82]

## DO YOU HAVE A PROBLEM?

**The Internet Addiction Test (IAT)**[83] can be used to measure Internet use in terms of mild, moderate, and severe levels of addiction. Kimberly Young, a professor at St. Bonaventure University and director of the Center for Internet Addiction Recovery, developed the IAT to assess symptoms of Internet addiction.

Based on the following five-point scale, select the response that best represents the frequency of the behavior described in the following twenty-item questionnaire.

0 = Not Applicable
1 = Rarely
2 = Occasionally
3 = Frequently
4 = Often
5 = Always

___How often do you find that you stay online longer than you intended?

___How often do you neglect household chores to spend more time online?

___How often do you prefer the excitement of the Internet to intimacy with your partner?

___How often do you form new relationships with fellow online users?

___How often do others in your life complain to you about the amount of time you spend online?

___How often do your grades or schoolwork suffer because of the amount of time you spend online?

___How often do you check your e-mail before something else that you need to do?

___How often does your job performance or productivity suffer because of the Internet?

___How often do you become defensive or secretive when anyone asks you what you do online?

___How often do you block out disturbing thoughts about your life with soothing thoughts of the Internet?

___How often do you find yourself anticipating when you will go online again?

___How often do you fear that life without the Internet would be boring, empty, and joyless?

___How often do you snap, yell, or act annoyed if someone bothers you while you are online?
___How often do you lose sleep due to late-night log-ins?
___How often do you feel preoccupied with the Internet when off-line, or fantasize about being online?
___How often do you find yourself saying "just a few more minutes" when online?
___How often do you try to cut down the amount of time you spend online and fail?
___How often do you try to hide how long you've been online?
___How often do you choose to spend more time online over going out with others?
___How often do you feel depressed, moody, or nervous when you are off-line, which goes away once you are back online?

After all of the questions have been answered, add the numbers for each response to obtain a final score. The higher the score, the greater the level of addiction and creation of problems resultant from such Internet usage. The severity impairment index is as follows:

**NONE 0–30 points**
**MILD 31–49 points:** You are an average online user. You may surf the Web a bit too long at times, but you have control over your usage.
**MODERATE 50–79 points:** You are experiencing occasional or frequent problems because of the Internet. You should consider their full impact on your life.
**SEVERE 80–100 points:** Your Internet usage is causing significant problems in your life. You should evaluate the impact of the Internet on your life and address the problems directly caused by your Internet usage.

--------

**The Bergen Facebook Addiction Scale**[84] is aimed specifically at Facebook use. Cecilie Andreassen, a researcher at the University of Bergen, and her colleagues list the following six basic criteria as a means of identifying possible addiction to Facebook. Participants are asked to give one of the following responses to each statement:

1 = Very Rarely
2 = Rarely
3 = Sometimes
4 = Often
5 = Very Often

___You spend a lot of time thinking about Facebook or planning how to use it.
___You feel an urge to use Facebook more and more.
___You use Facebook in order to forget about personal problems.
___You have tried to cut down on the use of Facebook without success.
___You become restless or troubled if you are prohibited from using Facebook.
___You use Facebook so much that it has had a negative impact on your job/studies.

Scoring "often" or "very often" on at least four of the six items may suggest that a person is addicted to Facebook, according to Andraessen.[85]

## WHAT HAPPENS IF WE TURN IT OFF?

"It's amazing how quickly, once we let go of that fear [of being disconnected from the Internet and social media], we wake up from the illusion," explains tech expert and former product philosopher at Google Tristan Harris. "When we unplug for more than a day, unsubscribe from those notifications . . . the concerns we thought we'd have don't actually happen. We don't miss what we don't see."[86] Don't allow yourself to get too wrapped up in waiting for the next friend request, like, or "follow." This is not the measure of a full life. According to Harris, many social media companies exploit an "asymmetry in perception." We get an invite from someone on Facebook or LinkedIn, for example, and reasonably assume that that person thought about us and decided that it would be nice to connect, so he or she reached out. But, Harris points out, most of the time a machine is behind it and leading the interaction. It's more likely that the person merely reacted to a prompt or suggestion

## TIPS AND APPS TO HELP YOU REGAIN YOUR BRAIN

- When it's time to use your brain, **get rid of the smartphone**. Put it away somewhere. Make sure it's out of sight. The physical presence of a smartphone—even if it is on silent mode or powered off—may distract your subconscious mind and reduce your brain's ability to function at high levels.[87]
- **Allow Notifications from People Only.** Most notifications come from machines and not people. This is a mistake, according to Time Well Spent. The mission of most automated notifications is to lure us back into apps. Take back some control by turning off all notifications on your phone except those that originate from real people—apps like WhatsApp, FB Messenger, or Messages.[88]
- **Offtime.** Offtime is an anti-app app that can help you regain focus and save time by limiting your access to time-wasting apps, including games, Facebook and other social media sites. This app enables you to cut back on the distractions and interruptions by imposing a bit of self-discipline on yourself toward the goal of being more productive and efficient.[89]
- **Distance Yourself from Unconscious Choices.** The next time you check your phone, notice all of the colorful icons there on the screen. They are there waiting to be tapped and played with, at possible cost of your maximum productivity. You don't need these distractions in your face every time you unlock your phone. Limit your first screen to apps you use for in-and-out tasks–like maps, camera, calendar, and notes. Move all of the rest—social media apps, in particular—off the first page and into folders.[90]
- **Create a Psychological Speedbump.** Time Well Spent advises setting up your phone so that you have to type in the name of the app in order to access it. This miniscule amount of work, they say, is just enough to make you ask yourself if you really care enough to open it up and engage.[91]
- **Stay in the Moment, with Moment.** Moment is an app (for Apple products) that allows you to automatically track how much you use your iPhone or iPad each day. Users can set daily limits and receive notifications when they go over. If you want, the app can force you off your device when reach your limit.[92]
- **Charge Your Device outside the Bedroom.** "Get a separate alarm clock in your bedroom," recommends Time Well

Spent, "and charge your phone in another room (or on the other side of the room). This way you won't get sucked into your phone before you even get out of bed."[93]

- **Adjust Your Settings.** Michael Schulson, a writer who focuses on technology issues, suggests turning off certain features of "compulsive design." These would include **auto-play** (the mechanism that automatically plays videos back to back on YouTube and Netflix) and **infinite scroll** (the mechanism that creates endless Facebook and Twitter feeds).[94]
- **Consider Using Adblock Plus.** This free and open-source program can cut down on the number of distracting ads you encounter online. It blocks banners, pop-ups, tracking, malware and more.[95]
- **Set Limits.** Common Sense Media, a parent advocacy group, recommends that users establish **media-free times** (mealtimes, one hour before bedtime) and/or **media-free zones** (bedrooms, cars) to restore some balance as well as support face-to-face conversation, healthy sleep, and safe driving.[96]

from the platform and complied with little conscious thought. But it may feel like a social obligation to "return the favor," so naturally you stop what you are doing and respond in kind. "Imagine millions of people getting interrupted like this throughout their day," Harris said, "running around like chickens with their heads cut off, reciprocating each other—all designed by companies who profit from it. Welcome to social media."[97]

Ashani, aged twenty-two, is a marketing assistant in the Cayman Islands. She believes that she could stop using social media, but she doesn't want to. "It would definitely be difficult. At my age, it seems you have more of a problem if you're not on social media than if you are. That being said, I have described my social media activity as an addiction before. I think I would attribute part of that 'diagnosis' to the mindless way I open Instagram without thinking about it—even when I've just closed it!"[98]

Michelle, aged forty-one, is a Texas business owner who suspects that she spends too much time on social media. "I once utilized an app to monitor myself for usage on devices and apps and although I expected it to be high, I was still surprised."[99] She loves Facebook for the "efficiency of communication with many people and the ease and speed with which you can reference personal information. I've had countless positive interactions. . . . I've caught up with old friends and made new ones. I have been able to contact and develop relationships with people I may not otherwise have had the opportunity to. I fostered and have further developed relationships in the community and 'real world' via social media that I likely would not have otherwise."

Michelle thinks that the worst thing about social media is the way it can distract you and rob time from your other priorities. She also had to deal with the discovery that her then twelve-year-old son had opened a Twitter account that had received tweets "of an adult nature," including some "displaying materials inappropriate for children." Michelle says that she was "shocked, even mortified" by this. Her son said he had deleted it, but he didn't understand that removing the app from his phone was not the same as deactivating the account; so it was still live.

Furthermore, Michelle is concerned that she spends too much time on social media, and using digital devices in general, and that she pays a price for it with negative changes in her eyesight, posture, attitude, and overall health. But she can't bring herself to stop using these platforms and devices because it benefits her business. "An analogy that comes to mind would be an alcoholic having to work in a bar serving alcohol and having to monitor themselves while not abstaining from [alcohol], but taking in only a controlled amount. It [social media] is no doubt addictive, and designed to segue you from one subject to another."

"It takes you away from the issues at hand in your real life," she said. "Oftentimes it's a needed break from work, but just as often a hindrance to it. . . . With some guidelines, boundaries or usage limits set and agreed within the home or workplace, it can be quite positive. If left to run rampant and unchecked, undoubtedly [it] can cause damage. [Spending time on social media sites] is a shallow form of entertainment. Overuse certainly can decrease your attention span, patience level, and ability to engage with people and other things, on a deeper level."

In one of life's silly little twists, Michelle says her spending a lot of time on social media used to be a source of irritation for her husband. But that is no longer the case—because Michelle encouraged him to start using it too, and now he's on it as much as she is. "It's not a source of conflict," she says, "but certainly [an] annoyance at times, for us both."

Leo Igwe, a forty-six-year-old researcher in Nigeria, spends six to eight hours per day on Facebook. He says he is concerned that he may be giving too much time to it, but stopping concerns him as well. He worries that pulling the plug would make him "restless and unable to concentrate fully on other things."[100]

---

## WHAT ABOUT THE CHILDREN?

*American Academy of Pediatrics recommends the following guidelines[101] for children using digital devices:*

- "For children younger than 18 months, avoid use of screen media other than video-chatting."
- "Parents of children 18 to 24 months of age who want to introduce digital media should choose high-quality programming, and watch it with their children to help them understand what they're seeing."
- "For children ages 2 to 5 years, limit screen use to one hour per day of high-quality programs."
- "For children ages 6 and older, place consistent limits on the time spent using media, and the types of media, and make sure media does not take the place of adequate sleep, physical activity and other behaviors essential to health."
- "Designate media-free times together, such as dinner or driving, as well as media-free locations at home, such as bedrooms."
- "Have ongoing communication about online citizenship and safety, including treating others with respect online and off-line."

---

## CUTTING BACK

Those who are concerned that their Internet/social media use is a serious problem might try reducing the time spent by simply making a clear decision to do so and then relying on willpower to make it happen. Reducing online time in small step-by-step increments might work well for some. Others might do better by cleaving their online time in half or more and moving on with life. The best way to tackle it depends on the individual.

Adding new activities might help. Replace one habit with another habit, so long as it's less problematic. Spend time with friends doing fun things that don't allow for screen time. Try hiking, archery, rock climbing, chess, running, singing in a choir, surfing, knitting—anything you think might keep you engaged and happy off-line.

Whenever possible, put some physical space between you and your smartphone, tablet, or laptop. The problem of mindless reaching for a device is eliminated when the device is out of reach. Try setting boundaries of time and place. No electronic devices after sunset, for example. No electronic devices allowed in the dining room and bedroom at any time, ever.

Those who continue to struggle can try one or more of the tech-

---

### YOU AIN'T SEEN NOTHING YET

The fast-changing landscape of social media is about to get even more interesting. Facebook's push to incorporate virtual reality into its platform,[102] for example, may be a significant move toward revolutionary changes, not just for social media but for our entire species. Virtual reality promises so much. We will spend time with faraway friends and family and it will feel as if they are in the room with us. We will be able to walk on the Moon, watch the Super Bowl from the vantage point of a premium seat, and stroll through the world's greatest museums at our own pace. VR is definitely something to be excited about—and to be worried about. If the current versions of Snapchat, Instagram, Twitter, and Facebook—which are nice but hardly mind-blowing—have been able to hook tens of millions of users, what will social media with VR do to us?

Alter, associate professor of marketing and psychology at New York University's Stern School of Business, is also concerned about where VR may take us: "Since mainstream VR is in its infancy, we can't be sure that it will dramatically change how we live. But all early signs suggest that it will be both miraculous and dangerous. . . . Wielded by big business and game designers [it may] prove to be a vehicle for the latest in a series of escalating behavioral addictions."[103]

nological aides listed previously in this chapter ("Tips and Apps to Help You Regain Your Brain"). It may seem odd that there are apps designed to help you stay off of apps, but it just might work. For others, however, this may be a problem that runs too deep and requires professional help. Full-blown Internet addiction, excessive time spent online, or suffering negative consequences from online activities that you can't stop might be too much to correct alone. As mentioned earlier, difficulties might be connected to a larger mental-health issue such as depression or anxiety. If there is a significant problem, the best advice is to seek out the necessary help. Do not ignore, deny, or surrender. No one should passively accept his or her ongoing behavior if it is diminishing the quality of life. Get help.

## WHO YOU CALLING AN ADDICT?

Some heavy social media users take a different view of spending countless hours online. They see no problem with devoting substantial chunks of their life online because time spent is not necessarily a measure of anything harmful. They claim that one has to consider the value in whatever it is people are doing on these sites and apps. Daniel K. Minto, aged thirty-one, is an electronics technician in the US Navy who says he spends about half of his waking hours on social media. And it's not a problem. To the contrary, he is sure that it enriches his life.

> I'm not concerned that I spend too much time on social media. I would say that online social connection is a truer form of interaction with regard to expression because it eliminates the stresses and constraints of physical presence. The worst thing about social media is its tendency to blur the line between the real world and a virtual one. However, I can't say that that's a bad thing; it's just different than what we've grown up with. We're a social animal and we thrive off interaction and expression. Social media allows for that in the easiest way we've ever thought of. To younger millennials and those who will come after them, social media is natural. In its beginnings, it sometimes seemed like people were spending less time interacting in "real life" and more time on social media, and that was considered a bad thing. Today, as social media becomes just another aspect of daily life, asking someone if they're spending too much time using it is like asking if they're using their eyes too much, or listening too often. I could stop using social

media at any time, but it would be a decision to seclude myself in the corner of the room with blinders on and earplugs in. Could I stop? Of course. Would I? Only if everyone else did at the same time. Otherwise, stopping the use of social media is a willful disconnect from each other. I don't think anyone can be addicted to social media, because it's a part of life now. You often hear people accusing each other of being "addicted to their phones," but what does that really mean? Interacting with friends, family, and colleagues too much? Watching and reading and listening to things that you like too much? Being relevant, opinionated, engaged, and educating yourself too much? Social media becomes a problem only when it's a distraction from responsibilities. But that goes for anything.[104]

Minto makes a crucial point. Though some people clearly do seem to have harmful compulsive disorders that involve social media, he is correct in that we can't be too loose and quick with our fears and condemnations. Someone spending many hours per day on social media may appear to some to be suffering from a negative addiction. But that cannot be determined without first analyzing what the person is actually doing on social media and how it is impacting his or her life. The behavior and long hours may be positive and productive for him or her. As such, you have to examine the net costs, net benefits, and the circumstances surrounding each individual's use. For example, social media may provide a substantial boost to the quality of life for some children and teens with autism.[105] Additionally, it may be useful to note that it's not as if everyone was devoting his or her available time to such illustrious activities as reading Plato, building homes for the homeless, practicing the violin, and running marathons before Facebook, Instagram, and Snapchat stormed onto the scene to become everyone's favorite time-sucks. Many of the hours eaten up in the silliest and most trite corners of social media today were once squandered in ways that were equally as, or even more, trivial in the past.

## BUT I'M SO INTERESTING

No matter what the circumstances, no man can completely escape from vanity.

—Shūsaku Endō, *Silence*[106]

Talking about oneself is a quintessential human move. We can't help ourselves. Self-exposure comes to us like breathing. We may mock and condemn the most arrogant, overexposed celebrities for being "so full of themselves" but, truth is, the stars are just excelling at the same game we all play. Even the humblest among us can't resist slipping into publicist mode and talking about him- or herself on a regular basis. It's natural, normal; it's human. One of the reasons social media is so attractive—addictive, perhaps—to many people is that it is such a convenient stage for sharing ourselves and for self-promotion. Research shows that we are highly motivated to communicate personal things about ourselves both off-line and online. We even get an internal chemical reward in our brains when we share something about our successes, failures, problems, hopes, and dreams with others. Self-disclosure, opening up, feels good to us, if not necessary. "People dedicate close to 40 percent of their time talking about themselves," write Diana Tamir of Princeton and Harvard's Jason Mitchell, researchers who conducted experiments on the value and rewards of self-disclosure.[107] "This number reaches 80 percent in [online] social networks with the possibility of feedback and immediate rewards. Self-disclosure was strongly associated with increased activation in brain regions that form the mesolimbic dopamine system. . . . Moreover, individuals were willing to forgo money to disclose about the self."

Yes, much as we humans tend to love money, it seems we are willing to sacrifice it simply to experience the pleasure of telling other people something about ourselves. "Just as monkeys are willing to forgo juice rewards to view dominant groupmates and college students are willing to give up money to view attractive members of the opposite sex," Tamir and Mitchell write, "our participants were willing to forgo money to think and talk about themselves."[108] Not everyone feels the need to share their lives on social media, however.

"I don't go anywhere near the stuff [social media] and just don't understand why anyone wants to," said John Higginson, an older resident of Manchester, England.[109] "I'm afraid I'm from a different generation. To be honest, I'm not really very interested in what other people are doing. And I certainly can't understand why they would be remotely interested in what I'm doing."

Andrea, a young Louisiana teacher, doesn't use social media, in part because she finds it all a bit too self-serving for her tastes.

I think it gives people the incorrect notion that they have something important to say every moment of the day and that other people want to hear it. The fact that there is a forum for all our status updates, and a place to post photos of what we had for lunch and comments on the last episode of, whatever, makes us feel self-important. My brother is a man of few words. He once said that chit-chat for the sake of it was like throwing up on a white couch just to add some color. Social media is like that scene from *Stand By Me* where everyone is projectile vomiting everywhere. Aren't the folks on Twitter referred to as "followers"? Weird. Like we can all be gurus of something. Most of us don't do much worth "following."[110]

Robert DeAngelo, a Florida editor/journalist, thinks younger users get hooked on social media because it gives them a break from reality. "It does seem like lots of young people are living more of a virtual life than a real life," he said. "They have Facebook 'friends' that they've never met and yet feel really close to. I think they are losing the ability to communicate with someone in person. E-mail and texting can be a good way to communicate, but nuance is lost. Facial expressions, tone, whether something is said with sarcasm— all of that is lost in translation with electronic communication."[111]

"There is also the online aspect of *creating* who you'd like to be, rather than [just being] who you actually are," DeAngelo continued.

Because you're not actually meeting the folks you're interacting with, you can create a persona and backstory to suit any purpose. That leads to being able to "say" things online that you'd never say in real life— see the comments section following any news story—and "talk" to people you'd never actually approach. And if it all goes horribly wrong, you just click out of that screen and move onto something else.

In some ways, you can't blame young people for getting hooked on the virtual world. The trials and tribulations, pain and loneliness, fear and anxiety of the real world don't exist there. But when they log off their devices, the real world that awaits them can seem like a letdown. Or at least not as dreamlike. So what's the solution? More time online. That's where the addiction forms. And that's why some people spend more time in their virtual life than in their actual one.

I'm not prepared to offer a blanket condemnation of social media simply because millions may use it to blow on the embers of vanity for a quick and shallow high. One shouldn't be too harsh in faulting people for being human or reaching for a bit of relief and distraction in an often tough, unfair world. However, a conscious awareness of this particular reason why social media might be so attractive can nudge us into more rational and productive use of it. Maybe don't stop expressing yourself about yourself, but be reasonable about the time and energy devoted to it. Don't thoughtlessly give up deeper intellectual pursuits or fun times with real-world friends just for a fleeting hit of dopamine that comes from a Facebook post or Instagram pic. Don't fall into the trap of working too hard for the insatiable beast that is social media. Maybe some can manage it, but it's just not possible for all of us to be always interesting and beautiful while leading lives of nonstop excitement.

Simple photos of your sleeping cat or another bland selfie don't measure up like they used to on social media these days. Many Instagram users today seem compelled or obligated to post a never-ending series of colorful and impactful photos that show how fun and exciting their lives are—even if their lives are not exciting. To feed this need, "Instagram playgrounds" may be the next big thing.[112] The Museum of Ice Cream,[113] for example, was a big hit in New York and is now taking California by storm.[114] Social media users loved it instantly because of its vibrant pink, photo-friendly atmosphere and unique theme, perfect for an Instagram fix. What's weird, however, is that the Museum of Ice Cream is not a museum of ice cream. It's a constructed false-reality that exists primarily for taking social media photos; and people pay $29 for the privilege. Booking it for a private event costs $180,000.[115] As a Hollywood set for civilians, it is a perfect fit for an age when stardom is supposedly within everyone's reach. For many social media users now, it seems that an image of a cool experience is less about experiencing something cool and more about the image itself. Don't be surprised if more similar themed backdrops pop up across the landscape. Maryellis Bunn, the twenty-five-year-old creator of the Ice Cream Museum, says she has had inquiries from Abu Dhabi and Japan, and she currently plans to open more in the United States.[116]

There is nothing new or bad about having fun with a few pretend or misleading photos, of course. But we might be cautious about going too far with this behavior on social media. Who is fooled most by an overly contrived and staged photo anyway? The audience or the person who posted it? When we pay money and put in work to produce a fake scene in our lives, what does it say about our actual lives and real experiences? And what's next along this avenue? Will millions of social media users soon be posting computer-generated fake videos of themselves climbing mountains, surfing, and playing fetch with a beautiful dog? An app already exists that can place a smile on your face if that selfie is too somber.[117] Yes, if you can't be bothered to actually go out and find something exciting to do, no worries, a filter will make you look as if you did in the all-important photo.

Minutes and hours spent photographically documenting yourself doing fake things for the sole purpose of posting it on social media is time that could have been spent doing something real and sharing that experience instead. All social media users should be conscious of how much time they devote to less-than-authentic persona building and answering the demands of a real or imagined online audience. At its best, social media reflects our actual lives and is a way to share the best of who we are and what we do. At its worst, social media is the sad simulation of what should have been our lives.

Never forget that participating, to any degree, in social media is work—work that contributes to someone else's bottom line. In his book *Terms of Service*, Jacob Silverman writes about this, calling it "digital serfdom": "The digital lords appear to be little more than caretakers fattening themselves on our data production."[118] He explains further, "We publicize our lives through social media to create an aspirational ideal for others and an idealized, possibly unfulfillable, version of ourselves. No one's life is as good and eventful as seen through Facebook, no one's life as shimmering and beautiful as viewed through the filters of Instagram."[119] Attempting to achieve the appearance of Pinterest-worthy lifestyles is a privilege, says Silverman: "We don't all have the luxury of time, knowledge, or resources to preserve our visibility, to try to achieve micro-fame. It's a constant process of cultivation, like bailing water from a leaky boat. It's a luxury of people who can spend the time needed to stay present and available on their networks. If you don't maintain this performance, if you don't keep bailing water, you'll sink out of view."[120]

This point is underscored by Harris, of Time Well Spent: "The ultimate freedom is a free mind, and we need technology to be on our team to help us live, feel, think and act freely. We need our smartphones, notifications screens and web browsers to be exoskeletons for our minds and interpersonal relationships that put our values, not our impulses, first. People's time is valuable. And we should protect it with the same rigor as privacy and other digital rights."[121]

The spectrum of social media use outcomes is long and wide for the individual. It runs from invaluable and wonderful all the way to frivolous and wicked. Take note of where you land most of the time. Regardless of whether or not Internet/social media addiction becomes a full-blown health issue sanctified in the pages of the *DSM*, we can work today from the knowledge that there is potential for harm here. For some people, social media is a negative or even a destructive factor in their lives. Perhaps one of the easiest ways for all of us to defend ourselves against letting social media degrade the quality of our lives to any degree is to ask one specific question, sincerely and often. At least once a month, I suggest, ask yourself: *Why?* Why am I doing this? Am I getting enough back for the time and mental energy I put into it? Is it worth it for me to engage with these apps and sites many times throughout the day? Be reflective, honest and, if necessary, be willing to modify your behavior. Answering or at least contemplating our reasons for engaging with social media can give us a fighting chance at using it more than it uses us.

# Chapter Four

# WHAT YOUR *OTHER* MIND DOES ON SOCIAL MEDIA

**You are not controlling the storm, and you are not lost in it. You are the storm.**
—Sam Harris, author, philosopher, and neuroscientist[1]

**We're entering an era of unprecedented psychological manipulation.**
—Bruce Schneier, computer security expert[2]

**Human stupidity has been one of the most powerful forces in human history.**
—Yuval Noah Harari, historian[3]

**Machines don't think, but neither do people.**
—César A. Hidalgo, director of the Macro Connections group at The MIT Media Lab[4]

I t's the twenty-first century; do you know where your mind is? That's not as silly a question as it seems, because most people don't know. The human brain today is an organ out of time. It evolved during and is best suited for life in the Pleistocene, a period from nearly two million years ago to about eleven thousand years ago. And yet here it is, having to make do in a modern, high-tech, increasingly wired, urbanized, and fast-changing world. The majority of people on Earth, right now, know little if anything about the brain's evolutionary history, its basic biology or psychological processes. This, perhaps, best explains why so few appreciate the value and urgent need for critical thinking in their lives. Enter the Internet and social media. Into this void of knowledge comes what may be the ultimate playground for cognitive bias, delusion, fraud, and stunning stupidity.

Why haven't critical thinking, skepticism, and a deep appreciation for the scientific method become prevalent at every level of
every society by now? Countless examples, from aviation to computers, show that science, evidence-based thinking, and respecting
reality work better than anything else for discovery, invention, and
simply getting things done. Do elevators go up and down, micro-
waves ovens cook food, and planes fly because we wish them to
while crossing our fingers? No, they work because of science and
engineering. Do we chart the accurate movements of the heavens
above by reading bird entrails and consulting astrologers? No, we
look to math and science for that. Computers, smartphones, and the
Internet work only because those who built them stuck to a trail
of discovery and facts, as opposed to one of magic and mysticism.
Yet here we are, a species so often delusional and deranged that
at times it can seem miraculous that we are able to feed and dress
ourselves. We have the answer to our most difficult challenges. We
know the way toward greater safety, efficiency, and productivity. It's
through science and reason. This is not to suggest that scientists
are always right or that science is always perfect. The scientific
process is a tool, one that can be used in many ways for many purposes. Science gave us antibiotics and vaccines as well as napalm
and thermonuclear weapons. The point here is that it works and
that scientific thinking is available to all of us. It's the means by
which anyone can cut through the nonsense and lies, to make one's
way closer to truth.

"Science is a way to call the bluff of those who only pretend
to knowledge," wrote Carl Sagan in his classic book about critical
thinking, *The Demon-Haunted World*. "It is a bulwark against mysticism, against superstition, against religion misapplied to where it
has no business being. If we're true to [science's] values, it can tell
us when we're being lied to. It provides a mid-course correction to
our mistakes. . . . Finding the occasional straw of truth awash in
a great ocean of confusion and bamboozle requires vigilance, dedication, and courage. But if we don't practice these tough habits of
thought, we cannot hope to solve the truly serious problems that
face us."[5] You and I must never forget that we are led around by
the subconscious workings of what is essentially a prehistoric brain
meant for the prehistoric environment. This is why we so often
default to the quick comfort of a guess dressed up as reason. Our

natural urges lead us to rely on instinct over intelligence, impulse over reflection. Look around and everywhere you will observe people who are busy fearing, hating, and worrying over the fabrications and exaggerations of their irrational minds. Humankind squanders immense, immeasurable amounts of time, energy, and resources upon various altars of madness. We have such capable, powerful brains but scarcely apply them to full effect. We are the brilliant-idiot rulers of Earth who fritter away so much of the potential within these massive thinking machines evolution gifted to us. We are like Ferraris stubbornly driving in reverse, top-end computers with screens dimmed to gray fog. And all the while we fool ourselves into believing that we are rational, sensible creatures loyal to logic and evidence. The hard truth is there to see for anyone who looks. We cling to made-up stories about ourselves and the world around us, mostly fictional narratives designed to comfort, confirm, and conform to whatever seems to work in the moment. But this way fails us again and again.

Good thinking matters. Every advancement that made our world better, and every human act that diminished or wasted human lives, tracks back to an idea, a success or failure of reason. It is only through self-awareness and humility that we might have a chance at overcoming the strange burdens and baggage that come with the ownership of a human brain. Billions eagerly use and rely on the products and benefits of science and critical thinking while simultaneously thinking and behaving in unscientific, uncritical, and irrational ways. A woman picks up her smartphone and accesses the Internet—two glorious examples of scientific thinking. She reads her horoscope and sends a text to her psychic—two sad examples of unscientific thinking. A man sits in his living room, where he reads and believes a fake news article on Facebook. The article, claiming new evidence that NASA faked the Moon landings, had been written only an hour ago, thousands of miles away from his home, and was delivered to his computer screen in part thanks to a satellite in space.

You may have moments in which you sense that you are out of place or disconnected to society because of all of the craziness that swirls around us. You might even feel as if you are thrashing about in an ocean filled with bobbing imbeciles, zealots, and maniacs. But this is where you belong. To be human is to be susceptible to nutty beliefs and behaviors. Don't be condescending. Don't attempt to deny or escape your membership in this club. Strive to make the best of it. Know the cognitive weaknesses, flaws, and foibles that come naturally to all of us. Then rise above them as often as possible.

For all our problems, human culture has made real progress. We are less violent.[6] We have more knowledge, more stored information, than ever before.[7] We have managed to turn on a light switch, yet most people insist on wearing a blindfold and continue to stumble around in the dark unnecessarily. Why is this the case? Why isn't rational thinking a universal goal, one that is on the lips of every teacher and politician? Why isn't every child on Earth, at least those fortunate enough to see the inside of a classroom, taught *how to think*? Why is the absurd notion that skepticism is negative so pervasive? Every achievement and all of our miseries alike are rooted in the consequences of thinking. For better or worse, our thoughts make the world we live in. Be aware of this, and also understand that by getting your own cognitive house in order you help nudge your society and all humankind toward a better place.

My travels across six continents and a deep curiosity for all things human have enlightened me to harsh realities. Most randomly selected twenty-first-century people are likely to know more myth than history, understand more astrology than astronomy, and be far more attentive to unproven supernatural forces that allegedly run their lives than they are to scientifically revealed natural forces that actually do run the universe. Given the high stakes of thinking, why do we place so little value on improving the quality and reliability of our perceptions, thoughts, and decisions? Societies train their brightest to be engineers, lawyers, doctors, astronauts, and so on. But not even the most highly educated elites are reliably taught in schools how unexpectedly strange and troublesome normal human minds are. The result is that relatively few of us understand how to improve safety, efficiency, and productivity through better thinking. I argue that scarcity of critical thinking is humankind's great unrecognized crisis. Therefore, given this planetwide and perpetual blind spot, it should be no surprise that weak critical thinking is a significant problem in such a vast subculture of human activity as social media. Make no mistake, we do import our cognitive shortcomings and subconscious weirdness into this new arena of communication and social interaction. And we suffer for it,

## WHAT IS GOOD THINKING?

*Good thinking is an umbrella term for understanding the human brain and using it in ways that enable one to make rational decisions, identify deception, and avoid or discard delusions as often as possible. It requires the following:*

- An understanding of the **evolutionary history of the human brain** and how it has left us with a thinking organ that goes about its business in unexpected ways that mislead us about reality.
- Knowledge of the **basic structures and functions of the human brain**, how vision and memory work, for example. How personal recollections and sensations can seem real and accurate even when they are not.
- An appreciation for the profound impact **nutrition, lifelong learning, and physical activity** have on the brain's health, performance, and longevity.
- Awareness of the prominent role of the **subconscious mind** in daily life, and the understanding that we inherited our brains from ancestors shaped by extremely competitive and dangerous environments that made fast subconscious reaction a priority over slower conscious reflection and imagination.
- An **alertness** to many of the natural and common mental biases and shortcuts that can undermine rational thought.
- The **courage and maturity** not only to question everything but also to accept the absence of answers and those answers that may contradict hopes and beliefs that appeal to us.
- **Sufficient humility** to prevent one from placing absolute trust in sensory perceptions, personal experiences, and even thoughtful conclusions. A willingness to always reconsider, revise, and change one's mind when better evidence demands it.

Source: Adapted from *Good Thinking: What You Need to Know to Be Smarter, Safer, Wealthier, and Wiser* (Amherst, NY: Prometheus Books, 2015).

just as we always have in other arenas throughout history. But you don't have to go this route. You can avoid most of the mental trip wires and potholes that others will walk straight into. All you have to do is think.

We carry, loaded into our skulls, three-pound blobs of electrochemical "magic" that have the potential to light up the dark and penetrate the densest fog with reason—*if* we care enough to try. Call me irrationally optimistic, but I view critical thinking as a cold meme, packed with universal potential, just waiting to catch fire and rage across all humanity via social media. (Perhaps if we somehow worked it into a cat video?) What is certain beyond doubt is that more of us need to recognize these problems of cognitive biases, deceptive perception of the world around us, emotional thinking, and subconscious shenanigans so that we may live more reasonable lives and build better societies.

"The history of science, medicine, politics, and business is littered with examples of obstinate adherence to old customs, irrational beliefs, ill-conceived policies, and appalling decisions," points out Dean Buonomano, a professor in UCLA's Departments of Neurobiology and Psychology. "Similar penchants are also observable in the daily decisions of our personal and professional lives. The causes of our poor decisions are complex and multifactorial, but they are in part attributable to the fact that human cognition is plagued with blind spots, preconceived assumptions, emotional influences, and built-in biases."[8]

I suspect one of the reasons critical thinking gets so little attention and respect from most people lies with the term itself. After years of giving many lectures hearing feedback from interviews, lectures, and writings, as well as having many conversations about thinking and irrational beliefs, I have learned that many people are just not sure what "critical thinking" means. Very few admit this up front because it's one of those things everyone feels they should know. For this reason, it is a mistake to casually toss around this phrase under the assumption that everyone is clear about what it is. Some people even become defensive when encouraged to "think critically" because they seem to sense that it may be a threat to them. But critical thinking is a threat only to lies and mistakes in reasoning, nothing else. It is both a valuable skill and an attitude we all need; yet I have had conversations with numerous people who were bright, positive, and clearly self-reflective—but who couldn't recognize a need for consistent critical thinking in their lives.

Many people seem to believe that critical thinking is an elitist catchphrase tossed about by professional philosophers and other intellectual weirdos who spend their days and nights worrying about whatever the hell is going on in Plato's cave or whether it's okay to push one fat man off a bridge in order to stop a train and save two children on the tracks. Maybe critical thinking is a bogus concept used by those who like to appear smarter or remind everyone that they are more educated than others. Maybe it's a sly way to insult people. Or, perhaps, it's a marketing scam to help sell books like this one. *No, no,* and *no.* Regardless of who we are, where are, or what we do, we all need critical thinking because being human and dwelling within human culture means being forever trapped in a fog of misperceptions and confusion. Critical thinking is *conscious* thinking, and it is the best way to cut through that fog and navigate our lives to better results. There simply is no rational reason to deny this need. Critical thinking skills are people skills, and they are readily available to everyone. Anyone can be an intellectual, a philosopher-scientist, and elite thinker, but only if reason and reality are valued. Ultimately it is our choice whether to think or not, and the quality of our own life hangs in the balance of that decision.

Toward making critical thinking more palatable to the masses, I have taken to referring to it as *good thinking.* Simple and positive-sounding, *good thinking* is easy for anyone to recognize and relate with as a positive trait or desirable behavior. Who doesn't want to think well, to be a good thinker? Who is going to say, aloud, "No, thanks. I'm sticking with *bad thinking*—just a better fit for me." I feel so strongly about this that I wrote a book titled *Good Thinking: What You Need to Know to Be Smarter, Safer, Wealthier, and Wiser.*[9] To warm up readers for deeper explorations of the key cognitive biases to come in this chapter, I have loosely excerpted the following primer from *Good Thinking.* This a brief rundown of common challenges every human must cope with while thinking and making decisions. Failing to keep these in mind guarantees you a consistent stream of mental mistakes with occasional bouts of idiocy on social media and elsewhere.

**THE DIRTY DOZEN**

Be aware of these standard weak points to make your mind less vulnerable to bad claims and bogus beliefs.[10]

1. **The Emotion Potion.** We are emotional creatures, and this often leads us to make irrational decisions, embrace bad ideas, and act in ways that work against our best interests. Emotions can intoxicate us, make us dumb. Be aware of this vulnerability. If someone tells you the world is going to end in fiery chaos soon, for example, don't let your fear of such an event distract you from rationally analyzing and challenging the claim. Don't think, "I'm scared." Instead, think, "This person doesn't have any good evidence to back up what he is saying."

2. **Popularity.** We are social animals. The relative safety of the crowd feels good. It can be cold and harsh out there all alone in the wilderness. But reality is not a popularity contest. Recognize how we all can be swayed by popular support of an idea no matter how destructive or ridiculous it may be. Never forget that truth and reality are not decided by vote. The majority of people have been wrong about many things many times throughout history. There were times when phrenology and bloodletting were respectable and popular ideas—but they were still wrong.

3. **Straw Person.** A common tactic people use to promote weak or worthless claims is to attack an easy-to-beat, diluted, or counterfeit version of the counterargument. Those who say, for example, that Earth is around 4.5 billion years old should not be swayed one bit on this point if a science denier were to tell them that there was a time when geologists didn't understand continental drift and still can't explain everything today about the structure and function of the Earth's core. Of course geologists don't know everything. But this does not refute the strong evidence for a 4.5-billion-year-old Earth.

4. **Loaded Questions.** Sometimes people try to make their point seem more sensible by slipping in an unproven claim or bit of nonsense as filler or padding. Example: "Another reason we know the Lost City of Atlantis is real is because

psychics and mediums have communicated with spirits of dead Atlanteans." Listen well and catch weak arguments or bad ideas within the larger claim. Challenge them all.

5. **Wishful Thinking.** This is simple but deadly to good thinking. We desire something, so we believe it to be true. This is a powerful human compulsion. Be aware of it and be tough with yourself. Always ask yourself, "Am I accepting this claim because it makes sense and is supported by strong evidence? Or do I just want to believe it so much that I am willing to pretend to know that it is valid?"

6. **False Dilemma.** Watch out for people who frame their case as an "either, or" proposition. Sometimes there is a third option, or perhaps many more options. For example, a politician might say that more prisons must be built or there will be more violent criminals on the streets. But what if we went with a third option? What if nonviolent offenders were released early or given lighter sentences, thereby freeing up space for more dangerous criminals to serve longer sentences?

7. **Explaining by Naming.** Giving a name to something is not the same as explaining it. For example, calling an event a "miracle" is not an explanation for what happened and by what process. Calling an expensive conversation with a psychic or medium a "reading" does not explain how mind reading or talking to dead people works. Watch out for this deceitful form of verbal carpet-bombing. When it happens, simply ask the person to explain the name or concept he or she attempted to pass off as an explanation itself. An inability to do so will reveal everything you need to know about the person's credibility and/or competence.

8. **Circular Reasoning.** This shows up frequently in online chats and comment threads where people try to make their case in few words. It occurs when someone attempts to prove "A" by pointing to "B." And then claims that "B" can be trusted because "A" proves it.

9. **Authority Worship.** Don't forget that we humans are primates; we are essentially chimps in shoes. And, just like them, we are obsessed with rank and power. This gives us a huge weak point in our brains, because our natural reaction is to snap to and obey when we view someone as our superior. I'm not suggesting that you should rebel

against everything an authority figure says, of course. But do try to think clearly about the validity of words from on high. Don't let a uniform, fancy title, or dominant posture hoodwink you into believing nonsense or buying a junk product.

10. **Special Pleading.** People who promote or believe in things that are unlikely to be true often scramble to change the game when they feel the walls of reality closing in on them. For example, a person who says acupuncture works because "one billion Chinese people can't be wrong" might not like hearing that only about 18 percent of China's population relies on acupuncture,[11] and that person might react by suddenly arguing that numbers don't matter.

11. **Burden of Proof.** The person who makes an extraordinary claim has the burden of backing it up. You and I don't have to prove that mediums can't talk to dead people or that Bigfoot is living among the Redwoods. It's not even fair to suggest that we should, because in many cases it is impossible to disprove such things. Instead, the believer must validate her beliefs.

12. **Ad Hominem Attacks.** If dealing with facts doesn't get you anywhere, try name-calling. Or don't, because this is a despicable tactic. If you are discussing astrology with a total jerk, remind yourself that being a jerk is irrelevant to whether or not astrology is a real thing. Focus on logic and evidence. It's better for everyone in the long run to kill a bad message rather than the messenger.

## CONTACT WITH ONLINE INFORMATION MATTERS

Beyond the "Dirty Dozen" mental mistakes listed above, there are many cognitive biases and other psychological phenomena about which we all should be as informed as possible. Every social media user can benefit from being aware of the *mere exposure effect* and the *illusion-of-truth effect*, because typical online activity includes consistent contact with inaccurate stories, lies, and misinformation that serves someone else's hidden agenda. The mere exposure effect is enough to lose sleep over when you think about how easily your judgment can be manipulated. Your subconscious mind remembers and makes use of far more than "you" will ever know. Contrary to our natural assumptions, simply being exposed to an idea can influence our thinking about it later. This often holds true even if the information is deemed to be trivial or meaningless in the moment, and even if we consciously forget about it. The old adages "There's no such thing as bad publicity" and "Repeat a lie often enough and it becomes the truth," pack a frightening punch. Subconscious familiarity can lead us to feel more favorable about something than we otherwise would have—regardless of whether or not there is a good reason to be positive about it. Think of how easy mistakes in reasoning can happen when simply bumping into an exaggeration, absurdity, or lie online can make it seem sensible and believable should you encounter it again later. This is a primary reason why advertising is so effective. We are bombarded daily with ads online and off. We may assume they don't really work on us but, thanks to the mere exposure effect, many ads do succeed. Our subconscious minds are paying attention and being influenced, even as our conscious minds tune them out. It's as if we are all sleepwalking, on our feet but not quite awake, not fully alert to what is going on around us. And, as the brilliant writer Ralph Ellison warned us: "There are few things in the world as dangerous as sleepwalkers."[12]

The mere exposure effect raises serious concerns about *all* "meaningless" comments, photos, and viral memes encountered on social media platforms. We may dismiss an image or string of words that we encounter online as inconsequential in the moment; but it's possible that—beneath our awareness or consciousness— we are falling in love with the idea. This gives you something to think about as you laugh off those insane political rants and weird claims you skim over on social media every day. Without your open consent, the simple fact of exposure to them may be nudging you toward feeling more positive about these claims and ideas, should they cross your path in the future.

The similar *illusion-of-truth effect* is another potential problem on social media in particular. This disturbing phenomenon entails repeat readings, hearings, or viewings of information that lead you to believe that the information is true. Think of it as the cognitive version of being beaten into submission. Where the mere exposure effect can cause you to feel positive about something, this other effect can leave you convinced that a false claim is factually correct—*just because we saw it before*. The particularly creepy aspect of it is that it works even when we can't remember seeing the claim before. Worse, the illusion-of-truth effect can occur even if you are initially informed that the information is false! It's almost as if knowingly bad information wears us down, tortures us until we believe. Be careful about wallowing in sketchy information daily in your social media ecosystems. Bad ideas may contaminate your judgment through the most basic and briefest exposures if repeated enough times. The Nazi propaganda machine of the 1930s did not convince sufficient numbers of Germans that Jews were to blame a litany of their problems the first time they made the claim. To gain real traction with the idea, they repeated it, again and again. In 2002, I interviewed Armin Lehmann, a former member of the Hitler Youth.[13] He also was Hitler's last courier, present in the Berlin command bunker during the final days of World War II. Lehmann told me that anti-Semitic propaganda was a near-constant theme in school.

The present danger of this standard psychological vulnerability—one we all have—is clear. Therefore, we should keep it in mind, for ourselves and for our societies. It certainly might explain in part the strange loyalties we see some people show for destructive ideologies such as ISIS and other negative movements. "The illusion-of-truth effect highlights the potential danger for people who are repeatedly exposed to the same religious edicts or political slogans," warns neuroscientist David Eagleman.[14]

"The more we hear a lie, the more likely we are to accept it as truth," adds Bo Bennett, an educator and author of *Logically Fallacious*.[15] When I interviewed him about this topic, he continued, "But this also has to do with how easy the information is to process. When a politician says, 'I am going to fix the healthcare problems and make our system the best in the world,' we tend to believe this because of its simplicity. If the same politician were to explain precisely what he or she will fix, using legal and economics jargon, that message is less likely to be believed. Sometimes the truth is simple, but sometimes it's not."

## WHAT HAPPENS WHEN YOU DON'T KNOW
## WHAT YOU DON'T KNOW?

### The Dunning-Kruger Effect

Is there anything worse than being ignorant, dumb, stupid, misinformed, misguided, and clueless? Yes, there most certainly is. Meet the *Dunning-Kruger effect*. The Dunning-Kruger effect is named after psychologists David Dunning and Justin Kruger. With a fascinating study that they coauthored, they exposed and described the phenomenon of believing we know more than we do. In other words, the Dunning-Kruger effect is the problematic and dangerous state of being unable to recognize the depths of one's own ignorance. It can lead to worse outcomes than simply not knowing, because when we underestimate lack of knowledge or skill we can be quick to adopt the role of an arrogant expert, eager to comment, decide, believe, and act—often with undesired or negative consequences. One might assume that ignorance would nudge us toward humility and caution in thought rather than arrogance and recklessness. But the human mind doesn't work that way.

Make sure you understand and never forget that we do a poor job of accurately assessing our own knowledge, skills, and reasoning abilities. This is a common human trait. Any typical D student, for example, is likely to perform worse than an A student on a test in the given subject, of course. But there's more to be concerned about here. Thanks to the Dunning-Kruger effect, the D student would also tend to be comparatively worse than the A student at estimating his or her own test performance. The D student struggles at getting an accurate feel for just how little he or she knows. When we find ourselves in over our heads, we tend to overestimate how much we know or how good we are at a skill, simply because we just don't know enough to know our shortcomings. Leonardo da Vinci excluded, this matters to everyone because out in real life most of us are "D students" in most subjects. An engineering or law degree alone doesn't make you an expert in geology or nuclear arms proliferation, but you may feel competent in the moment because of the Dunning-Kruger effect. The same lack of knowledge that makes a D student deficient in the first place also leaves him or her less able to recognize what she or he doesn't know. To make matters worse, we also do poorly at assessing the skills and abilities of *other people* in areas in which we lack expertise. This means that we can't consistently and accurately identify incompetence in politicians, medical doctors, lawyers, and so on because we don't know enough about their specific fields to evaluate them.

To see the Dunning-Kruger effect in action, just listen in on two typical Americans engaged in a heated discussion about politics. Before long, both are sure to verbalize unjustified expertise in a wide variety of fields and offer ready solutions to every complex problem from the economy to terrorism. This is not a "dumb people problem." Well-educated and brilliant people also stray from their areas of competence without a corresponding dialing down of confidence. You have done this. You will do this. I state that with confidence because everyone has this problem. No one is immune. We all struggle to recognize our limitations.

I have been aware of this problem for so long that my conversational speech has adapted to guard against it. Over the years, it has become my habit to sprinkle conversations with phrases that qualify and declare the limits of my knowledge and certainty. *I'm not sure, but . . .* ; *According to the data I've seen, it seems to me that . . .* ; *I don't know, but I lean toward . . .* ; *I could be wrong, but my strong hunch is . . .* ; *At the moment it seems reasonable to me that . . .*; and so on. I do this with such consistency that I sometimes worry I might sound like a paranoid lawyer trying to preempt a lawsuit stemming from the reckless use of a ladder or toaster. This also might seem to some to be wishy-washy or weak language, but it's not. Prefacing the statement of a claim or position with, "I don't know for sure but . . . " is not weak. It is a mark of strength and honesty. It makes everything to follow more powerful, not less, because it is not shrouded in lies, delusions, or false confidence. Qualifying important communications in this way serves two purposes. (1) It protects me from overreaching and thereby setting myself up for intellectual annihilation in conversation or debate, should I be wrong. (2) It also helps keep me authentic and focused within. It is more difficult to drown in your own hubris when you literally speak aloud the limits of your knowledge. Still, even with my regular linguistic safety catches, I fear that I sometimes slip into fake-expert mode.

Thanks to many years of running and weight training, I tend

to feel that I have it all figured out and can come up with a good answer to virtually any question on the topic of fitness. But I can't. I exercise a lot, and I've read a bunch of books on the subject. That's not the same as having earned a university degree in kinesiology or putting in twenty years as a head strength and conditioning coach for an NFL team. Yet for all my internal protocols and verbal speed bumps, I still catch myself speaking sometimes as if I am a credentialed expert in the field. But the reality is that there certainly are specific fitness topics about which I am so deeply ignorant that I can't even recognize how uninformed I am, so I should tread carefully and maintain cautious humility.

The good news is that simply being *aware* of the Dunning-Kruger effect can make us safer, more efficient, and rational when online. Humility can and should become a habit, the default setting. Yes, it's hard to be humble when half of your Facebook friends are certain that aliens built the Great Pyramids at Giza, but we must beat back these demons of overconfidence. Humility is the prerequisite to sound skepticism and consistent critical thinking.

Having the mere awareness and understanding that all people— yourself included—struggle to accurately assess competency levels can inspire the crucial and necessary pause, that moment of reflection before speaking, writing, clicking, liking, or swiping. Prior to declaring the "obvious answer" to gun violence, racism, sexism, or poverty—and then digging in to defend it—we must recall that confidence is not the same thing as knowledge. The Dunning-Kruger effect explains much of the loud, proud folly you find in social media. In a paper about their study, Dunning and Kruger write, "when people are incompetent in the strategies they adopt to achieve success and satisfaction, they suffer a dual burden: Not only do they reach erroneous conclusions and unfortunate choices, but their incompetence robs them of the ability to realize it. Instead . . . they are left with the impression that they are doing just fine."[16]

We struggle to know our own ignorance, always have and maybe always will. No one is an expert on everything, so everyone succumbs to the Dunning-Kruger effect at some point. This is an old cognitive challenge, one that will not cease tormenting us anytime soon. Some twenty-six centuries ago the Chinese philosopher Confucius is believed to have written or said: "To know when you know something, and to know when you don't know, that's knowledge."[17]

Socrates, regarded by some as the greatest thinker of all time, is believed to have inspired what we call the Socratic paradox: "I know that I know nothing."[18] William Shakespeare seemed to be aware of this problem as well, having written this line into his play, *As You Like It*: "The fool doth think he is wise, but the wise man knows himself to be a fool."[19]

Good thinkers resist the lure of arrogance and are quick to say, "I don't know." Good thinkers are always willing, even eager, to change their minds when shown enough contrary evidence that collides with a belief or conclusion.

A final warning: Don't allow your awareness of the Dunning-Kruger effect to paralyze you on social media or elsewhere. Be more thoughtful and cautious, of course, but this is not an excuse to shy away from or disengage from interactions and explorations into areas you don't know much about. Plunge forward into new frontiers and grow your mind. Only do it with a wisdom that comes from knowing that you don't know everything.

## WHY WE DON'T ROCK THE BOAT—EVEN WHEN IT'S SINKING

Building and maintaining social networks is one of humankind's greatest strengths. These connections allow us to accomplish things no individual could ever achieve alone. However, a significant problem often arises when we bind ourselves together off-line or in cyberspace. This is where *groupthink* enters the picture. Groupthink is the common and dangerous tendency to fall in line and agree, even when we should know better. In other words, it is the tendency to align our thoughts in pursuit of consensus; this can lead us to make regrettable decisions. In our positive efforts to maintain unity, get along, avoid alienating others, or lose friends, we go along with what we perceive to be the group's desired direction, idea, or outcome. But sometimes we agree with what seems to be the majority position even when our intellect or moral compass might point in a different direction.

Groupthink has long been and continues to be a serious problem for governments, corporations, religious organizations, and maybe for you on social media. Many disasters, near disasters, and just plain bad decisions might have been avoided if one or more people within a collaboration had resisted the dominant winds. This is not the same as someone not speaking up with an opposing viewpoint or idea because they are afraid of repercussions.

Groupthink is different than fear-based obedience. Instead, groupthink happens when people feel that agreeing and going along is the right thing to do. It makes sense that this would be common, because we are taught to value teamwork and loyalty to friends, colleagues, and allies. Saying no when everyone in the tribe is saying yes can be difficult. It not only makes one stand out for possible negative scrutiny within the social unit but also can be seen as abrasive, repugnant, or even a sign of dangerous disloyalty.

Groupthink can be a problem for social media users because platforms like Facebook and Twitter cater to it so well. For example, many Facebook users build a coalition of family members, real-world friends, coworkers, and online acquaintances. How many Facebook users post any and all opinions without any thought given to possible negative reactions from others? I suggest most don't. Within the mostly closed world of a particular Facebook community, groupthink can be a powerful and near-constant presence. What if the all or at least a majority of someone's Facebook friends post, share, and "like" a report about a dubious herbal concoction said to cure AIDS, diabetes, eczema, and low self-esteem? There is a good chance that this person will either join in by also giving the news story a "like" or react to it with silence, which itself can be a form of agreement and conformity. If groupthink comes into play, as it so often does, the least likely response from most people in these situations is to challenge it. For all of the talk about trolls and flame wars, most people go along to get along. Facebook, Instagram, and Twitter users know that great power is always at their fingertips and the fingertips of others. With a simple click they can banish or be banished from a community forever. Exiling was a common practice in some ancient societies. Some viewed it as a fate worse than death. And here we are again. Today, people are exiled from social media tribes every moment.

Perhaps a helpful way to think about this is to remember that old saying, "monkey see, monkey do." We're all primates, remember, and, like the monkeys of that cliché, we are prone to imitation and quite good at it. Imitation is one of the primary ways in which we learn new technical and social skills. Imitation has been a means of survival for a long, long time. You are a copycat. Keep this in mind while wading through all of those posts and comments on social media. Again and again, subconscious impulses will encourage you to do as you see your fellow primates doing—even, sometimes, when the behavior or idea is negative, a waste of time, or just plain dumb. "The extent to which imitation is engrained into the brains of humans is easy to underestimate," warns UCLA neuroscientist Dean Buonomano, "not because it isn't important, but rather because it is so important that, like breathing, it is automatic and unconscious"[20]

What social media users must do to avoid bogging down in a swamp of groupthink is first, realize and remember that the sensible goal is not consensus for the sake of consensus. The objective is to be correct, to have a clear view of a situation, and to avoid being an idiot. What good does it do you to be a loyal teammate when the team is running full speed toward the edge of a cliff?

What can you do to avoid groupthink? Build diverse social networks. If I encountered a Scientologist or a CrossFit fanatic who asked for advice on how to avoid groupthink, the first thing I would suggest is for him or her to diversity the social circle. Friend a few Buddhists. Connect with a couple of jujutsu enthusiasts. The more diverse the exposure and input, the better. It's difficult to think outside the box if you live your life inside a box.

Finally, understand that there are a variety of ways to raise objections and offer differing opinions within a group that do not involve being a rude, rebellious, jerk. Those who are concerned about offending friends, being blocked on Twitter, or instigating arguments need only take a soft but steady approach. Show studies, data, and expert opinions that support a view that contradicts group consensus. To soften the blow, preface it with: "Hey, just to careful, let's consider another possible answer." or "Do you think there is anything we should consider about this other idea?" Try to frame the exchange as less of a debate and more of team effort to get to the truth. Remember that the point is not to win arguments or achieve unanimous agreements one way or another. The goal is to make the right decision. One key to preventing or fixing groupthink on social media is to work hard at being tolerant. It's the same way we can escape filter bubbles. Don't reflexively unfriend, unfollow, or block every person who has an opinion that is different from yours. Ask questions before helping to ignite a fiery debate. Constructive, positive dialogue, at least from your end, has a much better chance of doing more good than immediate censorship and isolation. If, of course, you are connected with someone who is so persistent, stubborn, obnoxious, abrasive, or disappointing that you find the relationship too stressful, then unfriend and block away. There's no sense in suffering when relief is but a click away. Just know that social media works in a precise way that fuels groupthink. We actively connect ourselves to people who mostly share our backgrounds, experiences, and views. This is human nature. But while it might be comfortable, it is not intellectually healthy or safe in every situation.

## BEWARE THE BANDWAGON

We love jumping on bandwagons. Similar to groupthink, this too can seem irresistible at times. Who among us would not enjoy the warm and cozy feeling of riding off into the sunset with a bunch of people who are all on the same wavelength, chanting the same slogans, or perpetually patting one another on the back? It's obviously reassuring and empowering to be with the in-crowd or at least among allies. When surrounded by agreeable voices, we feel confident that we are right and that all is right in our immediate field of vision. But those who wish to be mature, wise, and reality-based in their thinking must acknowledge the obvious: Crowds can be wrong. Popularity is not a reliable measure of truth and reality. One of the most detrimental effects of social media is the way it exploits our natural weakness for assuming a real or perceived majority knows what it's talking about.

The *bandwagon effect* must be given due consideration while on social media. To fail in this is to ensure taking repeat journeys to fantasyland. It doesn't matter who you are; you will feel a rush of confidence when you think that your beliefs, ideas, or conclusions align with a majority or a substantial number of people. The mind automatically seeks reassurance and refuge in the crowd. Your subconscious will whisper to you: *How can all of these people be wrong?* But of course we know that large crowds can be wrong, and many are wrong every day. Consider as an example the world's three most popular religions, which account for more than half of the world's population. Based on their most basic, core claims and doctrines, Christianity, Islam, and Hinduism cannot all be correct. The only possibilities are for one of them to be correct or for all three of them to be wrong. It is not even possible for them to be logically compatible on so basic a matter as the number of deities: Islam's one god only/no divine son vs. Christianity's trinity of three-gods-in-one vs. Hinduism's millions of gods.[21] Therefore, on this point of religion, at least a few billion people are wrong.

Let's reiterate that point: *The crowd is often wrong.* It can be wrong even when the crowd numbers in the billions. And if billions of sane, honest, well-intentioned people can be mistaken about their beloved religious belief, how easy then is it for a crowd to be wrong about a political candidate, an alternative medical treatment, or a conspiracy claim? Keep this in mind when exposing yourself to impressive retweet, share, and "like" stats.

The bandwagon effect is not cut-and-dried. Sometimes a bit of bandwagon jumping is okay. We must necessarily do it at times for efficiency's sake. I'm happy to jump on the UNICEF, science, and critical thinking bandwagons, for example. I just know not to strap myself in so tight that I can't jump off if I should discover that I'm being taken off in the wrong direction. The key is to board a particular bandwagon only on the basis of very good reasons to do so and not for reasons of popularity, comfort, coercion, or emotional hunches. For example, "scientific consensus" is a bandwagon of sorts. When the world's scientists within a particular field generally converge on the same conclusion, those of us who value truth and reality can with some confidence jump onboard with them. But we do this not because they are a crowd. It is because we understand the scientific method and trust it to a significant degree. We *tentatively* accept the scientists' conclusion as probably true—because we know from past experience that science is the most effective means of discovery and figuring things out. But good thinking requires us to be ready to bail out at a moment's notice should better, contradictory evidence turn up.

## WELCOME TO THE SHADOW BRAIN[22]

Most of us have heard of something called "the subconscious mind," that mysterious other part of ourselves that somehow interacts with our normal mind. What few people grasp, however, is just how prominent and powerful an influence it is to our lives. This subconscious presence, I call it the *shadow brain*, is not a minor player who follows behind you only to occasionally whisper advice in your ear. No, it is you who follows the shadow most of the time. Believe it or not, "you" are the minor player in your life.

To help understand how important the shadow brain is to you, imagine looking down from high above and spotting a lone swimmer treading water at the center of an enormous lake. The swimmer is you, and the lake is your shadow brain. The swimmer is tiny and alone, with deep waters on all sides. The swimmer is also blindfolded. Currents and waves constantly pull and push one way or another. The blinded swimmer cannot consistently detect or make sense of these forces, because there are no points of reference. Sometimes the currents turn the swimmer a bit left or right. Sometimes they completely reverse the swimmer's course. Often the swimmer will stroke away at full effort but go nowhere. Sometimes the oblivious swimmer doesn't swim at all but makes fast progress across the lake nonetheless due to strong currents. In addition to this, unknown creatures swim around and beneath the swimmer. Sometimes they brush against the swimmer's legs with such a light touch that the swimmer doesn't notice. Some are small, some big. Many times they impact with such force that the swimmer knows something substantial is there but still has no idea what it is or what its intentions are.

The swimmer has no idea how wide or how deep the lake is. The shore could be ten meters away or ten thousand kilometers away. But the swimmer imagines it is nothing more than a small swimming pool because this is a comforting thought. The lake is a thousand times larger than that, however. If only the swimmer knew more about the lake, at least a hint of its size and maybe something about the currents, waves, and creatures as well. But the blindfold prevents the swimmer from understanding anything. In an attempt to make sense of it all and feel less anxiety, the swimmer constantly thinks up reasons, explanations, possibilities, and excuses for why the waters move, why strange things move around below the surface, and why no shore is ever reached. The swimmer keeps swimming, year after year, never realizing the bizarre truth: The lake is the greater part of the swimmer's life. The lake is the swimmer, too.

Good thinking can't take us out of the vast lake that is our shadow brain. But that's okay. We wouldn't want to leave it even if that were possible. We need our shadow brains to be our automatic-reaction force, to keep our involuntary systems functioning, and to find countless mental shortcuts through daily life for us. But good thinking does one invaluable thing for us. It takes off the blindfold.

Good thinking allows us to understand that we are that swimmer and that the lake is us too, influencing and controlling us. No longer blind and ignorant, we can now pause to reason when it is appropriate and possible, such as the moment before we make important decisions. We can pay attention and try to determine if we swam a northerly course for sensible reasons or if it was one of the creatures below that nudged us northward for irrational or unknown reasons. We will always be in the center of the lake; the lake is us as much or more than anything else in our lives. We will always find ourselves treading water and swimming with or against the currents of our subconscious. Simply recognizing this reality, however, gives us greater control and provides more opportunities to make good decisions.

**Are you in control of "you"?** It is difficult to overstate the influence and impact of the shadow brain on one's life. You don't even live your life in real time. It typically takes a fraction of a second for your shadow brain to receive, process, and act on input from your senses, significantly faster than your conscious mind. So when a friend yells your name from across the street, a cat rubs against your leg, or your phone rings, "you" are the last to know. Weirder still, your other brain is first to act even when "you" decide to do something! Researchers have observed related brain activity occurring before a person makes the conscious decision to act.[23] This means that at the precise moment you decide to stand up, for example, your shadow brain has already begun the cerebral processes related to standing up. It knew what you were going to decide and started working on it before "you" actually made the decision. What does this imply about free will? If your shadow brain has already decided to stand up before "you" did, then who is really doing the standing up? Who is in charge? Moreover, this "other you" that is so involved with your life is constantly feeding you input about how to react to the things, events, and people you encounter. Should you buy this or that? Is this person you just met okay or a bit too creepy? Trust me, while you might want to dither and ponder ethics or weigh a long list of pros and cons, the other you has already made the call. More often than not, "you" are relegated to the role of explainer in chief. You have to defend and make sense of decisions and actions your shadow brain is responsible for.

"To make our way in the world," warns Yale psychologist John A. Bargh, "we must learn to come to terms with our unconscious self."[24] Otherwise we can do little better than flounder in the middle of a deep lake—blindfolded. While in pursuit of good thinking, we have to acknowledge that the shadow brain is always there, looking over our shoulder, paying attention when we are not, working through problems we gave up on, and making countless split-second decisions that we then take credit or blame for. It may be common for us to second-guess the words and deeds of others. But modern science has made it clear that we should be in the habit of second-guessing ourselves as well.

## FALSE CONSENSUS EFFECT

It's reassuring and empowering when everyone agrees with us and, surprisingly, even when they don't. All who so much as dip a toe into social media are immediately subject to the *false consensus effect*. This psychological phenomenon is rampant, virtually unavoidable on Facebook, Twitter, Snapchat, Instagram, and so on. False consensus effect is yet another lie the shadow brain tells us to make us feel more comfortable with ourselves. It is the natural assumption, the stealthy bias that consistently bubbles up from down below to assure us that our thoughts, feelings, beliefs, attitudes, values, views, conclusions, and behaviors are not weird or unpopular—even when they are. False consensus effect is our tendency to overestimate how similar other people are to us. It is remarkable how common this bias is.

People often defend a pet belief or preferred conclusion by declaring that there must be something to it because "everyone believes it." I've heard this defense tactic countless times on six continents. It inevitably comes up while discussing everything from conspiracy theories and ghosts to astrology and alien abductions. It is clear to me that many of these believers have exaggerated and unrealistic notions of just how many people share their beliefs and are imbued with heightened confidence if not outright certainty as a result. This is the bandwagon effect without the bandwagon.

The key to understanding this challenge is to recognize that we not only seek belonging and acceptance but want others to agree with us. We yearn not for a few comrades, but for most or everyone who is good, sane, and smart to agree with us. This makes perfect sense because it makes us uncomfortable when good, sane, and smart people do not agree with us. Their contrary positions call into question the validity of our important beliefs and conclusions. They push us toward doubt and possibly revising or dropping beliefs, a journey many people don't wish to take. Enter the false consensus effect.

With a little help from the subconscious mind, we assume without much thought that everyone, or at least a significant number of people, see the world in the same way we do. Those who don't must be dim or defective in some way. I have fallen victim to the false consensus effect many times, and it can be jarring when reality comes crashing in. Because I have researched, written, and talked about irrational beliefs for so much of my life, many of these claims seem to me nearly impossible to be believed. When you know the real story behind the Roswell myth, for example, it can seem silly to take it seriously.[25] And even though I consciously know that millions of people do believe it, my subconscious mind sometimes ignores the data and leads me to just assume the person I'm chatting with couldn't possibly accept the claim that extraterrestrials crash-landed in a New Mexico desert back in 1947, were scooped up by the US military, and are on ice today in some secret facility. As a positive, constructive skeptic who wants to be polite and respectful when it comes to the wild things people believe, I have to consciously push back against the false consensus effect and remind myself that my perspectives are not synchronized with everyone I encounter on the street or on social media, not even when it comes to the most absurd and unlikely beliefs. False consensus effect has tripped me up more than once on the topic of conservation, for instance. I am a lifelong fan of life. I think that biodiversity, the beautiful and vital mix of life on our planet, is the ultimate treasure of our world and that squandering it within the flash of a few generations is a tragic mistake and colossal crime. To me this seems apparent and undeniable, so I tend to automatically assume that others feel the same way. Clearly, however, not everyone does, as I rediscover again and again. What may seem obvious to you is not necessarily so to others. Keep this in mind and you will be able to mount some defense, at least, against the false consensus effect.

The false consensus effect runs rampant on social media because of the fractured/filtered nature of online communities. When a group of like-minded people agree and reinforce one another, confidence tends to soar. People within these groups naturally believe that most people outside the group agree with them as well. After all, they figure, everybody I'm communicating with thinks this way, so the same must hold true for all of those I'm not communicating with as well. False consensus effect distorts attitudes even when people know that the majority doesn't align with them, because they may then assume that *enough* people do agree to validate their ideas and beliefs. Related to this is our habit of *thinking for the population*. When we have no idea how many people believe a certain claim, for example, we commonly project our own knowledge, experience, values, and beliefs into the imagined minds of hundreds, thousands, millions of others to decide how they think or feel.

## WATCH WHERE YOUR ANCHOR DROPS

The *anchoring effect* can cause our thinking to set sail for the wrong harbor. The human brain is demanding, one could say greedy, in its constant need for blood and oxygen. No other organ comes close to its requirements. The three-pound brain of a 150-pound adult accounts for just 2 percent of bodyweight but demands as much as 25 percent of the body's blood supply. The brain hungers for information in much the same way. The brain's mantra could be "keep it coming"; something is always preferable to nothing. Your shadow brain wants, craves, and covets input of any kind to serve you. Working behind the scenes, it is relentless in trying to help you stay alive and succeed. Most of the time it works out well. Sometimes, however, no good, accurate, or useful information is available. But the subconscious mind doesn't give up on its mission to serve you. So, for better or worse, it will seize the first thing available to work with. The absence of accurate, relevant, or timely information prior to decision making seems to be an uncomfortable or intolerable state for the subconscious mind; so, in a pinch, your shadow brain will make do with almost any extraneous input. The early information that hits a knowledge vacuum matters. It becomes the anchor around which later thinking and decision making grows.

A simple example of the anchoring bias can be found at car dealerships. A dealer puts a price on the car's window. That price is high, too high, but a typical potential buyer doesn't know how much the dealer actually paid for the vehicle wholesale, so a fair price is unknown. However, with that sticker price offered up as an anchor, the first bit of information, the buyer's subconscious has a starting point from which to work and, the dealer hopes, it will sway the buyer to estimate higher on what a fair price is.

It is remarkable, even scary, how anchoring bias can steer us toward answers and opinions with frivolous information. For example, if I were to mention or show you a large number, say 100,000, and later ask you to guess how many spoons or forks you have in your home, you likely would guess a higher number than if I had earlier exposed you to the number 10, 20, or some other lesser number. Because you didn't know how many silverware items you have, your subconscious mind would instantly scramble for input of any kind that might help you come up with a good answer. Having recently been exposed to a number, any number, could be enough to set your mind off in one direction over another—*even though that first number had nothing to do with the silverware count.*

To be clear, the anchoring effect is different from the mere exposure effect because it is based on our mind's willingness to rely on an anchor, a specific bit or bits of information, even though it is unrelated to the decision or task at hand. The mere exposure effect can betray our reasoning via nothing more than familiarity. It nudges us toward a feeling or belief based on nothing more than exposure. The anchoring effect has been well tested and shown to be remarkably consistent. For example, an experiment by psychologists Amos Tversky and Daniel Kahneman had people estimate what percentage of African countries are in the United Nations, a question at which most people could only guess.[26] But before guessing, participants had to spin a Las Vegas–style roulette wheel that was engineered to stop at the number 10 or the number 65. The test subjects were not told that this roulette-wheel spin and "winning" numbers had any connection to the percentage of African UN member nations. But those numbers dropped anchor in the subconscious minds of the wheel spinners anyway. Those who landed on 10 gave an average answer of 25 percent. Those who landed on 65, the higher number, guessed 45 percent, a higher answer. The meaningless whirl of a wheel influenced answers by a difference of twenty points!

The direct relevance of anchoring bias to social media comes into play when we consume news, posts, gossip, or images posted by friends and followers. The first input that hits your subconscious mind about a topic you are not reasonably familiar with sets the stage for your conscious thoughts and decisions about it. It may not matter if this information is inaccurate, exaggerated, biased, or completely irrelevant. It is input, and your subconscious mind will happily make use of it. The importance of first impressions cannot be overstated here. There is no cure for this challenge. Anchoring is a standard process of the human mind. So be warned: when you skim that News Feed on Facebook or scroll through tweets, your subconscious mind is sucking up input that may be put to use—beyond your awareness—when it's crunch time and you need to make a decision or form an opinion. The best we can do is know about the anchoring effect, respect it, and question ourselves at every turn. Use your mental faculties to seek out accurate, unbiased, and relevant information whenever and wherever possible to be more sensible and safer.

## OTHERS ARE MORE EASILY FOOLED THAN I AM

Another significant challenge for social media users is coping with the *third person effect*. This effect is our natural tendency to overestimate the impact of information on others while underestimating its impact on ourselves; in other words, it gives us a false sense of superiority. It is important to be aware of this effect because it can make us feel overconfident about our analytical and reasoning skills and, as a result, be more vulnerable to bad information. Who among us hasn't sighed and shook her head at the sad mental foibles of "those people"? Who hasn't wondered how in the world "they" can be so stupid? "Those guys" fall for anything, but I don't. Once again, a good general education or high IQ can't be relied on to save you from yourself. This is one more human cognitive trap no one can afford to ignore or dismiss, especially while wading around in the diverse content found on social media.

As I am writing this, one of the day's trending topics on social media is the work of "Prophet" Lethebo Rabalago, a South African Christian minister. During services he sprays what he claims is insecticide, "Doom Super Multi Insect Killer" to be specific, in the face of his congregates to "heal them."[27] Several photos of one insecticide healing event are posted on his Facebook page. As one might expect, many people immediately condemned or mocked Rabalago on social media. Most of those making negative comments probably felt a powerful sense of intellectual superiority over Rabalago and his flock. *They're dumb and I'm smart*, would be the most basic likely thought. But how many of these condescending critics are themselves believers in outlandish claims and practices? Given the right timing and context, we all are capable of being nudged onto strange paths of delusion. Humility is in order, everywhere and always. It is easy to find the fool without but never so simple to spot the one within.

The advertising industry can teach us a lot about the third person effect. Most people assume that the radio, television, and Web ads that greet us at every turn and fill so much of our daily world have a negligible effect on us, or none at all. It's just visual and auditory clutter to be ignored. Sure, advertising works on some people; it must, or corporations wouldn't spend billions of dollars on it every year. But it doesn't work on you and me, right? We're too sharp for that. The reality, however, is that these ads can and do work on all of us, to one degree or another, as numerous studies have shown.[28] Mere exposure—as in the mere exposure effect addressed earlier in this chapter—to a product or brand can make us more likely to buy it in the future. So while we assume advertising seduces, hypnotizes, or tricks all of those other gullible suckers but leaves us unscathed, it turns out that these ads are having an unnoticed effect on us. We like to imagine that we scan ads as cold, calculating robots who are impervious to deceptive words and images. We glance at ads just to make sure there isn't some new product we need or want or to see if there might be a great price to be taken advantage of. In reality, however, we are not cold robots; we are warm emotional pushovers being softened up in a way that makes us more likely to buy later.

One interesting component of the third person effect that everyone should be aware of is that it has been shown to have an even greater impact when we are confronted with information we don't know or care much about.[29] For example, if you were to read an article or some Facebook post about a person, topic, or event about which you had thought little before, it would be natural for you to assume that this information would impact others a lot more than it does you. After all, you don't care, right? The third person effect can also be particularly potent when the source has or seems to have a negative bias.[30] I suspect that this stems from our natural attraction to gossip. We find stories about others, especially those with a negative slant, to be irresistible. And for good reason. We use gossip to transmit and remember important information, especially warnings. Lisa Feldman Barrett, a Northeastern University professor of psychology, describes gossip as nothing less than a "vital thread in human social interaction."[31] Gossiping is perhaps the most effective means of sharing information about those we cannot trust or are at least suspicious of. Our gossip fixation, I believe, is one of the key reasons why so many absurd conspiracy theory claims are able to infect the minds of millions.

The important thing is to understand and be aware that information assumed to be irrelevant in the moment can have a significant impact on you later, should that person or topic come up again in a more important context. "You," your conscious self, may not even remember those brief minutes, seconds, or fractions of seconds you spent on that article or post; but there is a good chance that your subconscious mind will remember and reference it toward "advising" you on how to think, act, or decide. In light of this, virtually everything one skims or reads has potential for later subconscious influence. Something to keep in mind.

**Real for them, real for me? The conformity conundrum.** Several years ago while working as newspaper reporter, I covered the performance of a marginally popular faith healer. She shared her personal and emotional story of dying, going to heaven, and being sent back to Earth by Jesus to heal the sick. The extraordinary tale didn't come with any evidence, of course, but was fascinating nonetheless. And the audience certainly loved it. I watched as their excitement grew with each emotional high point in the story. At one moment during the presentation, a woman in the audience held up her hands and then reacted as if she had been electrocuted. I was close enough to hear her say after recovering that the "Holy Ghost" had touched her. This electrocution-like behavior spread around the room. Within minutes, several people indicated that they had felt the warm shock of the Holy Ghost.

I can't say for sure if an invisible supernatural entity was or was not in the room with us that night. But I do know enough about normal, natural human psychology to conclude that I most likely witnessed the power of conformity. We are social creatures. We tend to synchronize not only our physical behavior with those around us but even our deepest thoughts and feelings as well. There is no escaping this fundamental aspect of human existence. It's just how we big-brained primates roll. Most of us understand and agree with the obvious truth that family, friends, crowds, and culture influence us, but few recognize just how powerful and persuasive "the group" can be to our thinking processes as individuals.

Given its impact, we don't spend enough time contemplating our place in the hive. Sure, we think about status, rank, belonging, and rejection, but not nearly enough about how relationships and social networks influence our reasoning and decision making. Our connection to so many other minds, whether up close or via social media, has a great impact on our thinking, our perceptions, and our lives. The herd-like nature of social media can be disturbing when viewed from the outside. When I step back and think about the Facebook universe, for example, I see many vast digitized subcultures with their own particular slants, moods, and flavors. One of the primary reasons filter bubbles are such a problem in social media is that we are herd animals, more cow than bear. Social psychologists have shown over and over how easy group membership can influence our thinking—much of it taking place behind the curtains of our awareness. No human should go anywhere near social media without a keen awareness of this.

It is unsettling how social influence can alter perceptions of reality within a person's mind. Please do not underestimate this. Do the work to maintain independent thinking. Be brave enough to doubt and honest enough to change your mind when necessary. Solomon Asch's classic 1951 experiment presented college students with the task of making simple perceptual judgments about the length of lines on a sheet of paper. Unknown to them, however, was the presence of hired actors among them posing as fellow test subjects. The test was simple enough: Identify the longer of two lines. No tricks or optical illusions. The correct answer was obvious, or should have been. But again and again the actors chose the wrong line, and a large percentage of test subjects went along and agreed with it.[32] This should disturb and scare all thoughtful people who value truth and reality. There was a bright spot in the experiment, however. When one actor was tapped to play the lone dissenter and choose the correct line, the ratio of test subjects who selected the wrong line fell. I take hope and inspiration from that. One sensible voice in a sea of madness can sometimes make a difference.

It is difficult to know whether people who chose the wrong line truly believed their answer due to misperception or were lying to conform. But does it matter? When we are surrounded out on the streets and inside social media by a crowd of people who can't or won't keep themselves grounded in even the simplest of realities, what does it do to our own private perceptions of reality? When we see and admire the emperor's fine clothes, how can we be sure that he's not actually nude and that we have been hoodwinked by the intimidating weight of majority opinion?

## FALLING DOWN BY LOOKING UP

Authority bias is the tendency we have to trust in and be influenced by someone perceived to be an authority figure. Its grip can be so tight on us that in some situations we will believe, do, or buy virtually anything. This psychological phenomenon is not a workplace problem exclusively. This is a life problem. It happens everywhere, all the time. It is the reason actors wear white lab coats while telling us how white our teeth can be on TV commercials. Authority bias is an amazing thing to behold. Just about anything becomes credible and can be believed if the person speaking about it has some attachment to the magic of authority. We constantly underestimate the sway this bias has on us, often at the cost of money, time, dignity, or safety.

Authority bias is a significant problem in social media because of the way we endorse and share news, comments, and images. The mere act of receiving a news report from a trusted, intelligent friend on Facebook can infuse that article with the pixie dust of authority. Add to that the additional challenge of seeing through the silent authority claim that comes with information presented in the form of a news article created and published by a person or a company that wants you to believe and accept its product.

The authority bias is a slippery challenge in current times because traditional authority is under attack in so many spheres. But regardless of whether you already hate big government, don't trust the police, or are in the process of rebelling against formal religion, you need to be on top of this problem because authority bias is unbound by social borders or traditions. It comes at you from every direction. For example, Alex Jones, host of the InfoWars podcast and website, is a tireless promoter of some of the most absurd conspiracy claims. But he is nothing less than a trusted authority figure to his fans who don't trust mainstream news sources and government authority figures. I've never been to an anarchist pre-protest planning meeting, but I wouldn't be surprised if it's typical for someone in the room to assume an authoritative role, just to get things going.

Closely related to the problem of placing excessive trust in authority is what I call the *bleed-over effect*. An impressive title, rank, or credentials in one thing doesn't necessarily make one an expert in other things. Don't let someone's expertise bleed over to other topics without justification. This is a big problem on social media, where I see many people citing and quoting people as definitive voices of authority on something, even though they carry no real weight on that topic. *An expert in one thing is not an expert in everything*. Vague titles aren't enough. One can get a PhD in virtually anything these days—and from the comfort of one's couch. A chiropractor may wear a white lab coat and be called "Doctor," but we can't assume that he or she went to an accredited medical school like doctors who work in hospitals do. A security guard may wear a law-enforcement-style uniform and carry impressive tactical gear, but it doesn't necessarily mean he knows the law. All of this may seem obvious to you now, but it's easy to be overconfident in the moment and let down your guard. We forget the danger at key moments because of our innate attraction to and weakness for authority. Your shadow brain is more impressionable than you are. Isaac Newton may well have been the greatest genius of all time. But not everything he claimed can be trusted. For example, he seemed certain that the Earth will end by supernatural means one day. Great as Newton was at mathematics and astrophysics, I don't place any trust in his doomsday projections, because—unlike his work in math and celestial mechanics—he offered no compelling evidence in support of them.

To be clear, I should add here that it is almost always wise to listen to and consider new ideas and claims from anyone, regardless of their expertise. You can make a fair hearing brief, of course, and you don't want to waste time or brainpower going over the same nonsense again and again. But don't reflexively shut out everything that comes at you just because it may lack impressive credentials. Just as experts are sometimes wrong, so to can non-experts be correct. Superior critical thinkers work to maintain open minds.

Giving due respect and attention to those who have earned it with hard work and an impressive track record is necessary for efficiency in seeking good information and coming to the best conclusions. But never should we assume that truth and reality can be accurately assessed by the credentials of the messenger alone. Even when the source of information we are considering is legitimate, with real and obvious authority or expertise, we still can't afford to sleepwalk or go on autopilot. If it is about something important to you—the fair price of a house, which college to apply to, the fate of the planet, and so on—then don't rely on a single expert opinion, no matter how impressive that expert is. Second opinions are important not only for serious medical procedures. They can be valuable in all aspects of life.

It may be deep within us to fixate on authority figures and believe what they say, but you don't have to be an obedient little space monkey and snap to attention every time someone wearing a uniform, lab coat, or funny hat tells you what to believe, do, or buy. Always consider the claim in isolation, if only for a moment, as if it fell from the sky or emerged from the soil, unattached to anyone or anything. Develop this unnatural but necessary habit of seeing through the masks, titles, and crowns. With deliberate effort, *listen* to a claim, order, pitch, or promise. In your mind, separate it from the source as a way to push back against authority bias. Ask yourself if it would make as much sense coming from a pauper as it would from a prince. If not, there may be a problem.

## WHEN FINDING OUT THAT YOU ARE WRONG MEANS KNOWING YOU ARE RIGHT

Have you ever wondered, in a fit of red-faced frustration, why some people, when they are wrong, can't seem to recognize obvious facts and change their minds accordingly? Of course you have. Even worse, some people seem to become *more* confident about their bad idea or incorrect conclusion, no matter how many facts or how much evidence you present to them. It's like throwing wood on a fire when you are trying to put out the fire. What is wrong these people? There are two things you need to know about this: (1) Nothing is wrong with "these people" other than the fact that they are people. (2) You are one of "these people."

There is a name for this problem. It is called the *backfire effect* and most people are not only unaware of it but also have no idea how vulnerable they are to this common failure of reasoning. Contradictory as it seems, seeing evidence of a new reality before us that contradicts what we already think does not necessarily clear up our thinking and make us wiser. In fact, it can often make us dumber than we were before we encountered the new knowledge. This natural inclination of the shadow brain will have you feeling more confident about a position you hold, even as you encounter accurate and overwhelming evidence that says you're wrong.

"Giving people factual information isn't as convincing as people often think," says Brendan Nyhan, a social scientist who researches the confounding backfire effect.[33] Having once worked for a fact-checking website, Nyhan saw firsthand how difficult it can be for people to change their minds in the face of compelling evidence that warrants it. Contrary to what you might assume, it is not unusual for us to do an about-face and move in the opposite direction of reason and evidence. In the upside-down world of your brain on the backfire effect, exposure to more knowledge can make you dumber. An encounter with new information that is real and true can push you farther away from truth and reality.

Why would we react to good evidence by maintaining our belief with even *greater* conviction than we had before discovering the new evidence? Most would agree that teaching, debunking, enlightening, and exposing truth sound like great concepts. But they can cause us to tighten our cognitive grip on a belief or idea that is important to us. The shadow brain does this as means of keeping us feeling stable and content. *Reality be damned, we're not letting go,* cries the subconscious brain. This bias raises disturbing thoughts for someone, like me, who for many years has worked hard trying to bring more light and reason to the world. Have my books about critical thinking and science caused some readers to double down on a nonsense belief? Thanks to the backfire effect, this is probably so.

The backfire effect helps to explain why so many online debates are a waste of time. How often does someone on Facebook or Twitter write: "Wow, the evidence and logic you shared has changed my mind. Thanks!" No, in almost every case, heated exchanges about politics, the existence of gods, or the morality of twerking result in nothing more than people on both sides digging in their heels and walking away feeling more confident and committed to their original belief than ever before. Being aware of the backfire effect will help you during engagements with people—friends and foes alike—on social media. Understand that failing to see the obvious is merely human. Much begins to make sense when we comprehend the power and influence of the backfire effect. Your frustration with others is likely to lessen as well. Where you once pulled your hair out and wondered if this person was insane or if that person was maliciously pretending to hold a nonsensical position just to irritate you, now you can accept that this is normal behavior, something to be expected. I have been called names and wrongly accused of bad things a few times on social media but was able to process it and react to it with what I feel is a high degree of maturity and wisdom, because I understand just how easy it is for anyone to become overconfident and feel excessive passion for a lost cause. Yes, brain awareness can make us kinder and more forgiving. Consider this a nontrivial fringe benefit.

An understanding of the backfire effect can also be great motivation to be more accepting of awkward evidence and inconvenient ideas. The simple act of remembering that your shadow brain is consistently trying to "protect" your positions and your feelings about them by infusing your conscious mind with unjustified confidence and a distorted perception of the sensibility of your beliefs can keep you on your cognitive toes.

"As social media and advertising progresses, confirmation bias and the backfire effect will become more and more difficult to overcome," warns David McRaney, author of *You Are Not so Smart*.[34] "You will have more opportunities to pick and choose the kind of information which gets into your head along with the kinds of outlets you trust to give you that information." He continues:

> Advertisers will continue to adapt, not only generating ads based on what they know about you, but creating advertising strategies on the fly based on what has and has not worked on you so far. The media of the future may be delivered based not only on your preferences, but on how you vote, where you grew up, your mood, the time of day or year—every element of you which can be quantified. In a world where everything comes to you on demand, your beliefs may never be challenged. As information technology progresses, the behaviors you are most likely to engage in when it comes to belief, dogma, politics and ideology seem to remain fixed.[35]

I have learned through experience over the years that it is not enough to explain to someone why it is not rational to believe in extraordinary claims that aren't backed up with a lot of very good evidence. Based on the best current arguments and evidence, for example, it makes no sense to assert that psychics, demons, alien abductions, Bigfoot, and the Loch Ness monster are real. These and other such claims could be true but probably are not, because to date no one has been able to show that they are true. But deconstructing weak arguments and pointing to the absence of evidence is not enough, not in light of the backfire effect. The best way to counter such staunch support, I think, is to explain a few relevant brain processes that might be helping to support the claim. Knowledge of how human vision and memory work go a long way, for example, toward explaining why many people believe that they have seen alien spaceships in the sky. It helps to let people know that supernatural or paranormal claims are not the only riddles to be solved.

In fact, they are the easiest of all. People are better off, and wiser, when they recognize that the human brain presents the first hurdle and greatest obstacle toward reaching reasoned and intellectually sound destinations.

## CAN WE INOCULATE OURSELVES AGAINST BOGUS CLAIMS?

Dartmouth College associate professor Joshua Compton specializes in *inoculation theory*, a process that allows us to strengthen ourselves against being persuaded to believe in nonsense and accept bad ideas by exposure to limited or weak versions of them beforehand. "Inoculation theory as it applies to persuasion and influence is based on a process that's actually pretty familiar to most people—medical inoculation," Compton told me.[36] "In a typical medical inoculation, we get exposed to a weak version of a threat, like a flu virus, to prepare our body to fight off stronger versions that we might encounter later. And that's how persuasion inoculation works, too. When we get exposed to a weak version of a threat, like a persuasive argument, we get prepared to fight off stronger versions that we might encounter later."

Compton says that fifty-plus years of research shows that it works. Pre-exposure to weakened counterarguments, an intellectual vaccination, really does give us greater resistance to stronger counterarguments later: "One of the biggest takeaways from inoculation scholarship is that, in terms of resistance, it's usually better to confront counterarguments head on than it is to try to avoid them."

Compton thinks inoculation theory might prove useful in mitigating problems associated with filter bubbles and fake news. "Inoculation theory would suggest that exposure that is limited to just one side of an issue can result in what some attitude researchers have called a paper tiger effect—a position that looks really strong, but only looks strong because it's never been strongly challenged. These beliefs can crumple under the pressure of persuasive arguments. Inoculation, on the other hand, shores up these positions—challenges and bolsters them prior to exposure to stronger persuasive arguments encountered later."

"Inoculation theory suggests that attitudes and beliefs must be robust to fend off persuasive attacks on them—and that one way to make an attitude or belief more robust is to challenge it with weaker attacks before exposure to stronger ones," Compton continued. "Inoculation theory would seemingly work, then, on fake news about specific issues, like climate change, or perhaps even the very genre of fake news itself. The key is to not be taken by surprise by the threat, so that means being exposed to different opinions and beliefs, and study and analysis of these different opinions and beliefs, before exposure to persuasive attacks."

But wait, can a person be inoculated against good ideas? Unfortunately, inoculation theory is not a perfect fix—because it can work both ways.

"Inoculation doesn't guarantee a rational, informed response to persuasion, of course. The same process than can make a healthy position more robust could make an unhealthy position more robust, too. Some of the evidence does strongly suggest that inoculation elicits more thinking about an issue—and we hope that this thinking is informed by reason and fact, but that's not necessarily so. The one finding that probably gives me the most hope that inoculation leads to better thinking is that inoculation seems to motivate people—and equip them—to talk about the issue with others, in more conversations, with more conversational partners. If this boost to dialogue is leading to exposure to more perspectives, then that seems quite healthy to me. The strong effects of such inoculation—resistance effects, persuasion effects, increased talk about the issue, a boost to involvement and participatory behaviors—and the resilience of these effects—[can last] for weeks, if not months, if not years. . . . That keeps me hard at work on better understanding not just processes of resistance to influence, but also, the roles of facts and evidence and logic and truth in resistance to influence. Informed resistance seems the better goal than resistance."

## IT IS RATIONAL TO FEAR IRRATIONAL FEAR

Imagine a terrorist, some ski-mask-wearing, faith-fueled zealot with an AK-47, running toward you on a sidewalk. Now look back over your shoulder. That's not an approaching freight train, it's a tornado heading your way. See with your mind a ten-foot shark slicing effortlessly around you as you tread water far from the beach. Its dark-gray dorsal and top tail fin just break the surface. Finally, pull up a scene in your head of an intruder in your house, late at night, who has come to murder you. Scary stuff, right? Now imagine a severely depressed person sitting alone in a room, an automobile, and a pack of cigarettes on a table. These three images are not nearly as scary as the first few. But why is this the case? Look at the data in the box below and ask yourself why it is that we allow ourselves to become so easily terrified by some things more than others, even when the numbers don't support our fears.

## FEAR VS. DANGER

| US Deaths over a Ten-Year Period (1995–2005)[37] | | | | |
|---|---|---|---|---|
| **Terrorism** | 3,200 deaths | vs. | **Suicide** | 300,000 deaths |
| **Natural Disasters** | 7,000 deaths | vs. | **Automobile Accidents** | 450,000 deaths |
| **Murder** | 180,000 deaths | vs. | **Smoking** | 1,000,000,000 deaths |

The reason fear does not always align well with reality is that fear is a deep, fast emotion. When there is an immediate, grave danger, the luxuries of time and deep intellectual reflection are not practical. If the boulder is falling above your head, you need to jump out of the way now, not after you think about the size and weight of the boulder and what kind of damage it might do to your cranium. Terrorism terrifies us more than car crashes, despite the numbers, because our brains have evolved to panic over the threat of another life-form intentionally killing us. That intense fear of predators made sense for most of human and pre-human existence. Automobiles and cigarettes may kill more people, but it's not personal and they have not been around long enough to spark any similar primal horror within us. Intense fear surges up from a place in the brain that lies far below higher reasoning.

Fear is the necessary monster that lives in the darkest part of our shadow brain. Though it makes us uncomfortable and often causes us to worry needlessly and make bad decisions, we need our capacity for fast and thoughtless fear.

Without instinctual, emotional fear, we all would spend short lives walking across busy highways, throwing knives at each other for sport, and picking fights with UFC champions—and humankind would not last long. Fear ovolved to help keep us alive. Yesterday's primates who lacked sufficient fear no doubt were culled by predators, generation after generation. Their genes, for the most part, have been lost to the distant past. It is to this process that we owe our modern anxiety-riddled, and fearful minds. Unfortunately, fear is not always useful. Because it must be automatic and fast in order to work for us when it counts, fear is often inappropriate, misguided, and just plain unnecessary. Many of the natural fear-related instincts that were developed so long ago can sometimes be distracting and even destructive today. "Our evolutionary baggage encourages us to fear certain things because they comprised a reasonable assessment of what was harmful to our ancestors millions of years ago," explains UCLA neuroscientist Dean Buonomano. "But how appropriate are the prehistoric whispers of our genes in the modern world? Not very."[38]

Toward overall good thinking in the social media universe it is necessary for you to strive for a somewhat realistic connection between the degree of fear felt and the actual danger level of the stimulus causing it. To do this, two things must happen. First, you must recognize when your fear button is being pushed by digital input. If an image, post, or news article alarms you, angers you, or makes you feel intensely uneasy, acknowledge what your deeper brain is experiencing and the message it is sending you. The second step is to do the work of trying to figure out whether or not this fear is based on a credible threat. Take this seriously. Those who do not are soft clay in the hands of all who would use fear to manipulate. I'm a believer in fearing fear. Given how often it is used by governments, demagogues, corporations, religious leaders, and so on to influence or control people, it is rational to have a healthy respect for fear. The solution to our irrational fears is not bravery; it is good thinking. We can diffuse irrational fear to feel better and become more sensible by watching out for it, recognizing it, analyzing it, and, when appropriate, rejecting it. We can and should become better at distinguishing credible reasons to be afraid from all of the irrational and bogus stimuli that scare us. The latter, by the way, is often in the service of someone else's selfish agenda.

Bo Bennett, author, educator, and strong advocate for critical thinking, points to the availability heuristic as a key culprit behind many of our fear-based judgment errors. "The availability heuristic is the tendency to overestimate the likelihood of events with greater 'availability' in memory," he said, "which can be influenced by how recent the memories are or how unusual or emotionally charged they may be."[39] He continues:

> Most people who are terrified of being killed by terrorists don't lose a moment of sleep about being killed by lightning, even though they are many times more likely to die from being struck by lightning. Why? Because terrorist attacks are emotionally charged events that, as wrong as it sounds, have high entertainment value. When they occur, these events dominate the media for days, and sometimes months, like in the case of the 9/11 attacks. Based on this level of exposure, our emotions overpower our reasoning, and what is factually a statistical impossibility becomes a perceived "strong possibility." This bias affects our views on other issues such as white cops killing unarmed black men (if you consume more liberal media), or acts of heroism by cops (if you consume mostly conservative media). Besides making sure you get your information from an array of credible sources, realize that *all* media report on information that is interesting or entertaining, which skews our perception of the world.

**The anatomy of fear.** Two small but influential bundles of neurons are positioned about four inches directly behind each of your eyeballs. The amygdalae are ground zero for your deepest fears. Because of the significant impact the amygdalae often have on our conscious thinking, everyone should know something about what they are and how they work. About the same size and shape as an almond, an amygdala is panic central, a fear factory, our primal repository of terror. The amygdalae work by receiving input from the senses and making lightning-fast reactions, when deemed appropriate, to put you into a state of fear.

The amygdalae are relevant to social media use because your modern brain doesn't know that it is a modern brain. It never got the memo about the last several thousand years having happened. Civilization, urbanization, and computerization just kind of happened all of the sudden and your brain hasn't caught up yet. Vast portions of our twenty-first-century brains continue to function as if we were still in the prehistoric world—especially those amygdalae. This is the reason we so often react and think in such bizarre and irrational ways when afraid. Our decision-making abilities are compromised when under the influence of fear. Subconsciously, you may respond to a scary tweet about the general threat of terrorism in a way that is similar to how a *Homo erectus* individual a million years ago might respond if she caught a glimpse of a four-hundred-pound crouching predator cat half hidden in the bushes fifty feet away. But these two very different scenarios do not warrant the same automatic reaction. The *Homo erectus* would likely be helped by an instant fight-or-flight response to being in the presence of a threatening predator. Without time-consuming conscious thought, her heartrate rises in preparation of physical effort (such as running or fighting), metabolism cranks up to high-speed, muscles tighten, and pupils widen to maximize vision. This is all good, because being ready for action could be the difference between life and death for her. But a tweet about terrorism in the twenty-first-century is a much different scenario.

A general comment about terrorists killing random people may be cause for concern, but the physical impact and mental distractions of the flight-or-flight response are unnecessary. They are worse than unnecessary because the fear response degrades, corrupts, and smothers good thinking. Rational decision making becomes significantly more difficult, sometimes impossible, when your heart is racing, hands are trembling, and amygdalae scream "red alert!" No actual living terrorist is fifty feet away. The tweet cannot kill you. Adrenaline and widened pupils won't help you assess the information's credibility and relevance to you. Potentially important information comes at us constantly in daily life and as much of it as possible needs to be analyzed, considered, and processed by the prefrontal cortex, the very part of the brain that intense fear relegates to the sidelines. We don't want to miss warnings about real and immediate dangers, nor do we want to waste time and energy reacting to bogus or distant threats. When any kind of *information* scares us, the best reaction is to remember that words are not a crouching lion with sharp claws and dagger-like teeth. We do not need to run from or physically fight words. The better option is to calm down and defend ourselves with the human brain's higher reasoning abilities.

---

### TEN GOOD BOOKS FOR GOOD THINKING

- *The Demon-Haunted World: Science as a Candle in the Dark*, by Carl Sagan (New York: Random House, 1995).
- *Brain Bugs: How the Brain's Flaws Shape Our Lives*, by Dean Buonomano (New York: W. W. Norton, 2011).
- *How to Think about Weird Things: Critical Thinking for a New Age*, 6th ed., by Theodore Schick and Lewis Vaughn (New York: McGraw-Hill, 2010).
- *Brain Rules: 12 Principles for Surviving and Thriving at Work, Home, and School*, by John Medina (Seattle: Pear, 2014).
- *Brain: The Story of You*, by David Eagleman (New York: Pantheon, 2015).
- *Caveman Logic: The Persistence of Primitive Thinking in a Modern World*, by Hank Davis (Amherst, NY: Prometheus Books, 2009).
- *Pseudoscience and Extraordinary Claims of the Paranormal: A Critical Thinker's Toolkit*, by Jonathan C. Smith (Hoboken, NJ: Wiley-Blackwell, 2009).
- *The Believing Brain: From Ghosts and Gods to Politics and Conspiracies—How We Construct Beliefs and Reinforce Them as Truths*, by Michael Shermer (New York: Times Books, 2011).
- *Thinking Fast and Thinking Slow*, by Daniel Kahneman (New York: Farrar, Straus, and Giroux, 2013).
- *You Are Now Less Dumb: How to Conquer Mob Mentality, How to Buy Happiness, and All the Other Ways to Outsmart Yourself*, by David McRaney (New York: Gotham, 2013).

When a politician stokes fires of panic deep in our brains with exaggerated talk of war or financial ruin, many people pay attention. They worry and if they react with any kind of action it is often an ill-conceived and irrational response, because human brains are less analytical and contemplative when fear takes over. This is why it is so important that we consciously monitor our fear and tame or reconsider how we react to it.

Crime, unemployment, economic and moral collapse, terrorism, and various supernatural doomsdays have all been standard fodder for speeches and soundbites by many political candidates. "If a politician can unnerve the electorate, he or she can obscure the facts," warns Timothy J. Redmond, an adjunct professor at Daemen College. "And if a politician can obscure the facts he or she may be able to mobilize the public to support policies that the latter will come to regret. For as the English poet Samuel Taylor Coleridge noted, 'In politics, what begins in fear usually ends up in folly.'"[40] Don't fall prey to every scary post or news article that comes your way on social media. Quiet the siren and think. It is not impossible nor even all that difficult for you to step back from the fearmongering, recognize it for what it is, consult with reality in the form of reliable new and credible statistics, and tame the instinctual fear response within that finds such exaggerated warnings so believable and disturbing.

## HOW TO THINK LIKE A SCIENTIST

It is a common misconception that science is something reserved for scientists and is therefore off-limits or somehow beyond the reach of mere civilians. Nonsense. Science is a tool, a human invention available to all of us to use down in the trenches of our daily lives. Each of us—regardless of education, income, nationality, subculture, or age—can and should apply the scientific method often. Everyone stands to benefit by maintaining the intellectual stance of a good scientist. Remember that science is by far the best way we have to explore, discover, learn, and confirm the accuracy of claims. Why not use it for yourself?

What follows here is a simple, no frills guide for doing science in the real world. This is the scientific method stripped down, simplified, and humanized for everyday use by anyone. Become familiar with it and apply some or all of it often so that you may better identify and step clear of mistakes, frauds, and all of those crazy claims that stalk us in daily life. Fortunately, it works as well online as off-line, so keep it in mind while surfing the Web and engaging with all of those friends, followers, trolls, and bots who might lead you astray on social media. Science works, so why not use it?

**I. React like a scientist.** The most crucial step is the first step. When your travels throughout the social media drop something important or strange in your lap, it is crucial that you pause and think before making any decisive intellectual moves. Avoid granting immediate and total acceptance to anything that matters. Hold back, at least for a moment. Good scientists do not accept any big claims at first contact, and neither should you. They wait, they doubt, they consider, they check, they withhold judgment. And, even if everything checks out, they only accept the claim/idea to a degree. Everything is provisional in science; every conclusion is held on a tentative basis, no matter how overwhelming the current evidence may be. Revision is always welcome, no matter if it is unexpected, uncomfortable, or even embarrassing. The goal of science—and good thinking—is always to get to what is real and true, whatever that may turn out to be.

*Adopting a scientific stance will serve you well on social media.*

**II. Do your research.** Given the right context, a bad idea can take on the look and feel of legitimacy, at least at first glance. Even when we judge a source to be sensible, sober, honest, and reliable, we still cannot immediately accept unusual claims, not before doing some minimal research. Check everything that is weird, important, or new before believing it. The hard truth is that human beings cannot be trusted unconditionally when it comes to sharing information. People lie; people become confused; and even the most sensible and honest among us often get facts wrong. Therefore, we must check to see if the claim holds up to scrutiny.

Researching a social media post, image, or news share is usually an easy process. Most bad ideas and false claims wither and die when exposed to even a tiny bit of light. The only reason so many ridiculous lies and painful mistakes are able to rage through social media like wildfires is because sufficient numbers of people are intellectually lazy and pass them on unopposed.

---

### DOUBT IS GOOD

Doubt everything, more so initially and less later should the claim earn it, but keep doubting to an appropriate degree. Think of doubting things as essential bricks that construct a wall around you, one capable of holding back all of those barbarians at the gate. It is doubt that prevents us from embracing every bad idea and harmful lie that comes along.

Embracing doubt is not negative. Being skeptical doesn't mean closing your mind or being cynical. Applied properly, doubt is profoundly positive, the best protection we have against deception and delusion. Listening to and considering new and extraordinary ideas is generally a good idea. It does not become a problem so long as you always give a fair hearing to the skeptical voice within. Doubt is a pillar of wisdom. It lies at the core of good thinking and is essential to maneuvering through social media as the most rational, truth-seeking, reality-based person you can be.

---

One of the first things scientists do when confronted with a new idea is to explore what other sources are saying about it. Why make mistakes that others have already made? Why waste time and energy traveling down dead-end roads when others can tell you what's ahead? Do an online search to find out more information about the claim or news story. Do not, however, simply search the name of the claim or general topic. Doing this may present you with nothing more than sites and articles that stand to gain something from the claim in question. Once again, remember that Google is not your personal infallible, all-knowing god. It's a search engine. So make sure to do searches with keywords such as "investigation," "skeptic," "hoax," "fraud," "controversy," and "scam" along with your topic name. It's possible, of course, that this could just as easily leave you with a list of negative sources that also are not credible. Everybody and everything has haters. When you find information both for and against the claim, then the next step is to consider the sources. What kind of sites and people are confirming the topic under consideration, and what kind of sites and people are condemning it? Not always, but often a clear pattern emerges. If two podcasters and a supplement company are pushing some new miracle brain pills but *Consumer Reports*, the Food and Drug Administration, as well as *Skeptic* and *Skeptical Inquirer* magazines have declared it to be a scam or at best an unverified claim, then it should be obvious which way to lean.

After checking for mainstream news articles by reputable journalism sources, do a specific search for articles that have been published in reputable, peer-reviewed science journals. What are scientists saying about the claim? Does is it seem as if the scientific community is convinced that there is something to it? If not, ask yourself why not. Even the best scientists are not perfect; science is not free from corruption; and the absence of a consensus does not necessarily disprove anything. But understand that scientists make their living by dealing in reality, figuring out what works and what doesn't. Careers advance by blazing new knowledge trails using the light of evidence to guide them. It's a clear warning sign when scientists have not confirmed something despite it having been around for a while. But what if the claim or idea is so new that no scientist has had an opportunity to study it yet? This too is a reason to be wary.

In the case of little or no scientific research having been published, the claim may still be true, but a wait-and-see approach is probably the best course of action. Rarely do you have to accept or reject an extraordinary claim immediately. It is okay to defer a conclusion, to wait for more data. "I don't know at this time" is a perfectly reasonable position to take when warranted. It's often the only honest and sensible position when confronted with new ideas.

Finally, ask around. Revert to old-school tactics and communicate directly with other people. Isn't this just what social media is supposed to be for? Connect and communicate; ask questions about a claim before you believe it. Of course, this is not completely reliable either, because those you ask could be clueless or deluded about the particular claim or news item. But it's worth trying.

*Scientists rely on the work of other scientists to help them save time, work efficiently, and avoid stumbles. Always research a claim before believing it. Do smart searches and reach out to others to see if they know something about it that you don't.*

**III. Come up with your own hypothesis or theory.** Try to explain how a claim might be true or false. Speculate. Imagine. Could that blurry Bigfoot photo your friend just posted to Instagram be his wife in a cheap Halloween costume? Think of possible alternate explanations for the weird claim you just read on Twitter. Maybe the person who tweeted it is sincere but gullible, smart but drunk, or a liar—or maybe he just made an honest error in judgement.

When confronted with an outrageous or weird news article, think it through and consider alternate explanations. Yes, maybe the Loch Ness monster really was hooked and boated in Scotland yesterday. But consider this hypothesis: Maybe this is the product of a snickering, teenaged carnival barker somewhere in Moldova fishing for clicks by any means necessary in order to get paid.

*Imagine possible explanations for an idea or claim, then narrow them down to determine which of them is more likely to be true. This mental exercise can help you analyze and deepen your view of the topic, while also better positioning you to reach a well-reasoned conclusion later.*

**IV. Conduct your own experiment or test.** Some people love to talk all day about how confident they are in the validity of ghosts, psychic readings, and other such claims. Believe me, I know. I'm the guy who so often politely listens to the stories and takes notes. But, at the end of the day, talk is just talk. *Prove it*, says the good scientist. The good thinker asks: *How do you know?* Sometimes the best way to get to the truth is by running an experiment or two. Test the claim and respect the results. In sort, *do science*. Experiments don't just happen in laboratories, of course. Many people already conduct experiments all of the time without thinking much about it. They just need to be more thoughtful and methodical about it. When a typical person is looking to buy a car, for example, it's customary to take it out for a test drive. That can loosely be considered an experiment.

It's not always easy. Figuring out how to test a claim can be difficult, but it is doable more often than not. It is important to keep in mind that most claims we encounter in daily life are positive, meaning they declare that something exists, is true, or works in a certain way. Your challenge is not as hard as you might think, because you don't have to disprove the claim. You just want to see if an experiment can verify the claim as true. If the experiment fails, the claim might still be true but you now have a reason to be more skeptical. For example, if one of my Twitter followers declares that there is a real goddess who "grants wishes to anyone who sincerely asks for good things," then I can easily test this claim. If I'm tempted to believe the claim, then it's especially crucial that I conduct an experiment. Accepting it as true without any confirmation would mean I'm just another goofball willing to believe anything. To test this claim, I might recruit some people to help me and instruct them to close their eyes and make a wish to this goddess for an immediate end to global child hunger and malnutrition. If that doesn't happen, then I would have a stronger reason to remain skeptical of the claim and deny it entry into my own personal pantheon of beliefs. However, I still wouldn't go so far as to declare that I have absolute knowledge of the goddess's nonexistence or impotence when it comes to granting wishes. Who knows? Maybe this particular goddess is real and maybe she really does grant wishes but she was busy that day, or maybe my volunteers didn't project their wishes correctly. I'll keep an open mind, but I won't believe in her, in part because the experiment failed.

Don't forget about the second step in this process: Do the research. Find out as much as you can about what has already been done. The claim you are curious about or tempted to believe in may have already been tested by someone somewhere. Search around. *Skeptical Inquirer* and *Skeptic* have excellent, searchable online archives. Survey the work of longtime skeptics James Randi, Ben Radford, Joe Nickell, and others, to see if they have already tackled the claim. If it's a news item, check with Snopes.com and also see what older, respected news media companies are reporting.

If you find relevant studies or experiments published in journals or elsewhere, a key point to consider is sample size. In general, experiments that involve testing something with people benefit from larger sample sizes. A tiny pool of test subjects makes it easier for results to become skewed and lead to false conclusions. One or two outliers can throw the small data set out of whack. For example, a therapeutic touch study with a sample size of four would be suspect based on small sample size alone. Finally, check to see if the experiment was double-blind and placebo-controlled. This is the gold standard for experiments because it reduces the chance of unintentional bias by the researchers.

One experiment is not the final word. Experiments are meant to repeated. Many things can go wrong. If possible, do it again and again. Have someone else conduct your test and see if the results are the same. Of course, you should consider the cost of time, energy, and resources when considering a claim and determine whether it's worth the trouble. If someone claims to have invented a new exercise that will render me immortal, I'll probably not be willing to invest much time thinking about it because it's so very unlikely to be true. However, if someone tells me that they developed a new pullup technique guaranteed to add five reps to my personal best, I might want to check that out.

*Do science. Test unusual claims by conducting experiments when possible. Find out if others have already tested or investigated the topic.*

**V. Share your conclusion.** After pausing, doubting, hypothesizing, analyzing, researching, and testing a claim, it's time to make your decision about accepting or rejecting it. Remember that rejection in the scientific and good-thinking sense does not mean you necessarily have disproved or even denied that the claim is true, only that you are unconvinced at this time.

Once you decide to accept or reject the claim, you still aren't finished. Now it's time to ask other people to look for errors in your reasoning. Share your conclusion with the smartest, most sensible people you know. Let others consider, challenge, and pick apart your conclusion or decision. This is the street version of the tried-and-tested publication and peer-review process that helps make science so productive. Scientists put their work out in the light where other scientists can review it, tear it apart if possible, and repeat experiments toward confirming the result or exposing its flaws. When a scientist searches for errors in the work of another scientist, she or he is not engaging in devious backstabbing. It's just science.

When it comes to your important beliefs, conclusions, and ideas, the more good thinkers you can recruit to double-check your thinking, the better.

Finally, it is vital that you consider whatever input you receive from others and be willing to change your mind if necessary. If someone points out a mistake or a flaw in your reasoning, don't be too irritated or offended. Be grateful that you have been given the chance to move a little closer to truth and reality.

*No mind is an island. Sharing a conclusion with smart, sensible people is crucial because none of us is perfect. Asking others for input is not only necessary but also relatively easy to do these days, thanks to social media. Let those online networks work for you. Use them to strengthen your good thinking.*

## WISDOM, HUMILITY, AND THE EVER-PRESENT BLIND SPOT BIAS

I hope you have ignored that voice you heard in your mind from time to time throughout this chapter. That was your subconscious trying to make you feel secure and comfortable by convincing you that you're much too smart to fall for any of this stuff. That voice is the final cognitive bias we will consider here. This is the one that helps all of the others work so well against us. The *blind spot bias* reassures us by making us believe that we are rational and logical, that it's other people who are too emotional, too gullible, and just not sharp enough when it counts. Don't believe these lies. Be humble and stay grounded when the blind spot bias shows up. Be aware that we all tend to underestimate our vulnerability to cognitive biases. Research shows that it is natural for us to believe that we are better than most when it comes to critical thinking.[41] But this reflexive and unjustified confidence only puts us at even greater risk because it encourages a further lowering of defenses—which, in most cases, are far too weak already. Be diligent. Maintain awareness and admit to your many standard human vulnerabilities. Strive to keep them under control, but know that you never will. No one can tame all of them all of the time. It's impossible, because these automatic mental processes are an intimate part of who we are. But in trying, by working to be more rational and walk a path closer to reality, we open ourselves to living richer, more honest lives.

There is a chance that the avalanche of deception, delusion and confusion wrought by the Internet and social media today will turn out to be good for humanity in the long run. At some point, it may just be too much. Enough people will be victimized enough times, and frustrations will rise until critical mass is achieved. No one will be able to deny the need for good thinking if the world is drowning in lies. In the meantime, with so much nonsense and propaganda flying at us from every direction every moment, we face the choice now to either lie down as constant fools and hapless victims, or to wake up, stand up, and think critically. Filter bubbles, fake news, deceptive advertising, and so on present difficult challenges; but you and I can take them on and win more battles than we lose. A sharp mind, wielded by a committed and consistent good thinker, can dodge or destroy almost any bad idea.

*Chapter Five*

## THE QUEST FOR PRIVACY, SECURITY, AND THE PERFECT PASSWORD

**Surveillance is a central feature of modernity.**
—David Lyon, electronic surveillance expert[1]

**Perhaps you have broken no laws. You live what you think is an average and quiet life, and you feel you are unnoticed among the crowds of others online today. Trust me: even you are not invisible.**
—Kevin Mitnick, hacker turned cybersecurity consultant[2]

**Americans have a rich history of expressing outrage over privacy violations, before trading it all away for greater convenience.**
—*PC Mag*[3]

**Nothing that touches the Internet is secure.**
—Chris Swecker, former assistant director of the FBI[4]

**Privacy is the line we continually negotiate for ourselves as unique creatures of God and as social animals.**
—Gen. Michael Hayden, former director of the National Security Agency and CIA[5]

The dream led him deeper into a strange place, somewhere he had never been. The thick, damp forest glowed an almost-artificial neon green, nearly too bright for his eyes to take in. For two days and nights, the man walked among towering trees and endless blankets of ferns. Unsure of where he was going or why, the man knew only that he must keep moving. One morning, without warning, the journey ended. He emerged from the forest to find himself within sight of a vast city. He ran toward it without hesitation, across a flat field of grass.

Once in the city, the man walked its winding streets. He took in the sights, sounds, and smells of the busy megalopolis. *So many people*, he thought, *so much activity*. At every turn he encountered more beautiful, ugly, or fascinating faces to study. All of them were strangers. He wondered who each person was, what the unique stories of their lives might be. After walking for a while, the man stopped and stood in place. He marveled at the nonstop spectacle of humanity flowing around him and suddenly realized something profound. No one knew him here. No one called him by name or even glanced at him in recognition. It was as if he wasn't even there. The man began walking again. He moved freely through the currents of people and marveled at the strange sensation of invisibility.

To be unnoticed and unknown, he realized, was a kind of power, one he had never known. The man smiled. He realized in that moment that he could choose to be loud, kind, quiet, wise, or silly—anything he wanted. He felt lighter, unbound by personal history or external expectations. He was at once nothing and everything. He could reinvent himself a thousand times, if he chose to, become someone new on each street corner, if he desired. Today he was energetic and ambitious; but if he wanted to be lazy tomorrow, so be it, he could! No one would judge, because no one knew him. People were all around, eyes everywhere. But none watched. There was no past, no record to hold him down or push him this way or that way. For the first time, the man did not feel as if he were a character in a play. He was truly himself, whatever that would be. He was free.

And then he woke up.

## CAN PRIVACY SURVIVE?

**People will accept ideas presented in technological form that would be abhorrent in any other form.**
—Jared Lanier, *You Are Not a Gadget*[6]

Is privacy doomed to become in the future nothing more than a fantasy or sleepy dream as distant from reality as dragons and unicorns? Privacy never was a standard, inevitable feature of human

life. For most of our existence, we have been in close, intimate settings together. Secrets could not have been easy to keep in prehistoric hunter-gatherer societies. No doubt the villages and small
towns of our past were not very conducive to high levels of privacy
either. Even the cities that came later were mostly mash-ups of
many neighborhoods in which everyone knew everyone. By the late
twentieth century, however, a new perception of personal privacy
had become the expected norm for most people, at least among those
with the economic means to secure it. Privacy became common and
cherished by so many that it is probably difficult for many to accept
what has happened in the early twenty-first century.

Science fiction authors such as George Orwell in his classic book
*1984*, may have anticipated mass surveillance and the dissolving
of privacy among individuals, but few others did. The Internet has
provided the means for self-serving interests to monitor and learn
almost everything about us. In democratic societies today, we see
stunning levels of surveillance of citizens by governments and businesses. Social media may well turn out to be the next best way for
governments to control their citizens. China seems well along this
path now.[7] Even the worst, most notorious totalitarian regimes of
the past could not have dreamed of approaching the current situation. And it's not all being done by illegal or completely unethical
means. Hundreds of millions of people voluntarily give away many
of the details of their private lives to social media platforms, apps,
and websites. Moreover, this large-scale, unprecedented, high-tech
takeover and handover of personal privacy is only going to become
more pervasive in the near future as Internet-based tech reaches
deeper into our lives. Soon the "Internet of things" will be in full
bloom and everything from your vacuum cleaner to your toaster will
be online and potentially spying on you.[8]

Right now there are companies known as data brokers that
own vast amounts of personal information—the life details—of millions of people. Such data are worth incredible sums of money to
businesses, for marketing purposes. The digital reflection of your
life is a commodity, owned and controlled by companies. Once they
have it, they can legally do pretty much whatever they want with it
without your awareness and consent. Much of this activity results
in nothing more than harmless personalized advertising coming at
us. But that's not the entire picture, and there are many reasons

to be concerned, as this chapter will address. Further complicating matters, like everyone else, these companies are vulnerable to hacking by cybercriminals. "The problem with our being the product as opposed to the customer of massive data brokers is that we are not in control of our data and thus not in control of our destiny," warns Marc Goodman, a law enforcement technology expert and former FBI futurist-in-residence.[9] "The continued aggregation of this information, unregulated and insecure, sits as a ticking time bomb, with our every thought and deed available for the picking by a new and emerging class of bad actors whose intents are far worse than selling us discounted diapers and adjusting our insurance rates."

## HERE COMES THE LIGHT

We may soon reach a point when corporate and government entities have access to every relevant aspect of your life. In astonishing detail, they will know where you go; whom you spend time with; what you do at work and in your leisure time; what you eat, drink, watch, read, and listen to; how much money you earn, save, and spend; what you buy; your sexual activities and fantasies; every photo you take; every text, e-mail, comment, post, and image that you send and receive; how fit you are; and your health status. People you have never met or heard of will know you better than you know yourself. Amazing, perhaps irresistible, benefits and conveniences will flow from all of this, of course, but there will be a price. There will be a corresponding loss of privacy and, quite possibly, freedom. Control is much easier when those in power know every thought and can anticipate every new idea or behavior of those they oversee.

"In the heyday of European imperialism, conquistadores and merchants bought entire islands and countries in exchange for colored beads," writes historian Yuval Noah Harari.[10] "In the 21st century our personal data is probably the most valuable resource most humans still have to offer, and we are giving it to the tech giants in exchange for e-mail services and funny cat videos." An employee at a local coffee shop recommended I get their app so that I could take advantage of discounts and occasional free drinks. It sounded like a good idea, so I grabbed my phone, accessed the app online, and was about to download it, but I decided to take the unusual step of actually reading the terms of service agreement first. I discovered that before I could activate this "free" app, I had to allow it access to my photos, e-mail accounts and contact lists, text messages, and more. All that for an occasional free cup of tea? No thanks.

We are both victims and architects of a rapidly changing culture. Privacy is not what it once was. Social media users are being taken advantage of, even as they act as accomplices. By their actions, if not words or preferences, millions of people are not just going along with the wholesale dismantling of personal privacy but actively making it possible and contributing to it. Facebook and the rest don't have to steal our private lives—because we give them away for free. Clearly privacy is fading fast. But will we miss it when it's gone? "Who could deny that privacy is a jewel?" wrote the late poet Phyliss McGinley.[11] "It has always been the mark of privilege, the distinguishing feature of a truly urbane culture. Out of the cave, the tribal teepee, the pueblo, the community fortress, man emerged to build himself a house of his own with a shelter in it for himself and his diversions. Every age has seen it so. The poor might have to huddle together in cities for need's sake, and the frontiersman cling to his neighbors for the sake of protection. But in each civilization, as it advanced, those who could afford it chose the luxury of a withdrawing-place."

Will the next generation look back at personal privacy and think of it as a unique relic of the past, similar to how we view silent movies or the Acheulean hand ax today? Will they struggle to imagine twentieth-century people and the cultures that allowed them to so often experience relative invisibility and anonymity? Will some of them yearn for that lost age, a time without constant surveillance generating endless unseen judgments and manipulations? Will anyone comprehend what it was like to live without digital shadows, the personal-data files that now increasingly follow us through life? How will future generations understand a life free from cyber ghosts, no past mistakes and failures haunting them until death? A world without the mass harvesting of personal data, a time before algorithms defined and judged individuals, influenced perceptions, and determined opportunities will perhaps seem fantastical. Then again, maybe tomorrow is already here. Maybe we are that "future generation," living in a post-privacy world right now; only, most of us haven't realized it yet.

Electronic surveillance expert David Lyon recognized as far back as 1994 that privacy issues were going to surge and gain momentum:

"Surveillance should be a concern of both social analysis and political action because it has become a central feature of contemporary advanced societies."[12] Former US Supreme Court Chief Justice Earl Warren wrote the following even earlier, in 1963: "The fantastic advances in the field of electronic communication constitute a great danger to the privacy of the individual."[13] The concerns, fears, and even outrage heard over the loss of privacy in recent years should not be dismissed as mere paranoia because much has changed and much is changing fast. At the very least, we all would be wise to pay attention. I am not inciting panic here or suggesting we all opt for an off-the-grid existence, only more awareness and practical personal vigilance. The mass loss of privacy via the Internet and social media may not bring on the apocalypse, but it does matter.

William Gibson, a science fiction writer with many potent ideas about life in the digital age, believes that we are "approaching a theoretical state of absolute informational transparency, one in which 'Orwellian' scrutiny is no longer a strictly hierarchal, top-down activity, but to some extent a democratized one. As individuals steadily lose degrees of privacy, so, too, do corporations and states."[14] This is important to keep in mind. We—the everyday peasants on Facebook and Snapchat—are not alone in having to adapt on the fly while feeling the squeeze of shrinking privacy. Politicians, CEOs, generals, dictators, and every celebrities are caught in the same vortex. Our world is changing.

"Light is going to flow," declares David Brin, another science fiction writer. "You may try to stand athwart history with your hand out, shouting 'Stop!' but it will do scant good against a river."[15] He points out in the book *Chasing Shadows: Visons of Our Coming Transparent World* that old notions of privacy are changing fast so we—the public—had better get in the game and make the best of it. Brin believes that there are both good trends and bad trends at work right now, with far more balance than most news media and experts currently recognize or admit to. A high degree of transparency, he asserts, may be scary for us; but it could work out okay, especially when the light flows up as well as down. Transparency and a world with fewer secrets helps keep the abusive powers of governments and corporations in check. Public exposure, he points out, helped gays, lesbians, and trans people become more accepted in the West. "To everyone's surprise, light become their best friend."[16] Brin asks if we can "at least use light to enhance the things we cherish most, and to serve as—in the words of Justice Brandeis—a 'great disinfectant' of the bad?"[17]

More people are becoming aware of and concerned about privacy issues, even if their online behavior doesn't reflect it. Ninety-one percent of adult American Internet users surveyed by the Pew Research Center agree or strongly agree that they have lost control of their personal information online.[18] Many feel "confused, discouraged, or impatient" when they try to figure out how best to interact with online companies that ask for personal information. Younger people are more aware of privacy issues than older users are, but they also share more of their personal information online than do older people. A majority of Internet users, 68 percent, believe current laws do not do enough to protect people's privacy online.[19] Sixty-four percent think the government should do more to regulate how advertisers collect and use personal information.

"There is some information I don't mind social media sites collecting, as they connect me to products and services I'm interested in," said Elke Feuer of Florida.[20] "However, it does bother me how interconnected they are with other sites so they know where we've visited, [what we've] read or searched for, especially if it's private information. I find it unnerving when an ad or article pops up for a topic I didn't read on Facebook [but read elsewhere]. I try to set up as many security and privacy settings wherever possible to limit intrusion. As a business owner and author, it's difficult to avoid social media, as that's where a majority of my customers and readers hang out."

Because of former CIA employee and whistleblower Edward Snowden's revelations in 2013, many Americans are now aware that their government is probably monitoring them to some degree while they are on social media and engaged with other Internet activities. What might this knowledge mean for free speech? Nothing good, it seems. A 2016 study by Elizabeth Stoycheff, an assistant professor in the Department of Communication at Wayne State University, showed that public awareness of government surveillance "may threaten the disclosure of minority views and contribute to the reinforcement of majority opinion."[21] This means that people are less likely to speak up when they disagree with popular ideas. Stoycheff cites a "chilling effect" on people that discourages them from commenting and posting on social media as openly and honestly as they would otherwise.

---

**OUT OF CONTROL: THE STATE OF PRIVACY**

- According to a Pew Research Center study,[22] 91 percent of adults agree or strongly agree that consumers have lost control over how personal information is collected and used by companies.
- 70 percent of social-networking-site users say that they are at least somewhat concerned about the government accessing their information without informing them.
- 80 percent of adults agree or strongly agree that Americans should be concerned about the government's monitoring of phone calls and Internet communications.
- 88 percent of adults agree or strongly agree that it is very difficult to remove inaccurate information about them online.
- 80 percent of those who use social media say they are concerned about third parties like advertisers or businesses accessing the information they share on these sites.
- 64 percent believe the government should do more to regulate advertisers.

---

Jeremy Kocal, aged forty-one, of California is a heavy user of Facebook. He is active on Twitter and Instagram, and LinkedIn to a lesser degree. Kocal suspects that human culture is in transition. "I think the world of people living with privacy and secrets is almost dead and the days of full transparency are taking over, whether we choose that transparency or not," he said.[23] "I expect Facebook and other companies to steal my information, sell or give it to the highest bidder, rightfully be sued over it by keen observers, pay off the fines, and continue anyway. It concerns me, but deep down I think we want to know the private affairs of the citizens of Earth, and with the means to find everything out that is recorded online, it feels inevitable. If someone wants to know something about me, the president, the pope, etc., there is a way to get it. Facebook is a part of that 'sharing' experience; and by being a part of it, I get shared, even the parts of me I didn't want or expect to be shared."

## A GROWING DISCONTENT

> **Today's technologies refuse to let people alone, attempting to reconstruct people's past while authoring their future. The need to protect individual rights to lead a full and social life in the face of intrusive technology has never been greater.**
>
> —Lori Andrews, law professor and
> Internet privacy advocate[24]

Social media sites *should not* save any information about users for any amount of time. That is the opinion of 40 percent of adult Americans, according to the Pew Research Center.[25] Fourteen percent think that it is okay for sites to save information about them for "a few weeks"; 11 percent said they don't mind the sites saving data for "a few months'" and 5 percent are fine with them keeping it for "a few years." Four percent are okay with a social media site saving information about them for "as long as they need to." The latter, of course, most closely represents the reality of the current situation. Therefore, according to this survey, a mere 4 percent of social media users are content with how social media companies treat their personal data. The same Pew study found that just 1 percent of US adults are "very confident" that their social media site or sites will keep their information private and secure. Ten percent are "somewhat confident," and 45 percent are "not at all confident."[26]

People seem to be waking up to the fact that something less than desirable may be going on out of their view. Some people are getting incredibly rich off of the personal data of millions of people, and this equation doesn't feel right to some. "Their job is to extract value from the intimate details of our lives," explains social media expert Jacob Silverman.[27] "And you can be assured that shareholder value is more important to them than some sense of altruism or consumer rights." As Silverman states, "Facebook's great achievement has been to repeatedly chip away at the edifice of privacy and ensure that each move—each removal of a privacy control, each introduction of a new feature that exposes more user information—is eventually accepted. We are all frogs in the Facebook pot, slowly being brought to a boil."[28]

"I haven't had many bad experiences on social media because

I really try to keep my account private and don't post much," said Kelly, aged thirty-one. "I've had strange people try to 'friend' or 'follow' me online, and it's a creepy feeling. It's especially unsettling when you can tell that an ex-partner or people you barely know have searched specifically for you. I try to make my accounts as private as possible, but on the Internet, nothing is private."[29]

Facebook, the present dominant force of social media, has made it clear for years that it believes society should be more open. Users can't say they weren't warned. David Kirkpatrick writes in his book, *The Facebook Effect*, that Facebook co-founder Mark Zuckerberg makes several arguments for creating a more open, less private, world.[30] He quotes Zuckerberg as follows:

> "Having two identities for yourself is an example of a lack of integrity," Zuckerberg says moralistically. But he also makes a case he sees as pragmatic—that "the level of transparency the world has now won't support having two identities for a person." In other words, even if you want to segregate your personal from your professional information you won't be able to, as information about you proliferates on the Internet and elsewhere. He would say the same about any images one individual seeks to project—for example, a teenager who acts docile at home but is a drug-using reprobate with his friends.

It's time for everyone to be aware that a click, post, tweet, or page view is not the real game here. When that YouTube video some teenager recorded of his friend falling off a roof goes viral (spreads fast and far throughout the Internet) it supports the systems of surveillance. "Virality isn't just about apportioning fame or anointing that day's popular meme," writes Silverman in *Terms of Service*.[31] "It is intrinsically connected to the larger system of quantification of surveillance, and feedback loops that underlies social media. This same system is now roiling the journalistic world, transforming our relationship with media from passive readership to something far more complex and, perhaps, harmful to the culture." Silverman continues:

> In some sense, each of us is now a public figure, thanks to the development of digital systems designed to make sure that Internet users are always locatable and identifiable by their real names, all so that they can be connected to a digital profile that reflects their tastes and

habits. When these systems are combined with smartphone GPS data and the proliferation of advertising screens, sensors, cameras, and facial recognition throughout our urban environments, we are looking at a future where we will never be anonymous, even when walking down the street.[32]

## WHY INTERNET PRIVACY IS YOUR ISSUE

Abandon whatever comforting delusions you may have allowed yourself, and accept that online privacy and security are serious, relevant issues for all. Many people may shrug their shoulders and say they have nothing to hide, but this probably would not be the case should they give it more thought. Considering how much time we spend online and how much of our lives touch the Internet in one way or another, "who cares?" is just not a reasonable attitude to maintain these days. So much is now exposed to online surveillance, and so much can be gleaned from what we do on the Internet; this information includes our health status and history, finances, sexuality, religious beliefs, political loyalties or leanings, and shopping history. Sure, many people may reflexively say that they have nothing to hide, but how many of us would hand over our phone, wallet, and family photo album to a stranger—or a thousand strangers—to analyze, copy the contents, save forever, and then possibly use what they find to pass judgment on us? We are more agreeable to doing this kind of sharing online because we can't see the strangers; but they are there, nonetheless. Imagine sitting down for a job interview and being asked whether you are straight or gay, whether you are liberal or conservative, how much money is in your savings account right now, if you have ever visited a pornographic site, and if you have ever been prescribed antidepressant medication. The current reality is worse than this, actually, because potential employers who do their homework or hire a social media research firm don't even have to ask you. They already know. And if they don't like something they find, you never get as far as the job interview.

If you just experienced a slight ache or itch of discomfort down deep, that would most likely be cognitive dissonance. This is the unpleasant feeling that occurs when two contradictory beliefs collide inside your brain. You want to believe that all your web searches,

e-mails, and social media posts are private. But you also know you
should face up to the truth of how little privacy and security exist
online. Your subconscious mind probably prefers to avoid this conflict and pretend it's not happening, so it may nudge you to shrug
it off, change the subject, or conjure up some nonsense compromise
that allows you to believe that somehow both things can be true at
the same time. But you know they can't, so don't fall for it.

In addition to government and corporate data harvesting, be
aware that hacking is a serious problem, one with potentially severe
consequences; in fact, sometimes people die.

Ashley Madison, an online dating service that caters to married
people seeking extramarital affairs, was hacked in July 2015 by a
group or someone named "The Impact Team." A month later, more
than 25 gigabytes of company information and user data was leaked
online. More than 30 million people were exposed, potentially
revealing their real names, home addresses, credit card records,
and home addresses.[33] A pastor and professor at the New Orleans
Baptist Theological Seminary killed himself that summer and left a
note mentioning his sorrow for being on the list of Ashley Madison
users.[34] That same year, an ISIS fighter made a misstep on social
media and likely paid the ultimate price for it. He posted a selfie
taken at an ISIS command and control center. US Air Force analysts
at a base in Florida noticed it and, likely identifying geotag information within the photo, located and targeted the building within
hours. "It was a post on social media to bombs on target in less than
24 hours," said General Herbert J. "Hawk" Carlisle.[35] Chances are
you are not a philandering preacher or a careless terrorist, but the
point is that your online information can be accessed and used in
many different ways by many different people, governments, and
companies. No matter who you are or what you do, there likely are
at least a few things you would rather keep out of the reach of a
random stranger or someone who doesn't like you and might enjoy
causing you grief.

Be aware that an extensive and diverse list of people are or likely
will be looking at your online persona at some point and making
decisions that will have significant impacts on your life. Current
and potential employers can learn a lot about your "private" life
these days, and they can do it without you ever being aware that
they are checking on you. People you date, live next door to, or meet

at a casual party can conduct simple and quick online searches that reveal many personal details. One person I interviewed for this book lost a friend to suicide, related in part, he suspects, to Facebook: "I had a dear friend that had a very ugly and public breakup on Facebook that may have contributed to his suicide. People can easily and instantly inflict emotional damage on social media for all the world to participate in. It's really rough when it unfolds like that."

## NOTHING EVER GOES AWAY

> On the Internet, the words "delete" and "erase" are metaphorical: files, photographs, mail, and search histories are only removed from your sight. The Internet never forgets. The magnitude of this is hard to believe because one's first instinct is to find it unbelievable.
> —Sherry Turkle, Abby Rockefeller Mauzé Professor of the Social Studies of Science and Technology and director of the MIT Initiative on Technology and Self[36]

Perhaps those who are concerned about our rapidly vanishing privacy have it all wrong. Maybe our world would be better if we all would just be more open, more authentic and honest with each other. Could it be that we have been too private and secretive for our own good? Perhaps future societies will be more trusting, efficient, and prosperous thanks to more online connectivity and greater transparency. Maybe, but we aren't there yet. For many people, much of the Internet and social media today feels like too much, too fast when it comes to privacy and security. And they have a point; humans in the early twenty-first century are ill-prepared and ill-equipped to have everything they do surveilled, analyzed, and stored in order to manipulate and judge them. Yes, in the moment, one may feel safe, making it incredibly easy to launch a photo, comment, or joke into cyberspace. But that doesn't mean it *is* safe. What, then, are we supposed to do? Are we obligated to call in a team of consultants and confidants to discuss possible ramifications and long-term blowback before posting a one-sentence update on Facebook, a 140-character tweet, or an Instagram pic? That's ridiculous.

It's not fair that we should be obligated to be in editor/historian/

lawyer mode every moment of our lives simply because companies need our personal data to make money and governments want to spy on everyone. We need to be spontaneous, at least sometimes. No one should have to analyze and overthink every minor move online. But at the moment we can't be too carefree and impulsive. Not without risk. The problem with the typical social media user's understandable impulse to live in the moment is that every move made on social media comes with a long shadow of permanence. *Everything* is saved somewhere *indefinitely*. It's a very human thing to think in the short term. Our thoughts naturally dwell on the present and immediate future. It's difficult for us to imagine or care much about the potential difficulties a post or photo may pose to us in some distant future. We think it's safe now, and it probably is safe now, so we post it, thereby potentially putting ourselves in harm's way down the road. Keep in mind that neither individuals nor societies are stagnant. People change and perceptions of good and evil change, as do tastes in fashion, humor, and social mores in general. A mundane comment today might be embarrassing, seem scandalous, or possibly even rise to the level of a hate crime several years hence. A silly, harmless photo now might be devastating to one's personal or professional life later. The future is always uncertain. Therefore, we can never be completely confident that what is appropriate today will always be so. This places a heavy burden on all social media users because they are not only posting, sharing, and commenting in the moment for today, they are doing so potentially *forever*.

Consider how unfair this is to young people in particular. They should be allowed to grow and change. Forgiveness and forgetting are crucial to the long arc of a human life, and social media as it is today favors neither. "Would we have had a Mark Twain or a Bob Dylan if the Facebook doppelgängers of Samuel Clemens and Robert Zimmerman had dogged them at every step?" asks Jaron Lanier, a pioneer of virtual reality technology and social media critic.[37] "Strategic forgetting is part of personhood, and it is threatened. To be a person you have to find a sweet spot in which you both invent yourself and are real."

Lanier feels that social media is changing how young people live their lives. "The most effective young Facebook users . . . are the ones who create successful online fictions about themselves. They tend their doppelgängers fastidiously. They must manage offhand remarks and track candid snapshots at parties as carefully as a politician. Insincerity is rewarded, while sincerity creates a lifelong taint. Certainly, some version of this principle existed in the lives of teenagers before the web came along, but not with such unyielding, clinical precision."[38]

---

### WHAT YOU DON'T KNOW ABOUT CYBERSECURITY CAN HURT YOU

The Pew Research Center studied the American public's general knowledge of cybersecurity and revealed that most people are ignorant about basic, critical concepts.[39] The typical or median participant answered only five out of thirteen questions correctly. Only 1 percent of the study's participants achieved a perfect score. Before reading the next paragraph, consider taking the short test at this link and find out how much—or how little—you know about cybersecurity: http://www.pew internet.org/quiz/cybersecurity-knowledge/.

According to the Pew results, 54 percent of people wrongly think that all e-mails are encrypted. Some e-mail services provide this service, but many do not. It's also important to know that encryption needs to be end-to-end for the best level of security. This means only the sender and the recipient have the key to decipher the message. Fifty-five percent of those Pew tested hold the mistaken belief that all Wi-Fi traffic is encrypted by default on all wireless routers. Sixty-one percent don't know that their Internet service providers (ISPs) are able to see all of the sites they visit, even while using the "private browsing" mode on their browsers. Nearly 20 percent couldn't identify a secure password from a list of options.

---

Tim Raynor, aged fifty-two, is a Website design and development expert by day and musician by night. He views the Internet and social media as a big playground and shark tank, all rolled into one. "As far as where social networks are going," he said, "if I were to go by today's climate, I'd say more trolling, more ignorance, more fake news, more hate, and, of course, more echo chambers. In other words, I don't see a whole lot changing in the near future; but it will be interesting to watch." Raynor believes it is difficult, if not impossible, to be both online and private at the same time these days. The two just don't go together:

> Big brother can find you one way or the other. Google is still going to know you were thinking of buying Nutella on Amazon, and that drone you see flying around your neighborhood probably is watching you with all your blinds closed. However, since I'm not doing anything wrong, it really doesn't concern me. I do use identity protections to fight the hackers, but even that isn't a guarantee you won't eventually get nailed by one. It's happened to many of us, but it doesn't steer me away from the Internet. Flaws in Internet privacy just come with the territory, and doing whatever you need to to keep your privacy safe is all you can do. I don't believe any of us are 100 percent safe; but the rewards of having social interaction and friendships with people all over the world is worth the risk, in my opinion.[40]

This is a common sentiment. Many people think that they can do only so much, given the money and resources of those who own the social media platforms. If one feels he or she doesn't really have all that much to hide, then it's understandably difficult to get worked up about this issue.

"I don't care [about privacy online]," says Miles, a sixty-seven-year-old retiree living in Virginia:

> At my age, I don't have too much to offer or lose. Over time, I've lost quite a few followers by talking about atheism and left-wing subjects. And my connections have become more like-minded, but it doesn't bother me. Just as we seek out comfy couches, we like to be around comfy mentalities. Human nature. You may not be very broad-minded, but you won't be stressing with disturbing thought challenges. Most people enjoy human interaction. That's here to stay. The new big deal is that we do it over great distance and reach more people we know personally. Used to be radio kept you from feeling so alone, now that's gotten better and more fine-tuned. We used to write a magazine to get a specialized answer and wait a month for that answer; now Facebook channels offer instant access to experts in that field/hobby/concern. It used to be très cool to chat on the air on shortwave and CB radio. Now just use the keyboard and instantly find a new buddy in New Guinea. It's magical; I like it.[41]

Keven Hand, a freelance graphic artist and animator, lives in Missouri where he spends about two hours per day on social media, mostly Facebook. He isn't worried about details of his personal life being bought and sold behind his back or the possibility of strangers stalking him. He seems to have made philosophical peace with it all. "There are forces out there in the universe that I cannot control," Kevin said:

> The yearly revolutions of the Earth around the Sun, Saturn's ring color, and my cowlick. The universe has a plan and uses all these variables, good and evil, to forge my destiny. I could join a cult, or some other organization that would use its collective forces to challenge these variables as many have done in the past. But that takes time and I'm too busy. The light bill will not pay itself. Got to keep moving in this economy in order to keep liquid assets from hardening to a crispy outer shell. The time invested in caring about who is out to get me takes away from just how many hours I have before my next deadline. Divorce myself from worry? Unlikely, but the evil that exists in our world will never be extracted from the good. I cannot divest myself long enough to care about these evil doers that look to ruin me on social media. So, Russia, do your worst.[42]

Tim, Miles, and Kevin represent a sentiment that is common these days. Nothing unusual about people accepting what they feel they can't change. The problem, however, is that many people do have a few things to hide, perhaps nothing illegal, but something still personal enough to want to keep private. Personality and preference must be considered as here. Some activities or expressed ideas may seem harmless and noncontroversial, even trivial to me and you, but to someone else they might be intensely private. After all, there is a tremendous amount of individual and cultural variation present on this little world of ours.

Then there is the problem of revealed information that could reasonably be thought of as benign or neutral yet still has the potential to harm. Imagine, for example, a person who loves to hike. She posts numerous photos on social media that show her out in nature. No problem; what could possibly be wrong with that, right? But what if she attempts to rent an apartment and the owner looks over her Facebook page and decides that she is "one of those annoying tree-hugger types"? Anyone is made vulnerable when so much information is out there being interpreted by both algorithms and humans behind our backs. Your social media data may be subject to the personal tastes of others, taken out of context, or simply put into play against you beyond any reasonable expiration date.

By the way, the above hypothetical example of someone failing to get an apartment due to social media activity is not unrealistic; it's already happening. Rental property owners can hire a firm to assess and rate applicants based on social media history. Are you ready for this? Your ability to rent a particular apartment could hinge on some secret formula produced by a judgmental and unforgiving algorithm. A machine could scrape your social media accounts and then spit out a score that determines where you can live.[43]

Social media activity and the *quality* of your online friends and followers may also become a significant, if not a primary, factor in determining your credit score. Internet technology expert Marc Goodman: "Facebook may become the next FICO credit scoring agency as financial data aggregators take full advantage of your social data feeds to rate your financial stability. So as your mom used to warn you, choose your friends wisely."[44]

You have been warned.

## HOW TO PROTECT YOURSELF FROM TROLLS

As if spying governments, prying apps, data brokers, relentless algorithms, and hackers were not enough to worry about, we also have the problem of Internet trolls. This particular strain of human takes perverse pleasure from being mean to people; posting insults, harassment, threats, abusive language; and generally doing their best to stink up the place for everyone.

The troll name originates with either the grotesque monsters of Norse mythology or "trolling," as in fishing. Both make sense. The classic Internet troll behaves in a grotesque manner while fishing for chaos and anger. There are multiple explanations for troll behavior. Some of them are just standard-issue jerks, off-line as well as online, nothing too complicated about it. They probably never quite figured out how basic socializing works and may not even appreciate how cruel and inappropriate they are. We've all encountered people in life who for some reason just don't work and play well with others. Remember the worst kid on the playground in kindergarten? He probably grew up to be a troll.

The problem of trolls is not trivial. Millions of people encounter them, and many come away from it "extremely upset." Forty-one percent of Internet users in the United States have been the target of online harassment, and 66 percent say they have witnessed others suffer harassment online.[45] Thirty-nine percent report seeing "severe behaviors such as stalking, physical threats, sustained harassment, or sexual harassment" while online, most commonly on social media platforms.

Then there are the trolls who lead dual lives. Socially competent and pleasant enough out on the streets but monstrous inside a computer, these Jekyll-and-Hydes behave as if they are playing a first-person shooter game but with real people taking fire. Social media, for all the wonderful things it allows, is also a vast wilderness in which angry cowards feel empowered because they can provoke, harass, and threaten people at will and with impunity. Worse, trolls can drag others down into the gutter with them. Anger and threatening language are often contagious, which is why comment threads often descend into rage and circular frustration. So what can we do?

The first thing is to avoid being too condescending. As horrible as troll behavior can be, being mean to others is not exactly exotic human behavior. We are all capable of becoming the troll. Monsters lurk within everyone. It's not a comfortable thought, but it's true. Given the right context, the right sequence of events, you or I might post something inappropriate. The human brain can take a wrong turn at any moment. Consider the amygdalae, two small bundles of neurons that serve as the fear and anger centers of the brain. When something scares or enrages us, they take the helm to get us ready to run or fight. When this happens, we can't think as deeply and as clearly as we normally do, because the prefrontal cortex, the region of the brain where higher reasoning takes place, has been relegated to the sidelines for the moment. This is why you shouldn't tweet if you're angry or comment on somebody's photo while you are upset. Pause and calm down first so that you will have a better chance of choosing the right words, words you won't regret later.

## TROLL NATION

A 2017 Pew Research Center study[46] on the frequency and forms of harassment online surveyed 4,248 US adult Internet users and found the following:

- A majority of those who have been harassed online, 66 percent, said it happened to them most recently on a **social media site or app**.
- **Young people** are more likely to be victims. Seventy percent of Internet users aged eighteen to twenty-four say that they have been harassed.
- Of those who have personally endured online harassment, 27 percent have been called **offensive names**. Eight percent have been **physically threatened**. Eight percent have been **stalked** and 6 percent have been **sexually harassed**.
- **Young women** aged eighteen to twenty-four are harassed at the highest rate. Twenty-six percent have been stalked, and 25 percent were sexually harassed.
- **Who are the trolls?** More than half of those harassed online do not know the identity of the person targeting them.
- Among all of those harassed, 27 percent, found their most recent experience **"extremely or very upsetting."** Thirty-eight percent of harassed women said this about their most recent harassment experience.
- Twenty-seven percent of US adults say that they have **"refrained from posting something online after witnessing the harassment of others,"** and 13 percent stopped using an online service because of the harassment they observed inflicted on others.

I reviewed numerous expert opinions on how best to handle trolls. There are many recommendations—counter their lies with facts; use humor to disarm them; report them to site moderators; be nice to win their hearts, and so on—but I believe one defensive tactic outperforms all others by far. It's called silence. A tried-and-true method of dealing with trolls is to hit back with nothing more than cold, hard silence. Just ignore them. Don't react, don't reply, don't engage. The old saying, "Don't feed the trolls," is a good one. When you explode, scream back in all-caps, and trade threat for threat, you give them the win. Deny trolls the reaction they seek.

Victims of harassment should know that trolls are often empowered by feelings of anonymity. They feel that they can say anything because nobody knows who they are. But the joke is on them, because nobody is anonymous on the Internet anymore. Yes, there was a time years ago when no one on the Internet knew you were a dog.[47] Today, however, many people know you're a dog. A sophisticated hacker may still be able to get away with total anonymity, but the days of just anyone being able to run around the World Wide Web and do anything, free of consequences, are long gone.

The victim of harassment may not know the troll's identity, but somebody will. Let's not forget about all of those algorithms out there working day and night to identify, quantify, and commodify everyone online—trolls included. Anyone who makes a habit of using abusive or threatening language while online may be at risk of having significant problems later when he or she applies for a job, seeks an apartment to rent, submits to a credit check, joins a dating site, and so on. It will not be difficult for firms that provide background-check services to identify someone who behaves like a creep online.

## DEFINED BY DATA

Yes, Internet users may be on their way to passively and agreeably surrendering all of their privacy; but this current period may also be the calm before the storm. Some of the social media users I speak to about this are stunned when they hear the basic realities of what is going on behind their screens. They just haven't tuned in to this issue and, as a result, haven't been concerned or worried. But every moment of every day, governments and companies suck up oceans of personal data from billions of lives around the world. They do this for diverse reasons that include everything from serving and protecting people to suppressing, manipulating, exploiting, and profiting off of them. This much is clear, however: privacy is gone, at least the kind of privacy that previous generations knew. It has been snatched away by secret algorithms. Our personal lives were kidnapped without violence; our thoughts and movements surrendered, imprisoned without protest inside countless unseen servers. But in most cases, we have no right to call this a crime, because we agreed to give it all away. Perhaps some future generation will fight to regain control of their identities, to take them back from the governments and corporations. What we passively hand over with little thought or concern they may view as an invaluable treasure. Or perhaps they will be content to enjoy colorful and complex lives enhanced by a wired world and fully networked humanity. What is important now is that social media users understand, first, that this transformation is taking place and, second, that they are making it possible by their online activities.

"Facebook is unilaterally redefining the social contract—making the private now public and the public now private," writes Internet privacy activist Lori Andrews in her chilling book, *I Know Who You Are and I Saw What You Did: Social Networks and the Death of Privacy*.[48] She continues, "Private information about people is readily available to third parties. At the same time, public institutions, such as the police, use social networks to privately undertake activities that previously would have been subject to public oversight." For example, if police are not able to obtain a search warrant, they may search a home anyway by analyzing social media photos. Furthermore, merely conducting an online search for information about the side effects of antidepressants could end up being harmful to a person if that information makes it into the hands of an employer or college admissions officer.[49]

"Everything you post on a social network or other website is being digested, analyzed, and monetized," Andrews warns. "In essence, a second self—a virtual interpretation of you—is being created from the detritus of your life that exists on the Web. Increasingly, key decisions about you are based on that distorted image of you. Whether you get a mortgage, a kidney, a lover, or a job may be determined by your digital alter ego rather than by you."[50] The trail we leave on social media matters and can have a significant impact on our lives outside of social media. Randi Zuckerberg, former Facebook director of market development and spokesperson as well as the sister of Facebook co-founder Mark Zuckerberg, says she never posts anything online "that I wouldn't be comfortable having reprinted on the front page of a newspaper."[51]

---

**ATTACK OF THE APPS**

Apps, the popular programs millions of people download to mobile devices, can be incredibly useful and fun. There's one for just about everything, it seems. But have you ever wondered why so many of them are free? Did you really think that people invest all the time and money necessary to create an app simply because they love humanity and wanted to give back? No, in most cases they are making money off of the app by using it to suck up your data and send it back to them to sell. The game Angry Birds (more than two billion downloads) was so popular and so good at this that the NSA (National Security Administration) began secretly intercepting data from Angry Birds users because it enabled the spy agency to save so much time and effort. Thanks to one silly little game, the NSA collected personal data such as location and sexual orientation on millions of people.[52]

While apps can be great, some even difficult to live without, we shouldn't be too casual about downloading them onto our smartphones and tablets, because we don't really own or control them. They are not our friends. Apps are doing their real work for someone else.

---

There seems to be no limit to the depths and precision data brokers will go in compiling personal information about people that can be sold to businesses that want to target the right people with their marketing.[53] One US company discussed in a *60 Minutes* report sold lists of people who had a sexually transmitted disease, and another one of people who have purchased pornographic materials and sex toys. Further complicating things, there are many websites that are little more than data traps, deceitful ambushes set up to fool you into giving away your personal data. A Florida company named 5 Solutions, for example, operates seemingly straightforward and helpful websites with names like "GoodParenting Today.com" and "T5 HealthyLiving.com." Visitors to these sites are encouraged to post personal information about their families and their health. Untold numbers of visitors give away their data for the purpose of enriching someone without ever realizing what they've done. Children are easy targets for this kind of thing, too.

## A SCANDAL DOWN UNDER

In 2017, the *Australian* reported seeing a leaked twenty-three-page internal Facebook document that detailed how the company was mining data from Australians and New Zealanders and offering them up for targeted ads.[54] Nothing revelatory there, but what made this secret document particularly unsettling is that it gives an idea of how far Facebook and its clients are willing to go. According to the document, Facebook was offering to help advertisers, in real time, target kids as young as fourteen when they were most vulnerable, at moments when they were feeling "worthless," "defeated," "overwhelmed," "anxious," like a "failure," "stupid," and "useless."

The report further claims that Facebook can do more than detect current emotions; it can also follow and predict the emotional rhythms of young people from day to day. According to the *Australian*, the document states: "Anticipatory emotions are more likely to be expressed early in the week, while reflective emotions increase on the weekend. Monday–Thursday is about building confidence; the weekend is for broadcasting achievements."

This report was specific to the Australia region, but there is little reason to assume that similar activities involving children and teenage social media users won't happen in other regions. Facebook apologized in reaction to the leaked document. The company promised an internal investigation, disciplinary action if appropriate, and denied that Facebook targets people based on their emotional state. Former Facebook product manager Antonio Garcia-Martinez wasn't buying it. "I believe they're lying through their teeth," he wrote in the *Guardian*.[55]

The dark potential of this kind of emotion-based precision marketing is not difficult to imagine. Will young males who have been identified by social media algorithms as being at risk for suicide one day be targeted with ads for cheap handguns?

## YOUR BOSS IS A CYBER STALKER

CareerBuilder and Harris Poll conducted a study in 2016 and found that 60 percent of employers use social media sites to research candidates before hiring them.[56] Jobseekers aren't the only ones impacted by social media reviews, however. More than a quarter of employers have reprimanded or fired employees as a direct result of content found on their social media accounts. Furthermore, 92 percent of professional job recruiters use social media to analyze the "private" lives of candidates.[57] "Tools such as Facebook and Twitter enable employers to get a glimpse of who candidates are outside the confines of a resume or cover letter," said Rosemary Haefner, chief human resources officer of CareerBuilder. "And with more and more people using social media, it's not unusual to see the usage for recruitment to grow as well."[58]

| Who Uses Social Media to Learn about Job Candidates?[59] | |
| --- | --- |
| IT | 76 percent |
| Sales | 65 percent |
| Financial Services | 61 percent |
| Health Care | 59 percent |
| Retail | 59 percent |
| Manufacturing | 56 percent |
| Professional and Business Services | 55 percent |

## WHAT PROSPECTIVE EMPLOYERS DO NOT WANT TO SEE ON SOCIAL MEDIA

| What Prospective Employers Do Not Want to See on Social Media[60] | |
| --- | --- |
| Provocative or inappropriate photographs, videos or information | 46 percent |
| Information about candidate drinking or using drugs | 43 percent |
| Discriminatory comments related to race, religion, gender, etc. | 33 percent |
| Candidate bad-mouthed previous company or fellow employee | 31 percent |
| Poor communication skills | 29 percent |

There's a good chance the following thoughts just flew through your mind: *I had better max out the privacy settings on my Facebook page, leaving almost nothing for just anyone who comes along to see. And I'll delete every controversial comment, every crazy photo I've ever posted or tweeted anywhere.* Sorry, but that may not be the answer. If only it were that simple. The CareerBuilder / Harris Poll study found that 41 percent of employers say they are less likely to interview someone if his or her online presence is minimal or nonexistent. Bottom line, it seems that in order to maximize your chances in the job market, these days it is necessary to have a substantial social media presence, yet one with nothing that hints of anything offensive, risky, or unethical. This is difficult, if not impossible, to achieve, of course, because almost anything can potentially offend someone. When social media reveals all, what happens when a vegan interviews a job candidate who is a hunter in his "private life"? How might an atheist fare in the job application process if the potential employer is a religious fundamentalist, or vice versa? What if the interviewer simply hates the candidate's taste in music and movies, as revealed by a quick scan of her Facebook page? Likability is a huge factor in landing a job, and getting someone to like you can be a delicate, fickle thing. Answers to questions potential employers cannot legally ask a job candidate can be easily found out anyway, thanks to social media. Much that was once private and out of bounds is now on the table because of social media. Good luck.

Here's another charming reality to keep in mind: All social media users are being used as guinea pigs. All your tweeting and posting is akin to a lab rat running around in a maze in pursuit of some elusive speck of cheese while shadowy figures in white coats hover above, taking notes just out of view. If you are on social media, you are being observed, studied, and experimented on, constantly, in an effort to learn new and better ways to keep you engaged and coming back. Never forget that social media sites make their money by keeping you on them for as long as possible and having you share as much about yourself as possible so that they can learn more about you in order to help advertisers target you. The priority is to figure out what makes you stay. The stark truth here is that you are outmanned and outgunned in this arena. Too many smart people with lots of money and plenty of computing power are working hard to ensnare you and then translate your existence into a profitable commodity.

Social media expert Silverman asserts that Google, Facebook, and others are engaged in "nothing less than social engineering on a broad scale, pushing us to share and share under the pretense of improving our lives and building [a] global community when, in fact, they want nothing more than to target us with ads that they deem 'relevant' and urge us to buy products from their part-ners."[61] He continues, "Whether or not they actually believe in their grand prophecies only matters insofar as it provides cover for their assaults on user privacy, identity, self-expression, and autonomy. Under the paternalistic hands of Google and Facebook, we have been building digital lives only to give them away wholesale, all because the services were convenient and free and we told ourselves that we didn't know any better."

Yet another twist to all of this (about which most people are unaware) is that it's not only the owner of a particular website you visit that may be tracking you and harvesting data from you. It is now very common for many—dozens, possibly hundreds—of third-party companies to be there, waiting to track you as well. Some of this goes on without the host site even knowing about it.

Florida newspaper editor and photojournalist Robert DeAngelo might be living the life of an off-grid hermit in the eyes of some, but it works for him. LinkedIn is the only social media platform he cur-rently uses. So far, so good, he says. He doesn't lie in bed at night crying over missed likes and unread tweets. "To me, social media is an extension of the younger generation's desire to be celebrities," he said.[62] "Their thought process seems to be: 'I need to put these images online, and post every little detail about my life, because people are interested in what I think, what I do, how I'm feeling, etc.' Lots of young folks don't long to be famous for a particular talent; they seek whatever version of fame they can acquire through social media to feel accepted. I don't think I'm missing out on anything. I believe I'm well-read and up-to-date on current events through traditional sources."

DeAngelo thinks posting "too much" personal information online is a danger not worth indulging in, given relatively meager returns. He continues:

> It's definitely a mistake. How many times do people need to see the results of hacking or identity theft before they get the message? Nothing online is absolutely safe. Ask any celebrity whose private nude photos end up on some websites. Employers often research a potential hire's social media to see what types of things he or she is posting. Embarrassing photos, racially insensitive tweets, cyber-stalking an ex—these are all things that can derail an otherwise good candidate. The other aspect is that what's posted online has the potential to stay there forever. What you might have thought funny at age sixteen a prospective employer or mate might not find so amusing when you're twenty-five and seeking a job or spouse or home loan.

## THE QUEST FOR THE PERFECT PASSWORD

Most cybersecurity experts recommend using passwords that do not contain actual words. There are programs, easily available to anyone, that churn through huge numbers of dictionary words at high speed, trying to find a match. Safer passwords contain a combination of letters (both uppercase and lowercase), numbers, and some symbols, such as & or *. Avoid repeating letters or numbers, and don't use sequences of letters or numbers that are recognizable (e.g., *QWERTY, 54321*). It may be a burden, but experts discourage the use of the same password for multiple accounts. Don't enter passwords into public computers, where malware can easily get them. It's also a good idea to change your passwords periodically.

Elite hacker turned Internet security consultant Kevin Mitnick

## HOW TO LEAVE FEWER FOOTPRINTS

Is it possible for a typical person to conduct Internet searches and visit webpages without being identified and having every move surveilled, logged, analyzed, and saved? Probably not. However, there are some steps you can take to reduce exposure and minimize your vulnerability to tracking.

Consider using a VPN (virtual private network). This would allow you to create a more secure connection between your computer and the Internet. Some VPNs are free, and some charge a monthly fee. VPNs are a huge boost to security when using public Wi-Fi. Some critics point out that many VPN providers see everything you do online, so total privacy is not achieved. Here are some more options to increase online privacy:

- **Ghostery** (www.ghostery.com) is a program that deletes and blocks many tracking technologies. According to the company, "The Internet sucks. Ghostery makes it suck less."[63]
- **Privacy Badger** (www.eef.org/privacybadger) blocks many tracking cookies.
- **Duck Duck Go** is a search engine company that promises to never save your data or track you.
- **Delete Me** (www.abine.com) works to scrub the Internet of your personal data.
- **Tor** (www.torproject.org/about/overview.html.en) allows for more anonymous Internet activity by utilizing thousands of relays and encryption to make it difficult for a third party to monitor and track you.
- **TrackMeNot** (https://cs.nyu.edu/trackmenot/) will jumble your search history into a noisy mess aimed at frustrating the data miners.

points out that most people, even those in high places with a lot of responsibility, can be lazy when choosing passwords. For example, Michael Lynton, the executive who was hacked in the 2014 Sony data-breach incident, was using the password "sonyml3."[64] It probably took the hackers less than five seconds to crack that one.

Here are some examples of popular but terrible passwords that no sentient life-form in the twenty-first century should be caught using: *12345, QWERTY, 121212, password,* and *password1.* If you are using those or anything close to them, you may as well go print out every document, e-mail, and photo you own right now and stack them on the sidewalk of a major city. Experts recommend long passwords, from ten to twenty-five random characters, and it's best if they are a random sequence of letters, numbers, and symbols. Remember: no dictionary words or even a long string of words with a number thrown in at the end, as in "rosesareredvioletsareblue99." An example of a safer password would be something like "Xei+odjge#$^vm*)&rt9!E%kS."

The obvious problem here is that no one wants to take the time to memorize a long string of gobbledygook. So what to do? Consider using a password manager. Mitnick recommends open-source password managers, such as KeePass and Password Safe, because they don't store data online.[65] It all stays on your computer. LastPass seems like a good one, too. LastPass stores your passwords on its servers, but they're encrypted and so should be safe. Using the same password for multiple accounts is one of the most common mistakes people make. Don't do it. Each account should have its own unique password. That's inconvenient, of course; but it's not as much of an inconvenience as being hacked might be. Also remember that password managers make dealing with multiple passwords much easier.

It might seem risky and perhaps feel a bit prehistoric in these times, but I suggest writing down your long, ultra-complex passwords on paper. If you don't use a password manger, this can ease your mind about forgetting your passwords. Writing them down might not be wise or even allowed in the workplace, but for your private accounts and home use, I think it makes some sense. After all, it is better to use a password that you can't easily remember, because they're more likely to be long, random, and harder to break than one that's easy to remember (but easy to crack). If you do write down your passwords, however, don't identify that it's a list of passwords by writing

"Passwords," and don't include any usernames on the same paper. It's also important not to indicate what the password is for by writing "Gmail," "Facebook," or "bank account" on the same piece of paper, for example. And avoid carrying this piece of paper around in your wallet or car. If you simply must have it with you on the go, I suggest burying passwords within an endless field of letters, numbers and symbols on a page or, better, on a document saved to your laptop or tablet. Make a multipage document that is dense with text, and place your password or passwords somewhere in among a stream of similar gibberish. Just be sure to do it in such a way that you will easily remember where it is. Something like the third line of the third paragraph on the third page might work. And, of course, do not include "password" in the document title when you name it.

It helps to think of hackers as predators. As such, just like lions and sharks, they prefer an easy kill over hard work. No lion or shark worth its apex predator status will expend energy chasing the strongest and fastest member of a group if there is a slow and feeble target sitting there as an available option. If you have a strong password, there is a good chance random hackers will pass you by for someone with a weak password.

If you don't want to write down your passwords and instead opt to memorize them, then make acronyms your friends. A good trick is to use the first letter of a long phrase you won't forget. For example, "Neil Armstrong and Buzz Aldrin walked on the Moon Apollo XI 1969" would be "naabawotmaxi1969." Don't make the phrase too simple or recognizable. Avoid using "Mary had a little lamb" or "the rain in Spain." The longer and less common, the better. Ideally, make it personal: "I have a small scar on my left knee," IHASSOMLK. To make the password better, toss in some random numbers that you can remember (not your birth date or family members') and a few symbols too.

Experts seem near unanimous in their recommendations to use two-step or two-factor authentication for anything you care about keeping secure. This is a simple process to opt into with most sites and services. It usually requires entering a short code that is texted to you in addition to your password.

Another important way to keep your passwords and accounts safer is to avoid using public Wi-Fi whenever possible. Security expert Mitnick describes public Wi-Fi as "merely convenient" and

## HOW TOUGH ARE YOUR PASSWORDS?

Check the strength of your passwords at "How Secure Is My Password?" (https://howsecureismypassword.net). This free site, sponsored by a password manger company called Dashlane, gives you an estimate of how long it might take a program to crack your password. It also offers helpful analysis of why your password may be weak. It may shock you how easy it can be to beat passwords with widely available computer programs. I entered a variety of typical/easy and complex/tough passwords to see the variation. One of the easier ones I submitted could be cracked in an estimated "300 microseconds," according to the site. Another password that I had assumed was pretty good might last no more than three seconds under algorithmic assault. However, the site estimated it would take from a hundred years to 89,000 years to beat some of the better passwords I entered. The experts appear to be right. Make your passwords long and random, and include a mix of uppercase and lowercase letters, numbers, and symbols. Avoid obvious patterns, and (it merits repeating) don't use one password for all of your accounts.

The brutal truth is that nothing we do online is 100 percent safe—no matter how diligent we are. Everything is hackable now. If you have never been hacked, it's probably only because nobody good at it has tried. Programs are sold or given away online these days that can give anyone a good chance of successfully hacking a site or e-mail account. Some of these programs are so simple and user-friendly that you don't even have to have coding skills. Cybersecurity professional Garth Humphreys says that with this easy availability of hacking programs, it often comes down to motivation. How badly does someone want to break into your online life? Don't make it easy for the hacker. "It can be a quite terrifying experience if you're a victim of cybercrime," Humphreys said.[66] "We have our whole lives online; every day, every aspect of who we are is streamed or uploaded. I don't think people should be scared or paranoid, but they should be more aware of the things that they put online and take the necessary steps to safeguard themselves against becoming a victim. I think in most areas of our [off-line] lives people are more or less aware of the associated risk of doing a particular action; somehow, when they go online, they tend to drop their guard—and this opens them up to being taken advantage of."

Humphreys cites the tragic case of fifteen-year-old Amanda Todd[67] as an extreme example of just how dangerous hacking can be. "She was blackmailed into showing her breasts on a webcam," he said. "The blackmailer wanted to see more of her body and told her if she didn't, he would release the photos he stole from her. The blackmailer released the photos of her and even created a fake profile in Amanda's name. He 'friended' her real family and friends and then posted the nude pics on the fake profile for her family and friends to see. As a result of this, she was bullied and teased by people at school. She even moved to a different school, and this blackmailer kept following her online. Sadly, it was too much for her and she committed suicide. All this was done by a twisted and motivated individual with zeros and ones."

"incredibly insecure."[68] And, finally, never use public PC terminals, like those available in hotel business centers and airport lounges, to access your social media accounts, e-mail accounts, or anything else you want to keep private. There are programs, malware, that hackers load on them to record passwords keyed in by anyone hapless enough to use these terminals. "Assume the person who last used it installed malware—either consciously or unconsciously," warns Mitnick.[69]

## PERSPECTIVE

It may be easy to dismiss social media privacy concerns as instigations to unwarranted panic. I wouldn't call it fearmongering exactly, but sometimes it all does seem a bit over the top. *My life will be ruined because some company knows I like green tea and stalks me with ads for tea everywhere I go online. So what? I ain't got time to care about that.* Who wants to waste time and energy worrying about something that seems like such a vague and unlikely danger?

## BASIC SECURITY TIPS IN BRIEF

- **Log off and turn off.** If you don't need to be online while using your computer, then don't be. If you aren't using your computer, then turn it off. Going off-line or powering off does not eliminate the risk of being hacked but does significantly reduce the danger.
- **Backup your data.** If your data is backed up frequently, you are less vulnerable to ransomware or a virus.
- **Understand that social media can impact your off-line life.** Social media is an increasingly popular source of information about individuals. You may be analyzed and judged by potential employers, renters, school administrators, romantic interests, loan officers, and so on, based on your social media activity.
- **Don't trust pirated materials.** Downloading a large file from a stranger who doesn't own the rights to it is asking for trouble.
- **Delete apps you don't use.** Think of apps as little spies who live in your phone. The fewer of them, the better. If you can live without an app, get rid of it.
- **Don't share *everything* about yourself on social media.** Criminals, creeps, and trolls can exploit personal information you post online.
- **Update Software Often and Always**. Don't ignore prompts for software updates. Software companies are locked in an endless war with hackers, and you want the fixes and upgrades they fight back with.
- **Don't fill out online questionnaires.** Many websites exist just to suck up data from visitors. Don't make it easier for data brokers by answering every question a site asks. Don't fill in personal details unless you really need something on the other side of that form.
- **Beware of USB drives.** They are common carriers of malware.
- **Think before sexting.** Sending private sexually explicit photos or messages is dangerous for several reasons. If you're tempted, pause and consider possible consequences before you do it.

- **Use strong passwords.** Don't use common words or phrases. The longer it is, the better. Include random numbers and symbols. Change passwords often. Don't use the same password for multiple accounts.
- **Use two-step authentication.** Adding one small step can be a big leap for personal security.
- **Don't be stupid.** Recognize and accept that you can be a victim of cybercrime or online harassment. Everyone is a target.

Even government and police surveillance of social media are not immediately terrifying. *Come on*, you think to yourself, *why would anyone care about me and my humble, run-of-the-mill Facebook account?* I get it. It's not like you are a member of an al Qaeda cell. You've probably never posted anything that is criminal or truly horrible. As discussed earlier in this chapter, however, what you consider trivial or benign might become a serious problem in the hands of the wrong person or in a different time and context. For example, women have been fired from their jobs for dressing provocatively— not while at their workplace but as seen in photos posted to social media.[70] So maybe something is out there, one of countless digitally fossilized moments from your busy, complex life. Maybe you can't remember it. But it will be out there, nonetheless.

Frankly, I discourage paranoia. Our species is plagued with too much irrational fear already. I do, however, recommend reasonable caution and common sense when it comes to social media. Users need to have a general awareness about how social media participation works. "Your" images and words on social media are not yours. They stopped being exclusively yours the moment you posted them. Now they belong to the company that owns the platform to which they were uploaded. This was explained in the terms of agreement you didn't read but agreed to anyway. The platform owns your images, your words, and whatever emotional confessions and expressions you leave behind—potentially *forever*. Still don't care? Think back. Have you ever posted any regrettable photos? At least one image of you in an awkward, embarrassing, possibly reputation-damaging situation? Maybe you didn't post it but a "friend" did and tagged you by full name without asking. What about that one little comment you once posted to social media a few years ago? You know, that micro-rant where you lost your cool, just for a moment, and typed something mean, stupid, or out of character. Here's the least you need to know: Even if you went back and dutifully scrubbed the potentially troublesome post from your Facebook page, Twitter feed, or Instagram account, it's still out there somewhere in the digital universe. It never goes away. It is, at the very least, almost certainly still in the possession of the company; after all, you gave it the right to keep everything you do on its platform. Sleep well.

## E-MAIL IS SCARY, TOO

Never forget that delete doesn't mean what your subconscious mind wants you to believe it means. When you zap an embarrassing or potentially damaging e-mail into apparent oblivion, it only feels like it's gone for good. Clearing out that "sent" file might reassure those who have secrets; but they are only fooling themselves. Nothing has been disintegrated or banished from the known universe. Like your Facebook and Instagram pics, e-mails live on indefinitely in the host servers of your e-mail provider because they keep copies of *everything*. Ponder this for a moment: Every e-mail you have ever sent to or from all of the usual carriers—AOL, Gmail, Apple, Yahoo, AT&T, Microsoft, Comcast—still exists and is in the legal possession of people you don't know.[71]

> *Your privacy is very important to us.*
> —Facebook, Terms of Service

"Privacy is, above all, the currency we draw on to pay for a range of free Internet services, most notably social networks," writes Jacob Silverman in *Terms of Service*.[72] He continues, "We offer Google and Facebook information about ourselves, while simultaneously being assured that our data is being used responsibly and that we have a wide range of privacy controls. It's more accurate, then, to say that privacy is submitting to market pressure, becoming increasingly commoditized. Your privacy has been taken, chopped up into packets of data, and circulated through commercial transactions beyond your view." And what about the cloud? Storing "personal" data there may change things legally, warns Mitnick. "A huge concern about using the cloud is that your data does not have the same Fourth Amendment protections that it would if were stored in a desk drawer or even on your desktop computer. The only true protection is to understand that anything you put up there can be accessed by somebody else and to act accordingly by encrypting everything."[73]

Social media users give away more key information about their personal lives than they realize. For example, one doesn't have to post a clear declaration of political beliefs, religion, or sexuality for such information to be gleaned by clever algorithms. So dial down the confidence and reconsider that comforting belief that your online movements are suitably vague to prevent unseen agents from building an accurate and useful profile of who you are. University of Cambridge researchers showed that a computer program's analysis of social media users' digital footprints was more accurate in forecasting their lives—predicting significant things about them—than their friends, family, spouse, colleagues, and so on were.[74] Can that be true? Are there really algorithms that know as much as or more about you than those who are closest to you? Apparently so.

The University of Cambridge study looked at only "likes" on Facebook, nothing else, and was able to produce remarkable results. The computer program was 88 percent accurate in identifying the sexual preferences of male users; 95 percent accurate in identifying racial or ethnic affiliations; and 85 percent accurate in spotting Democrats and Republicans. Christians and Muslims were correctly identified 82 percent of the time. Analyzing only these likes allowed accurate insights into one's relationship status and even problems with substance abuse. What makes this study so remarkable is that the results didn't rely on obvious clues such as a user "liking" a Facebook page or group dedicated to Islam, the Republican Party, or some other obvious indicator. It relied on the accumulation of tiny details as revealed by many "likes" of many and diverse things within the social media ecosystem. The researchers said, for example, that less than 5 percent of the gay people in the study had anything that directly and obviously indicated that they were gay, but the program selected them correctly at a rate of nearly 90 percent.[75] Our "likes" tell intimate stories about us, and there are algorithms that can hear them far better than most human ears can. The scary implications of this should be clear in a world that still harbors so many prejudices. Gays and atheists, for example, can be jailed or executed in some societies today.[76]

It's important to keep in mind that technology is improving fast, as are the reach and creative capabilities of hackers who would manipulate, embarrass, rob, or otherwise do you harm online. It is possible now, for example, for cyber thieves to access your iPhone or other devices simply by using your fingerprints as shown on a mere photograph. Yes, biometrics, viewed by some as the gold standard of tech security, may turn out to be a relatively easy way in.[77] But often the critical information that has the potential to allow someone access to do damage doesn't have to be stolen by supervillain means; so many people make it available to anyone who wanders by. Facebook is, to some degree, a convenient digital scrapbook, diary, and/ or logbook for your life. But having strangers and companies pick through your life events might lead to problems. The least you can do is tighten up your social media accounts. Be warned, however, that this is often confusing and more difficult than it should be. Social media companies clearly want users to be more open and less secretive about their lives, because their economic model is based on sharing, not withholding. The more you reveal about your activities, thoughts, and preferences, the more valuable you are to them.

It may feel uncomfortable to mentally run through an imagined list of the people who are surveilling you and taking notes, but we all should do this because it can help motivate us to maintain some level of vigilance about what we do online. Someone or some algorithm is out there, right now, Googling your name, reviewing your Twitter and Instagram feeds, or scanning your Facebook photo gallery, and so on, for anything that will assist her, him, or it in knowing you better and possibly passing judgment on you.

Facebook users also should be aware of the potential problem of friends adding them to groups without asking. Why Facebook allows this is a mystery. I have had to remove myself from several groups that I did not join and had no interest in being associated with. For me this has been a mild annoyance, but it could cause serious problems for some people. Imagine a young gay person who has not come out to family and friends for fear of ostracization or violence suddenly being joined to several gay-themed Facebook pages by one of his or her "friends." The results could be terrifying, even deadly.

It is strange how we can be aware of a significant risk but still proceed anyway, as if there's no problem. Our subconscious minds, eager to keep us happy in the present, whisper: "Relax, nothing bad will happen to you." Even though we know that text messages, e-mails, online photos, and social media accounts are highly vulnerable to hacking and that almost all online communications are vacuumed up and stored in NSA super-servers somewhere, we keep launching things out into cyberspace that would be embarrassing or damaging if made public. Why? How does a relatively reasonable, sober person look into the frame of an electronic screen and make the decision to drop a private thought or image into the open jungle that is the Internet? MIT professor and social media expert Sherry Turkle thinks she knows:

> [It is] the paradox of electronic messaging. You stare at the screen on your desk or in your hand. It is passive, and you own the frame; these promise safety and acceptance. In the cocoon of electronic messaging, we imagine the people we write to as we wish them to be; we write to that part of them that makes us feel safe. You feel in a place that is private and ephemeral. But your communications are public and forever. This disconnect between the feeling of digital communication and its reality explains why people continue to send damaging e-mails and texts, messages that document them breaking the law or cheating on their spouse.[78]

The game has changed. This we can all be sure of. Accept that we are the first generation of people in the history of civilization to live in a state of near total and constant surveillance. Our communications, movements, behaviors, likes, dislikes, desires, strengths, weaknesses, hopes, fantasies, purchases, and so on are being recorded and archived by governments and corporations at unprecedented levels. Medieval lords may have kept a watchful eye on the serfs; Stalin had his KGB; and J. Edgar Hoover spied on Martin Luther King Jr. and many other of his fellow Americans; but what we see going on today is something completely different. Even Stasi agents, the infamous secret police of the former East Germany who monitored and documented the lives of citizens in

## TRIM DOWN YOUR SOCIAL MEDIA IDENTITY

*Vague is safer.* That might be a good mantra for social media users to live by. Keep in mind that no one forces us to engage in social media activity—not yet anyway. Sure, maybe one day all citizens will vote for president on Facebook and shop for groceries on Instagram, and all students will tweet their test answers. But for now all of this activity is voluntary, so be smart about it. Don't feel coerced or required to give away more of yourself online than you may be comfortable with or than may be in your best long term interest. There is no law that compels us to pour out all of our lives on social media— not yet. Make it a habit to share less rather than more. You don't have to give up as much information as you probably do. For example, why not hold back your birthdate and/or your place of employment? Yes, it's nice to get all of those "happy birthday" messages on social media, but that one date could also be the key bit of information that helps a hacker break into your digital life. Telling the world where you work might be a mistake, too. Why not be vague and just state the general field you work in? Knowing precisely where you work could encourage and enable some troll turned stalker to harass you there. If you don't walk around telling every stranger on the street how old you are and where you live, work, and play, then why would you post all of that information online, where the maximum number of strangers can see it?

Keep in mind what can be discovered about you on the social media platforms you use whenever you fill out security questions and information for important online activities such as banking. For example, if you are on Facebook, it probably wouldn't be too difficult for an identify thief to learn your mother's maiden name, your pet's name, your hometown, the high school you graduated from, and so on. Therefore, it is too risky to use this kind of information for your security questions on other sites.

astonishing detail, never came close to this. It is not much of an overstatement to say that *everyone* is being spied on *all the time* by somebody somewhere. Such is life in the wired age.

## TERMS OF SERVICE

To make matters stranger, much if not most online surveillance and data harvesting is only possible because hundreds of millions of people passively surrender to terms of service agreements. To be able to plunge into whatever fun and benefits social media participation brings, you must first give the platform owner the legal right to convert your online activities and movements into profitable ones and zeros. These companies digitize and summarize their users, with the end product being something that is supposed to be a rich target for advertising. But is it really us?

We can't know how accurately we are represented online, remember, because we aren't allowed to peek behind the corporate firewalls and review the data that increasingly define us. Advertisers want these digital biographies, and pay handsomely for them, because knowing us to some degree allows them to be more efficient and cost-effective at targeting us with ads.

It is remarkable how people have been trained by corporations to sign or agree (by clicking) to terms of service contracts without even *trying* to read them. Corporate legal teams broke the will of the public long ago. Why would we read them? It's easy to anticipate what awaits. People learn through experience early in life that terms of service agreements are almost always composed of confusing, mind-numbing legalese. They are dense thickets of words designed to protect the company rather than inform us. But I strongly recommend resisting this habit with social media use.

Take a few minutes and read, or at least skim, the terms of service for all of the platforms you currently use or are considering. Do it if only to gain a whiff of enlightenment and perhaps a more realistic sense of potential problems. You may be surprised by how straightforward some of it is; and the simple act of reading these things may resonate and awaken you—not necessarily to scare you away from using social media, but to motivate you to be more cautious and at least understand the exploitive nature of these for-profit companies. "You give us permission," states Facebook's current terms of service, "to use your name, profile picture, content, and information in connection with commercial, sponsored, or related content (such as a brand you like) served or enhanced by us. This means, for example, that you permit a business or other entity to pay us to display your name and/or profile picture with your content or information, without any compensation to you."[79] Translation: *We can and will make money off the details of your personal life. You are the commodity by which we prosper.*

Snapchat, a social media platform favored by the young, is widely seen as offering a less invasive, less creepy, and lighter version of today's social media experience. Its creative photo filters and fun features, such as bunny ears and vomiting rainbows that can be superimposed over selfies, promote a feeling of carefree and silly entertainment. Nothing silly about Snap's numbers, though. After only five years of existence, some 158 million people use the app an average of eighteen times daily. Snap was valued at about $34 billion in early 2017. That valuation puts it ahead of traditional media powerhouse CBS and makes it worth about three times more than Twitter, which was founded six years earlier than Snap.[80] Further, it has a higher valuation than Ferrari, Best Buy, Hershey, Viacom, Hilton, and American Airlines.[81]

Snapchat offers more than creative filters that enhance photos. The app also allows users to send to their friends a photo that disintegrates ten seconds after being viewed. "Stories" vanish after twenty-four hours. In other words, there are (seemingly) no mistakes hanging around to embarrass later. Seems reassuring enough, right? However, "disintegrate" and "vanish" are relative terms here. I have extracted a few trees from the dense forest of Snap's terms of service agreement to show that the reality doesn't quite match users' perception. What follows is a series of excerpts from the current Snapchat terms of service, with relevant comments in boldface.[82]

- We [Snap Inc.] collect different kinds of information from or about you. **Things you do and information you provide**. . . . This can include information in or about the content you provide, such as **the location of a photo** or the date a file was created.
- Keep in mind that, while our systems are designed to carry out

our deletion practices automatically, **we cannot promise that deletion will occur within a specific timeframe**. . . . Finally, **we may also retain certain information in backup for a limited period of time** or as required by law.[83]

- You grant Snap Inc. and our affiliates a **worldwide, royalty-free, sublicensable, and transferable license** to host, store, use, display, reproduce, modify, adapt, edit, publish, and distribute [your] content.[84]
- When you appear in, create, upload, post, or send Live, Local, or other crowd-sourced content, you also grant Snap Inc., our affiliates, and our business partners the unrestricted, world-wide, **perpetual right and license to use your name, likeness, and voice**.[85]

Snap is not unique. Here is a short list of privacy-related items from Facebook's Data Policy:[86]

- We collect content and information that other people provide when they use our Services, **including information about you**, such as when they share a photo of you, **send a message to you**, or upload, sync or import **your contact information**.
- We collect information about **the people and groups you are connected to** and **how you interact with them**. . . . We also collect contact information you provide if you upload, sync or import this information (such as an **address book**) from a device.
- If you use our Services for purchases or financial transactions (like when you buy something on Facebook, make a purchase in a game, or make a donation), **we collect information about the purchase or transaction**.
- **We collect information from or about the computers, phones, or other devices** where you install or access our Services, depending on the permissions you've granted. . . . [This may include:] **device locations, including specific geographic locations, such as through GPS, Bluetooth, or WiFi signals.** Connection information such as the name of your mobile operator or ISP, browser type, language and time zone, **mobile phone number and IP address.**
- **We collect information when you visit or use third-**

> **party websites and apps** that use our Services. This includes . . . your use of our Services on those websites and apps, as well as information the developer or publisher of the app or website provides to you **or us**.
>
> - **We receive information about you and your activities on and off Facebook from third-party partners**, such as information from a partner when we jointly offer services or from an advertiser about your experiences or interactions with them.
> - **We receive information about you from companies that are owned or operated by Facebook,** in accordance with their terms and policies.
> - Information associated with your account will be **kept until your account is deleted** . . .

Doesn't some of this sound more like a national spy agency's mission statement or some dictator's wish list for Orwellian-level surveillance rather than free social media platforms meant for fun and networking? But why? The answer, of course, is because Snapchat, Facebook, Instagram, Twitter, and all of the others need their users' personal data to generate income. That's the purpose of these platforms. Cute doggie-face pics and flower crowns are but means to an end.

We also embrace the hardware that makes this new level of surveillance possible. We walk around with smartphones in our pockets that track us. We bring electronic devices, such as baby monitors and "intelligent personal assistants," into our homes that can enable others to see and hear us. The only reasonable conclusions are that we are either in denial and refuse to recognize the obvious, or we don't really care about our privacy. One of my Facebook friends posted a comment about this: "They already have us used to the idea of carrying cameras with microphones and GPS trackers around with us voluntarily. Maybe they will make it mandatory, like driving with your license, or purchasing a product like 'health insurance' to collect even more data. We even now install listening devices in our homes that collect data on us. Imagine that data transferred to a robot sent to destroy you."

He was joking, I think. But there is serious issue here to consider. Billions of people now carry tiny potential spies, in the form of smartphones, with them everywhere they go. A smartphone can be an effective bug, even when it appears to be turned off. The US government has used this technique for years, according to Edward Snowden.[87] Worse yet, any phone or Internet-connected object that has speakers—no microphone needed—might be turned into a listening device as well. "The fact that headphones, earphones and speakers are physically built like microphones and that an audio port's role in the PC can be reprogrammed from output to input creates a vulnerability that can be abused by hackers," explained Yuval Elovici, director of the Ben-Gurion University Cyber Security Research Center.[88] There is one very simple step that could eliminate the risk of hackers and user-installed apps from listening and watching without the owner's awareness. The manufacturers of these phones could include *physical* on/off switches that disable the microphone and camera, putting them beyond the reach of external threats.[89] And, to make things even safer and more sensible, why not have a physical on/off power switch for the phone itself? That way no one could be tricked by hackers into thinking that his or her phone is off when it is quietly spying on them. Imagine that.

## A RISKY PROPOSITION

Sex is on the short list of primary driving forces within the human animal. Therefore, it should surprise no one that, among billions of people with smartphones, some will use these devices in ways that are related to sex. The equation is plain and the answer predictable:

Phone Camera + Instant Communication + Humans =
An Endless Avalanche of Personal Nude Pics
Flying around the Internet

However, sexting—sharing private nude photos of oneself or sexually explicit messages with another person through a phone service provider, e-mail, or social media site—may be fun and exciting, but it is extremely risky for two primary reasons. The obvious reason is that nothing is safe on the Internet, everything is hackable, and just about everything seems to live on somewhere, regardless of whether you delete your copy. The second reason to pause and think before sexting is that sending a sexual and potentially embarrassing photo demands a tremendous amount of trust in the recipient. And that trust is often misplaced. An Indiana University study[90] found that most people who engage in sexting, 73 percent, do so with an expectation of privacy. They believe the images will not go any further than the person they send them to. However, researchers discovered that 23 percent of people who receive these sexual images admit to sharing them with others. That's a betrayal-of-trust rate of almost one in four.

Younger and less experienced people who may be new to the emotional rollercoaster of romance need to understand that love and lust can be an erratic game. Great confidence and feelings of permanence often accompany the thrills of early-stage sexual attraction and the first stirrings of love, but the reality is that most relationships end, and of those some end bitterly, with resentment and anger. The sweetest, most attractive person in your life today may turn out to be tomorrow's monster hell-bent on embarrassing you publicly, getting you fired from your job, and/or ruining your next relationship. It happens. Don't let yourself believe that sexting is a stupid person's problem or something reserved for sexual deviants. For most people who do it, this is probably an impulsive act done in the heat of the moment while communicating online with someone they like and want to like them back.

American teens today rely heavily on social media to seek, secure, maintain, and sometimes destroy romantic relationships. According to a Pew Research Center study, more than half of teens aged thirteen to seventeen, 55 percent, have used social media to flirt or let someone know that they are attracted to them.[91] Ten percent of teens say that they have sent "flirty or sexy" pictures or videos of themselves to someone. While no studies to date show that sexting is rampant among teens, the young people I spoke with about it certainly seem to believe it is. I heard the following claims: "Everyone does it"; "A ton do it all the time"; and "There is a whole website for the photos [that have been sexted at my school]." Exaggerations aside, I suspect it may be a problem, though probably nowhere near pandemic proportions. Of course, that is no comfort to an individual child or teen who ends up making a mistake and suffering for it.

Revenge porn is yet another disturbing reality brought to us by the Internet.[92] This is the act of sharing or posting personal sexual photos of a former lover, partner, or acquaintance without permission for the purpose of humiliating and/or causing harm to him or her. This is a danger that should be taken seriously by anyone tempted to share a nude or compromising photo of himself or herself with a love interest. Revenge porn is illegal in some countries and illegal in about half of the states in the United States. But don't take solace in that. Its illegality doesn't mean it isn't happening to someone every moment of every day. Its illegality doesn't mean it can be remedied quickly and easily, should it happen to you. Try to imagine the nightmare scenario of having personal nude photos of yourself plastered across the Internet and then trying to get them taken down from websites. This can prove very difficult, if not impossible, to do with complete success. If the images are not selfies but are consensual photos taken by someone else, things can get even more complicated. For example, if a former boyfriend or girlfriend took the photos, it would mean that this person—not the victim—owns the rights to the photo, which makes it more difficult to get them removed.

Carrie James, of Harvard's Project Zero,[93] focuses much of her work on the digital, moral, and civic lives of young people. She told me that it is vital for parents to show genuine interest in their children's online activities. "Crucially, though, this interest should not simply be keyed to behaviors that might get youth into trouble online and ways to avoid such consequences," she explained.[94]

> Adults should be striving to listen for the social, creative, civic, and emotional implications of their social media worlds. Key questions adults might be asking include: What excites and engages youth on their social networks? How do they take up the creative affordances of apps like Musical.ly, Instagram, and Snapchat? How are social media sparking an interest in social justice issues and civic engagement? What ideas and perspectives are youth seeing on their networks and what might be missing? How are their social media experiences contributing to their emotional well-being? When and how might digital time-outs support personal well-being as well as reflection about the moral and ethical dimensions of their tweets, texts, and online pics?[95]

James promotes what she calls "conscientious connectivity" for young people online. This is a call for them to be "mindful or reflective of the ethical implications of online choices." James continues:

I see this approach as a counter to the largely individualistic, myopic, and shortsighted mind-sets about online life that I heard youth embracing in the studies my colleagues and I carried out. To be clear, this is not to say that youth should not be thinking about how their tweets, Instagram photos, or Snapchat [stories and images] might affect or come back to haunt them as individuals. Rather, their thinking should attend to such personal concerns in balance with moral and ethical considerations. Being a conscientious digital citizen requires having ethical thinking skills or capacities—for example, complex-perspective-taking—the ability to consider the perspectives of near and distant individuals, of larger systems and publics that may be audiences for or affected by one's tweets, Instagram pics, or Snaps. Yet, having such skills isn't enough. Youth also need to be sensitive to opportunities to engage in ethical thinking. They need to spot ethical dilemmas when they come up. . . . In short, living in a digital world means that our words and deeds may have far-reaching impact. Nurturing habit of minds to think through those impacts is essential.[96]

**Is Snapchat safe for private photos?** It's the last thing a parent wants to think about, but many teens send sexually explicit messages and images through social media. Snapchat, with its vanishing-photos feature, seems tailor-made for this kind of activity. When the pic is opened for viewing, a countdown ensues, and it "vanishes" ten seconds later. No smoking gun. No evidence. No regrets. If only former US congressman and New York City mayoral candidate Anthony Weiner had restricted his sexting to Snapchat, he might have avoided a lot of personal grief. Then again, maybe not, because there is a lot of false confidence swirling around Snapchat these days. Sure, using this app to send sexually explicit images may be *less* risky than posting potentially scandalous information and images on Facebook or Instagram, but Snapchat is far from risk-free. Users who receive a sexy pic that they consider a keeper can save it simply by taking a screenshot of it or by utilizing other image-capturing technology. Snapchat is no sanctuary for secrets or private photos. Finally, one should be aware that the parent company, Snap, seems to reserve the right to keep all user images, videos, and messages indefinitely. It has a deletion policy that may seem comforting at a glance but read closely it is too vague and noncommittal to reassure anyone.[97]

The critical question to ask before launching that provocative pic out into the electronic ether is whether or not you have total confidence that the recipient is not going to attempt to do harm with the image now, or ever. The problem is that this cannot be known with certainty in the present because people can change and no one knows the future. But the worst must be considered because the consequences can be brutal. No one wants to think about possible breakup and animosity when a relationship is new and exciting, or entertain unpleasant thoughts about a new flame. But breakup and the possibility of revenge had better come to mind before putting yourself at risk.

A current member of the US military told me that sharing sexual photos on social media is common in military culture and sometimes leads to blackmail:

> Women prey on men, especially the younger guys, using dating apps like Tinder, asking them to trade sexual photos, and then black-mailing them for money by threatening to upload the private photos to a public Facebook page and then tagging the sailor's command and family members, etc., to the photos so everyone will see. They are often blackmailed in this way when women take pictures of them underage drinking at parties, cheating on their girlfriends, using illegal drugs, etc. They will go to popular bars, clubs, or party spots, specifically tar-geting young males to take photos and blackmail them later. Another big problem, which you've probably heard on the news recently, is the sexual harassment of female Marines, sailors, soldiers, and airmen on social media. In this case, it's almost always males targeting females. The males take photos or videos of the females without their knowledge in locker rooms, showers, or berthing areas, and then upload them onto Facebook or Snapchat. They do this for fun or to haze the females. The DoD [Department of Defense] is 100 percent against this behavior, and they're doing everything they can to stop sexual harassment.

## MORE REASONS TO CARE

> **Privacy is completely and utterly dead, and we killed it.**
> —Jacob Morgan,
> futurist and author of *The Future of Work*[98]

Those who still see no reason for concern about so much personal data ending up in the hands of corporations might consider what could happen if a company's culture changes, say, if a new board of directors takes over and decides to chart a new course. Google's official motto had been "Don't Be Evil" since its founding, but the company dropped it in 2015.[99] I'm not suggesting that Google is evil, only that things can change. Who knows what the future holds? asks security expert Mitnick: "Given what Facebook knows about its [more than one] billion subscribers, the company has been fairly benevolent—so far. It has a ton of data, but it, like Google, has chosen not to act on it. But that doesn't mean it won't."[100] Imagine what could happen if your insurance company bought the data recorded by an online health or exercise tracker that you use? They might raise your premiums because you haven't been consistent with your running, or maybe your heartrate is just a little too high. But you'll never know. It will just happen. It may not be wise to get on the wrong side of your government now or in the future. For example, if you are an American citizen, or have ever communicated online with any American citizen or US entity, you should be aware that the NSA (National Security Agency) maintains a $2 billion data complex in Utah.[101] Have no doubt, some or all of your e-mails, texts, and social media posts are in there somewhere, waiting, just in case someone wants to take a close look at your life one day.

---

### FACEBOOK IS FOREVER

Want to delete your Facebook account and get rid of whatever digital trail you left on it? Sorry, you can't. It doesn't belong to you, remember? All of that data, including your family pics and the personal posts you made when you fell in love, don't belong to you. You can take it off the Web, assuming no one out there has saved everything and posted it elsewhere. But, according to Facebook, every one of your photos, comments, and "likes" will lie dormant, presumably waiting for the inevitable day when you regain your senses and return to the Facebook family. Facebook will not allow you to open a new account if you come back. You can only reactivate your old one. And, of course, you have no choice but to go along with all of this because you agreed that everything you posted, shared, and received while on Facebook became the property of Facebook—forever.[102]

---

We are weird, contradictory creatures when it comes to our privacy. On one hand, we want it. *Leave me alone. Mind your own business. Stay out of my life.* The idea of someone or some organization peeking into our personal space alarms and angers most of us. But, remember, we are simultaneously social creatures. We need others to know us. We desperately want to be connected and liked by others. Many want to be famous as well, especially, perhaps, those who are enamored by the ongoing Kardashian-ization of pop culture. To be famous for being famous seems to be a respectable goal now, one to which much of social media caters. Human culture today has been twisted and engineered to attempt to satisfy these conflicting desires. But it can't work. Ultimately something has to give. Either our desire for privacy will wither and die or we will stop giving it all away and governments and corporations will cease their invasions into our private lives. It's difficult to imagine humankind traveling a road of such deep contradiction forever.

Privacy issues are not new. Humans have been peeping on one another for a long, long time. Rulers have always felt the need to keep a close eye on those they rule. "Mass surveillance itself is clearly not a novel phenomenon," writes security expert David Lyon. "It emerged as a vital aspect of the growth of modern societies; indeed it helps to define such societies. So while the scale and pervasiveness of contemporary surveillance would be impossible without computer power, computers have not created the situation that citizens of advanced societies find themselves in today. We were 'data-subjects' long before any supposed technical revolution occurred."[104]

When I visit a website in search of a new pair of running shoes or a book but ultimately decide not to buy, I am haunted by ads of shoes and books for days, if not weeks, after. With facial recognition technology improving rapidly and becoming more affordable, we can be identified and tracked on public sidewalks, in shopping malls, in parking lots, and so on. Personalized ads will one day probably greet us almost everywhere. So be careful what you do online; it could get embarrassing. Does anyone want to walk through a subway station during rush hour and be stalked by constantly reappearing ads for jock-itch relief or erectile dysfunction treatments? As the science fiction film *Minority Report* showed, digital billboards, walls, floors, ceilings, even the sky may become high-tech fishing lures that see us coming and light up in an effort to hook us, utilizing whatever our

## WHAT IS ENCRYPTION AND DO WE WANT IT EVERYWHERE?

Encryption is the solution to all of our privacy problems—or it's a source of bigger problems, depending on whom you ask. Encryption is the process of turning your information into an indecipherable jumble of characters that only you and those you allow can translate back into readable information. Many experts and critics of social media's personal data collection issues believe that encryption is the necessary fix. But a collision of opposing desires has complicated things. At issue is personal privacy versus public safety. We can assume that most users of Facebook, Instagram, Snapchat, and other social media platforms would opt for privacy when given a clear choice to have it. Encrypting everything sounds like a great idea. But some governments lean toward a position that says mass encryption of data would be catastrophic for the security of society because it would make it significantly more difficult to gather intelligence on terrorists. Given all of the known failures, lies, and excesses that can be pinned on political leaders and law enforcement agencies, it may seem sensible to dismiss their argument. But we shouldn't. There is a balance here that can and must be found. We don't want Mark Zuckerberg and his algorithms documenting and analyzing every trip we take to the bathroom. But neither do want to make it easier for religious fanatics to blow us up while flying at 35,000 feet.

Clear and tough regulation seems to be the best answer. If governments don't want to see everything encrypted, then how about they show some concern for the people by reigning in these huge companies that are destroying personal privacy as a means to make billions of dollars? At the minimum, social media users should have a right to know in unambiguous language what is being collected by whom and for what purposes. Users should also have a right to request and see whatever digital biographies of them companies hold. We can do this with our credit reports, why not our secret digital dossiers? This way we can at least know what's in there and try to correct any errors that may harm us. The need for this should be obvious when you consider that the Federal Trade Commission estimates that roughly a quarter of all consumer credit

> reports contain errors—despite some regulation and over-
> sight—and Acxiom, a data broker, has admitted that as much
> as 30 percent of the data they hold about people like you and
> me may be flat-out wrong.[103]

secret cyber biography reveals about our wants and needs. We may
soon find ourselves under constant sensory and emotional assault
from sounds and images seeking to extract money from us. There
may be no end to it, no peace. For example, many toilets, private and
public, may one day be Internet-enabled and capable of analyzing
our waste to alert us if something seems amiss with our health.[105]
Sure, having a toilet warn you about a current or imminent health
problem sounds nice. But, of course, this also would open the window
for personalized ads to be projected onto the surface of the water, for
instance. Today, we can turn off the computer, put down the smartphone if we want a moment of peace. Tomorrow may be different.

## WHAT DID EDWARD SNOWDEN REVEAL?

In 2013 Edward Snowden, a one-time CIA employee and relatively low-level private contractor working for the National
Security Agency, stole and gave to journalists documents
revealing that the US NSA and the United Kingdom's coun-
terpart, GCHQ, were harvesting vast amounts of data from
their own citizens, most of whom were not under investigation by any law enforcement agency. E-mails, text messages,
photos, videos, social media comments—*everything* was up
for grabs. The stated goal of such unprecedented mass surveillance may have been reasonable and defensible—stop terrorists before they kill—but that doesn't necessarily mean spying
on everyone all of the time is legal, moral, or even the most
productive course to take in the fight against terrorism.

Snowden is still a source of great controversy, of course;
he is seen as a traitor by some, and a hero by others. History
will have to sort that out, I suppose. In the meantime, we all
would be wise to at least appreciate the awareness we now
have about what is happening to our "private" communications and online activities.

Has a crime occurred when one person willingly gives something of value to another? No, that would be called "giving." But what if one doesn't understand the value of the thing given or that there may be serious consequences of having given it to this other person? It's still not a crime, perhaps; fleecing the gullible makes up much of the world's economy. If nothing else, however, we do seem to have come up on a gray moral area. If someone takes your personal information by legal yet mostly mysterious means and then profits from it, have you been victimized? Does it matter if you don't understand just how much of personal data has been taken or the ways in which it will be used? Some worry. Some condemn. Most, however, just don't care. They give it little thought, if any. They agree to terms of service—without reading—and proceed to share some of the most intimate aspects of their lives with people they do not know somewhere behind the screen, people who will sell or use this data with little or no oversight.

Facebook has developed a deep learning program, called Deep-Face, that can identify people in photos. Facebook claims that it is better at recognizing faces than humans are, scoring a 97 percent accuracy rate. Understand what this means to your ability to walk around in pubic as an anonymous person. You could be in a crowd at Disney World or on a New York City sidewalk, and if some random tourist takes a photo of something while you happen to be walking by in the background, and then posts it on social media, you might be identified online by name in a photograph you never knew was taken of you. Under pressure in Europe from privacy advocates and the European Union, Facebook deactivated facial recognition from user accounts there.[106]

Privacy may not be dead and gone, but's it's in trouble. And there is a good chance that no one can save it but us. Governments and corporations have their own interests at stake on this matter, and those interests do not always coincide with the public's. Therefore, it likely remains with us, the people who use the Internet and social media, to say "enough is enough" and push back.

## IS IT TOO LATE?

**The same rights that people have off-line must also be protected online, including the right to privacy.**
—United Nations[107]

After so many pages of doom and gloom, it bears repeating something I wrote in the introduction to this book: I do not view the Internet or social media as a lost cause or a failed experiment. I still use social media, and I rely on the Internet for many things. I remain hopeful. Everyday people leading conventional lives are the ultimate source of all of these billions of dollars the social media companies earn. At any moment, they can demand something better, more respect for their privacy from companies and better protections from their governments. And if users don't get what they want, then at some point they may log off and never come back. I can't see everyone turning their back on the Internet, of course, but individual social media companies? Sure, that's possible. Or maybe new companies will come along with evolved and enhanced forms of Facebook, Twitter, Instagram, Snapchat, and so on. Maybe they will make do with business plans that don't rest on selling our private lives. To be blunt, the current winners of the social media landscape should have already done the right thing. It's overdue, and they don't have any excuses, given the brains and resources at their disposal. The world loves to marvel at today's titans of cyberspace for being so brilliant and creative. But if they really are all that, then why haven't they figured out how to make their money without constantly chiseling away at our privacy and risking user revolt? Maybe I am guilty of overestimating the wisdom and power of billions of Internet users. But I hope that these companies are shown to be guilty of underestimating the wisdom and power of their users.

"A more responsible Facebook or Google would not simply offer better or straightforward privacy settings," writes social media expert Silverman in *Terms of Service*. "They would decline to collect this data in the first place, much less share or trade it with so many outside partners. They would encrypt all data they transmit, encourage the adoption of other security measures, and use the court system to fight government data requests. They would also diversify their business practices so that their financial prospects were not contingent upon surveilling users and manipulating them into passivity with promises of better advertisements for prescription drugs or cheap electronics."[108]

I find it encouraging that optimistic thoughts come up so often in discussions about the issue of online privacy. Many people do have at least some hope that the Internet and social media will become a more welcoming, sensible, and less-exploitive environment, enough to save some semblance of privacy.

"I think it's a pendulum and just starting to swing in another direction," said veteran editor/journalist Robert DeAngelo.[109] "I believe young people will begin to realize maybe social media isn't all it's cracked up to be, at least in terms of posting anything and everything. I think folks will start to be more judicious with the types of things they reveal about themselves on social media. Definitely not predicting social media will go away—it's probably here to stay. But it might evolve into something that allows the social interaction some desire without giving up one's privacy entirely."

Cybersecurity expert and futurist Marc Goodman believes that great things are possible, including much better privacy and security online. But we have to make it happen. "The techno-utopia promised by Silicon Valley may be possible, but it will not magically appear on its own," he writes in his book *Future Crimes*.[110] "It will take tremendous intention, effort, and struggle on the part of citizens, government, corporations, and NGOs to ensure that it comes to fruition. A new battle has begun between those who will leverage technology to benefit humanity and those who prefer to subvert these tools, regardless of the harm caused to others. This is the battle for the soul of technology and its future. It rages on in the background, mostly sub rosa, heretofore well hidden from the average citizen."

Andreas Weigend, the founder and director of the Social Media Lab and former Amazon chief scientist, is one of the world's foremost experts on Big Data. Like many others, he declares privacy as we knew it a lost cause, "a blip in human history" and today only "an illusion," as he puts it.[111] Nevertheless, Weigend offers hopeful words for the future in his book *Data for the People*: "'Data for the People' is not some empty slogan. . . . The traditional 'Mad Men' of marketing have been replaced by data scientists running algorithms on the multitudinous digital traces that a billion people leave behind every day. Even more important than the exponential growth in our data set is the change in our mindset. To be full participants in the social data revolution, we must shed the old mindset of passive 'consumers,' who take in whatever is placed before us, and embrace a new mindset, that of active co-creators of social data. . . . This is how data of the people and by the people can and will become data for the people."[112]

Privacy, according to my best hunch, will never again be what it was in, say, 1890, or, for that matter, 1990. It will, however, likely mount a comeback of sorts. More consistent and higher levels of privacy may become available in the near future. But it will come with a price. I say this with some confidence because whenever and wherever there is great demand, someone almost always shows up to sell a product or service that satisfies it.

"As the value for data increases, there will be a call to put a clearer monetary value on, in particular, personal information," predicts technology expert Kenneth Cukier.[113] "It will be tempting to make personal privacy a property right, in order to better protect it. Firms will need to get clearer permission to use personal data and suffer greater economic damages if they fail to protect privacy or misuse the data. . . . Hitherto free services like Facebook and Google will come with a price tag unless we are willing to cough up the data. So privacy in 2050 will probably be a luxury good, like flying business class or owning a second home."

Let's hope purchased privacy will be more affordable to most than flying business class or owning a second home is today. But the return of privacy may be inevitable on some level at least. People are already concerned about what has happened—remember, 91 percent of Americans feel that they have lost control of their personal information[114]—so the demand is there and is likely to grow. Hopefully the coming years will see the widespread availability of cheap and effective cyber walls, shields, scramblers, barriers, and force fields capable of repelling some or all of those prying people and programs. Don't count on it, though. And don't wait. You have work to do now. Maintain awareness and make sure that what remains of your privacy is hard to steal. Take reasonable actions. Short of living in a lead-lined bunker and sleeping in a Faraday cage, do whatever you can. Don't be a soft target for hackers and data brokers. And strengthen those passwords. Right now.

*Chapter Six*

# WHAT'S NEXT?

We find ourselves in a thicket of strategic complexity, surrounded by a dense mist of uncertainty.

—Nick Bostrom, professor, University of Oxford;
director, Future of Humanity Institute;
director, Strategic Artificial Intelligence Research Centre[1]

We and our technological creations are poised to embark on what is sure to be a strange and deeply commingled evolutionary path.

—Arati Prabhakar, former director of DARPA[2]

No individual path of evolution of any kind can be predicted, either at the beginning or even toward the end of its trajectory. Natural selection can bring a species to the brink of a major revolutionary change, only to turn it away.

—Edward O. Wilson, naturalist[3]

After centuries of hard-won understanding of nature that now permits us, for the first time in history, to control many aspects of our destinies, we're on the verge of abdicating this control to artificial agents that *can't* think, prematurely putting civilization on autopilot.

—Daniel C. Dennett, Austin B. Fletcher Professor of Philosophy and co-director of the Center for Cognitive Studies, Tufts University[4]

The Internet is the first thing humanity has invented that humanity doesn't understand.

—Eric Schmidt, former Google executive[5]

Once, we were microscopic shadows of existence, not quite something yet more than nothing. We fell short of whatever mark it is that life is supposed to measure up to. But then we lived. We spread throughout a vast ocean on a small, lonely planet. We tumbled along a perilous path of ever-increasing complexity and intelligence until we landed on our feet atop solid ground. One of many, our precise brand of primate out-competed and out-lucked most others. We organized ourselves into small hunter-gatherer societies, then chiefdoms, followed by ultra-complex states. Along the way, we had tamed fire to turn away the darkness and all its monsters. We acquired languages and told stories. We had spread across a challenging and unforgiving world and won the ultimate victory—continued existence. We made music and wrote stories. We loved and we enjoyed sexual connections, even as we butchered ourselves in one conflict after another. We invented science. We captured the Sun's magic and used it for energy and for war. We touched the Moon and looked back at the beginning of time.[6] Now we find ourselves at a strange new place, a moment and setting that seems to be sneaking up on us, even as we engineer it. We are poised to become closer to each other than ever before, but only if we first place machines between us.

> **Abstract thinking by biological brains has underpinned the emergence of all culture and science. But this activity—spanning tens of millennia at most—will be a brief precursor to the more powerful intellects of the inorganic, posthuman era.**
>
> —Martin Rees, former president of the Royal Society,
> emeritus professor of cosmology and astrophysics,
> University of Cambridge[7]

We have come far. So, where exactly are we? And what comes next? In previous chapters, we explored key issues related to the Internet and social media, including filter bubbles, fake news, addiction, privacy, and some of the cognitive biases that cause problems for people online. Another important consideration, however, cannot be explored in the same way—because it does not yet exist. But we must try anyway. We need to consider what comes next, prepare for . . . something, I'm not sure what. The future is out there, and it's rushing toward us. What we will have, what we will do, and who or what we will be tomorrow is an urgent concern because the pace of change is quickening. But in looking forward, let's not be naive and disrespectful to the pain and suffering of the millions of people who are still waiting on the basic comforts and conveniences of the last century to show up in their lives. Let's acknowledge that not every human today has the luxury of imagining, worrying about, or cheering on the next big thing to come out of Silicon Valley. The spectrum of the human experience is so wide right now that it can be difficult to comprehend. One person tours the Louvre in virtual reality from the comfort of her couch at home. She looks at a time-less work of Greek art. Inspired, she ponders the meaning of life, as well as the possibility of immortality via next-gen tech and medi-cine. In that same moment on the same planet, a person dies slowly from dysentery while crying unanswered prayers. She looks up at an empty sky and ponders the meaningless of her misery and death.

The hope, of course, is that fast-improving computer technology will lift all boats. Everyone, including the millions of human babies who die each year from malnutrition and preventable diseases, will benefit from the approaching waves of technology and social media innovations. But we might end up with a world just like the present one, in which some people are born into hellholes with no hope of escape and others enter life with a ticket to the ultimate toy factory in hand.

## WHAT IS THE FUTURE OF THE INTERNET AND SOCIAL MEDIA?

There are many questions, and the answers will not come easy. But the act of asking is constructive. I ask questions not because you or I can answer them now but because we need to be thinking about them now. Wondering, imagining, and a bit of evidence-based guessing can help us avoid total blindness and perhaps reduce our vulnerability to error and abuse. For example, does empowering our technology weaken us? If we end up as a species of hyper-connected cyborgs marching about within one global superorganism, will that mean we will have sacrificed some or all of our humanity? What is "our humanity" anyway? Does becoming more machine and less

flesh leave us less alive? Are we in the process of exiting the realm
of "life"? How can we answer such questions when we haven't yet
agreed on a definition of life? How does one call for sensible caution
in the face of explosive, disruptive technological progress without
slipping into the dreaded Luddite zone? Will social media make
us more tribal or less tribal, more self-destructive or less so? Does
making the Internet more important in our lives lessen or enhance
the importance of our lives? Will the public have enough of a say in
how the Internet and social media shape society? Will the public
have any say? Can social media do more than merely facilitate connection and communication? Can online social networks improve
the overall quality of human discourse? Will the Internet free us,
enslave us, or bring about something in between? Will it enrich all
of humankind, or only a fortunate few? Can we trust what may be
one of the most profound and consequential leaps in cultural evolution to a handful of billionaires and politicians? None of this is arm-
chair philosophy meant to merely pass the time. There are serious
and immediate challenges tied to these questions, and we must
work to get them right or risk running ourselves straight into one
avoidable problem after another.

An example of a challenge in need of immediate attention is
our excessive and often thoughtless reliance on computers, smartphones, and apps. Millions place unwarranted trust in "Googling
answers," for example. "Google is God" may be an old Internet joke,[8]
but some people today really do seem to believe that Google is a
modern-day oracle, omniscient god, or, at the very least, a wise and
trustworthy scholar. But it's none of those things. Google is a search
engine. Resist the lazy mind. Be vigilant. Maintain an awareness
of the role and prominence of technology in your life. The best tools
are there for us to use—and not the other way around. "For today's
younger generation, the world has been turned upside down," writes
John Markoff, author of *Machines of Loving Grace*.[9] "Rather than
deploying an automaton to free them to think big thoughts, have
close relationships, and exercise their individuality, creativity, and
freedom, they look to their smartphones for guidance. What began
as Internet technologies enabling their users to share preferences
efficiently has become a growing array of data-hungry algorithms
that make decisions for us. Now the Internet seamlessly serves up
life decisions for us."

## TWO QUESTIONS FOR THE FUTURE

*Writer, educator, and futurist Bryan Alexander[10] has high hopes for social media but also some concerns. I asked him two questions about where all of this liking and tweeting may lead.[11]*

**There is plenty of negative reporting about social media these days—privacy loss, filter bubbles, trolls, etc.—will the good overcome the bad, long-term?**

**Alexander:** I think social media is a net positive for humanity, unless we truly screw it up. There are so many benefits, including spurring creativity, increased access to different people and cultures, grounding for democratic storytelling, access to diversity information sources, emotional support, new ways of gathering and sharing information, the ability to find one's creative voice through different media, and more.

We're in a frantic period now, partly driven by old media frenzy and post-2016-election fallout. This isn't a good time for lucidity. For example, few are addressing media criticism from before 2016. Nobody's criticizing television—arguably the most powerful source for polarization and misinformation in the current landscape.

There are some realistic criticisms. Troll swarms have attacked some women, racial minorities, and trans people. We *can* spread bad information easily—hence the heroic role of Snopes.com. Some of the major social media platform owners, Facebook, notably, are not trustworthy in responding to these challenges. But I think the advantages are strong, and capable of being realized generally. I suspect we'll improve our collaborative use of social media as skills increase, digital literacy grows, and trolling gradually backfires.

**What is likely for the future of the Internet and social media?**

We could see social media bifurcating into levels based on money, control, and prestige, like the old divide between broadcast and community TV. Imagine gated communities with stronger content controls than there are now, moderated by a mix of humans and AI, accessible through a fee. In contrast would be a Wild West of more chaotic, less slick-looking sites.

What happens if video, rather than text or images, becomes central to our social media experience? Will it be harder to bully or abuse people whose animated faces you see? Will it be easier or more difficult to spread misinformation?

It could be a more authoritarian future. That is, governments are already using social media to protect themselves. Platform providers can take a stronger role in policing content—think of Facebook and Google running mixed human and AI teams to scout for bad information, or Twitter kicking off selected bad users. There's also a new wave of love for old-school media, including newspapers and TV news. All of these are based on individual users ceding power to authorities.

It could be a more democratic future. Digital literacy, which includes information and media literacy, should empower individuals to interact with information and each other in a more critical, careful way. In this future, users gain, rather than cede authority.

Carries James of Harvard's Project Zero is optimistic about the future. "The Internet is in some ways a grand stage for expressing all these qualities and perhaps a unique one, given its special affordances," she said.[12]

We can see it used in profoundly humane, socially positive ways—for example, communities of support for youth who feel marginalized and isolated due to their sexuality, experiences with bullying, struggles with a medical condition, etc. We also see the deeply inhumane uses, such as the Steubenville [High School rape] case,[13] that suggest deep disconnects. Given potentials on both sides, it's hard to argue that the Internet/digital technologies "make us" more or less human or humane. What's more important is how we use these technologies—in reflective versus unreflective ways—and with what purposes. I want to feel hopeful that we'll see more of the humane uses going forward, but we are challenged right now by a modeling/mentorship gap. When our most powerful leaders use social media to mock, taunt, and bully, it's hard to feel optimistic that others won't simply follow suit. But, being in education, as I am, is a hopeful choice; so I will continue to focus my energies on supporting humane ways of being digital.

## FACEBOOK IS COMING FOR YOUR BRAIN

**The merging of humans and machines is happening now.**
—Headline of a *Wired* magazine article, January 27, 2017[14]

Will Facebook ever be satisfied? Apparently not. Despite having more than two billion users, harvesting incomprehensible amounts of valuable user data, and earning more than $25 billion in yearly advertising revenue,[15] Zuckerberg and crew want more. Now Facebook is after your brain. The company is investing time and money into the development of a brain-computer interface that would enable users to engage with social media via thoughts alone.[16] The plan was announced by Regina Dugan at Facebook's annual F8 conference in April 2017. Dugan leads the effort and comes to it with impressive credentials. She is a former director of DARPA, the US military's fringe-and-beyond research department. She also once led Google's experimental ATAP research group. Facebook's basic goal for a brain-computer interface would be to allow its users to type with their thoughts at a rate of 100 words per minute. Dugan says they hope to demonstrate this ability within two years.

Facebook is not the only one chasing this prize. Elon Musk, founder of Tesla and SpaceX, is trying to build what his team calls a "direct cortical interface."[17] The goal is to build small devices that can be implanted in the brain and enable a person to "upload and download thoughts." Facebook is also working to develop a bizarre but fascinating technology that would allow human skin to hear. The company has already produced an "artificial cochlea" toward this end.[18]

What all of this means is that some extremely interesting, game-changing breakthroughs may be coming to the social media scene in the not-too-distant future. Facebook users might be able to post comments to their pages, conduct chats with friends, add or delete images and videos, and so on, *all from inside their head.* And you thought privacy issues, hacking, and malware were problems now. Imagine the accidental status updates that might occur during a good dream. Think of what it would mean to have the occasional brain fart and disturbing private thought published and archived in the cloud, within reach of data miners and hackers forever. Still, it's fascinating to consider what it would be like if something anywhere close to this were to be realized on a massive, societal scale. It would be something close to actual telepathy, the hollow fantasy of so many for so long, finally made real and delivered to us by science and engineering. The most intriguing aspect of all of this, of course, is not having the ability to type with thoughts. It is the down-road potential for two or more minds meeting up in cyberspace, connecting in an intimate, unprecedented way that would place our species on to a very different plane of existence. It would be, I suppose, the ultimate manifestation of our compulsion to connect, share, and socialize. Perhaps by 2050 or so these brain-computer interface initiatives by Facebook and others will be seen as the historic baby steps that led to the moment when humans transitioned into more durable and capable robot bodies, or went all the way and became immortal holograms. Keep your eyes on the ball. Things are moving quickly. Do you remember when e-mail was cool, cutting-edge technology? Now e-mailing someone seems weirdly formal and cumbersome. It feels like two tin cans with a string between them.

"It is change, continuing change, inevitable change, that is the dominant factor in society today," wrote Isaac Asimov, the prolific science and science fiction writer, many years ago.[19] "No sensible decision can be made any longer without taking into account not only the world as it is, but the world as it will be. . . . This, in turn, means that our statesmen, our businessmen, our everyman must take on a science fictional way of thinking."

Jake Farr-Wharton, of Australia, is a projects director and host of *The Imaginary Friends Show*, a popular podcast. He appreciates the benefits of social media and has high hopes for its future. "I feel that it provides an opportunity for people to share their experiences, culture, knowledge, and opinions," he said.[20] "One day, I'd love to have a chip in my brain that connects me to the neural net, giving me access to all information on everything all of the time—and enough cloud based memory so I can process all that information without frying my brain."

## WHY ARE WE DOING THIS?

**We don't have Wi-Fi, so you'll just have to talk to each other.**
—Sign in a café window

Writing more than a century and a half ago in *Walden* (an essential read I suggest for those who spend large amounts of time in the digital environment), Henry David Thoreau reminds us that communication for the sake of communication doesn't necessarily mean much. It is, rather, the *quality* of what we say, write, and read that matters. "Our inventions are wont to be pretty toys, which distract our attention from serious things," he writes. "They are but improved means to an unimproved end, an end which it was already but too easy to arrive at; as railroads lead to Boston or New York. We are in great haste to construct a magnetic telegraph from Maine to Texas; but Maine and Texas, it may be, have nothing important to communicate."[21] When tackling the challenges of our Internet and social media use, both globally and for the individual, we would be wise to make sure we do not mistake "improved means to an unimproved end" for meaningful and positive progress.

"The Internet is not about technology, it is not about information, it is about communication," writes Michael Strangelove, a lecturer in the Department of Communication at the University of Ottawa and the author of *Empire of Mind*.[22] "The Internet is mass participation in fully bidirectional, uncensored mass communication. Communication is the basis, the foundation, the radical ground and root upon which all community stands, grows, and thrives. The Internet is a community of chronic communicators." So *what* are we communicating? How much of the Internet is used up with flagrant hate and blatant stupidity? *Too much* is the answer. I sometimes worry that the World Wide Web might become a lost cause, turn out to be nothing more than crowded, seedy shopping mall, a gaudy distraction-contraption that falls well short of being or doing anything uplifting for humanity. I know there are many examples of wonderful things made possible only via the Internet today, but so much of the potential good is just not being realized. Even as we stumble around in cyberspace without ever finding real satisfaction, we can't help but feel that the Internet doing great things for us. But how many and how great? A line by science fiction writer William Gibson's *Neuromancer* comes to mind: "Cyberspace, a consensual hallucination experienced daily by billions."[23]

Sir Tim Berners-Lee, father of the World Wide Web, Knight Commander of the Order of the British Empire, and Turing Award winner, is not happy about our current social media situation either. He is concerned about what has become of his creation as we come to the end of its first three decades of existence. He released a statement in 2017 acknowledging this, pointing out that the Internet has become "more of a purveyor of untruth than of truth because of the way the adverting revenue model encourages people to put things online which will be clicked on."[24] Berners-Lee continued:

> I've become increasingly worried about three new trends, which I believe we must tackle in order for the web to fulfill its true potential as a tool which serves all of humanity. . . . Even in countries where we believe governments have citizens' best interests at heart, watching everyone, all the time is simply going too far. It creates a chilling effect on free speech and stops the web from being used as a space to explore important topics, like sensitive health issues, sexuality or religion. I may have invented the web, but all of you have helped to create what it is today. All the blogs, posts, tweets, photos, videos, applications, web pages and more represent the contributions of millions of you around the world building our online community. . . . It has taken all of us to build the web we have, and now it is up to all of us to build the web we want—for everyone.[25]

To make something of the Internet and social media that we can really be proud of, we must, as individuals, feed into it something more than our shallowest hopes, fears, and vanities. Technology will not uplift us as a species any more than stone tools alone did. Even the most finely crafted and sharpened rock meant nothing without the fingers of a motivated, focused, and ambitious *Homo erectus* wrapped around it. We must give purpose to this tool and not wait for it to tell us what to do. It is our responsibility to influence the Internet more than it influences us. Of course, we can't all be as interesting as Daniel Dennett or Stephen Hawking, perhaps, but we can try. With effort, we might do better tomorrow than we did yesterday. No one should have to hold back ideas and opinions on social media, but neither does anyone have to make spewing hate a personal hobby. At their best, social media sites and apps are megaphones for positive expression. They can show the best of who we are; what we do; what we care about, dream about, and work for. At their worst, however, they can be deep pits of hate and jealousy. Dark places where many users spend time they can never get back being mean to strangers or trying to impress people they barely know with staged presentations of something that only vaguely resembles their real life.

Many people find that the role of social media in their lives evolves over time, becoming more or less important. New York City teacher Shanika took an eight-month break from Facebook in 2016. She explained to me, "My desire to leave was triggered by a post by a friend who took a picture posing near her grandmother's tombstone. Something about it felt very superficial. Things like this cheapen the human experience, turning them into mere spectacles, and cheapen our relationships with people."

Shanika's reaction to her friend is not all that uncommon; it is something even Jacob Silverman touches on in *Terms of Service*. There he writes about the tendency many users have of plastering too much of themselves on social media. "The ones who are most blissfully, unself-consciously happy baffle me most. Where is their neuroticism, their self-consciousness about sharing and laying their lives bare? How easily they've assimilated themselves to this lifestyle, tending to their profiles, little gardens of personality in which only pleasantries bloom and life's setbacks, even a death in the family, are presented with such overwrought sentimentality that it's possible to think that such tragedies are welcomed, because they offer an opportunity to share and be embraced by the social-media cocoon."[26]

Linda Stone, a former Apple Computer and Microsoft executive, also harbors all-too-common feelings of loss and remorse related to a tool, the Internet, that could be far more of a boost than a burden: "Before the Internet, I made more trips to the library and more phone calls. . . . I walked more, biked more, hiked more, and played more. I made love more often. . . . The Internet stole my body, now a lifeless form hunched in front of a glowing screen. My senses dulled as my greedy mind became one with the global brain we call the Internet."[27]

We can't afford to let the Internet go to waste or, worse, degrade and corrupt the best things about us. We must not stumble and fall under the weight of our own banality and boorishness. The Internet, social media, smartphones, all of it, can help us to do more and be more. For instance, there are apps that can bring stationary cyclists around the world together for mass virtual reality races against one another in real time.[28] The Internet can allow for more ambitious and safer hiking by connecting us with information about location, terrain, weather, and plant and animal life. I frequently use the Internet and digital technology to discover and buy new books, the kind I can hold and feel. Like all tools, the Internet and social media are what we make of them. "This is the *new* human way," said Natasha, an attorney, "Social media is not going to go away, so the best thing to do is invest your time and energy into flooding the various platforms with *truth and knowledge*, as opposed to alternative facts and Kim Kardashians. Like everything else, social media will evolve."[29]

John Michael Strubhart of Texas says he places a high value on thinking "long and hard" about his life and how he interacts with the world. Like Natasha, he believes that there is a lot of good here if we look for it, or build it. He is confident that his social media activities do not threaten his deeper intellectual activities. However, he does recognize the potential for problems: "I think that social media has the potential to be anti-intellectual. I know several people who would readily say, 'I saw it online. I believe it! You can't change my mind!' *Get off-line and read a book, develop an interest, commune with nature, explore another culture, do something tangible to make the world a little better* is good advice for everyone. The worst thing about social media is that it is too easy to consume. It takes very little effort to get a feeling of satisfaction from it. It can be a very lazy way to experience something."[30]

Strubhart thinks that social media may offer us a means to enhancing the better aspects of our existence, but it's up to us ultimately: "I think that the only lasting way to achieve that is to do so from the inside. Digital connectivity can lead you there, but it cannot in itself transform one into a more humane and human person. Online networks, like any other technology, can bring out the best and the worst in people. If history is any true indicator, we will make progress and have setbacks as a direct result of this technology, but progress will get the greater share of that action. Of course, I could be wrong."

Joy Holloway-D'Avilar, a registered nurse, thinks that social media may have stimulated or unleashed "a part of humanity that

## WILL BIG DATA KNOW EVERYTHING ABOUT EVERYONE?

Today's big business of Big Data; mass surveillance; individually targeted advertising; increasingly complex and perceptive algorithms; better, faster, smaller, and cheaper hardware; and greater Internet reach will move humanity into a weird existence in which every move made—every thought and action, past, present, and even future—may be observed and tracked by computers. This will have a massive impact on billions of lives, for better and worse. Based on current trends, I predict that machines will know a person's past in great detail and far more accurately than he or she does because human memory is limited and fallible. Human memory has no chance against that of a computer. Stranger still, computers will be able to predict an individual's *future* thoughts and movements with remarkable accuracy. By sifting through massive amounts of personal data, a computer program will be able to anticipate what someone wants or needs before it even crosses the person's mind. This brings to mind the shadow brain, discussed in chapter 4. The powerful combination of social media, Big Data, and complex algorithms soon may become a larger, more problematic *artificial* shadow brain that we must account for. Like the natural subconscious mind, this one will know things about us that even we are not aware of. It will silently nudge or shove us toward specific decisions and behaviors. It will influence us to lean toward love, fear, hate, or indifference. Unlike the subconscious mind, however, this data-driven algorithmic shadow brain is likely to be loyal to companies or governments lurking somewhere in the dark. Google can already predict now, with impressive accuracy, where millions of users will be, say, a week from next Thursday at 7:23pm. One day soon, companies are likely to know where you would want to spend your vacation, not only in the current year but five or ten years hence as well. Algorithms will know if a romantic relationship will succeed long-term—before the first date.

It's not difficult to imagine how Stalin and Hitler might have used Big Data to further their murderous agendas. What might happen if a modern dictator or rogue government were to make full use of complex algorithms to identify early trends or disparate factors that indicate a citizen might become disloyal or less loyal in the future? Every revolution could be stopped before it began, every dissident silenced before speaking. Scary stuff, no doubt, but historian Yuval Noah Harari believes that evil dictators armed with algorithms are not the greatest threat to the current version of humanity: "The individual is more likely to disintegrate gently from within than to be brutally crushed from without," he writes in *Homo Deus: A Brief History of Tomorrow*.[31] "Today most corporations and governments pay homage to my individuality, and promise to provide medicine, education, and entertainment customized to my unique needs and wishes. But in order to do so, corporations and governments first need to deconstruct me into biochemical subsystems, monitor the subsystems with ubiquitous sensors, and decipher their working with powerful algorithms. In the process, the individual transpires to be nothing but a religious fantasy. Reality will be a measure of biochemical and electronic algorithms, without clear borders, and without individual hubs."

always lay deep beneath the surface," and this is not all bad:

There's this need to have a platform, to shout, to be heard and seen on some greater level. Maybe most of us were dormant extroverts, and this just gave to humanity what humans always wanted but never knew how to go about having. After all, humans have the need to express themselves in grand ways; take, for example, the pyramids in Egypt and South America, the cave drawings, extravagant ground carvings—heck, Stonehenge and the heads on Easter Island. We can now socialize without having to leave home. But I have also seen social media draw people out of their homes to physically connect, so I don't knock it. It is all how we use it; take, for example, a phone is very useful, but people could spend hours on it yapping away all sorts of nonsense, wasting their time and lives. I say it's all in how you use the tools you have available to you. I for one am quite focused, so these transitory flashy things don't dissuade me from my focus and pursuit of all things intellectual. As they say, small things amuse small minds. If you're really about anything and are focused, social media cannot distract you from your ability to be mindful and present. I say, make social media work for you. As someone that has family in four countries, I need it to stay connected. If you are a goal-oriented and focused individual, nothing can take you off your game. You must have laser focus in life, or everything that comes along will be a distraction. And one must always take time, whether in meditation, hiking, or something else, to reflect and go inward and put these things on pause.[32]

## SOCIAL MEDIA AND YOUNG PEOPLE: A TEACHER'S PERSPECTIVE

Timothy Redmond is a social studies teacher at Williamsville East High School, an adjunct professor at Daemen College, an associate director for the Summer Institute for Human Rights and Genocide Studies of Buffalo, and the director for the Holocaust Resource Center of Buffalo's annual Conference for Educators on Human Rights and Genocide Studies. He has a master's degree and doctorate in political science, and he also writes the Examined Life, a column published in the *East Aurora Advertiser* that encourages critical thinking in the realm of American politics. He shared with me some of his observations and thoughts[33] about how social media impacts his students:

> Because of social media today, students are never able to escape social judgment, and it is addictive. Some students exhibit a compulsion to check their phones immediately when the bell rings, and sometimes during class. Students describe the stress that is associated with "Snap Streaks," a streak of days posting on Snapchat. It has become a badge of honor to have a long streak of posts with your friends; and if an extended streak, some in excess of over one year, is broken, many students are heartbroken. When parents take away their phones, they give their friends their account information so their friends can post for them, thereby preserving the streak. Friends who forget to post and break the streak will earn the wrath of their partner.

Students get a social media account because they don't want to feel left out. Trends happen on social media, and you don't want to be left out of conversations in school the next day. So you have to constantly be checking so you don't miss out on something. It is heartbreaking when you see your circle of friends is out and [has] shared something on their [social media] accounts. You see it while at home because you were not invited.

There is also stress waiting for validation. Students want their posts to be retweeted and liked, and there is an element of a popularity contest involved as students continually compare the number of friends, followers, retweets, and likes they have compared to their peers. Screenshots enable a student's life to persist—a bad picture or a post that one comes to reqret can be copied and shared instantly and broadly. Before and after class, they are often playing games on their phones. One of the most striking differences I have found is how much quieter my classroom has become before and after class. Students used to talk to each other, but now many of them are on their phones, playing games. This could, perhaps, stunt their social skills.

*Socrates feared the printed word.*

They may be reading more, but perhaps their attention span is shorter. They read headlines and click to the next story; maybe they have a harder time reading large amounts of text. I have students comment on "how long" a three- or four-page article is; but all of this is, of course, anecdotal—many don't complain, and I forgot how I felt when I was fifteen. But, then again, our actions rewire our brain, so perhaps there is a real difference.

This is a world I didn't grow up in, so am I just that guy who is all upset because Elvis is moving his hips? Socrates feared the printed word; Neil Postman feared television. But, if Shakespeare had to memorize Homer, he would have never had the time to create *Hamlet*. I learned more from watching [Ken] Burns's documentary on the Civil War than from any book. There will always be something lost with the rise of a new technology, but there will also be something gained. I think there are incredible positives to social media, but obviously also some real concerns.

*We have met Big Brother and he is us.*

My biggest fear about social media [in general, for all ages] is that we increasingly engage in self-censorship. We have met Big Brother and he is us. Our social media feeds have become our soma. Social media is a tool that encourages our confirmation bias; it encourages us to think like lawyers rather than scientists. And that is dangerous because the echo chambers that result engender polarization and extremism. [As] someone who studies politics and human rights, I am gravely concerned about this. I just returned from Rwanda this summer and was confronted daily with the horror that an echo chamber can leave in its wake. When we essentially become our own publishers and editors, we eliminate all contrary points of view, and our critical-thinking skills will simply atrophy. My advice: Seek information, not ammunition. Therefore, (1) do not unfriend people who express different points of view, in fact, (2) seek out people on Twitter, etc., who are from [your] opposing political party, etc.

I was not surprised by the presence of fake news, per se—that was already present in such things as the birther movement. But I was surprised at the business of fake news, the incredible amounts of money that people could amass by doing nothing more than sitting at home and generating one false, outrageous story after another. I think human beings, in general, are gullible—some more than others, to be sure—but I think when you combine our difficulty with thinking critically with social media, you have a perfect storm, one that is tailor-made for the explosion of fake news.

*We need critical-thinking courses*
*in high school as well as college.*

What needs to happen is we need to begin emphasizing critical thinking far more in our educational system. It is not that teachers are not teaching critical thinking; it is just not presented to students in one package. So they learn about checking sources in one class and confirmation bias in another and the difference between correlation and causation in yet another, but I am not sure they see how they are all connected. We need critical-thinking courses in high school as well as college.

My fear is that [the Internet and social media] will really broaden the information gap. People who are interested and curious will become more informed, and those who don't want to watch the news don't have to anymore because there are so many other options. I fear that these choices will continue to divide people. We won't have any shared experiences or any shared knowledge. When I was in college, everyone talked about the latest episode of *Seinfeld*. Now it is so divided. Some people watch *Game of Thrones* and others watch *Orange Is the New Black*, etc. We all can't keep up. On the one hand, it is incredible the amount of quality programs that are being produced; it really is astounding. But, at the same time, we are just drowning in content, and we don't have any shared experiences that help bring us together.

I am an optimist, so I believe that we will become more rational. I believe that the power of truth will continue to work away at irrationality. It may seem imperceptible at times—like a river eroding a rock—but I believe that, in the long run, reason and evidence will prevail. But there is so much work to be done.

Camille, aged forty, is a thoughtful person and avid social media user with concerns about how we are using Web-based technologies. She says that one of the problems is that there aren't Internet education classes for everyone to take, which leads to things like millions of people wrongly believing that Google reliably serves up correct answers to any question. She thinks that the best thing about social media is that it keeps you in touch with your family and friends. And the worst thing about it is that it keeps you in touch with your family and friends. "Seeing the interests and opinions of people that I thought were sound of mind posting things online that makes me question their sanity every day," Camille said,[34] "it can feel like I got punched in the face while wearing my rose-colored glasses. Social media definitely makes you question your social circle."

Although Camille says she can't see herself ending her relationship with Facebook or Instagram anytime soon, she does struggle with posting photos of her baby.

I try to be mindful of what and how much I share, for a multitude of reasons. I'm careful not to post anything that would be embarrassing to my son when he gets older. Who knows what his generation will think about social media or how they will use it? Either way, I have to be mindful that I'm not inadvertently creating his social presence before he does. I also get concerned with how Facebook will use Big Data and facial recognition to analyze content from my posts to target him the moment he becomes an online citizen. I use social media, but I do hate many things about it. I don't particularly like or trust the owner of Facebook [Mark Zuckerberg], and I'm fully aware that I am the commodity which makes Facebook billions of dollars. My data. My information. My content. They sell my info. But social media is so engrained into everyday life that it's pretty difficult to avoid.

Camille continued:

There are lots of intellectuals creating amazing, interesting content and sharing it online. But we live in a time where reality shows, Twitter wars and viral videos of cats playing the piano are the distraction of choice for the average person. I think social media has reprogrammed many people to seek out meaningless validation for themselves through "likes" and has encouraged us to be inadvertently insincere about how we feel when we respond to status updates. . . . All the social media companies seem to have been created by people with less-than-desirable social skills, so it could explain a lot of what's currently wrong. I don't see social media going away anytime soon. People have always been compelled to share. [Before the advent of social media,] we wrote books, we composed music, we created art. We like to share ideas, good and bad. Social media is a great tool for that, and I think that need to share will keep it going.

## DON'T BLINK, YOU MIGHT MISS THE FUTURE

> **Predicting the future of the Internet is easy: anything that it hasn't yet drastically transformed, it will.**
> —Chris Dixon, technology expert and investor[35]

When you ask knowledgeable people about what the near- and long-term futures of the Internet and social media might be like, you never know what kind of response is coming. I have yet to hear the same answer twice. There are two basic themes, however, that seem most popular. The first is that this will all go to hell. No doubt about it, the

Internet will collapse under the weight of too much hate, stupidity, censorship, freedom, corruption, and/or exploitation. Or it will be torn apart by the conflicting demands of a highly intelligent species suffering from an obvious personality disorder. There will be too much control and regulation, while simultaneously not nearly enough, of course. The Internet will flounder because of too much secrecy, while also never allowing enough privacy. Social media users revolt, finally fed up with working so hard to make somebody else rich off their lives. Maybe the cyberterrorists and hackers will, in the end, win by stealing, stopping, and freezing *everything*. When it's humans versus humans, humans always lose; this we can be sure of. But, wait, maybe the doomsayers are wrong and we're all in for a great time ahead.

The second prediction is that the Internet and social media will basically allow us to download utopia. Some people are certain that things will be wonderful in the future, a global Disney theme park for all. The Internet will fulfill the promise of the cyber-utopians who told us it would end war, alleviate poverty, and fix stupidity by joining our minds, showering us with knowledge and wisdom, and setting us free, finally, from our collective past of dirt and stone. It's not quite the singularity—no one gets raptured up to the warm womb of the iCloud—but it's a very nice sentiment nonetheless. And then there are my favorites, the people who see futures before us that are so weird we can't even reliably judge them as mostly positive or mostly negative because we are trapped in the limited perspective of now, restricted by the suffocating confines of an organic shell and a natural past. I am always reluctant to scoff at or outright dismiss wild claims made about where the computer power, the Internet, and social media are going because I do think it makes sense to expect the unexpected in this case. Social media may well transform humankind into a single superorganism, for example. This is not crazy talk; one can argue that this is the course we're on right now. "Once we had neurons," observes Ted Anderson, curator of the TED conferences and TED Talks. "Now we're becoming the neurons."[36]

"As we speak, nerds in the best universities of the world are mapping out the brain, building robotic limbs, and developing primitive versions of technologies that will open up the future where your great grandchild will get high by plugging his brain directly into the web," speculates Cesar Hidalgo, an associate professor at the MIT Media Lab and the author of *Why Information Grows*.[37] He continues:

The augmentation that these kids will get is unimaginable to us, and is so bizarre for our modern ethical standards, that we are not even in a position to properly judge it (it would be like a sixteenth century puritan [sic] judging present day San Francisco). Yet, in the grand scheme of the universe, these new human machine networks will be nothing other than the next natural step in the evolution of our species' ability to beget information. Together, humans and our extensions—machines—will continue to evolve networks that are enslaved to the universe's main glorious purpose: the creation of pockets where information does not dwindle, but grows.

---

Less than 1 percent of the world's population was using the Internet in 1995. Today, approximately half the world's population is online. That's more than 3.5 billion people, and this number is growing at a rate of around ten people every second.[38] Facebook owner Mark Zuckerberg is working to pick up the pace. He wants to bring cheap or free Internet access to the billions not yet online. It's a Tony Stark–ish plan that involves giant solar-powered drones staying airborne for three months straight and beaming the Internet to people with lasers.[39]

---

Are you ready for the noosphere? Some people are rooting for a day when all human minds unite via the Internet or something like it to form one colossal, super-intelligent and super-creative mega-brain. The noosphere concept traces back in part to a Jesuit priest who wrote about it the 1920s.[40] Imagine complete cognitive connection for the species. Something like everyone on Earth walking around with a smartphone in his or her head, listening to and contributing to one big planetwide conference call that never ends. The noosphere, or some precursor to it, would allow a person to see, hear, and feel what anyone else is seeing, hearing, and feeling, anywhere else in the world. Want to be an elderly Albanian nanny in Florence, Italy, for a few hours, or at least share headspace with one? No problem. Just send a friend request and, if accepted, you're in.

Imagine true global connectivity with everyone online. We could observe the lives and thoughts of all humanity in real time all the time; virtually travel the planet, to anywhere, in a flash; be with anyone, do anything. Have the contents of a thousand books poured into your brain in less than a second. Tap into not only the present lives of billions of people, but also their memories and imagination. Of course, being who we are, it's a sure bet that somebody would attempt to hack this global brain and load it up with malware and viruses, or simply steal your data—which is you at this point. And you thought we had serious privacy and security issues now. It is also possible that collective super-connectivity may lead to a "collective superintelligence,"[41] a single, mass brain arising from billions of individual brains. This could happen by design or by accident. All of this may lead the minds of *Star Trek* fans straight to the Borg.

These fictional uber-villains of the twenty-fourth century are a collection of numerous species bound together by a wireless hive mind. Think noosphere with a wicked mission statement. The Borg roam the galaxy, attempting to "assimilate" every intelligent life-form they encounter. More machine than life, the Borg strip victims of all individuality and add their consciousness to the collective mind. They exist in a state of zombie-like servitude to algorithms and network demands. Being Borg means total connection, no privacy, and every experience shared. It's a lot like the Internet and social media experience today, only without the annoying ads.

Could some version of this be in our future? Let's hope not because the Borg of *Star Trek* lore don't look happy, nor do they ever seem imaginative or inspired. Maybe what we have now—billions of mostly isolated brains constantly bumping into one another and hungering for connection—makes for a more productive and creative environment than one gigantic merged brain would. Then again, given our deep need for social connection, maybe something approaching a Borg-like existence—even if it meant no joy and bad skin tone—would be too tempting. Given the choice between isolation or assimilation, I think most people would choose the latter. Perhaps a merge with machines wouldn't degrade our humanity and turn us into cybernetic zombies but would instead finally free us to be *more* human. It's possible. Some may scoff at the idea of people in the future connecting brain-to-brain, losing much of their individuality and all of their privacy, sharing thoughts, memories, emotions, and experiences in such an extreme, intimate way. Yeah, how ridiculous; it's not like we have an example or trend to point to that might suggest such a thing could ever happen. Well, excluding the two billion people on social media right now.

## THE SINGULARITY:
## FUTURE FANTASY OR INEVITABLE REALITY?

The much-hyped technological singularity describes a moment in the near future when computers become so smart and evolve so fast that they rocket past our ability to understand their thoughts and actions. Humankind suddenly would be the intellectual equivalent of something like bacteria on the sole of Einstein's shoe. It's fascinating to think about the possibility of a machine we made to become something like a god, all-powerful and incomprehensible, no faith required. But can it happen?[42]

Some very smart people are working on AI right now, in many countries, as billions of dollars are being invested in this research. Some experts are convinced that the sudden arrival of unimaginably powerful AI is not only inevitable but also extraordinarily dangerous because of the many unknowns. Nick Bostrom, a professor at the University of Oxford and director of the Strategic Artificial Intelligence Research Centre, is one who worries about how it may play out: "Before the prospect of an intelligence explosion, we humans are like small children playing with a bomb. . . . Superintelligence is a challenge for which we are not ready now and will not be ready for a long time. We have little idea when the detonation will occur, though if we hold the device to our ear we can hear a faint ticking sound."[43] Writing in his important book, *Superintelligence: Paths, Dangers, Strategies*, Bostrom continues:

> For a child with an undetonated bomb in its hands, a sensible thing to do would be to put it down gently, quickly back out of the room, and contact the nearest adult. Yet what we have here is not one child but many, each with access to an independent trigger mechanism. The chances that we will *all* find the sense to put down the dangerous stuff seem almost negligible. Some little idiot is bound to press the ignite button just to see what happens. Nor can we attain safety by running away, for the blast of an intelligence explosion would bring down the entire firmament. Nor is there a grownup in sight."

The singularity will happen at some point, many say, because current trends and the momentum of progress can't be denied. Others argue, however, that AI will hit a wall. Computers may beat us at chess and drive our cars for us, but they will never rule the Earth. Still more experts predict an inevitable merging of machine and human, a singularity that we get to see from the inside rather than standing on the sidelines and watching in confusion. We can see evidence of this already as millions of people live cyborg lives today with insulin pumps, retinal implants, heart and brain pacemakers, and cochlear implants. As the machines get smarter, faster, and smaller, where will we end up? Visionary writer H. G. Wells, author of science fiction classics *The Time Machine* and *The War of the Worlds*, also thought seriously and wrote often about humankind's future prospects. He wrote the following in 1945: "Man must go steeply up or down and the odds seem to be all in favor of his going down and out. If he goes up, then so great is the adaptation demanded of him that he must cease to be a man."[44]

Ray Kurzweil, inventor, author, and Google's director of engineering, went on record with the following prediction in his 2005 book, *The Singularity Is Near*: "I set the date for the Singularity—representing a profound and disruptive transformation in human capability—as 2045. The nonbiological intelligence created in that year will be one billion times more powerful than all human intelligence today."[45]

It should be obvious that the evolved biological algorithms of our brains are not coping very well with the complex demands of the information age. We so easily fall for lies and nonsense, misperceive reality, and struggle to make effective big-picture, long-term plans. What happens when the combination of Big Data, artificial algorithms, and super-intelligent machines are superior to us in most things? "When cars replaced horse-drawn carriages," observes historian Yuval Noah Harari, "we didn't upgrade the horses—we retired them."[46] Could that be our fate?

The relevance of the singularity to social media is that the billions of people who are connecting online and sharing their lives today may be contributing to the rise of AI or superintelligence. It is possible that an electronically joined humanity, with so much of its knowledge, creativity, fears, and hopes digitized and socialized—a noosphere-in-the-making, perhaps— could be a critical step toward the singularity.

Miki Hardisty, a computer technology professional with more than twenty years of experience in the field, imagines our relationship with social media possibly ending up at religion. "In less than five years, societies will completely distrust social media and Internet content, which will give rise to two movements: machine-aided telepathy and blockchain sharing for social content."[47] Block-chain began as a way to move around cryptocurrencies like Bitcoin securely, but it can be applied to other online information, too. Block-chain relies on data sharing across a network of many people and many computers in a way that makes it very difficult for hackers to manipulate or corrupt the data. A document becomes much safer when it has many eyes on many copies of it.[48] Hardisty continues: "Blockchain will transcend the financial use-case and will grow to be [the] only source of shared/trusted content. Specialized 'uber-super-computers'—let's call them UCSs—will be created [and] used to mine blockchains for social content. To power these USCs, scientists and engineers will strive to go beyond Moore's law."[49]

"Over the next twenty to fifty years," Hardisty speculates, "machine-aided telepathy technology will grow to connect social groups in a hive mind with membership tightly controlled. Schools and training centers will erect to train the mind to reduce telepathic dependencies on machines. Growing telepathic powers without being aided by machines will be easiest in the physical proximity of others exercising their telepathic skills. Practice-centers, community centers for people to physically connect will draw practitioners. These centers in the next one hundred years will become dogmatic and evolve into a religious community, or several religious communities, based on faith in the power of the mind. These religious factions will openly shun computers."

Historian Harari also sees the possibility of weird new religions materializing somewhere over the Internet rainbow:

As the global data processing system becomes all-knowing and all-powerful, so connecting to the system becomes the source of all meaning. Humans want to merge into the data flow because when you are part of the data flow you are part of something much bigger than yourself. Traditional religions assured you that your every word and action was part of some great cosmic plan, and that God watched you every minute and cared about all your thoughts and feelings. Data religion now says that your every word and action is part of the great data flow, that the algorithms are constantly watching you and that they care about everything you do and feel. Most people like this very much. For true-believers, to be disconnected from the data flow risks losing the very meaning of life. What's the point of doing or experience anything if nobody knows about it, and if it doesn't contribute something to the global exchange of information?[50]

## ON SOCIAL MEDIA, NO ONE CAN HEAR YOU SCREAM

Maya Indira Ganesh is an insightful expert on many Internet issues. Currently she is the director of applied research for Tactical Technology Collective, a Berlin-based nonprofit that "explores the political and social role of technology in our lives."[51] Ganesh's areas of work include digital security, activism, ethics, and privacy. "Social media is now at a point of being somewhere like television was twenty or twenty-five years ago," she told me.[52]

> Personalities and celebrities are creating influence just by their presence, advertising is practically unavoidable, and it's a good place for breaking news and entertainment. For people in these sectors, social media can be profitable. But it doesn't seem to be the sort of place for someone who is struggling for visibility or voice. Messages can be manipulated, and messages cannot be nuanced. As much as there is the sense that you can participate and 'have a voice,' this isn't entirely true. Social media has started to mimic a media broadcaster, and most of us just exist in small filter bubbles; or we mobilize around events that occur locally.

Ganesh encourages social media users to learn how these platforms work, how they track users and save their data. "It's always a good idea to know how something you use a lot works, whether that thing is a medication, technology, whatever. Understand its effects on you. It's a good idea to know about how social media basically creates photocopies [of] every single action and keeps a record of it, and with access to that data, it's possible to create a profile of you. This profile, whether it is accurate or not, is being used as a de facto ID card; but it is more than an ID card, because we use the Internet and social media for so many personal and intimate things as well. It's important to think about the kinds of social, personal, and professional situations you're in and how these will be affected by having this profile of yourself visible and accessible to a number of different agencies, from the government to tax authorities to potential employers."

Tactical Technology Collective offers several free resources that can help people gain more control over their data and privacy. The website myshadow.org offers practical options for those who would like to minimize their online profile. They even have an eight-day "digital detox" plan available.

"I think there is increasing awareness of Big Data and the data industry and how algorithmic regulation of everyday life, society, politics, and identity is taking place," said Ganesh. "But there isn't much that consumers can use right now to hold the data industries to account for what they do with users' personal information and how they profit from it. This is one of the reasons Tactical Tech's work tries to intervene at the point of educating users and empowering them to address the information asymmetries that exist. So we *hope* that users will be more empowered and aware about privacy through the activism and advocacy happening in many parts of the world."

Media developer Christoph, of Atlanta, Georgia, points out that the Internet and social media are still relatively new and people continue to figure out how to use them well:

> Social networks show us the human animal pretty accurately right now. People seem to show more of themselves when they don't feel the need to filter themselves. It has cast a huge light on how humans think. That said, now that the social networks are starting to run filters and warn people of possible offensive speech, I think people will be less inclined to use it. There was a freedom once, a freedom to say whatever you felt. Now here comes the Network Nanny, telling you that you are offensive and that they are going to flag your comment. No one likes being told what to do or how to think. As soon as people start getting these messages that someone is watching, people will stop posting what they really think. They will start acting like they are in church; the grand experiment will be over. People will lose interest, and it will become just another MySpace, Napster, or Farrah Faucet poster in the trash heap of pop culture. If there is anything that can be gleaned from human nature on social media, it better be collected now. That door is starting to close.[53]

Less-than-perfect visions of social media's future like Christoph's are not difficult to find. Cameron M. Smith is a Portland State University anthropologist with eclectic interests. In addition to his archaeological work, he has written about topics as far-ranging as how the colonization of space might impact human evolution. He says:

> I think it's a plausible future that as many peoples' lives become more intolerable, they will go to an online world where they can feel dignity and freedom and other things they don't get in real life. It was tried with Second Life,[54] but I don't think that really worked too well. I think when the tech improves, an alternate world like this is where many might do their socializing. That scenario is convincingly made, to me, in [the science-fiction novel] *Ready Player One*.[55] Interestingly, in the end it is all described as rather sad that it was how things worked out for humanity. But there it is.[56]

Musician and writer Jeremy Kocal, aged forty-one, of Pasadena, California, doesn't think the future of social media will be problem-free, but he votes moving full speed ahead, anyway:

> It feels like we are massively shifting and evolving as humans. I appreciate where we came from, and progress is inevitable. Maybe the Earth knows something we do not, like an asteroid is on its way, and we will need to get off the planet quite soon. If that's the case, or something similar, unknown, or not-yet-understood forces, could be driving us toward these shifts so that we can solve these issues together. We are fighting about so many cultural and religious issues right now. But I am encouraged that we are talking about them now, even if it's an ugly version of many of these conversations. There is a heightened awareness of many issues that were not "appropriate" to discuss, and now they are everywhere. I asked myself the other day: "When did I first give any thought to whether or not the egg that I am eating came from a chicken that had a life free from cages?" These bits of awareness are creeping up on so many topics. The point may be that we are combining forces to collectively solve our own planetwide problems. Digital connectivity is the ultimate opportunity to unite every location, every language, and every person for a common goal. It's scary, but it's also wonderful, and in my opinion, worth the angst, annoyance, and risk involved in forging ahead![57]

When I reached out to social media users as part of my research for this book, I had expected responses to be more homogeneous than they turned out to be. After all, most people who consistently watch football on TV love football. Most people who own a BMW love their BMW. Social media is different. Many people seem conflicted. It appears that a significant number of users engage with it daily despite not fully buying in, or at least having serious concerns about what it may be doing to them and the world. For example, the people quoted below—Nathan, Ashani, Cheryl, and Ashley—are of different ages and live in different countries yet all appreciate social media while also worrying about its impact.

Nathan Lee, a twenty-one-year-old pre-med student, says he is not anti-technology and recognizes all of the good that comes from it. However, he thinks that it has negatively impacted "the aspect of personal relationships with people. People need to get outside and see God's creation by hiking, biking, and living life rather than being cooped up inside and staring at a screen for hours and hours every day. All in all, social media and other online social media networks do have positives, but they also have negatives that I believe are dangerous to the advancement of society."[58]

"I think the Internet has helped us to become more human," says Ashani, a twenty-two-year-old marketing student. She highlights the positive impact of the Internet and social media as "being a part of movements and groups and being connected to people that you may never have dreamed of being connected with before. We are more connected with each other more than ever before."[59]

Floridian Cheryl sees social media as a complex jumble of good and bad that can take a hard turn down either path at any time for an individual: "In some ways, it has made us meaner. People say things on social media that they probably would not say in a normal human conversation. In other ways, it's great because you find out about current local and world events in an instant. I also see lost pets being found, neighbors helping each other by giving advice on which handyman to use, and lots of happy birthday wishes. It can certainly go either way."[60]

Ashley, aged thirty, is an attorney who joined Facebook in 2004, the year of its launch.

I think of social media as an extension of who we are as humans. . . . The behaviors users exhibit on social media are all the classic human behaviors: compassion, hatred, curiosity, intolerance, grief, inspiration, etc. Folks do have an opportunity to selectively reinvent themselves, be anonymous, or highlight particular sides of themselves; however, I feel that is all very human too—those are things folks do when they go into a new environment, meet new people, etc. I think social media has the potential to be a force of good, [a] force of evil, and a neutral force. I think the future of social media will continue to parallel—and perhaps exaggerate—human behaviors.[61]

## WILL THE INTERNET AND SOCIAL MEDIA MAKE US SMARTER AND NICER?

Can a more wired world and connected humanity positively impact reason and rational decision making? Will it connect our species to higher levels of compassion and rational thinking? We certainly could use some help. Keep in mind that you live in a time in which tens of millions of girls do not go to school simply because they are girls.[62] While some women command missions in space, millions of other women down here on twenty-first-century Earth aren't allowed to get a driver's license.[63] Ours is an age in which flat-Earth belief is enjoying a comeback[64] and "witches" are still feared and sometimes killed.[65] There may be good reason to think that the Internet will become a more polite and respectful place in the coming years. The idea of a peaceful Internet may seem absurd today, given the terrible troll culture found in so many of its corners, but this behavior of screaming at strangers in all-caps, hating, and threatening murder and rape over trivial issues was cultivated and enabled by the high degree of anonymity users experienced during the early days of the Internet. This is no longer the case, however. Because social media platforms like Facebook push users to use their real names, and because people are tracked and surveilled everywhere they go online now, increasing numbers of people may feel a greater sense of responsibility for what they say online.

If virtual reality becomes a major factor for social media and throughout the Internet experience, as many experts are certain it will,[66] then it may have a positive influence on human affairs. Researchers at Stanford have been studying how certain scenarios presented in VR can impact participants' emotions and behaviors afterward.[67] You can, for example, spend time virtually with a family of a different nationality, religion, or skin color to help recognize your humanity and kinship with them. You might experience nature in VR settings to realize the beauty and importance of biodiversity. The problem with all of this, of course, is that VR technology could be used just as easily to make someone more fearful and nationalistic, more sexist or racist, or less concerned about the natural environment.

I remind readers that there is always a human lurking somewhere behind even the flashiest technology. Don't be misled by automation and algorithms; a human being has or had direct influence on every bit of hardware and software you encounter at some point, for better or worse. Sure, good people may do marvelous things for the world with increasingly powerful computer technology, but don't count on bad people to play nice with it, too. It is for this reason that I tend to be less concerned about Terminators and Skynet than I am the humans who write the software or hold the remote controls. We don't know yet if intelligent machines can be evil, but there is no doubt that people can be.

## IS GOVERNMENT REGULATION THE ANSWER TO ALL OF OUR WOES?

An important and growing challenge today is understanding how fast-changing technology impacts political campaigns and governance. Brendan Nyhan, professor of political science at Dartmouth College, believes that he and other social scientists are still coming to grips with the role that social media, and Facebook in particular, currently plays in American democracy. Where this research leads and what it uncovers will have implications for all countries and all forms of government. Socialists, democratic leaders, and dictators of all types can make use of social media and other Internet-based technologies to manipulate and control populations. As Nyhan puts it:

> Facebook has a remarkable level of influence on the information people see in our democracy. They [Facebook management] are starting to take responsibility for the way they enabled fake news during the

2016 election, but there are some broader and more difficult questions about one company having that level of influence on what people see. I don't think we should be comfortable with this. They are trying to be neutral, but it's difficult to do so. . . . I simply don't know that one single company should have that level of control over the news that people see, but nor do I have a solution about what to do about it.[68]

Nyhan is not sure that government regulation is the answer: "I'm very reluctant to endorse regulatory solutions. A lot of it wouldn't stand up to a First Amendment [free speech] challenge. Government regulation is a very blunt instrument to use in the marketplace of ideas. We should rely on civil society, hopefully, to address these kinds of problems. But if Facebook doesn't address this problem, the political system may force them to do so. We are already seeing these steps being taken in Europe, where there is less protection of free speech and governments are more willing to intervene in the private market. Facebook may not be able to operate in this kind of Wild West state of limited regulation for much longer."

The public has real power to force change here, according to Nyhan: "The public shaming of Facebook has had a big influence on their behavior already. They recognize that the status quo is not tenable for their standing as a prominent company. Their own employees were upset about the role Facebook played in the 2016 election. Pressure from the public and their employees can play an important role. Whether it will be sufficient or not remains to be seen. At least they aren't still pretending that they don't have a problem."

José van Dijck of the Netherlands is one of the world's leading researchers of Internet media. She is Distinguished Professor at Utrecht University and the first woman elected president of the Royal Netherlands Academy of Arts and Sciences. She told me that an obvious obstacle to positive progress for social media is that the underlying and overriding reason the providers offer their services to users has little or nothing to do with making life better for them. "Of course, what we want these platforms to do is mostly to improve connectedness—the way that we relate to each other, to come together as humans and to intensify our relationships through better communication and bonding. However, what most online platforms are after is connectivity—the 'datafication' and commodification of informal social interaction through the automated or algorithmic architecture of platforms. In my most optimistic version, I would like to see public space carved out on the Internet for truly noncommercial, human interaction, a space void of nontransparent business models where users have control over their own data."[69]

Imagine that: public safe spaces on the Internet. No secret snooping by businesses, no algorithmic mischief, no data harvesting or government spying, just free and open cyberzones where people can come together, communicate, and share experiences. Van Dijck sees two specific problems that need to be overcome for social media to flourish and reach the potential its most optimistic cheerleaders envision:

> Lack of transparency, vis-à-vis algorithmic selection, and lack of control, vis-à-vis data. Individuals, unfortunately, can do very little to push back against these problems because corporate platforms keep their algorithms carefully hidden business secrets, and virtually all users sign away rights to control their data the minute they check the box and use a free app. I think we will increasingly realize that regulation is necessary to keep the platform society open and responsible. Whether this can be done best by government regulators, self-regulation or co-regulation is a pressing question. But indeed, users need to be protected from nontransparent exploitation of private information and the hidden filtering of information.

Is a more open, honest and user-friendly Internet even possible? Without such a major transformation, could more people getting access to Internet and social media as is help turn us into a more sensible life-form? Peter Boghossian, assistant professor of philosophy at Portland State University, doesn't have a confident prediction about where things are going but speculates that the problems of some national governments blocking content from their people will probably get worse as better technology to do so becomes available. It may become easier for them to stop or slow social and intellectual progress by controlling the flow of information. "This will increasingly not be pornographic content [that governments block]," he said, "but alternative epistemologies. This will mostly fall into the domain of religion but will also include economic and other broad political topics. I also think it will be increasingly difficult to access prohibited materials online, as governments enact stricter regulations and get better at weeding out objectionable content. [The future of the Internet and social media is] a mixed bag. We know from interview-based studies religious organizations have conducted, that the main reason people abandon their faith is because of the Internet. Alternatively, I also think this radicalizes people who were on the fringe. So, it's a mixed bag."[70]

Do the Internet and social media humanize or dehumanize us? Texas business owner Michelle, aged forty-one, would like to see our collective digital-wired culture become more human: "It's moving too fast for us to appreciate the implications, as is so much technology, in my opinion. I have hope that in the future we will find some balance as a society and return to unplugged endeavors, like getting outside more, spending family time together. But then again, I'm an optimist."[71]

Michelle's hopeful tone infused with some concern represents a common theme I found among many social media users I interviewed for this book. It seems that people want certain things from our technology but think that they have no say, that somehow there are forces out there too overwhelming and powerful to steer. Whether it is the momentum of progress or the agendas of business and governments, something has given people a deep sense of powerlessness when it comes to where humankind is going with the Internet and related technologies.

Social media critic Jacob Silverman believes that nothing but a combination of grassroots revolt, government regulation, and users supporting those who are demanding change can improve the situation. He suggests: "Educate yourself. Protest the bad politics of the tech giants, which are today's robber barons. Seek out the dissidents of the tech industry, the whistleblowers and malcontents, the digital-rights activists and the small companies doing weird things or forsaking traditional commercial models. Like any large influential industry, social media companies should be regulated, in this case by the FCC, FTC, and other applicable agencies," he told me.[72] "Any company that is in the business of filtering what people see and hear—and in collecting massive amounts of personal data on them in the process—wields a great deal of influence, and it's the responsibility of informed lawmakers and regulators to look out for the people's best interests."

Silverman warns that failure to act soon could be disastrous:

It's hard to generalize, but I worry about the development of filter bubbles, the proliferation of false information, and the use of social media to propagandize and surveil large populations. I think one day we're going to see a massacre or genocide abetted by social media—just as radio broadcasts, for instance, helped spur Hutus in Rwanda to kill their Tutsi neighbors. Some platforms, perhaps those with more moderation, may become trusted sources of news and information, but heavy curation has just as many pitfalls, particularly with promoting a kind of unified, apolitical, advertiser-friendly environment. The great promise of social media is to provide free or cheap, mostly unmediated communications between human beings all over the world. It, of course, allows people the means for public self-expression and organizing. I don't think there's anything inherently utopian about social media, but a best-case scenario would find us with ways of communicating and sharing that don't surveil users, monetize their data, or jeopardize their privacy. These flaws are essentially baked into the models used by today's tech giants, so without major reforms on their end, I don't see this medium reaching its potential.[73]

The daunting, near overwhelming challenge of meaningful reorganization that Silverman speaks of may seem more hopeful if we keep in mind that all of this, the Internet and every social media site and app, came from human hands and thoughts. And as such, these things can be remolded by hands and thoughts. UK science writer Oliver Morton stresses that we must never lose sight of the fact that *humans* create all of this technology that infiltrates and dominates so much of our daily lives. As he puts it, "technologies can never be relied on to solve problems in the absence of social action; one of the dangers of fetishizing technology as an actor in its own right is that it obscures this point. Good solutions will rarely, if ever, be implemented through technology alone. And technology will never be the last word on anything. . . . The centuries of ceaseless technological change are not going to come to an end; they may only just be getting going. A clear understanding that technology does not have its own agenda but serves the agenda of others, and that it necessarily creates new needs almost as effectively as it meets old ones, will make this change easier to navigate responsibly."[74]

We *can* make the Internet and social media better for us. Ability does not guarantee action, however. The possibility of change does not mean the necessary work will get done to achieve it, of course. Bo Bennett, vocal advocate for critical thinking and author of

*Uncomfortable Ideas*, spends a lot of his time confronting and combatting bad ideas and the natural tendency we have to believe in them. But despite his view from the trenches of the often messy and dispiriting battle for rational thought, Bennett envisions a brighter future for the Internet and social media:

> Our ability to use technology is part of being human. Social media is just another form of communication—or perhaps a facilitator of communication. We are starting to see the problems with it, such as its effect on political polarization, but I have no doubt that the problems will be addressed, or at least mitigated. As much as I love the movie *Idiocracy*, I am much more optimistic about our future. I do believe that good ideas will beat bad ideas in the market of information. I would love to see this happen purely driven by the users, but [if it takes] corporate or government intervention, so be it. Overall, I am optimistic.

If we want a better Internet and World Wide Web, one with more helpful and constructive social media, more privacy, less fake news, fewer or more porous filter bubbles, and some restraints for the secretive efforts to addict us and exploit every move we make online, then *we* must make it happen. Maybe the billionaire owners of these companies will do the right thing because they care more about you than they care about money. But don't count on it. Maybe honest politicians will rise up and fight on your behalf. But don't count on it. You and I, most likely, are the only solution. You have to care and—and this is the hard part—actually do something. But what?

## PUSHING IN THE RIGHT DIRECTION

Spread knowledge. Make sure that everyone you know is aware of what is really going on with these popular social media sites. Explain to family and friends how Facebook, Snapchat, Instagram, and others make their money off user data. Tell them that teams of smart engineers are working hard every day to hook them to these sites and apps and keep them engaged with them for as long as possible—regardless of whether doing so might be detrimental to the user's quality of life. "Media," a god in the 2017 Starz television series *American Gods*, described the current state of social media well when she said, "Time and attention—better than lamb's blood."[75]

Enlighten people around you to the fact that the main purpose of many apps is to spy on the user. Pressure politicians to enact regulations that protect you online. Don't vote for candidates of any party who are not serious about protecting your current rights and working to get you more rights. When sitting politicians favor a big company's need for profit over your need for online safety and privacy, tweet some constructive rage at them for a change instead of attacking some anonymous stranger for liking the wrong sports team.

Never stop learning about the human brain, science, and more effective ways to apply science in your life. Commit to good thinking and maintain a skeptical posture; do this first for yourself and then encourage others to start making better use of their brains, too. Keep your guard up, not only to protect yourself from the crooks and crackpots that may reach you through your social media accounts, but most of all to protect yourself *from yourself*. Know this and never forget it: Your brain is weird. Left unchecked, it's highly vulnerable to falling for nonsense and then working overtime to convince you that it makes perfect sense. Your subconscious mind has a mind of its own. It may have nice intentions, but if you let it, it will take you by the hand and lead you down many nutty, embarrassing, expensive, and dangerous paths. Embrace good thinking now and forever.

At times while writing this book I flirted with unleashing an anti-Internet/social media rant, my condemnation of a failed experiment. I might have come close, but a review of the transcript will reveal that I did not. Something held me back. And it wasn't warm optimism so much as a cold honesty. Not only do I find myself incapable of hating or giving up on the Internet, social media, and all things digital, I hold a deep affection, if not outright love, for almost all of it. I feel this way because I have realized what the Internet, its billion websites, and all of social media are. They are honest reflections of humankind. Despite what you might hear from one of your kooky friends on Facebook, the Internet is not the creation of nefarious extraterrestrials from an alien world, draped over our planet like a fishnet to distract, control, and eventually enslave us. Nor is it a government conspiracy meant to keep us staring down at our smartphones so that we won't look up at the chemtrails above us. No, the Internet is us. When I go online, I feel as though I am looking into a mirror. I see myself and the rest of humanity—in all its wonderful, weird, pathetic glory—staring back at me.

Social media is full of lies and lunacy because it is full of people. Why *wouldn't* the Internet be a superhighway with hardcore pornography zipping along at near light speed in a lane right next to an emoji-laden "Happy Birthday" e-mail making its way to Grandma's house? Why *wouldn't* social media be overflowing with lies, hoaxes, and videos of fainting goats? This is who we are. For every photo of a Walmart shopper who forgot her pants at home, fake news article, or conspiracy theory that is posted somewhere, there is a life-changing book, mind-expanding article, love-inspiring poem, or transcendent painting somewhere else online to balance it out. Okay, I admit, maybe the ratio is not exactly one to one, but the point is that there is an abundance of intelligent and uplifting material online. Much of the content and activities that make up the World Wide Web and social media may be corrupt, stupid, and mostly pointless, but a good bit of it is very cool and undeniably dazzling. Stupid *and* dazzling. Doesn't that remind you of one particularly plucky bunch of apes who climbed down, stood up, and walked in the general direction of great achievements?

The Internet—and the worst of the detritus that flows through it—are human creations, expressions of our beautiful ugliness, raw and pure. If all Facebook friends were devoted to spreading facts and wisdom, if every tweet were sweet, and no Instagram pic fell short of inspiring, then we would not recognize such an online world. It would be foreign, not ours or of us. It is human imperfection, our inclination to use the most powerful brains on Earth to imagine and then believe the unbelievable that makes us both enduring and endearing. Besides, perfection seems like it might be boring. Our messiness and madness often provide us the requisite fertile ground for our best moments. The first computers were built as an offshoot of war, to help militaries break codes and guide missiles. Sixty years ago, during the Cold War, the United States and the Soviet Union found themselves in a phallic competition to see who could build the biggest rocket. But from reckless playground posturing came nine voyages to the Moon and six spectacular landings. Members of our species walked on the lonely, cratered surface of another world, in a sophisticated and stylish achievement for all to be proud of. The Apollo Moon program is perhaps a perfect example of how we tend to do things. It's so often a case of either dumb motivations with brilliant outcomes or brilliant motivations with dumb outcomes. That's us. Own it.

In a time when changing technology threatens to disrupt so much so fast, we may find some reassurance within our social media activities, no matter how silly or cantankerous. The machines may be coming to take away our steering wheels, our jobs, and perhaps even our status as rulers of the planet, but we have not been made redundant yet. We know this because the proof is before our eyes, right there on the World Wide Web. We still run this show. Cyberspace, for all its cold, uncaring ones and zeros, still belongs to us. It carries the indelible stamp of flesh-and-blood humanity—and if you don't believe me, I have a few flat-Earth YouTube videos I'd love to show you. We all can justify and enjoy a little optimism here. Even a famous chess grandmaster and former world champion who was publicly beaten at his own game by a machine, is looking up these days. "The more that people believe in a positive future for technology, the greater chance there is of having one," writes Gary Kasparov in his book, *Deep Thinking: Where Machine Intelligence Ends and Human Creativity Begins.* "We will all choose what the future looks like by our beliefs and actions. . . . Nothing is decided. None of us are spectators. The game is underway and we are all on the board."[76]

Yes, AI is certain to fly by us in many arenas. Complex social media algorithms will deliver us more fun and conveniences while also making online networks more invasive and problematic. But there is something the machines will still need us for. We are the only ones who can give meaning to the meaningless. We are the necessary wildcard, the inevitable flukes who think about thinking, and brilliant lunatics who actually believe our own most ridiculous claims. What would the universe be without our quirkiness, fun, blind faith, stubborn stupidity, and goofy contributions? Out of human fears, hopes, and madness come invented purpose, the lies made into truths that we use to confront the dark void of existence with courage and resilience. Who but humans can *consciously decide* that decision making is beyond conscious power, that free will is an illusion? We are the ones who laugh, cry, create, and destroy for profound reasons or none at all. Let the machines top that.

It is unlikely that a true digital utopia will materialize around

us anytime soon. If it were to do so, we likely would find it too clean
and perfect anyway, an uncomfortable environment for creatures
like us. We may dream of and work toward a danger-free and flaw-
less existence, but we'll probably never get there. And that's okay—
because we don't need perfection. We are human; and that's good
enough.

# NOTES

## INTRODUCTION

1. David Ingram, "Facebook Hits 2 Billion-User Mark, Doubling in Size Since 2012," Reuters, June 27, 2017, https://www.reuters.com/article/us-facebook-users-idUSKBN19I2GG (accessed July 16, 2017).

2. Statista, "Number of Monthly Active WhatsApp Users Worldwide from April 2013 to January 2017 (in Millions)," https://www.statista.com/statistics/260819/number-of-monthly-active-whatsapp-users/ (accessed July 16, 2017); YouTube, "YouTube by the Numbers," https://www.youtube.com/yt/about/press/ (accessed July 16, 2017).

3. DMR, "18 Amazing QQ Statistics," http://expandedramblings.com/index.php/qq-statistics/ (accessed July 16, 2017); Statista, "Number of Monthly Active WeChat Users from 2nd Quarter 2010 to 1st Quarter 2017," https://www.statista.com/statistics/255778/number-of-active-wechat-messenger-accounts/ (accessed July 16, 2017).

4. DMR, "By the Numbers: 72 Amazing Baidu Statistics and Facts," http://expandedramblings.com/index.php/baidu-stats/ (accessed July 16, 2017).

## CHAPTER 1: WILD AND WIRED

1. Mark Zuckerberg, quoted in Randi Zuckerberg, *Dot Complicated: Untangling Our Wired Lives* (New York: Harper Collins, 2013), p. 22.

2. *Contact*, directed by Robert Zemeckis (Los Angeles, CA: Warner Brothers, 1997).

3. Sherry Turkle, *Reclaiming Conversation: The Power of Talk in a Digital Age* (New York: Penguin, 2015), p. 346.

4. B. J. Mendelson, *Social Media Is Bullshit* (New York: St. Martin's Press, 2012), p. 179.

5. Hande Boyaci, Tayyab Shah, Amanda Hurley, et al., "Structure, Regulation, and Inhibition of the Quorum-Sensing Signal Integrator LuxO," *PLOS Biology* 14, no. 5 (2016): e1002464, DOI: 10.1371/journal.pbio.1002464; PLOS, "Silencing Cholera's 'Social Media,'" *Science Daily*, May 24, 2016, www.sciencedaily.com/releases/2016/05/160524144701.htm (accessed April 29, 2017).

6. Jacqueline Humphries, Liyang Xiong, Jintao Liu, et al., "Species-Independent Attraction to Biofilms through Electrical Signaling," *Cell* 168, nos. 1–2 (January 12, 2017), DOI: 10.1016/j.cell.2016.12.014; University of California–San Diego, "Bacteria Recruit Other Species with Long-Range Electrical Signals," *Science Daily*, January 12, 2017, www.sciencedaily.com/releases/2017/01/170112141216.htm (accessed April 29, 2017).

7. Nic Fleming, "Plants Talk to Each Other Using an Internet of Fungus," BBC, November 11, 2014, http://www.bbc.com/earth/story/20141111-plants-have-a-hidden-internet (accessed April 29, 2017).

8. University of California–Davis, "Plant Parasite 'Wiretaps' Host," *Science Daily*, August 4, 2008, www.sciencedaily.com/releases/2008/07/080731140231.htm (accessed March 19, 2017).

9. Jacob Poushter, "Smartphone Ownership and Internet Usage Continues to Climb in Emerging Economies," Pew Research Center, February 22, 2016, http://www.pewglobal.org/2016/02/22/smartphone-ownership-and-internet-usage-continues-to-climb-in-emerging-economies/ (accessed April 21, 2017).

10. David Ingram, "Facebook Hits 2 Billion-User Mark, Doubling in Size Since 2012," Reuters, June 27, 2017, https://www.reuters.com/article/us-facebook-users-idUSKBN19I2GG (accessed July 16, 2017).

11. Statista, "Number of Monthly Active WhatsApp Users Worldwide from April 2013 to January 2017 (in Millions)," https://www.statista.com/statistics/260819/number-of-monthly-active-whatsapp-users/ (accessed July 16, 2017).

12. YouTube, "YouTube by the Numbers."

13. Josh Constine, "Facebook Messenger Hits 1.2 Billion Monthly Users, up from 1B in July," Tech Crunch, April 12, 2017, https://techcrunch.com/2017/04/12/messenger/ (accessed July 17, 2017).

14. Statista, "Number of Monthly Active WeChat Users from 2nd Quarter 2010 to 1st Quarter 2017," https://www.statista.com/statistics/255778/number-of-active-wechat-messenger-accounts/ (accessed July 16, 2017).

15. Daniel Sparks, "Top 10 Social Networks: How Many Users Are on Each?" Motley Fool, https://www.fool.com/investing/2017/03/30/top-10-social-networks-how-many-users-are-on-each.aspx (accessed July 16, 2017).

16. Ibid.

17. Ibid.

18. Statista, "Most Famous Social Network Sites Worldwide as of April 2017, Ranked by Number of Active Users," https://www.statista.com/statistics/272014/global-social-networks-ranked-by-number-of-users/ (accessed July 16, 2017).

19. Sparks, "Top 10 Social Networks."

20. Ibid.

21. Statista, "Most Famous Social Network Sites."

22. Ibid.

23. Ibid.

24. Ibid.

25. Ibid.

26. Aaron Smith, "Record Shares of Americans Now Own Smartphones, Have Home Broadband," Pew Research Center, January 12, 2017, http://www.pewresearch.org/fact-tank/2017/01/12/evolution-of-technology/ (accessed April 21, 2017).

27. Poushter, "Smartphone Ownership."

28. Ibid.

29. Craig Wigginton, "2016 Global Mobile Consumer Survey: US Edition," 2016, https://www2.deloitte.com/us/en/pages/technology-media-and-telecommunications/articles/global-mobile-consumer-survey-us-edition.html (accessed April 6, 2017).

30. Ibid.

31. Bernard Marr, "4 Mind-Blowing Ways Facebook Uses Artificial Intelligence," *Forbes*, December 29, 2016, https://www.forbes.com/sites/bernardmarr/2016/12/29/4-amazing-ways-facebook-uses-deep-learning-to-learn-everything-about-you/#4246410accbf (accessed March 31, 2017).

32. Smith, "Record Shares of Americans."

33. Poushter, "Smartphone Ownership."

34. Andy Coghlan, "Social Brains Grown in a Dish," *New Scientist*, January 14, 2017, p. 12.

35. Alexis C. Madrigal, "The iPhone Was Inevitable," *Atlantic*, June 29, 2017, https://www.theatlantic.com/technology/archive/2017/06/the-iphone-was-inevitable/531963/ (accessed June 29, 2017).

36. Sherry Turkle, "Sherry Turkle: Connected, But Alone?" TED, video, 19:48, from a TED Talk delivered February 2012, https://www.ted.com/talks/sherry_turkle_alone_together#t-149287 (accessed March 6, 2017).

37. Sherry Turkle, *Alone Together: Why We Expect More from Technology and Less from Each Other* (New York: Basic Books, 2011), p. 283.

38. Janelle Randazza, *Go Tweet Yourself* (Avon, MA: Adams Media, 2009), pp. ix–x.

39. Peter Rubin, "Facebook's Bizarre VR App Is Exactly Why Zuck Bought Oculus," *Wired*, April 18, 2017, https://www.wired.com/2017/04/facebook-spaces-vr-for-your-friends/ (accessed July 28, 2017).

40. Jeremy Bailenson, quoted in Adam Alter, *Irresistible: The Rise of Addictive Technology and the Business of Keeping Us Hooked* (New York: Penguin, 2017).

41. Jerry Kane, "Social Media . . . You Haven't Seen Anything Yet | Jerry Kane | TEDxLongwood," YouTube video, 19:25, from a TEDx Talk, posted by "TEDx Talks," July 7, 2014, https://www.youtube.com/watch?v=KzcQzM8CgIc (accessed February 15, 2017).

42. Gerald Kane, interview with the author, February 15, 2017.

43. Tom Standage, *Writing on the Wall: Social Media—The First 2,000 Years* (New York: Bloomsbury USA, 2013).

44. June Cohen, "The Rise of Social Media Is Really a Reprise," in *Is the Internet Changing the Way You Think? The Net's Impact on Our Minds and Our Future*, ed. John Brockman (New York: Harper Perennial, 2011), p. 38.

45. Ibid., p. 39.

46. Edward O. Wilson, *The Creation: An Appeal to Save Life on Earth* (New York: W. W. Norton, 2006), p. 12.

47. Maria Konnikova, "The Limits of Friendship," *New Yorker*, October 7, 2014, http://www.newyorker.com/science/maria-konnikova/social-media-affect -math-dunbar-number-friendships (accessed March 21, 2017). See also R. I. M. Dunbar, "Do Online Social Media Cut through the Constraints That Limit the Size of Off-line Social Networks?" *Royal Society Open Science*, January 20, 2016, DOI: 10.1098/rsos.150292, http://rsos.royalsocietypublishing.org/ content/3/1/150292 (accessed April 4, 2017).

48. Moya Sarner, "Alone in the Crowd," *New Scientist*, July 22, 2017, p. 32.

49. Chris Baraniuk, "World Wide Warp," *New Scientist*, February 20, 2016, p. 38.

50. Andrew Sullivan, "I Used to Be a Human Being," *New Yorker*, September 18, 2016, http://nymag.com/selectall/2016/09/andrew-sullivan -technology-almost-killed-me.html (accessed June 28, 2017).

51. Jaron Lanier, *You Are Not a Gadget: A Manifesto*, p. 26.

52. Ibid., p. 200.

53. Ibid., p. 4.

54. Ibid., p. 87.

55. Alexis C. Madrigal, "Facebook Doesn't Understand Itself," *Atlantic*, May 23, 2017, https://www.theatlantic.com/technology/archive/2017/05/the -big-assumption-in-facebooks-leaked-content-moderation-guidelines/527628/ (accessed June 29, 2017).

56. Rory Cellan-Jones, *"Stephen Hawking Warns Artificial Intelligence Could End Mankind," BBC News,* December 2, 2014, http://www.bbc.com/ news/technology-30290540 (accessed July 10, 2017).

57. "What If . . We Create Human-Level Artificial Intelligence?" *New Scientist* 232, no. 3100 (November 19, 2016).

58. "NGA 2017 Summer Meeting—Introducing the New Chair's Initiative 'Ahead of the Curve,'" YouTube video, 1:26:50, streamed live July 15, 2017, posted by National Governors Association, https://www.youtube.com/ watch?v=2C-A797y8dA (accessed July 17, 2017).

59. Paul Mozur, "Google's AlphaGo Defeats Chinese Go Master in Win for A.I.," *New York Times*, May 23, 2017, https://www.nytimes.com/2017/05/23/ business/google-deepmind-alphago-go-champion-defeat.html (accessed July 8, 2017).

60. PwC, "UK Economic Outlook," March 2017, http://www.pwc.co.uk/

economic-services/ukeo/pwcukeo-summary-report-march-2017-v2.pdf (accessed July 7, 2017), p. 3.

61. Martin Rees, "Organic Intelligence Has No Long-Term Future," in *What to Think about Machines That Think: Today's Leading Thinkers on the Age of Machine Intelligence*, ed. John Brockman (New York: Harper Perennial, 2015), p. 9.

62. Sean Prophet, interview with the author, March 22, 2017.

63. See Ray Kurzweil, *The Singularity Is Near* (London: Duckworth, 2016).

64. Randall, interview with the author.

65. Kelly, interview with the author.

66. Bong Manding, interview with the author, March 29, 2017.

67. Elke Feuer, interview with the author, April 1, 2017.

68. ScienceDaily, "How to Get More Followers on Twitter," May 2, 2013, www.sciencedaily.com/releases/2013/05/130502115517.htm (accessed July 13, 2017).

69. Dean Burnett, interview with the author, February 28, 2017.

70. Leticia Bode, interview with the author, March 4, 2017.

71. Richard Dawkins, "Net Gain," in *Is the Internet Changing the Way You Think? The Net's Impact on Our Minds and Our Future*, ed. John Brockman (New York: Harper Perennial, 2011), p. 9.

72. Thomas Rid, *Rise of the Machines: A Cybernetic History* (New York: W. W. Norton, 2016), p. 2.

73. Skynet is the fictional net-based artificial intelligence featured in the Terminator films.

74. Oliver Morton, "Concluding Reflections: Lessons from the Industrial Revolution," in *Mega Tech: Technology in 2050*, ed. Daniel Franklin (New York: Economist Books / Public Affairs, 2017), p. 226.

75. Kelly Frede, interview with the author, April 8, 2017.

76. Comment posted to "Quit Social Media | Dr. Cal Newport | TEDx Tysons," YouTube video, 13:50, from a TEDx Talk in June 2016, posted by "TEDx Talks," September 19, 2016, https://www.youtube.com/watch?v=3E7hkPZ-HTk (accessed August 18, 2017).

77. "Charles Barkley Thinks Social Media Is for Losers," CNET video, https://www.cnet.com/videos/charles-barkley-thinks-social-media-is-for-losers -ces-2017/ (accessed January 10, 2017).

78. Turkle, *Alone Together*, p. 1.

79. Sebastian Junger writes about the decline of deep and vital human relationships in his book *Tribe: On Homecoming and Belonging* (New York: Twelve, 2016).

80. *New Scientist*, "Oh, Lonesome Us," July 22, 2017, p. 3.

81. Moya Sarner, "Alone in the Crowd," *New Scientist*, July 22, 2017, pp. 31–32.

82. Ibid., p. 30.

83. Hugues Sampasa-Kanyinga and Rosamund F. Lewis, "Frequent Use of Social Networking Sites Is Associated with Poor Psychological Functioning

among Children and Adolescents," *Cyberpsychology, Behavior, and Social Networking* 18, no. 7 (July 2015): 380–85, https://doi.org/10.1089/cyber.2015.0055 (accessed July 30, 2017).

84. University of Pittsburgh Schools of the Health Sciences, "Social Media Use Associated with Depression among U.S. Young Adults," March 22, 2016, http://www.upmc.com/media/NewsReleases/2016/Pages/lin-primack-sm -depression.aspx (accessed July 30, 2017).

85. Ibid.

86. Keith Hampton, Lee Rainie, Weixu Lu, Inyoung Shin, and Kristen Purcell, "Social Media and the Cost of Caring," Pew Research Center, January 15, 2015, p. 12, http://www.pewinternet.org/2015/01/15/the-cost-of-caring/ (accessed August 3, 2017).

87. Andrew G. Reece and Christopher M. Danforth, "Instagram Photos Reveal Predictive Markers of Depression," *EPJ Data Science*, August 8, 2017, https://doi.org/10.1140/epjds/s13688-017-0110-z (accessed August 9, 2017).

88. Ibid.

89. Jean M. Twenge, "Has the Smartphone Destroyed a Generation?" *Atlantic*, September 2017, p. 61.

90. David Burnham, *The Rise of the Computer State* (New York: Random House, 1983), p. 9.

91. University of Cambridge, "Computers Using Digital Footprints Are Better Judges of Personality Than Friends and Family," *Science Daily*, January 12, 2015, https://www.sciencedaily.com/releases/2015/01/150112154456.htm (accessed March 2, 2017).

92. Ronald Goldfarb, ed., *After Snowden: Privacy, Secrecy, and Security in the Information Age* (New York: Thomas Dunne, 2015).

93. Jacob Silverman, interview with the author, January 31, 2017.

94. Louise Story, "F.T.C. to Review Online Ads and Privacy," *New York Times*, November 1, 2007, http://www.nytimes.com/2007/11/01/technology/01Privacy .html (accessed March 22, 2017).

95. Lori Andrews, *I Know Who You Are and I Saw What You Did: Social Networks and the Death of Privacy* (New York: Free Press, 2011), p. 29.

96. Ibid.

97. Jessica Guynn, "Mark Zuckerberg Publishes Manifesto to Save the World," *USA Today*, February 16, 2017, https://www.usatoday.com/story/tech/ news/2017/02/16/mark-zuckerberg-publishes-manifesto-save-world/98007574/ (accessed July 18, 2017).

98. Steve Kroft, "The Data Brokers: Selling Your Personal Information," *60 Minutes*, August 24, 2014, http://www.cbsnews.com/news/data-brokers -selling-personal-information-60-minutes/ (accessed February 7, 2017).

99. Guglielmo Marconi, quoted in Jacob Silverman, *Terms of Service: Social Media and the Constant Price of Connection* (New York: HarperCollins, 2015), p. 2.

100. Ibid., p. 4.

101. William Poundstone, interview with the author, February 28, 2017.

102. Randi Zuckerberg, *Dot Complicated: Untangling Our Wired Lives* (New York: Harper Collins, 2013), p. 78.

103. Danah M. Boyd and Nicole B. Ellison, "Social Network Sites: Definition, History, and Scholarship," *Journal of Computer-Mediated Communication* 13, no. 1 (October 2007): 211.

104. Poundstone, interview with the author.

105. Chuck Palahniuk, *Fight Club* (New York: Norton, 1996), p. 166.

106. Shona Ghosh, "Analyst: Snapchat's Valuation Numbers Don't Add Up," *Business Insider*, March 15, 2017, http://www.businessinsider.com/analyst -snapchats-valuation-numbers-dont-add-up-2017-3 (accessed April 6, 2017).

107. Natasha, interview with the author.

108. ICT Data and Statistics Division, *ICT: Facts and Figures* (Geneva, Switzerland: International Telecommunication Union, May 2015), https:// www.itu.int/en/ITU-D/Statistics/Documents/facts/ICTFactsFigures2015.pdf (accessed February 7, 2017).

109. Rachel Nuwer, "What If the Internet Stopped Working for a Day?" BBC, February 7, 2017, http://www.bbc.com/future/story/20170207-what-if -the-internet-stopped-for-a-day (accessed April 27, 2017).

110. Alexandre Aragão, "WhatsApp Has a Viral Rumor Problem with Real Consequences," BuzzFeed, May 31, 2017, https://www.buzzfeed.com/alexandre aragao/whatsapp-rumors-have-already-provoked-lynch-mobs-a?utm_term=.ht Nn1Lw63#.icKvlB15R (accessed June 1, 2017).

111. Bill Kovach and Tom Rosenstiel, *Blur: How to Know What's True in the Age of Information Overload* (New York: Bloomsbury, 2011), p. 6.

112. Ibid., p. 7.

113. Facebook, "Stats," https://newsroom.fb.com/company-info/ (accessed July 18, 2017).

114. Pew Research Center, "Social Media Fact Sheet," January 12, 2017, http:// www.pewinternet.org/fact-sheet/social-media/#data (accessed July 18, 2017).

115. Pew Research Center, "Social Media Fact Sheet," January 12, 2017.

116. Michael Tomasello, "The Ultra-Social Animal," *European Journal of Social Psychology* 44, no. 3 (April 2014): 187–94, doi: 10.1002/ejsp.2015 (accessed August 13, 2017).

117. Susan Cain, *Quiet: The Power of Introverts in a World That Can't Stop Talking* (New York: Random House, 2013), p. 3.

118. Robert Putnam, *Bowling Alone: The Collapse and Revival of American Community* (New York: Simon & Schuster, 2000), p. 108.

119. Ibid.; "Social Capital Primer," *Bowling Alone*, 2017, http://bowling alone.com/?page_id=13 (accessed January 19, 2017).

120. Ibid., p. 19.

121. Putnam, *Bowling Alone*, p. 27.

122. Ibid., pp. 288–331; "Social Capital Primer," *Bowling Alone*.

123. Putnam, *Bowling Alone*, p. 22.

124. Ibid., p. 23.

125. Ibid., p. 170.

126. Aaron Smith, "6 New Facts about Facebook," Pew Research Center, February 3, 2014, http://www.pewresearch.org/fact-tank/2014/02/03/6-new -facts-about-facebook/ (accessed March 21, 2017).

127. Jeffrey Gottfried, Michael Barthel, Elisa Shearer, and Amy Mitchell, "The 2016 Presidential Campaign—a News Event That's Hard to Miss," Pew Research Center, February 4, 2016, http://www.journalism.org/2016/02/04/the -2016-presidential-campaign-a-news-event-thats-hard-to-miss/ (accessed April 29, 2017).

128. *Wikipedia*, s.v. "Braco (Faith Healer)," last modified April 5, 2017, https://en.wikipedia.org/wiki/Braco_(faith_healer) (accessed May 24, 2017).

129. David W. Moore, "Three in Four Americans Believe in Paranormal," Gallup, June 16, 2005, http://www.gallup.com/poll/16915/three-four-americans -believe-paranormal.aspx (accessed April 2, 2017).

130. Linda Lyons, "Paranormal Beliefs Come (Super) Naturally to Some," Gallup, November 1, 2005, http://www.gallup.com/poll/19558/ paranormal -beliefs-come-supernaturally-some.aspx (accessed April 2, 2017).

131. Ibid.

132. Frank Newport, "In US, 42% Believe Creationist View of Human Origins," Gallup, June 2, 2014, http://www.gallup.com/poll/170822/believe -creationist-view-human-origins.aspx (accessed December 1, 2014).

133. Kurt Andersen, *Fantasyland: How America Went Haywire* (New York: Random House, 2017), p. 6.

134. Ibid., p. 8.

135. Guy P. Harrison, *Good Thinking: What You Need to Know to Be Smarter, Safer, Wealthier, and Wiser* (Amherst, NY: Prometheus Books, 2015).

136. US Senate, Permanent Subcommittee on Investigations, of the Committee on Homeland Security and Governmental Affairs, "ISIS Online: Countering Terrorist Radicalization and Recruitment on the Internet and Social Media," July 6, 2016, pp. 1–2, https://www.gpo.gov/fdsys/pkg/CHRG -114shrg22476/pdf/CHRG-114shrg22476.pdf.

137. Emerson T. Brooking and P. W. Singer, "War Goes Viral: How Social Media Is Being Weaponized," *Atlantic*, November, 2016, p. 72.

138. Ibid.

139. US Senate, "ISIS Online."

140. Ruth Pollard, "Islamic State Propaganda: What the West Doesn't Understand," *Sydney Morning Herald*, July 9, 2015, http://www.smh.com .au/world/islamic-state-propaganda-what-the-west-doesntunderstand-201507 08-gi86qu.html (accessed March 22, 2017).

141. Ibid.

142. Krishnadev Calamur, "Twitter's New ISIS Policy," *Atlantic*, February 5, 2016, https://www.theatlantic.com/international/archive/2016/02/twitter -isis/460269/ (accessed July 18, 2017).

143. Emily Dreyfuss, "Facebook's Counterterrorism Playbook Comes into Focus," *Wired*, June 17, 2017, https://www.wired.com/story/facebook-counter terrorism/ (accessed July 18, 2017); Monika Bickert, "Hard Questions: How We Counter Terrorism," Facebook, June 15, 2017, https://newsroom.fb.com/ news/2017/06/how-we-counter-terrorism/ (accessed July 18, 2017).

144. "The Importance of Social Media," New America, https://www.newamerica .org/in-depth/terrorism-in-america/why-do-they-commit-terrorist-acts/ (accessed February 10, 2017). Nearly half of jihadis, 46 percent, have some form of a social media profile with jihadist material or have utilized encryption to conspire.

145. Brendan I. Koerner, "Why ISIS is Winning the Social Media War," *Wired*, April 2016, https://www.wired.com/2016/03/isis-winning-social-media -war-heres-beat/ (accessed July 18, 2017).

146. Scott Shane, "The Lessons of Anwar al-Awlaki," *New York Times*, August 27, 2015, https://www.nytimes.com/2015/08/30/magazine/the-lessons -of-anwar-al-awlaki.html (accessed June 27, 2017).

## CHAPTER 2: WELCOME TO YOUR VERY OWN CUSTOMIZED, BIASED BUBBLE OF PSYCHOLOGICAL REINFORCEMENT, MANIPULATION, AND LIES

1. David Kirkpatrick, *The Facebook Effect* (New York: Simon & Schuster, 2010), p. 276.

2. Brendan Nyhan, interview with the author, March 7, 2017.

3. Michael P. Lynch, "Googling Is Believing: Trumping the Informed Citizen," *New York Times*, March 9, 2016, https://opinionator.blogs.nytimes .com/2016/03/09/googling-is-believing-trumping-the-informed-citizen/ (accessed February 8, 2017).

4. Eli Pariser, *The Filter Bubble: What the Internet Is Hiding from You* (New York: Penguin, 2011), p. 9.

5. Eli Pariser, "Beware Online 'Filter Bubbles,'" TED Talk, March 2011, https://www.ted.com/talks/eli_pariser_beware_online_filter_bubbles (accessed March 29, 2017).

6. Daniel J. Boorstin, *The Image: A Guide to Pseudo-Events in America* (New York: First Vintage Books, 1992), p. 240.

7. Yuval Noah Harari, *Homo Deus: A Brief History of Tomorrow*, p. 323.

8. Ibid., p. 334.

9. Ibid., p. 356.

10. Richard Gray, "Lies, Propaganda, and Fake News: A Challenge for Our Age," BBC, March 1, 2017, http://www.bbc.com/future/story/20170301-lies-propaganda-and-fake-news-a-grand-challenge-of-our-age (accessed July 19, 2017).

11. Pariser, *Filter Bubble*, pp. 15–16.

12. Natasha, interview with the author.

13. Camille, interview with the author.

14. John Michael Strubhart, interview with the author, March 22, 2017.

15. Angela Russell, interview with the author, March 31, 2017.

16. Dean Eckles, Twitter post @deaneckles, October 7, 2016, 10:37 a.m., https://twitter.com/deaneckles/status/784447589236236288 (accessed August 3, 2017).

17. Read Across the Aisle, "Intro to Read Across the Aisle," introductory video, 2:17, http://www.readacrosstheaisle.com/ (accessed July 19, 2017).

18. The Dr. Bo Show, 2017, https://www.thedrboshow.com/tools/qa/Bo/The DrBoShow.

19. Bo Bennett, interview with the author, March 9, 2017.

20. Michael Shermer, *The Believing Brain: From Ghosts and Gods to Politics and Conspiracies—How We Construct Beliefs and Reinforce Them as Truths* (New York: Times Books, 2011), p. 278.

21. Francis Bacon, quoted in Raymond Nickerson, "Confirmation Bias: A Ubiquitous Phenomenon in Many Guises," *Review of General Psychology* 2, no. 2 (1998): 176.

22. Sean Prophet, interview with the author, March 22, 2017.

23. Davies Robertson, *Temptest-Tost* (Toronto: Penguin Canada, 2006), p. 107.

24. See Harrison, *50 Popular Beliefs That People Think Are True* (Amherst, NY: Prometheus Books, 2012), pp. 154–60.

25. See ibid., pp. 89–99.

26. Drew Weston, quoted in Shermer, *Believing Brain*, pp. 261, 363; D. Westen, P. S. Blagov, K. Harenski, C. Kilts, and S. Hamann, "Neural Bases of Motivated Reasoning: An fMRI Study of Emotional Constraints on Partisan Political Judgment in the 2004 US Presidential Election," *Journal of Cognitive Neuroscience* 18, no. 11 (November 2006): 1947–58.

27. Ian Liberman, interview with the author, March 23, 2017.

28. *Wikiquote*, s.v. "Voltaire," last modified April 14, 2017, https://en.wikiquote.org/wiki/Voltaire (accessed February 10, 2017); Robert Andrews, ed., *Columbia Dictionary of Quotations* (New York: Columbia University Press, 1993), p. 633.

29. Allister Heath, "Fake News Is Killing People's Minds, Says Apple Boss Tim Cook," *Telegraph*, February 10, 2017, http://www.telegraph.co.uk/technology/2017/02/10/fake-news-killing-peoples-minds-says-apple-boss-tim-cook/ (accessed January 11, 2017).

30. Timothy J. Redmond, "Political Obfuscation," *Skeptic* 21, no. 4, 2016, p. 57.

31. Eliza Collins, "Poll: Clinton, Trump Most Unfavorable Candidates Ever," *USA Today*, August 31, 2016, https://www.usatoday.com/story/news/politics/onpolitics/2016/08/31/poll-clinton-trump-most-unfavorable-candidates-ever/89644296/ (accessed July 19, 2017).

32. American Press Institute, "'Who Shared It?': How Americans Decide What News to Trust on Social Media," March 20, 2017, https://www.americanpressinstitute.org/publications/reports/survey-research/trust-social-media/ (accessed July 19, 2017).

33. Nieman Lab, "People Who Get News from Social or Search Usually Don't Remember the News Org That Published It, Survey Finds," July 19, 2017, http://www.niemanlab.org/2017/07/people-who-get-news-from-social-or-search-usually-dont-remember-the-news-org-that-published-it-survey-finds/ (accessed July 20, 2017).

34. Sue Halpern, "How He Used Facebook to Win," *New York Review of Books*, June 8, 2017, http://www.nybooks.com/articles/2017/06/08/how-trump-used-facebook-to-win/ (accessed July 8, 2017).

35. Ibid.

36. David J. Helfand, "Surviving the Misinformation Age," *Skeptical Inquirer* 41, no. 3 (May/June, 2017): 39.

37. Jeff Jones and Lydia Saad, "Gallup Poll Social Series: Governance," Gallup, September 7–11, 2016, http://www.gallup.com/file/poll/195575/Confidence_in_Mass_Media_160914%20.pdf (accessed February 8, 2017).

38. Ibid.

39. Art Swift, "Americans Trust in Mass Media Sinks to New Low," Gallup, September 14, 2016, http://www.gallup.com/poll/195542/americans-trust-mass-media-sinks-new-low.aspx (accessed February 8, 2017).

40. *Guardian*, "David Remnick on the rise of fake news and the era of misinformation," June 19, 2017, https://www.theguardian.com/canneslions/2017/jun/19/david-remnick-deception-fake-news-cannes?CMP=share_btn_tw (accessed June 19, 2017).

41. Richard Gray, "Lies, Propaganda, and Fake News: A Challenge for Our Age," BBC, March 1, 2017, http://www.bbc.com/future/story/20170301-lies-propaganda-and-fake-news-a-grand-challenge-of-our-age (accessed July 19, 2017).

42. Kelsey Sutton, "Trump Calls CNN 'Fake News,' as Channel Defends Its Reporting on Intelligence Briefing," Politico, January 11, 2017, http://www.politico.com/blogs/on-media/2017/01/trump-refusing-to-answer-question-from-cnn-reporter-you-are-fake-news-233485 (accessed February 6, 2017).

43. Aaron Blake, "President Trump's Simplistic, Illogical Worldview, in One Tweet," *Washington Post*, February 6, 2017, https://www.washingtonpost.com/news/the-fix/wp/2017/02/06/president-trumps-simplistic-illogical-worldview-in-one-tweet/?utm_term=.00d1b079d2c0 (accessed February 7, 2017).

44. Amnesty International, "Syria: Human Slaughterhouse; Mass Hang-

ings and Extermination at Saydnaya Prison, Syria," February 7, 2017, https://www.amnesty.org/en/documents/mde24/5415/2017/en/ (accessed July 21, 2017).

45. Michael Isikoff, "Exclusive: Defiant Assad Tells Yahoo News Torture Report Is 'Fake News,'" Yahoo News, February 10, 2017, https://www.yahoo.com/news/exclusive-defiant-assad-tells-yahoo-news-torture-report-is-fake-news-100042667.html (accessed February 10, 2017).

46. Oxford Dictionaries, "Oxford Dictionaries Word of the Year 2016 Is . . .," https://www.oxforddictionaries.com/press/news/2016/12/11/WOTY-16 (accessed July 30, 2017).

47. Mackenzie Weinger, "John Fleming Links to *Onion* Story," Politico, February 6, 2012, http://www.politico.com/story/2012/02/congressman-links-to-onion-story-072507 (accessed February 6, 2017).

48. Alexandra Topping, "Ex-FIFA Vice President Jack Warner Swallows *Onion* Spoof," *Guardian*, May 31, 2015, https://www.theguardian.com/football/2015/may/31/ex-fifa-vice-president-jack-warner-swallows-onion-spoof (accessed February 6, 2017).

49. Jon Bershad, "FoxNation.com Reposts Anti-Obama Article from the *Onion*, Doesn't Mention It's a Joke," Mediaite, November 26, 2010, http://www.mediaite.com/online/foxnation-com-repurposes-anti-obama-article-from-the-onion-forgets-to-mention-its-a-joke/ (accessed February 6, 2017).

50. Henry Chu, "Beijing Newspaper Retreats, Apologizes for Capitol Gaffe," *Los Angeles Times*, June 13, 2002, http://articles.latimes.com/2002/jun/13/world/fg-whoops13 (accessed February 6, 2017).

51. "One Giant Slip in Bangladesh News," BBC News, September 4, 2009, http://news.bbc.co.uk/2/hi/south_asia/8237558.stm (accessed February 6, 2017).

52. Stanford History Education Group, *Evaluating Information: The Cornerstone of Civic Online Reasoning* (Stanford, CA: Stanford History Education Group, November 22, 2016), p. 3, https://sheg.stanford.edu/upload/V3LessonPlans/Executive%20Summary%2011.21.16.pdf (accessed May 24, 2017).

53. Ibid., p. 4.

54. Ibid., p. 7.

55. Ibid., pp. 4–5.

56. Ibid., p. 10.

57. Ibid.

58. Ibid., p. 17.

59. Ibid., p. 23.

60. Ibid., p. 24.

61. Sam Wineburg and Sarah McGrew, "Most Teens Can't Tell Fake from Real News," *PBS NewsHour*, December 13, 2016, http://www.pbs.org/newshour/updates/column-students-cant-google-way-truth/ (accessed February 8, 2017).

62. Ibid.

63. Ibid.

64. Jessica Guynn, "Google Tweaks Search to Root Out 'Fake News,'" *USA Today*, April 25, 2017, https://www.usatoday.com/story/tech/news/2017/04/25/google-tweaks-search-root-out-fake-news/100864892/ (accessed April 22, 2017).

65. Brendan Nyhan, interview with the author, March 7, 2017.

66. "Project Zero," Harvard Graduation School of Education, 2016, http://www.pz.harvard.edu/who-we-are/about (accessed May 24, 2017).

67. Carrie James, interview with the author, March 20, 2017.

68. Christine Elgersma, "News Literacy 101: Follow These Steps to Help Kids (and You!) Resist Fake News, Fact-Check, and Think Critically about News and Information," Common Sense Media, February 23, 2017, https://www.commonsensemedia.org/blog/news-literacy-101 (accessed May 24, 2017).

69. Out of Eden Learn, http://learn.outofedenwalk.com/ (accessed May 24, 2017).

70. "Dialogue Toolkit," Out of Eden Learn, http://learn.outofedenwalk.com/dialogue-toolkit/ (accessed May 24, 2017).

71. Camila Domonoske, "Man Fires Rifle Inside DC Pizzeria, Cites Fictitious Conspiracy Theories," NPR, December 5, 2016, http://www.npr.org/sections/thetwo-way/2016/12/05/504404675/man-fires-rifle-inside-d-c-pizzeria-cites-fictitious-conspiracy-theories (accessed February 2, 2017).

72. Adam Goldman, "The Comet Ping Pong Gunman Answers Our Reporter's Questions," *New York Times*, December 7, 2016, https://www.nytimes.com/2016/12/07/us/edgar-welch-comet-pizza-fake-news.html (accessed February 2, 2017).

73. BBC, "The Saga of 'Pizzagate': The Fake Story That Shows How Conspiracy Theories Spread," December 2, 2016, http://www.bbc.com/news/blogs-trending-38156985 (accessed July 23, 2017).

74. Domonoske, "Man Fires Rifle."

75. Matthew Rosenberg, "Trump Adviser Has Pushed Clinton Conspiracy Theories," *New York Times*, December 5, 2016, https://www.nytimes.com/2016/12/05/us/politics/-michael-flynn-trump-fake-news-clinton.html?_r=0 (accessed February 2, 2017).

76. Ibid.

77. Howard Gardner, quoted in Rory O'Connor, *Friends, Followers, and the Future* (San Francisco: City Light Books, 2012), p. 217.

78. Howard Gardner, "The Good: Can We Have It in the Absence of Truth?" December 13, 2016, http://thegoodproject.org/the-good-can-we-have-it-in-the-absence-of-truth/ (accessed February 2, 2017).

79. Anthony C. Adornato, "Forces at the Gate: Social Media's Influence on Editorial and Production Decisions in Local Television Newsrooms," *Electronic News* 10, no. 2, May 9, 2016, http://journals.sagepub.com/doi/abs/10.1177/1931243116647768?journalCode=enxa (accessed January 19, 2017).

80. O'Connor, *Friends*, p. 30.

81. Darrell Etherington, "President Obama on Fake News Problem: 'We Won't Know What to Fight For,'" Techcrunch, November 17, 2016, https://techcrunch.com/2016/11/17/president-obama-on-fake-news-problem-we-wont-know-what-to-fight-for/ (accessed November 19, 2016).

82. Meriam Metzger, interview with the author, March 1, 2017.

83. Lauren Feldman, "The Hostile Media Effect," in *The Oxford Handbook of Political Communication*, ed. Kate Kenski and Kathleen Hall Jamieson (New York: Oxford University Press, 2014), http://www.oxfordhandbooks.com/view/10.1093/oxfordhb/9780199793471.001.0001/oxfordhb-9780199793471-e-011 (accessed April 30, 2017).

84. Meet the Press, "Conway: Press Secretary Gave 'Alternative Facts,'" http://www.nbcnews.com/meet-the-press/video/conway-press-secretary-gave-alternative-facts-860142147043 (accessed July 23, 2017).

85. Michael P. Lynch, "Googling Is Believing: Trumping the Informed Citizen," *New York Times*, March 9, 2016, https://opinionator.blogs.nytimes.com/2016/03/09/googling-is-believing-trumping-the-informed-citizen/ (accessed April 30, 2017).

86. Ibid.

87. Matt Taibbi, "The End of Facts," *Rolling Stone*, February 23–March 9, 2017, p. 29.

88. Kurt Andersen, *Fantasyland: How America Went Haywire* (New York: Random House, 2017), p. 7.

89. Kurt Andersen, "How America Lost Its Mind," *Atlantic*, September 2017, https://www.theatlantic.com/magazine/archive/2017/09/how-america-lost-its-mind/534231/ (accessed August 20, 2017).

90. Craig Silverman et al., "Hyperpartisan Facebook Pages Are Publishing False and Misleading Information at an Alarming Rate," BuzzFeed, October 20, 2016, https://www.buzzfeed.com/craigsilverman/partisan-fb-pages-analysis?utm_term=.wdaKZL1NnG#.px7BVneAJR (accessed November 16, 2016).

91. Brendan Nyhan, interview with the author, March 7, 2017.

92. Craig Silverman, "This Analysis Shows How Viral Fake Election News Stories Outperformed Real News on Facebook," BuzzFeed, November 16, 2016, https://www.buzzfeed.com/craigsilverman/viral-fake-election-news-outperformed-real-news-on-facebook?utm_term=.bxlZ6dMw5Y#.vme21gBbZN (accessed November 19, 2016).

93. Ibid.

94. Ibid.

95. Jessica Wolf, "Political Affiliation Can Predict How People Will React to False Information about Threats," *Science Daily*, February 2, 2017, www.sciencedaily.com/releases/2017/02/170202141851.htm (accessed May 24, 2017).

96. Craig Silverman and Lawrence Alexander, "How Teens in The Balkans Are Duping Trump Supporters with Fake News," BuzzFeed, November 3, 2016, https://www.buzzfeed.com/craigsilverman/how-macedonia-became-a-global

-hub-for-pro-trump-misinfo?utm_term=.paDOyRwW7k#.nwyjXPNbA3 (accessed November 19, 2016).

97. Ibid.

98. Ibid.

99. Office of the Director of National Intelligence, "Assessing Russian Activities and Intentions in Recent US Election," January 6, 2017, https://www.dni.gov/files/documents/ICA_2017_01.pdf (accessed June 27, 2017).

100. Julia Munslow, "Ex-CIA Director Hayden: Russia election Meddling Was 'Most Successful Covert Operation in History,'" Yahoo News, July 21, 2017, https://www.yahoo.com/news/ex-cia-director-hayden-russia-election-meddling -successful-covert-operation-history-212056443.html (accessed July 23, 2017).

101. John Whitehouse, "This Viral Lie about Denzel Washington Is the Perfect Illustration of Facebook's Fake News Crisis," Media Matters, November 15, 2016, http://mediamatters.org/blog/2016/11/15/viral-lie-about-denzel -washington-perfect-illustration-facebooks-fake-news-crisis/214460 (accessed November 15, 2016).

102. David Mikkelson, "Gun Flight," Snopes, October 30, 2016, http://www .snopes.com/hillary-clinton-bought-137-million-worth-of-illegal-arms/ (accessed November 16, 2016).

103. Tatianna Amatruda, "That Trump Quote Calling Republicans 'The Dumbest Group of Voters'? Fake!" CNN, November 10, 2016, http://www.cnn .com/2016/11/10/politics/trump-quote-facebook-trnd/ (accessed November 16, 2016).

104. Silverman and Alexander, "How Teens in the Balkans."

105. Ibid.

106. Julia Love and Kristina Cooke, "Google, Facebook Move to Restrict Ads on Fake News Sites," *Reuters*, Nov 15, 2016, http://www.reuters.com/article/us -alphabet-advertising-idUSKBN1392MM (accessed November 17, 2016).

107. Nyhan, interview.

108. Mark Zuckerberg, Facebook post, November 12, 2016, 10:15 p.m., https://www.facebook.com/zuck/posts/10103253901916271 (accessed November 16, 2016).

109. Zeynep Tufekci, "Mark Zuckerberg Is in Denial," *New York Times*, November 15, 2016, http://www.nytimes.com/2016/11/15/opinion/mark -zuckerberg-is-in-denial.html (accessed February 1, 2017).

110. Jose van Dijck, interview with the author, January 21, 2017.

111. Dan Primack, "Business Media Has Its Own Fake News Problem," AXIOS, April 10, 2017, https://www.axios.com/business-media-has-its-own -fake-news-problem-2353912512.html (accessed April 10, 2017).

112. Josh Constine, "Facebook Shows Related Articles and Fact Checkers before You Open Links," Techcrunch, April 25, 2017, https://techcrunch .com/2017/04/25/facebook-shows-related-articles-and-fact-checkers-before-you -open-links/ (accessed April 25, 2017).

113. Ibid.

114. *Wikipedia*, s.v. "Jayson Blair," last modified May 3, 2017, https://en.wikipedia.org/wiki/Jayson_Blair (accessed February 2, 2017).

115. Mike Wall, "New Conspiracy Theory: Children Kidnapped for Mars Slave Colony," Space.com, June 30, 2017, https://www.space.com/37366-mars-slave-colony-alex-jones.html (accessed July 30, 2017).

116. Graham Lanktree, "Alex Jones Refuses to Apologize for Sandy Hook Conspiracy Theory," *Newsweek*, June 19, 2017, http://www.newsweek.com/alex-jones-megyn-kelly-sandy-hook-infowars-627129 (accessed July 30, 2017).

117. David Corn, "Here's the Alex Jones Story Megyn Kelly and Other Reporters Should Probe: What Is Trump's Relationship to the Nation's Most Dangerous Conspiracy Theorist?" *Mother Jones*, June 13, 2017, http://www.motherjones.com/politics/2017/06/alex-jones-megyn-kelly-donald-trump/ (accessed July 30, 2017).

118. Maksym Gabielkov, Arthi Ramachandran, Augustin Chaintreau, and Arnaud Legout, "Social Clicks: What and Who Gets Read on Twitter?" *ACM SIGMETRICS / IFIP Performance 2016* (conference papers, Antibes Juan-les-Pins, France, June 2016), https://hal.inria.fr/hal-01281190 (accessed May 26, 2017).

119. Caitlin Dewey, "6 in 10 of You Will Share This Link without Reading It, a New, Depressing Study Says," *Washington Post*, June 16, 2016, https://www.washingtonpost.com/news/the-intersect/wp/2016/06/16/six-in-10-of-you-will-share-this-link-without-reading-it-according-to-a-new-and-depressing-study/?utm_term=.16c5792fb4d9 (accessed July 23, 2017).

120. James Vincent, "New AI Research Makes It Easier to Create Fake Footage of Someone Speaking," Verge, July 12, 2017, https://www.theverge.com/2017/7/12/15957844/ai-fake-video-audio-speech-obama (accessed July 23, 2017).

121. Xiaoyan Qiu, Diego F. M. Oliveira, Alireza Sahami Shirazi, Alessandro Flammini, and Filippo Menczer, "Limited Individual Attention and Online Virality of Low-Quality Information," *Nature Human Behaviour* 1, no. 0132 (2017), doi:10.1038/s41562-017-0132 (accessed June 26, 2017).

122. Nyhan, interview.

123. Benjamin Radford, e-mail communications with the author, March 12, 2017.

124. John Pavley, "Trolls Are USA," Blog Pav Blog, November 10, 2016, http://www.pavley.com/2016/11/12/trolls-are-usa/ (accessed November 19, 2016).

125. Ibid.

126. Jacob Silverman, *Terms of Service: Social Media and the Constant Price of Connection* (New York: HarperCollins, 2015), p. 151.

127. Kate Losse, "'Fake News,' Authorship, and the Battle for Narrative Power," *Kate Losse* (blog), December 22, 2016, http://www.katelosse.tv/latest/2016/12/22/notes-on-fake-news-narration-power (accessed January 18, 2017).

128. Michael Kaplan and Ellen Kaplan, *Bozo Sapiens: Why to Err Is Human* (New York: Bloomsbury, 2009). p. 2.

129. Radford, interview with the author.

130. *Idiocracy*, directed by Mike Judge (Austin, TX: Twentieth Century Fox, 2006). *Idiocracy* is a 2006 comedy about the dumbing down of America. Many began calling it prophetic in 2016.

131. Timothy Snyder, *On Tyranny* (New York: Tim Duggan Books, 2017), p. 65.

## CHAPTER THREE: SOCIAL MEDIA ADDICTION

1. Anderson Cooper, "What Is 'Brain Hacking'? Tech Insiders on Why You Should Care," CBS News *60 Minutes*, April 9, 2017, http://www.cbsnews.com/news/brain-hacking-tech-insiders-60-minutes/ (accessed April 18, 2017).

2. Sherry Turkle, *Reclaiming Conversation: The Power of Talk in a Digital Age* (New York: Penguin, 2015), p. 40.

3. Cooper, "What Is 'Brain Hacking'?"

4. Chuck Palahniuk, *Fight Club* (New York: Norton and Norton, 1996), p. 29.

5. Andrew Thompson, "Engineers of Addiction," Verge, May 6, 2016, http://www.theverge.com/2015/5/6/8544303/casino-slot-machine-gambling-addiction-psychology-mobile-games (accessed April 19, 2017).

6. Lesley Stahl, "Slot Machines: The Big Gamble," CBS News *60 Minutes*, January 7, 2011, http://www.cbsnews.com/news/slot-machines-the-big-gamble-07-01-2011/ (accessed November 11, 2016).

7. Alice Robb, "Why Are Slot Machines So Addictive?" *New Republic*, December 5, 2013, https://newrepublic.com/article/115838/gambling-addiction-why-are-slot-machines-so-addictive (accessed January 21, 2017).

8. Thompson, "Engineers of Addiction."

9. Aaron Smith, "Record Shares of Americans Now Own Smartphones, Have Home Broadband," Pew Research Center, January 12, 2017, http://www.pewresearch.org/fact-tank/2017/01/12/evolution-of-technology/ (accessed April 21, 2017).

10. Ibid.

11. Physiological Society, "Stress in Modern Britain," 2017, http://www.physoc.org/sites/default/files/page/1736%208%20page%20report%20%283%29.pdf (accessed July 30, 2017), p. 3.

12. Ibid., p. 5.

13. TeleNav, "Survey Finds One-Third of Americans More Willing to Give Up Sex Than Their Mobile Phones," http://www.telenav.com/about/pr-summer-travel/report-20110803.html (accessed July 30, 2017).

14. Cooper, "What Is 'Brain Hacking'?"

15. "Your Phone Is Trying to Control Your Life," *PBS NewsHour*, January 30, 2017, http://www.pbs.org/newshour/bb/phone-trying-control-life/ (accessed April 18, 2017).

16. Tristan Harris, "How Technology Hijacks People's Minds—from a Magician and Google's Design Ethicist," May 19, 2016, TristanHarris.com, May 19, 2016, http://www.tristanharris.com/essays/ (accessed January 31, 2017).

17. Ibid.

18. Shona Ghosh, "Analyst: Snapchat's Valuation Numbers Don't Add Up," *Business Insider*, March 15, 2017, http://www.businessinsider.com/analyst -snapchats-valuation-numbers-dont-add-up-2017–3 (accessed April 6, 2017).

19. Andrew Perrin, "One-Fifth of Americans Report Going Online 'Almost Constantly,'" Pew Research Center, December 8, 2015, http://www.pew research.org/fact-tank/2015/12/08/one-fifth-of-americans-report-going-online -almost-constantly/ (accessed February 17, 2017).

20. Michael Winnick, "Putting a Finger on Our Phone Obsession," dscout, June 16, 2016, https://blog.dscout.com/mobile-touches (accessed May 1, 2017).

21. Adam Felber, Matt Gunn, Bill Maher, et al., *Real Time with Bill Maher*, episode 15, season 15, directed by Paul G. Casey, aired May 12, 2017 (Los Angeles, CA: HBO, 2017).

22. Mike Elgan, "Social Media Addiction Is a Bigger Problem Than You Think," ComputerWorld, December 24, 2015, http://www.computerworld.com/ article/3014439/internet/social-media-addiction-is-a-bigger-problem-than-you -think.html (accessed March 26, 2017).

23. Adam Alter, *Irresistible: The Rise of Addictive Technology and the Business of Keeping Us Hooked* (New York: Penguin, 2017), p. 319.

24. Evan Asano, "How Much Time Do People Spend on Social Media?" Social Media Today, January 4, 2017, http://www.socialmediatoday.com/ marketing/how-much-time-do-people-spend-social-media-infographic (accessed March 29, 2017).

25. Common Sense Media, *The Common Sense Census: Media Use by Tweens and Teens* (San Francisco: Common Sense Media, 2015), https://www .commonsensemedia.org/research/the-common-sense-census-media-use-by -tweens-and-teens (accessed April 20, 2017). Please note that users must have an account to access this report online.

26. GlobalWebIndex, *GWI Social: GlobalWebIndex's Quarterly Report on the Latest Trends in Social Networking* (New York / London: GlobalWebIndex, 2017), p. 5.

27. Jason Mander, "Social Media Captures 30% of Online Time," *Global-WebIndex* (blog), June 8, 2016, http://blog.globalwebindex.net/chart-of-the-day/ social-media-captures-30-of-online-time/ (accessed April 20, 2017).

28. Craig Wigginton, "2016 Global Mobile Consumer Survey: US Edition," Deloitte, 2017, https://www2.deloitte.com/us/en/pages/technology-media-and -telecommunications/articles/global-mobile-consumer-survey-us-edition.html (accessed April 6, 2017).

29. Ibid.

30. Ibid.

31. APA Staff, "Can You Be Addicted to the Internet?" American Psychiatric Association, July 20, 2016, https://www.psychiatry.org/news-room/apa-blogs/apa-blog/2016/07/can-you-be-addicted-to-the-internet (accessed April 20, 2017).

32. Perrin, "One-Fifth of Americans Report."

33. Eduardo Guedes, Federica Sancassiani, Mauro Giovani Carta, Carlos Campos, Sergio Machado, Anna Lucia Spear King, and Antonio Egidio Nardi, "Internet Addiction and Excessive Social Networks Use: What about Facebook?" *Clinical Practice and Epidemiology in Mental Health* 12 (June 28, 2016): 43–48, doi: 10.2174/1745017901612010043, https://www.ncbi.nlm.nih.gov/pmc/articles/PMC4926056/#R30 (accessed April 24, 2017).

34. "Twitter Usage Statistics," Internet Live Stats, http://www.internet livestats.com/twitter-statistics/ (accessed April 25, 2017).

35. Perrin, "One-Fifth of Americans Report."

36. GlobalWebIndex, *GWI Social*, p. 5.

37. *Time*, "For the Record," March 13, 2017, p. 6.

38. Common Sense Media, *Common Sense Census*.

39. Braun Research, Inc., "Trends in Consumer Mobility Report" (Princeton: Bank of America, 2015), http://newsroom.bankofamerica.com/files/doc _library/additional/2015_BAC_Trends_in_Consumer_Mobility_Report.pdf (accessed May 24, 2017).

40. Mary Meeker, *Internet Trends 2016—Code Conference* (Menlo Park / San Francisco: Kleiner, Perkins, Caufield, Byers, June 1, 2016), http://www .kpcb.com/internet-trends (accessed March 20, 2017).

41. Alter, *Irresistible*, p. 319.

42. Ibid., pp. 319–20.

43. Bianca Bosker, "The Binge Breaker," *Atlantic*, November 2016, https://www.theatlantic.com/magazine/archive/2016/11/the-binge-breaker/501122/ (accessed April 19, 2017).

44. Time Well Spent, "Calling All Technology Makers," http://www .timewellspent.io/designers/ (accessed July 24, 2017).

45. Andrew K. Przybylski and Netta Weinstein, "Can You Connect with Me Now? How the Presence of Mobile Communication Technology Influences Face-to-Face Conversation Quality," *Journal of Social and Personal Relationships* 30, no. 3, July 19, 2012, http://journals.sagepub.com/doi/abs/10.1177/0265407512453827 (accessed December 22, 2016).

46. "Craving Facebook? UAlbany Study Finds Social Media to be Potentially Addictive, Associated with Substance Abuse," news release, University of Albany New Center, December 9, 2014, http://www.albany.edu/news/56604.php (accessed March 27, 2017).

47. Lawrie McFarlane, "Prices Paid for Social Media Use," in *Social Media and Your Brain*, ed. C. G. Prado (Santa Barbara, CA: Praeger, 2017), p. 119.

48. "FAQ," Center for Internet Addiction, 2013, http://netaddiction.com/faqs/ (accessed January 9, 2017).

49. McFarlane, "Prices Paid for Social Media," p. 126.

50. T. Ryan, A. Chester, J. Reece, and S. Xenos, "The Uses and Abuses of Facebook: A Review of Facebook Addiction," *Journal of Behavioral Addictions* 3, no. 3 (September 2014): 133–48, doi: 10.1556/JBA.3.2014.016.

51. Common Sense Media, *Technology Addiction Concern, Controversy, and Finding Balance* (San Francisco: Common Sense Media, 2016), p. 35.

52. Gary Small and Gigi Vorgan, *iBrain: Surviving the Technological Alteration of the Modern Mind* (New York: William Morrow, 2008), p. 48.

53. Ibid., pp. 48, 50.

54. Lesley McClurg, "After Compulsively Watching YouTube, Teen Girl Lands In Rehab," April 17, 2017, https://ww2.kqed.org/futureofyou/2017/04/17/theres-growing-consensus-the-internet-is-addictive/ (accessed June 29, 2017).

55. William J. Netzer, "Poor Sleep May Be Linked to Alzheimer's Disease," Fisher Center for Alzheimer's Research Foundation, 2017, http://www.alzinfo.org/articles/poor-sleep-may-be-linked-to-alzheimers-disease/ (accessed January 30, 2017).

56. Katie Moisse, "5 Health Hazards Linked to Lack of Sleep," ABC News, June 11, 2012, http://abcnews.go.com/Health/Sleep/health-hazards-linked-lack-sleep/story?id=16524313 (accessed November 2, 2014).

57. Caroline Williams, "What's the Best Way to Go to Sleep?" *New Scientist* 230, no. 3075, May 28, 2016, p. 36.

58. Ibid.

59. McClurg, "After Compulsively Watching YouTube, Teen Girl Lands in Rehab," April 17, 2017.

60. Ibid.

61. Kimberly Young, "What the US Can Learn from China and Korea to Treat Internet Addiction," Center for Internet Addiction, November 6, 2014, http://netaddiction.com/chinas-internet-addiction-treatment-camps/ (accessed April 20, 2017).

62. Ibid.

63. "FAQ," Center for Internet Addiction.

64. American Psychiatric Association, ed., *Diagnostic and Statistical Manual of Mental Disorders*, 5th ed. (Arlington, VA: American Psychiatric Association, 2013), https://www.psychiatry.org/psychiatrists/practice/dsm (accessed April 21, 2017). It does include, however, a recommendation for further study of "Internet gaming disorder."

65. "FAQ," Center for Internet Addiction.

66. Common Sense Media, "Dealing with Devices: The Parent-Teen Dynamic, Are We Addicted?" Common Sense Media, 2016, https://www.commonsensemedia.org/technology-addiction-concern-controversy-and-finding-balance-infographic (accessed April 20, 2017).

67. Susanna Cline, interview with the author, March 24, 2017.

68. Alera, interview with the author.

69. Randall, interview with the author.

70. Aalto University, "Movie Research Results: Multitasking Overloads the Brain: The Brain Works Most Efficiently When It Can Focus on a Single Task for a Longer Period of Time," *Science Daily*, April 25, 2017, www.science daily.com/releases/2017/04/170425092429.htm (accessed April 25, 2017); Juha M. Lahnakoski, Iiro P. Jääskeläinen, Mikko Sams, and Lauri Nummenmaa, "Neural Mechanisms for Integrating Consecutive and Interleaved Natural Events," *Human Brain Mapping*, April 5, 2017, DOI: 10.1002/hbm.23591.

71. Lahnakoski et al., "Neural Mechanisms."

72. William Poundstone, *Head in the Cloud: Why Knowing Things Still Matters When Facts Are So Easy to Look Up* (New York: Little, Brown, 2016), p. 295.

73. Frances Booth, interview with the author, April 10, 2017.

74. The Radicati Group, *Email Statistics Report, 2015–2019* (London, UK: Radicati Group, March 2015), http://www.radicati.com/wp/wp-content/uploads/2015/02/Email-Statistics-Report-2015–2019-Executive-Summary.pdf (accessed April 25, 2017).

75. Daniel J. Levitin, *The Organized Mind* (New York: Dutton, 2016), pp. 101–102.

76. Ibid.

77. Turkle, *Alone Together: Why We Expect More from Technology and Less from Each Other* (New York: Basic Books, 2011), pp. 293–94.

78. Shanika, interview with the author.

79. Adrian F. Ward, Kristen Duke, Ayelet Gneezy, and Maarten W. Bos, "Brain Drain: The Mere Presence of One's Own Smartphone Reduces Available Cognitive Capacity," *Journal of the Association for Consumer Research* 2, no. 2 (April 2017): 140–54, https://doi.org/10.1086/691462 (accessed June 28, 2017).

80. *Newswise*, "The Mere Presence of Your Smartphone Reduces Brain Power, Study Shows," June 23, 2017, http://www.newswise.com/articles/the-mere-presence-of-your-smartphone-reduces-brain-power-study-shows (accessed June 28, 2017).

81. Ward, Duke, Gneezy, and Bos, "Brain Drain."

82. Cooper, "What Is 'Brain Hacking'?"

83. "Internet Addiction Test (IAT)," Center for Internet Addiction, 2013, http://netaddiction.com/internet-addiction-test/ (accessed March 30, 2017).

84. Cecilie Schou Andraessen, Torbjørn Torsheim, Geir Scott Brunborg, and Ståle Pallesen, "Development of a Facebook Addiction Scale," *Psychological Reports* 110, no. 2 (April 2012): 501–17, DOI: 10.2466/02.09.18.PR0.110.2.501 -517, https://www.researchgate.net/publication/225185226_Development_of_a _Facebook_Addiction_Scale (accessed June 14, 2017).

85. Ibid.

86. Harris, "How Technology Hijacks."

87. Ward, Duke, Gneezy, and Bos, "Brain Drain."

88. Time Well Spent, http://www.timewellspent.io/ (accessed July 24, 2017).

89. Off Time, http://offtime.co/.

90. Time Well Spent.

91. Ibid.

92. In the Moment, https://inthemoment.io/ (accessed July 24, 2017).

93. Time Well Spent.

94. Common Sense Media, *Technology Addiction Concern*, p. 33.

95. Adblock Plus, https://adblockplus.org/ (accessed July 24, 2017).

96. Common Sense Media, *Technology Addiction Concern*, p. 29.

97. Harris, "How Technology Hijacks."

08. Ashani, interview with the author.

99. Michelle, interview with the author.

100. Leo Igwe, interview with the author, March 28, 2017.

101. American Academy of Pediatrics, "American Academy of Pediatrics Announces New Recommendations for Children's Media Use," October 21, 2016, https://www.aap.org/en-us/about-the-aap/aap-press-room/pages/american-academy-of-pediatrics-announces-new-recommendations-for-childrens-media-use.aspx (accessed July 29, 2017).

102. Peter Rubin, "Mark Zuckerberg's VR Selfie Is a Bigger Deal Than You Realize," *Wired*, October 17, 2017, https://www.wired.com/2017/04/facebook-spaces-vr-for-your-friends/ (accessed July 28, 2017).

103. Alter, *Irresistible*, pp. 142–43.

104. Daniel K. Minto, interview with the author, March 30, 2017.

105. Suzi Parker, "The Benefits of Connecting Kids with Autism to Social Media," *Take Part*, March 4, 2014, http://www.takepart.com/article/2014/03/04/digital-literacy-autism-expressed (accessed April 24, 2017).

106. Shūsaku Endō, *Silence* (New York: Picador, 2017), p. 166.

107. D. I. Tamir, J. P. Mitchell, "Disclosing Information about the Self Is Intrinsically Rewarding," *Proceedings of the National Academy of Sciences* 109, no. 21 (May 22, 2012): 8038–43, doi: 10.1073/pnas.1202129109 (accessed February 19, 2017).

108. Ibid.

109. John Higginson, interview with the author, April 18, 2017.

110. Andrea, interview with the author.

111. Robert DeAngelo, interview with the author, April 15, 2017.

112. Alyssa Bereznak, "Can Real Life Compete with an Instagram Playground?" *Ringer*, August 9, 2017, https://www.theringer.com/tech/2017/8/9/16110424/instagram-playground-social-media (accessed August 10, 2017).

113. Museum of Ice Cream, https://www.museumoficecream.com/ (accessed August 11, 2017).

114. Susan Adams, "The 25-Year-Old Behind The Museum Of Ice Cream,"

*Forbes*, May 19, 2017, https://www.forbes.com/sites/forbestreptalks/2017/05/19/the-25-year-old-behind-the-museum-of-ice-cream/#61fe89f02e4e (accessed August 11, 2017).

115. Ibid.

116. Ibid.

117. FaceApp: Neural Face Transformations, Wireless Lab OOO, https://www.faceapp.com/.

118. Jacob Silverman, *Terms of Service: Social Media and the Constant Price of Connection* (New York: HarperCollins, 2015), p. 265.

119. Ibid., p. 24.

120. Ibid., p. 206.

121. Harris, "How Technology Hijacks."

## CHAPTER FOUR: WHAT YOUR *OTHER* MIND DOES ON SOCIAL MEDIA

1. Sam Harris, *Free Will* (New York: Free Press, 2012), p. 14.

2. Chris Baraniuk, "World Wide Warp," *New Scientist*, February 20, 2016, p. 38.

3. Sam Harris, "Reality and the Imagination: A Conversation with Yuval Noah Harari," March 19, 2017, https://www.samharris.org/podcast/item/reality-and-the-imagination (accessed April 29, 2017).

4. Cesar Hidalgo, "2015: What Do You Think of Machines That Think? Machines Don't Think, But Neither Do People," *Edge*, 2015, https://www.edge.org/response-detail/26176 (accessed December 25, 2016).

5. Carl Sagan, *The Demon-Haunted World: Science as a Candle in the Dark* (New York: Random House, 1995), pp. 38–39.

6. Steven Pinker, *The Better Angels of Our Nature: Why Violence Has Declined* (New York: Viking Books, 2011).

7. Jon Stewart, "Global Data Storage Calculated at 295 Exabytes," BBC, http://www.bbc.com/news/technology-12419672 (accessed July 26, 2017).

8. Dean Buonomano, *Brain Bugs: How the Brain's Flaws Shape Our Lives* (New York: W. W. Norton, 2011), pp. 143–44.

9. Guy P. Harrison, *Good Thinking: What You Need to Know to Be Smarter, Safer, Wealthier, and Wiser* (Amherst, NY: Prometheus Books, 2015).

10. Excerpted from Harrison, *Good Thinking*, pp. 20–22.

11. Paul Offit, *Do You Believe in Magic? Vitamins, Supplements, and All Things Natural: A Look behind the Curtain* (New York: Harper Paperbacks, 2014), p. 42.

12. Ralph Ellison, *Invisible Man*, 2nd ed. (New York: Vintage International, 1995), p. 5.

13. Guy P. Harrison, "Embraced by Evil," *Caymanian Compass*, December 5, 2002, pp. 15–16.

14. David Eagleman, *Incognito: The Secret Lives of the Brain* (New York: Vintage Books, 2012), p. 65.

15. Bo Bennett, interview with the author, March 9, 2017.

16. Justin Kruger and David Dunning, "Unskilled and Unaware of It: How Difficulties in Recognizing One's Own Incompetence Lead to Inflated Self-Assessments," *Journal of Personality and Social Psychology* 77, no. 6 (December 1999): 1121–34, http://gagne.homedns.org/~tgagne/contrib/unskilled.html (accessed April 29, 2017).

17. Robert Eno, trans., *The Analects of Confucius* (Bloomington: Indiana University Bloomington, 2015), p. 7, http://www.indiana.edu/-p374/Analects _of_Confucius_(Eno-2015).pdf (accessed November 20, 2016).

18. *Wikipedia*, s.v. "I Know That I Know Nothing," https://en.wikipedia .org/wiki/I_know_that_I_know_nothing (accessed June 6, 2017).

19. William Shakespeare, *As You Like It*, act 5, scene 1.

20. Buonomano, *Brain Bugs*, p. 81.

21. For more on this, see Guy P. Harrison, *50 Reasons People Give for Believing in a God* (Amherst, NY: Prometheus Books, 2008) and *50 Simple Questions for Every Christian* (Amherst, NY: Prometheus Books, 2013).

22. Excerpt from Guy P. Harrison, *Good Thinking: What You Need to Know to Be Smarter, Safer, Wealthier, and Wiser* (Amherst, NY: Prometheus Books, 2015), pp. 155–57.

23. Benjamin Libet, Curtis Gleason, Eldwood Wright, and Dennis Pearl, "Time of Conscious Intention to Act in Relation to Onset of Cerebral Activity (Readiness Potential)," *Brain* 106, no. 3 (September 1983): 623–42.

24. John A. Bargh, "Our Unconscious Mind," *Scientific American*, January 2014, p. 32.

25. My book, *50 Popular Beliefs That People Think Are True* (Amherst, NY: Prometheus Books, 2012) includes a chapter on the Roswell claim.

26. A. Tversky and D. Kahneman, "Judgment under Uncertainty: Heuristics and Biases," *Science* 185, no. 4157 (1974): 1124–31, doi:10.1126/ science.185.4157.1124.

27. Thabile Vilakazi, "South African Pastor Sprays Insecticide on Congregants 'To Heal Them,'" CNN, November 23, 2016, http://edition.cnn .com/2016/11/23/africa/south-african-insecticide-prophet/index.html (accessed November 23, 2016).

28. Demetrios Vakratsas and Tim Ambler, "How Advertising Works: What Do We Really Know?" *Journal of Marketing* 63, no. 1 (January 1999): 26–43.

29. Richard M. Perloff, "Third-Person Effect Research 1983–1992: A Review and Synthesis," *International Journal of Public Opinion Research* 5, no. 2 (1993): 167–84, doi: 10.1093/ijpor/5.2.167.

30. Ibid.

31. Eric Anderson, Erika H. Siegel, Eliza Bliss-Moreau, and Lisa Feldman Barrett, "The Visual Impact of Gossip," *Science* 332, no. 6036 (June 17, 2011): 1446–48.

32. S. E. Asch, "Effects of Group Pressure on the Modification and Distortion of Judgments," in *Groups, Leadership and Men: Research in Human Relations*, ed. H. Guetzkow (Pittsburgh, PA: Carnegie, 1951), pp. 177–190.

33. Michael Enright, "Does the Backfire Effect Explain Donald Trump's Startling Success?" CBC Radio, June 19, 2016, http://www.cbc.ca/radio/thesundayedition/america-guns-and-violence-remembering-beaumont-hamel -the-backfire-effect-1.3637113/does-the-backfire-effect-explain-donald-trump-s -startling-success-1.3637123 (accessed December 19, 2016).

34. David McRaney, "The Backfire Effect," *You Are Not So Smart* (blog), June 10, 2011, https://youarenotsosmart.com/2011/06/10/the-backfire-effect/ (accessed March 2, 2017).

35. Ibid.

36. Joshua Compton, interview with the author, March 30, 2017.

37. Buonomano, *Brain Bugs*, p. 121.

38. Ibid., p. 122.

39. Bennett, interview with the author.

40. Timothy J. Redmond, "Political Obfuscation," *Skeptic* 24, no. 6 (2016), p. 57.

41. Joyce Ehrlinger, Thomas Gilovich, and Lee Ross, "Peering into the Bias Blind Spot: People's Assessments of Bias in Themselves and Others," *Personality and Social Psychology Bulletin* 31, no. 5 (May 2005): 1–13, doi:10.1177/0146167204271570.

## CHAPTER FIVE: THE QUEST FOR PRIVACY, SECURITY, AND THE PERFECT PASSWORD

1. David Lyon, *The Electronic Eye: The Rise of Surveillance Society* (Minneapolis: University of Minnesota Press, 1994), p. 37.

2. Kevin D. Mitnick and Robert Vamosi, *The Art of Invisibility* (New York: Little, Brown, 2017), p. 5.

3. Evan Dashevsky, "Admit It, You Don't Care about Digital Privacy," *PC Mag*, March 25, 2014, http://www.pcmag.com/feature/321880/admit-it-you -don-t-care-about-digital-privacy (accessed April 22, 2017).

4. Ted Claypoole and Theresa Payton, *Protecting Your Internet Privacy: Are You Naked Online?* (Lanham, MD: Rowman & Littlefield, 2017), p. ix.

5. May Wong, "Former NSA Director Defends Surveillance Programs," Stanford Center for International Security and Cooperation, October 10, 2014, http://cisac.fsi.stanford.edu/news/former-nsa-director-defense-surveillance -programs (accessed January 10, 2017).

6. Jared Lanier, *You Are Not a Gadget: A Manifesto* (New York: Alfred A. Knopf, 2010), p. 48.

7. Alexander Klimburg, *The Darkening Web: The War for Cyberspace* (New York: Penguin, 2017), p. 273.

8. Maggie Astor, "Your Roomba May Be Mapping Your Home, Collecting Data That Could Be Shared," *New York Times*, July 25, 2017, https://www.nytimes.com/2017/07/25/technology/roomba-irobot-data-privacy.html (accessed August 5, 2017).

9. Marc Goodman, *Future Crimes: Everything Is Connected, Everything Is Vulnerable and What We Can Do About It* (New York: Random House, 2015), p. 80.

10. Yuval Noah Harari, *Homo Deus: A Brief History of Tomorrow* (New York: Harper, 2017), p. 346.

11. "A Lost Privilege," in *The Province of the Heart* (New York: Viking Press, 1960.

12. Lyon, David. *The Electronic Eye: The Rise of Surveillance Society* (Minneapolis: University of Minnesota Press, 1994), p. 214.

13. Nicholas Carr, *Utopia Is Creepy: And Other Provocations* (New York: W. W. Norton, 2016), p. 255.

14. David Brin, ed., *Chasing Shadows: Visions of Our Coming Transparent World* (New York: Tom Doherty Associates, 2017), p. 87.

15. Ibid., p. 323.

16. Ibid., p. 324.

17. Ibid.

18. Lee Rainie, "The State of Privacy in Post-Snowden America," Pew Research Center, September 21, 2016, http://www.pewresearch.org/fact-tank/2016/09/21/the-state-of-privacy-in-america/ (accessed March 3, 2017).

19. Ibid.

20. Elke Feuer, interview with the author, April 1, 2017.

21. Elizabeth Stoycheff, "Under Surveillance: Examining Facebook's Spiral of Silence Effects in the Wake of NSA Internet Monitoring," *Journalism and Mass Communication Quarterly* 93, no. 2 (March 8, 2016), http://journals.sagepub.com/stoken/rbtfl/1jxrYu4cQPtA6/full (accessed April 18, 2017).

22. Mary Madden, "Public Perceptions of Privacy and Security in the Post-Snowden Era," Pew Research Center, November 12, 2014, http://www.pewinternet.org/2014/11/12/public-privacy-perceptions/ (accessed April 17, 2017).

23. Jeremy Kocal, interview with the author, March 29, 2017.

24. Lori Andrews, *I Know Who You Are and I Saw What You Did: Social Networks and the Death of Privacy* (New York: Free Press, 2011), p. 59.

25. Rainie, "State of Privacy."

26. Ibid.

27. Jacob Silverman, *Terms of Service: Social Media and the Constant Price of Connection* (New York: HarperCollins, 2015), p. xiv.

28. Ibid., p. 293.

29. Kelly, interview with the author.

30. David Kirkpatrick, *The Facebook Effect: The Inside Story of the Company That Is Connecting the World* (New York: Simon & Schuster, 2010), p. 199.

31. Silverman, *Terms of Service*, p. 99.

32. Ibid., pp. 156–57.

33. *Wikipedia*, s.v. "Ashley Madison Data Breach," last modified May 17, 2017, https://en.wikipedia.org/wiki/Ashley_Madison_data_breach (accessed April 16, 2017).

34. Laurie Segall, "Pastor Outed on Ashley Madison Commits Suicide," CNN, September 8, 2015, http://money.cnn.com/2015/09/08/technology/ashley-madison-suicide/index.html (accessed April 16, 2017).

35. Jamie Seidel, "US General Tells How Social Media Fails Have Helped Agents Identify Islamic State Targets," News.com.au, June 5, 2015, http://www.news.com.au/world/us-general-tells-how-social-media-fails-have-been-assisting-agents-identify-islamic-state-targets/news-story/6f524ab55e78a069 26b913c87234f157 (accessed February 27, 2017).

36. Sherry Turkle, *Alone Together: Why We Expect More from Technology and Less from Each Other* (New York: Basic Books, 2011), p. 260.

37. Jaron Lanier, *You Are Not a Gadget: A Manifesto* (New York: Alfred A. Knopf, 2010), p. 200.

38. Ibid., pp. 70–71.

39. Kenneth Olmstead and Aaron Smith, "What the Public Knows about Cybersecurity," Pew Research Center, March 22, 2017, http://www.pew internet.org/2017/03/22/what-the-public-knows-about-cybersecurity/ (accessed March 22, 2017).

40. Tim Raynor, interview with the author, April 2, 2017.

41. Miles, interview with the author.

42. Kevin Hand, interview with the author, April 11, 2017.

43. Caitlin Dewey, "Creepy Startup Will Help Landlords, Employers and Online Dates Strip-Mine Intimate Data from Your Facebook Page," *Washington Post*, June 9, 2016, https://www.washingtonpost.com/news/the-intersect/wp/2016/06/09/creepy-startup-will-help-landlords-employers-and-online-dates-strip-mine-intimate-data-from-your-facebook-page/ (accessed February 9, 2017).

44. Goodman, *Future Crimes*, p. 75.

45. Maeve Duggan, "Online Harassment 2017," Pew Research Center, July 11, 2017, http://www.pewinternet.org/2017/07/11/online-harassment-2017/ (accessed August 4, 2017).

46. Ibid.

47. *New York Times*, "Cartoon Captures Spirit of the Internet," December 14, 2000, http://web.archive.org/web/20141030135629/http://www.nytimes .com/2000/12/14/technology/14DOGG.html (accessed August 4, 2017).

48. Lori Andrews, *I Know Who You Are and I Saw What You Did: Social Networks and the Death of Privacy* (New York: Free Press, 2011), p. 5.

49. Ibid., p. 28.

50. Ibid., p. 19.

51. Randi Zuckerberg, *Dot Complicated: Untangling Our Wired Lives* (New York: Harper Collins, 2013), p. 55.

52. Goodman, *Future Crimes*, p. 121.

53. Steve Kroft, "The Data Brokers: Selling Your Personal Information," CBS News *60 Minutes*, August 24, 2014, http://www.cbsnews.com/news/data-brokers-selling-personal-information-60-minutes/ (accessed February 7, 2017).

54. Darren Davidson, "Facebook Targets 'Insecure' Young People," *Australian*, May 1, 2017, http://www.theaustralian.com.au/business/media/digital/facebook-targets-insecure-young-people-to-sell-ads/news-story/a89949ad016eee7d7a61c3c30c909fa6 (accessed May 27, 2017).

55. Antonio Garcia-Martinez, "I'm an Ex-Facebook Exec: Don't Believe What They Tell You about Ads," *Guardian*, May 2, 2017, https://www.theguardian.com/technology/2017/may/02/facebook-executive-advertising-data-comment (accessed May 26, 2017).

56. CareerBuilder, "Number of Employers Using Social Media to Screen Candidates Has Increased 500 Percent over the Last Decade," April 28, 2016, http://www.careerbuilder.com/share/aboutus/pressreleasesdetail.aspx?ed=12/31/2016&id=pr945&sd=4/28/2016 (accessed April 18, 2017).

57. Kimberlee Morrison, "Survey: 92% of Recruiters Use Social Media to Find High-Quality Candidates," Business Insider, September 22, 2015, http://www.adweek.com/digital/survey-96-of-recruiters-use-social-media-to-find-high-quality-candidates/ (accessed April 18, 2017).

58. CareerBuilder, "Number of Employers Using Social Media."

59. Ibid.

60. Ibid.

61. Silverman, *Terms of Service*, p. 7.

62. Robert DeAngelo, interview with the author, April 15, 2017.

63. Ghostery, "About Ghostery," https://www.ghostery.com/about-ghostery/ (accessed August 2, 2017).

64. Mitnick and Vamosi, *Art of Invisibility*, p. 13.

65. Ibid., pp. 15–18.

66. Garth Humphreys, interview with the author, March 19, 2017.

67. Associated Press, "Amanda Todd's Accused Cyberbully Sentenced to 11 Years in Dutch Prison," *Global News*, March 16, 2017, http://globalnews.ca/news/3313729/amanda-todd-cyberbullying-aydin-coban-sentenced/ (accessed August 2, 2017).

68. Mitnick and Vamosi, *Art of Invisibility*, pp. 129–30.

69. Ibid., p. 141.

70. Andrews, *I Know Who You Are*, pp. 5–6.

71. Mitnick and Vamosi, *Art of Invisibility*, p. 30.

72. Silverman, *Terms of Service*, p. 281.

73. Mitnick and Vamosi, *Art of Invisibility*, p. 231.

74. Michal Kosinski, David Stillwell, and Thore Graepel, "Private Traits and Attributes Are Predictable from Digital Records of Human Behavior," *Proceedings of the National Academy of Sciences* 110, no. 5 (April 9, 2013), www.pnas.org/cgi/doi/10.1073/pnas.1218772110 (accessed March 20, 2017); Wu Youyou, Michal Kosinski, and David Stillwell, "Computer-Based Personality Judgments Are More Accurate Than Those Made by Humans," *Proceedings of the National Academy of Sciences* 112, no. 4 (January 27, 2015): 1036–40, doi: 10.1073/pnas.1418680112 (accessed March 20, 2017).

75. Michal Kosinski, David Stillwell, and Thore Graepel, "Private Traits and Attributes Are Predictable from Digital Records of Human Behavior," *Proceedings of the National Academy of Sciences* 110, no. 5 (April 9, 2013), www.pnas.org/cgi/doi/10.1073/pnas.1218772110 (accessed March 20, 2017); Wu Youyou, Michal Kosinski, and David Stillwell, "Computer-Based Personality Judgments Are More Accurate Than Those Made by Humans," *Proceedings of the National Academy of Sciences* 112, no. 4 (January 27, 2015): 1036–40, doi: 10.1073/pnas.1418680112 (accessed March 20, 2017).

76. Abby Ohlheiser, "There Are 13 Countries Where Atheism Is Punishable by Death," *Atlantic*, December 10, 2013, https://www.theatlantic.com/international/archive/2013/12/13-countries-where-atheism-punishable-death/355961/ (accessed August 3, 2017); Max Bearak and Darla Cameron, "Here Are the 10 Countries Where Homosexuality May Be Punished by Death," *Washington Post*, June 16, 2016, https://www.washingtonpost.com/news/world views/wp/2016/06/13/here-are-the-10-countries-where-homosexuality-may-be-punished-by-death-2/?utm_term=.7a7ef1539e87 (accessed August 3, 2017).

77. "A Fingertip to the Wise," *Newsweek* 168, no. 12, April 7, 2017, p. 49.

78. Turkle, *Alone Together*, p. 258.

79. Facebook, "Data Policy," last revised September 29, 2016, https://www.facebook.com/about/privacy/ (accessed May 25, 2017).

80. Michael J. de la Merced, "Snap Shares Leap 44% in Debut as Investors Doubt Value Will Vanish," *New York Times*, March 2, 2017, https://www.nytimes.com/2017/03/02/business/dealbook/snap-snapchat-ipo.html?_r=0 (accessed March 3, 2017).

81. Anna Escher and Katie Roof, "Snapchat Is Already More Valuable Than These 9 Companies," TechCrunch, March 2, 2017, https://techcrunch.com/2017/03/02/snapchat-is-already-more-valuable-than-these-9-companies/ (accessed March 3, 2017).

82. Snap, "Privacy Policy," Snap Inc., January 10, 2017, https://www.snap.com/en-US/privacy/privacy-policy/ (accessed April 4, 2017).

83. Snap, "Privacy Policy," January 10, 2017, https://www.snap.com/en-US/privacy/privacy-policy/ (accessed April 4, 2017).

84. Snap Inc. Terms of Service, https://www.snap.com/en-US/terms/ (accessed June 27, 2017).

85. Ibid.

86. Facebook, "Data Policy," last modified September 29, 2016, https:// www.facebook.com/policy.php (accessed August 18, 2017).

87. Kim Komando, "Can You Spy on a Phone When It Is Turned Off?" *USA Today*, June 20, 2014, https://www.usatoday.com/story/tech/columnist/ komando/2014/06/20/smartphones-nsa-spying/10548601/ (accessed April 17, 2017).

88. *Science Daily*, "Malware Turns PCs into Eavesdropping Devices," November 22, 2016, http://www.sciencedaily.com/releases/2016/11/1611221 23955.htm (accessed July 13, 2017).

89. Toby Percira, "Phones Would Be Safer If 'Off' Meant 'Off,'" *New Scientist*, January 4, 2017, https://www.newscientist.com/letter/mg23331072-900- -phones-would-be-safer-if-off-meant-off/ (accessed March 30, 2017).

90. Justin R. Garcia, Amanda N. Gesselman, Shadia A. Siliman, Brea L. Perry, Kathryn Coe, and Helen E. Fisher, "Sexting among Singles in the USA: Prevalence of Sending, Receiving, and Sharing Sexual Messages and Images," *Sexual Health*, 2016, doi: 10.1071/SH15240.

91. Amanda Lenhart, Monica Anderson, and Aaron Smith, "Teens, Technology, and Romantic Relationships," Pew Research Center, October 1, 2015, http://www.pewinternet.org/2015/10/01/teens-technology-and-romantic -relationships/#fn-14598–2 (accessed April 17, 2017).

92. If you are a victim of revenge porn, these websites may offer some help: www.endrevengeporn.org, www.withoutmyconsent.org, and www.women againstrevengeporn.com.

93. "Project Zero," Harvard Graduate School of Education, http://www .pz.harvard.edu/who-we-are/about (accessed May 25, 2017).

94. Carrie James, interview with the author, March 20, 2017.

95. Ibid.

96. Ibid.

97. Snap, "Privacy Policy."

98. Jacob Morgan, "Privacy Is Completely and Utterly Dead, and We Killed It," *Forbes*, August 19, 2014, https://www.forbes.com/sites/jacob morgan/2014/08/19/privacy-is-completely-and-utterly-dead-and-we-killed -it/#6f3a12f431a7 (accessed January 6, 2017).

99. Tanya Basu, "New Google Parent Company Drops 'Don't Be Evil' Motto," *Time*, October 4, 2015, http://time.com/4060575/alphabet-google-dont -be-evil/ (accessed August 3, 2017).

100. Mitnick and Vamosi, *Art of Invisibility*, p. 105.

101. Hadas Gold, "10 Things to Know about the NSA," *Politico*, June 12, 2013, http://www.politico.com/story/2013/06/10 things-to-know-about-the-nsa -092651 (accessed August 3, 2017).

102. "Facebook Privacy," Electronic Privacy Information Center, 2017, https://epic.org/privacy/facebook/ (accessed May 25, 2017).

103. Goodman, *Future Crimes*, p. 133.

104. Lyon, *Electronic Eye*, p. 41.

105. Christopher Mimms, "Most People Are Cool with 'Smart Toilets' That Share Their Personal Data," *Atlantic*, December 17, 2013, https://www.the atlantic.com/technology/archive/2013/12/most-people-are-cool-smart-toilets -share-their-personal-data/356230/ (accessed August 3, 2017).

106. Bernard Marr, "4 Mind-Blowing Ways Facebook Uses Artificial Intelligence," *Forbes*, December 29, 2016, https://www.forbes.com/sites/ bernardmarr/2016/12/29/4-amazing-ways-facebook-uses-deep-learning-to-learn -everything-about-you/#4246410accbf (accessed March 31, 2017).

107. James Vincent, "UN Condemns Internet Access Disruption as a Human Rights Violation," *Verge*, July 4, 2016, https://www.theverge.com/ 2016/7/4/12092740/un-resolution-condemns-disrupting-internet-access (accessed August 3, 2017).

108. Silverman, *Terms of Service*, p. 311.

109. Robert DeAngelo, interview with the author, April 15, 2017.

110. Goodman, *Future Crimes*, p. 4.

111. Andres Weigend, *Data for the People: How to Make Our Post-Privacy Economy Work for You* (New York: Basic Books, 2017), p. 47.

112. Ibid., p. 13.

113. Kenneth Cukier, "The Data-Driven World," in *Mega Tech: Technology in 2050*, ed. Daniel Franklin (New York: Economist Books/Public Affairs, 2017), pp. 172–73.

114. Madden, "Public Perceptions of Privacy."

## CHAPTER SIX: WHAT'S NEXT?

1. Nick Bostrom, *Superintelligence: Paths, Dangers, Strategies* (Oxford, UK: Oxford Press, 2014), p. 314.

2. Arati Prabhakar (former director of DARPA), "The Merging of Humans and Machines Is Happening Now," *Wired*, January 27, 2017, http://www.wired .co.uk/article/darpa-arati-prabhakar-humans-machines (accessed April 28, 2017).

3. Edward O. Wilson, *The Social Conquest of the Earth* (New York: Liveright, 2012), p. 21.

4. Daniel C. Dennett, "The Singularity—An Urban Legend?" in *What to Think about Machines That Think: Today's Leading Thinkers on the Age of Machine Intelligence*, ed. John Brockman (New York: Harper Perennial, 2015), pp. 85–86.

5. Sam Parker, "16 of the Wisest Things Anyone Ever Said about the Internet," BuzzFeed, May 15, 2013, https://www.buzzfeed.com/samjparker/quotes-about-the-internet?utm_term=.onNAw8Qgm#.ewPXK6Q9q (accessed March 6, 2017).

6. Lawrence M. Krauss, "A Scientific Breakthrough Lets Us See to the Beginning of Time," *New Yorker*, March 17, 2014, http://www.newyorker.com/tech/elements/a-scientific-breakthrough-lets-us-see-to-the-beginning-of-time (accessed August 5, 2017).

7. Martin Rees, "Organic Intelligence Has No Long-Term Future," in Brockman, *What to Think about Machines That Think*, p. 11.

8. "Google Is God," Googlism, http://www.thechurchofgoogle.org/proof-google-is-god/ (accessed August 5, 2017).

9. John Markoff, "Our Masters, Slaves, or Partners," in Brockman, *What to Think about Machines That Think*, p. 26.

10. Bryan Alexander, https://bryanalexander.org/.

11. Bryan Alexander, interview with the author, July 9, 2017.

12. Carrie James, interview with the author, March 20, 2017.

13. Michelle Dean, "The Lessons of Steubenville," *New Yorker*, January 11, 2013, http://www.newyorker.com/culture/culture-desk/the-lessons-of-steubenville (accessed April 27, 2017).

14. Prabhakar, "Merging of Humans and Machines."

15. Shona Ghosh, "Analyst: Snapchat's Valuation Numbers Don't Add Up," Business Insider, March 15, 2017, http://www.businessinsider.com/analyst-snapchats-valuation-numbers-dont-add-up-2017-3 (accessed April 6, 2017).

16. Josh Constine, "Facebook Is Building Brain-Computer Interfaces for Typing and Skin-Hearing," TechCrunch, April 19, 2017, https://techcrunch.com/2017/04/19/facebook-brain-interface/ (accessed August 9, 2017).

17. Cade Metz, "Elon Musk Isn't the Only One Trying to Computerize Your Brain," *Wired*, March 31, 2017, https://www.wired.com/2017/03/elon-musks-neural-lace-really-look-like (accessed April 28, 2017).

18. Liat Clark, "Facebook Is Working on Tech That Will Read Your Thoughts and Let You 'Hear' with Your Skin," *Wired*, April 20, 2017, http://www.wired.co.uk/article/facebook-messenger-bots-developer-conference-2017 (accessed April 28, 2017); Nick Statt, "Facebook Is Working on a Way to Let You Type with Your Brain," *Wired*, April 19, 2017, http://www.theverge.com/2017/4/19/15360798/facebook-brain-computer-interface-ai-ar-f8-2017 (accessed April 28, 2017).

19. Isaac Asimov, "My Own View," in *The Encyclopedia of Science Fiction* ed. Robert Holdstock (London: Cathay Books, 1978); later published in *Asimov on Science Fiction*, by Isaac Asimov (London: Panther, 1981).

20. Jake Farr-Wharton, interview with the author, March 31, 2017.

21. Henry David Thoreau, *Walden and Other Writings by Henry David Thoreau* (New York: Random House, 1992), p. 49.

22. Michael Strangelove, quoted in Robert Putnam, *Bowling Alone: The Collapse and Revival of American Community* (New York: Simon & Schuster, 2000), p. 171.

23. William Gibson, *Neuromancer* (New York: Ace, 1984), p. 51.

24. Sir Tim Berners-Lee, quoted in Klint Finley, "Tim Berners-Lee, Inventor of the Web, Plots a Radical Overhaul of His Creation," *Wired*, April 4, 2017, https://www.wired.com/2017/04/tim-berners-lee-inventor-web-plots-radical-overhaul-creation/ (accessed August 9, 2017).

25. Sir Tim Berners-Lee, "Three Challenges for the Web, According to Its Inventor," World Wide Web Foundation, March 12, 2017, http://webfoundation .org/2017/03/web-turns-28-letter/ (accessed April 18, 2017).

26. Jacob Silverman, *Terms of Service: Social Media and the Constant Price of Connection* (New York: HarperCollins, 2015), p. 46.

27. John Brockman, ed., *Is the Internet Changing the Way You Think? The Net's Impact on Our Minds and Our Future* (New York: Harper Perennial, 2011), pp. 218–19.

28. Matt Burgess, "Future of Fitness: VR Cycling Kit to Let You Exercise in Virtual Worlds," *Factor*, February 13, 2015, http://factor-tech.com/feature/future -fitness-vr-cycling-kit-let-exercise-virtual-worlds/ (accessed August 5, 2017).

29. Natasha, interview with the author.

30. John Michael Strubhart, interview with the author, March 22, 2017.

31. Yuval Noah Harari, *Homo Deus: A Brief History of Tomorrow* (New York: Harper, 2017), p. 350.

32. Joy Holloway-D'Avilar, interview with the author, March 23, 2017.

33. Timothy J. Redmond, interview with the author, March 1, 2017.

34. Camille, interview with the author.

35. Chris Dixon, quoted in Rory O'Connor, *Friends, Followers, and the Future* (San Francisco: City Light Books, 2012), p. 34.

36. Ted Anderson, "The Hive Mind," in Brockman, *What to Think about Machines That Think*, p. 284.

37. Cesar Hidalgo, "2015: What Do You Think of Machines That Think? Machines Don't Think, But Neither Do People," *Edge*, 2015, https://www.edge .org/response-detail/26176 (accessed December 25, 2016).

38. Rachel Nuwer, "What If the Internet Stopped Working for a Day?" BBC, February 7, 2017, http://www.bbc.com/future/story/20170207-what-if -the-internet-stopped-for-a-day (accessed April 27, 2017).

39. Dave Gershgorn, "The Unbreakable Genius of Mark Zuckerberg," *Popular Science*, August 23, 2016, http://www.popsci.com/mark-zuckerberg (accessed February 1 2017).

40. "A Globe, Clothing Itself with a Brain," *Wired*, June 1, 1995, https:// www.wired.com/1995/06/teilhard/ (accessed August 6, 2017).

41. Nick Bostrom, *Superintelligence: Paths, Dangers, Strategies* (Oxford: Oxford University Press, 2014), pp. 58–59.

42. To learn more about AI, superintelligence, and the singularity, I recommend the following three books: Nick Bostrom, *Superintelligence: Paths, Dangers, Strategies* (Oxford: Oxford Press, 2014); Ray Kurzweil, *The Singularity Is Near* (New York: Viking, 2005); James Barrat, *Our Final Invention: Artificial Intelligence and the End of the Human Era* (New York: St. Martin's Griffin, 2015).

43. Bostrom, *Superintelligence*, p. 319.

44. H. G. Wells, *Mind at the End of Its Tether* (London: William Heinemann, 1945), p. 30.

45. Kurzweil, *Singularity Is Near*, p. 136.

46. Harari, *Homo Deus*, pp. 393–94.

47. Miki Hardisty, interview with the author, April 25, 2017.

48. BlookGeeks, "What Is Blockchain Technology? A Step-by-Step Guide for Beginners," https://blockgeeks.com/guides/what-is-blockchain-technology/ (accessed August 6, 2017); Robert Hackett, "Wait, What Is Blockchain?" *Fortune*, May 23, 2016, http://fortune.com/2016/05/23/blockchain-definition/ (accessed April 26, 2017).

49. Thomas L. Friedman, "Moore's Law Turns 50," *New York Times*, May 13, 2015, https://www.nytimes.com/2015/05/13/opinion/thomas-friedman -moores-law-turns-50.html?_r=0 (accessed April 26, 2017).

50. Harari, *Homo Deus*, p. 391.

51. Tactical Tech, https://tacticaltech.org/ (accessed August 6, 2017).

52. Maya Indira Ganesh, interview with the author, March 14, 2017.

53. Christoph, interview with the author.

54. Emanuel Maiberg, "Why Is 'Second Life' Still a Thing?" *MotherBoard*, April 29, 2016, https://motherboard.vice.com/en_us/article/z43mwj/why-is -second-life-still-a-thing-gaming-virtual-reality (accessed August 7, 2017).

55. Janet Maslin, "A Future Wrapped in 1980s Culture," *New York Times*, August 14, 2011, http://www.nytimes.com/2011/08/15/books/ready-player-one -by-ernest-cline-review.html (accessed August 7, 2017).

56. Cameron M. Smith, interview with the author.

57. Jeremy Kocal, interview with the author, March 29, 2017.

58. Nathan Lee, interview with the author, March 27, 2017.

59. Ashani, interview with the author.

60. Cheryl, interview with the author.

61. Ashley, interview with the author.

62. ABC News, "Top 10 Facts You Don't Know about Girls' Education," ABC News, October 7, 2013, http://abcnews.go.com/International/10-facts -girls-education/story?id=20474260 (accessed April 27, 2017).

63. "Seven Things Women in Saudi Arabia Cannot Do," *The Week*, September 27, 2016, http://www.theweek.co.uk/60339/nine-things-women-cant-do -in-saudi-arabia (accessed April 27, 2017).

64. "Flat Earth. The Awakening. This Story Is Not for Everybody,"

YouTube video, 56:39, posted by MG TV, April 16, 2017, https://www.youtube
.com/watch?v=PCq_bSjyj9Q (accessed April 29, 2017).

65. Tonny Onyulo, "Witch Hunts Increase in Tanzania as Albino Deaths
Jump," *USA Today*, February 26, 2015, https://www.usatoday.com/story/news/
world/2015/02/26/tanzania-witchcraft/23929143/ (accessed April 29, 2017).

66. Virtual Human Interaction Lab, Stanford University, https://vhil
.stanford.edu/ (accessed August 7, 2017).

67. Ibid. and Marlene Cimons, "Using Virtual Reality to Make You More
Empathetic in Real Life," *Washington Post*, November 12, 2016, https://
www.washingtonpost.com/national/health-science/using-virtual-reality-to
-make-you-more-empathetic-in-real-life/2016/11/14/ff72ee7a-a06e-11e6-a44d
-cc2898cfab06_story.html?utm_term=.2a1ca2fecbe3 (accessed April 29, 2017).

68. Brendan Nyhan, interview with the author, March 7, 2017.

69. José van Dijck, interview with the author, January 21, 2017.

70. Peter Boghossian, interview with the author, January 17, 2017.

71. Michelle, interview with the author.

72. Jacob Silverman, interview with the author, January 31, 2017.

73. Ibid.

74. Oliver Morton, "Concluding Reflections: Lessons from the Industrial
Revolution," *Mega Tech: Technology in 2050*, ed. Daniel Franklin (New York:
Economist Books / Public Affairs, 2017), p. 226.

75. *American Gods*, episode one, Starz, July 2017.

76. Gary Kasparov, *Deep Thinking: Where Machine Intelligence End and
Human Creativity Begins* (New York: Public Affairs, 2017), p. 258.

# SELECT BIBLIOGRAPHY

Allen, John. *Online Privacy and Hacking*. San Diego: Reference Point, 2015.

Alter, Adam. *Irresistible: The Rise of Addictive Technology and the Business of Keeping Us Hooked*. New York: Penguin, 2017.

Angwin, Julia. *Dragnet Nation*. New York: Times Books, 2014.

Atkins, Larry. *Skewed: A Critical Thinker's Guide to Media Bias*. Amherst, NY: Prometheus Books, 2016.

Baron, Naomi S. *Words Onscreen: The Fate of Reading in a Digital World*. New York: Oxford University Press, 2015.

Bauerlein, Mark. *The Dumbest Generation: How the Digital Age Stupefies Young Americans and Jeopardizes Our Future*. New York: Jeremy P. Tarcher/Penguin, 2008.

———. *The Digital Divide: Arguments for and against Facebook, Google, Texting, and the Age of Social Networking*. New York: Penguin, 2011.

Boog, Jason. *Born Reading*. New York: Touchstone, 2014.

Bostrom, Nick. *Superintelligence: Paths, Dangers, Strategies*. Oxford, UK: Oxford Press, 2014.

Brin, David, ed. *Chasing Shadows: Visions of Our Coming Transparent World*. New York: Tom Doherty Associates, 2017.

Brockman, John, ed. *What to Think about Machines That Think: Today's Leading Thinkers on the Age of Machine Intelligence*. New York: Harper Perennial, 2015.

Brotherton, Rob. *Suspicious Minds: Why We Believe Conspiracy Theories*. New York: Bloomsbury Sigma, 2015.

Caballo, Frances. *Avoid Social Media Time Suck*. Santa Rosa, CA: ACT Communications, 2014.

Carr, Nicholas. *The Glass Cage*. New York: W. W. Norton, 2014.

———. *The Shallows: What the Internet Is Doing to Our Brains*. New York: W. W. Norton, 2010.

Chabris, Christopher, and Daniel Simons. *The Invisible Gorilla and Other Ways Our Intuitions Deceive Us*. New York: Crown, 2010.

Christakis, Nicholas A., and James H. Fowler. *Connected: The Surprising Power of Our Social Networks and How They Shape Our Lives*. New York: Little, Brown, 2009.

Clark, Andy. *Natural-Born Cyborgs: Minds, Technologies, and the Future of Human Intelligence*. New York: Oxford University Press, 2003.

Clark, Lynn Schofield. *The Parent App: Understanding Families in the Digital Age*. New York: Oxford University Press, 2013.

Colevile, Robert. *The Great Acceleration*. New York: Bloomsbury, 2016.

Davidow, William H. *Overconnected: The Promise and Threat of the Internet*. Harrison, NY: Delphinium Books, 2011.

Davis, Hank. *Caveman Logic: The Persistence of Primitive Thinking in a Modern World*. Amherst, NY: Prometheus Books, 2009.

Eagleman, David. *Brain: The Story of You*. New York: Pantheon, 2015.

Eply, Nicholas. *Mindwise*. New York: Alfred A. Knopf, 2014.

Epstein, Joseph. *Gossip: The Untrivial Pursuit*. Boston: Houghton Mifflin Harcourt, 2011.

Franklin, Daniel, ed. *Mega Tech: Technology in 2050*. New York: Economist Books / Public Affairs, 2017.

Goodman, Marc. *Future Crimes: Everything Is Connected, Everything Is Vulnerable and What We Can Do about It*. New York: Random House, 2015.

Hallinan, Joseph. *Why We Make Mistakes*. New York: Broadway Books, 2009.

Harari, Yuval Noah. *Homo Deus: A Brief History of Tomorrow*. New York: Harper, 2017.

Harrison, Guy P. *Good Thinking: What You Need to Know to Be Smarter, Safer, Wealthier, and Wiser*. Amherst, NY: Prometheus Books, 2015.

———. *Think: Why You Should Question Everything*. Amherst, NY: Prometheus Books, 2013.

Hines, Terrence. *Pseudoscience and the Paranormal*. Amherst, NY: Prometheus Books, 2003.

Horst, Heather A., and Daniel Miller. *Digital Anthropology*. New York: Bloomsbury Academic, 2012.

Jarrett, Christian. *Great Myths of the Brain*. West Sussex, UK: John Wiley and Sons, 2015.

Jones, Meg Leta. *Ctrl + Z: The Right to Be Forgotten*. New York: New York University Press, 2016.

Kahneman, Daniel. *Thinking, Fast and Slow*. New York: Farrar, Straus, and Giroux, 2011.

Kaku, Michio. *The Future of the Mind: The Scientific Quest to Understand, Enhance, and Empower the Mind*. New York: Doubleday, 2014.

Keen, Andrew. *The Internet Is Not the Answer*. New York: Atlantic Monthly, 2015.

Keizer, Garrett. *Privacy*. New York: Picador, 2012.

Kelly, Kevin. *The Inevitable: Understanding the 12 Technological Forces That Will Shape Our Future*. New York: Viking, 2016.

Marcus, Gary F. *Kluge: The Haphazard Construction of the Human Mind*. New York: Houghton Mifflin, 2008.

Mayer-Shonberger, Viktor, and Kenneth Cukier. *Big Data: A Revolution That Will Transform How We Live, Work, and Think*. New York: Eamon Dolan, 2013.

McFedries, Paul. *Twitter, Tips, Tricks, and Tweets*. Indianapolis, IN: Wiley, 2009.

McRaney, David. *You Are Now Less Dumb: How to Conquer Mob Mentality, How to Buy Happiness, and All the Other Ways to Outsmart Yourself*. New York: Gotham, 2013.

Medina, John. *Brain Rules: 12 Principles for Surviving and Thriving at Work, Home, and School*. Seattle: Pear, 2008.

Mendelson, B. J. *Social Media Is Bullshit*. New York: St. Martin's Press, 2012.

Merino, Noel, ed. *Privacy*. Farmington Hills, MI: Greenhaven, 2015.

Mooney, Carla. *Online Privacy and Social Media*. San Diego: Reference Point, 2015.

Nakaya, Andrea C. *Internet and Social Media Addiction*. San Diego: Reference Point, 2015.

Naughton, John. *From Gutenberg to Zuckerberg: Disruptive Innovation in the Age of the Internet*. New York: Quercus, 2012.

Nisbet, Richard E. *Mindware: Tools for Smart Thinking*. New York: Farrar, Straus, and Giroux, 2015.

Orwell, George. *1984*. New York: Signet Classics / Harcourt, 1949.

Palfrey, John, and Urs Gasser. *Born Digital: Understanding the First Generation of Digital Natives*. New York: Basic Books, 2008.

Parks, Peggy. *The Digital Divide*. San Diego: Reference Point, 2013.

Penenberg, Adam L. *Viral Loop*. New York: Hyperion, 2009.

Powers, William. *Hamlet's Blackberry*. New York: Harper, 2010.

Prado, C. G., ed. *Social Media and Your Brain*. Santa Barbara, CA: Praeger, 2017.

Putnam, Robert. *Our Kids: The American Dream in Crisis*. New York: Simon & Schuster, 2015.

Radford, Benjamin. *Media Mythmakers: How Journalists, Activists, and Advertisers Mislead Us*. Amherst, NY: Prometheus Books, 2003.

Ross, Alex. *The Industries of the Future*. New York: Simon & Schuster, 2016.

Rudder, Christian. *Dataclysm: Who We Are (When We Think No One's Looking)*. New York: Crown, 2014.

Rumsey, Abby Smith. *When We Are No More: How Digital Media Is Shaping Our Future*. New York: Bloomsbury, 2016.

Sales, Nancy Jo. *American Girls: Social Media and the Secret Lives of Teenagers*. New York: Alfred A. Knopf, 2016.

Schmidt, Eric, and Jared Cohen. *The New Digital Age*. New York: Alfred A. Knopf, 2013.

Schneier, Bruce. *Data and Goliath: The Hidden Battle to Collect Your Data and Control Your World*. New York: W. W. Norton, 2015.

Solove, Daniel J. *Nothing to Hide: The False Tradeoff between Privacy and Security*. New Haven: Yale University Press, 2011.

Standage, Tom. *Writing on the Wall*. New York: Bloomsbury USA, 2013.

Tucker, Patrick. *The Naked Future*. New York: Current, 2014.

Weigend, Andres. *Data for the People: How to Make Our Post-Privacy Economy Work for You*. New York: Basic Books, 2017.

Weinberger, David. *Too Big to Know*. New York: Basic Books, 2011.

Whiting, Jim. *Online Communication and Social Networking*. San Diego: Reference Point, 2012.

# ABOUT THE AUTHOR

Guy P. Harrison is a passionate advocate for science and reason. He calls the challenge of good thinking a moral issue and points to poor reasoning as humankind's great unrecognized crisis. Guy enjoys sharing his positive, constructive style of skepticism and science appreciation with people whenever possible. He has a degree in history and anthropology and has visited more than thirty countries on six continents. Having seen some of the best and worst of our world, he believes that we can do better. Guy maintains that if more people embraced critical thinking and had a better understanding of basic brain processes such as sensory perception, memory, and subconscious biases, we could eliminate a significant amount of human suffering and become much more efficient, safer, and productive as a species.

As a journalist, Guy has worked in many roles, including editorial writer, world-news editor, sports editor, reporter, feature writer, and columnist. He won the Commonwealth Award for Excellence in Journalism and the WHO (World Health Organization) Award for Health Reporting. Guy has also interviewed many leading scientists and significant historical figures. He has written about many diverse topics, including poverty in the developing world, conservation issues, religion, war, racism, gender discrimination, space exploration, and human origins.

Although he says he's an introvert, Guy never misses a chance to spread science and reason with others. He has been a guest on more than one hundred radio shows and podcasts and was a featured speaker at a science festival in New Zealand and at a Random House conference in San Diego, California.

Guy is the author of six previous books that have been popular with readers and highly acclaimed by critics. They are: *Good Thinking: What You Need to Know to Be Smarter, Safer, Wealthier, and Wiser*; *Think: Why You Should Question Everything*; *50 Simple*

*Questions for Every Christian*; *50 Popular Beliefs That People Think Are True*; *50 Reasons People Give for Believing in a God*; and *Race and Reality: What Everyone Should Know about Our Biological Diversity*. Random House selected *Think* as part of its national First Year Experience/Common Reads program, which promotes it as recommended reading for first-year university students.

Guy is a lifelong fan not only of science and history but also of science fiction. He says he's not ashamed to confess his deep love for robot uprisings, time machines, and interstellar travel. He lives in Southern California, where he enjoys running, hiking, biking, and writing.

Guy is also an "expert blogger" for *Psychology Today*. Read his essays at *About Thinking*, www.psychologytoday.com/blog/about -thinking. Visit his website at www.guypharrison.com.

# INDEX

Numbers in **boldface** indicate text boxes.